Chinese Animation

Harvard Contemporary China Series 21

Chinese Animation

Multiplicities in Motion

Edited by
Daisy Yan DU (Lead Editor)
John A. CRESPI
Yiman WANG

Published by the Harvard University Asia Center
Distributed by Harvard University Press
Cambridge (Massachusetts) and London 2025

Published by the Harvard University Asia Center, Cambridge, MA 02138

The Harvard University Asia Center publishes a monograph series and, in coordination with the Fairbank Center for Chinese Studies, the Korea Institute, the Reischauer Institute of Japanese Studies, and other faculties and institutes, administers research projects designed to further scholarly understanding of China, Japan, Korea, Vietnam, and other Asian countries. The Center also sponsors projects addressing multidisciplinary and regional issues in Asia.

The Harvard Contemporary China Series is designed to present new research that deals with present-day issues against the background of Chinese history and society. The focus is on interdisciplinary research intended to convey the significance of the rapidly changing Chinese scene.

Library of Congress Cataloging-in-Publication Data

Names: Du, Daisy Yan, editor. | Crespi, John A., editor. | Wang, Yiman, editor.
Title: Chinese animation : multiplicities in motion / edited by Daisy Yan Du (lead editor), John A. Crespi, Yiman Wang.
Other titles: Chinese animation (Harvard University. Asia Center) | Harvard contemporary China ; 21.
Description: Cambridge : Harvard University Asia Center, 2025. | Series: Harvard contemporary China series ; 21 | Includes bibliographical references and index.
Identifiers: LCCN 2024018046 | ISBN 9780674297531 (paperback) | ISBN 9780674301160 (ebook)
Subjects: LCSH: Animated films--China--History and criticism. | Animated film industry--China--History. | Animated films--Political aspects--China--History. | Women in the motion picture industry--China--History. | Motion pictures and literature--China--History and criticism. | Animation (Cinematography)--China--History.
Classification: LCC NC1766.C6 C485 2025 | DDC 791.43/340951--dc23/eng/20240919
LC record available at https://lccn.loc.gov/2024018046

Index by Steven Moore

♾ Printed on acid-free paper

Printed in the United States of America

Contents

Figures and Video

FOREWORD

Modern Chinese Literature, Film, and Animation

DAVID DER-WEI WANG

Chinese Animation: Multiplicities in Motion undertakes a daunting task in mapping the immense terrain of animation in the Chinese context and beyond. As the first of its kind, it seeks to assess Chinese animation as a new field of research emerging from modern Chinese literature and film studies. It approaches Chinese animation as a multiform of media, a cultural industry, a "structure of feeling," and a contact zone through which social imaginary, political agenda, and affective dynamics are brought into play.[1] In fifteen essays, the project presents a kaleidoscopic vista of Chinese animation, touching on issues such as its roots and ramifications, technological acquisitions and innovations, as well as conceptual engagements and historical implications. As the editors indicate in their introduction, the volume does not seek to define Chinese animation as a field in conventional terms; instead, these essays seek to open Chinese animation to as many disciplines and topics as possible so as to demonstrate its amorphous potential, its "multiplicities in motion."

Animation has long inhabited the way we make sense of the world—and ourselves. In the simplest terms, animation is an art medium in which still figures are manipulated to appear as moving images. It covers subgenres from cartoons to comics, AI-generated pictures, and computer games. Animation is often associated with a specific form of film production, though in the ontological sense, all film is composed of animated images. Early animations were drawn by hand on transparent celluloid sheets

1 Raymond Williams and Michael Orrom, *Preface to Film* (London: Film Drama Limited, 1954), 1-50.

and then photographed and exhibited on film. Today, most animations are made with computer-generated imagery (CGI). An archaeologist of animation can take us from premodern times, when figures were enlivened by using an optic device like the magic lantern, to postmodern times, where our daily lives are populated by digitally rendered phantasmagoria of the most vivid kind.

Animation has prodded us to engage with philosophical questions such as anthropomorphic fantasy versus mechanical repetition or reproduction; the pros and cons of "framing" the world like a picture in the Heideggerian sense. Above all, animation touches on the kinetics of art that enacts the "stills" of life.

Etymologically tracing the word provides clues to our theoretical engagement with the term. "Animation" is derived from the Latin "animātiōn," stemming from "animātiō," meaning "a bestowing of life."[2] One of the Chinese translations of the word, *donghua* 動畫, means "picture in motion." The most important dictum in the discourse on classical Chinese painting, *qiyun shengdong* 氣韻生動, or rhythmic vitality, highlights precisely the ancients' fascination with the kinetic potential of pictorial art. By disassembling the compound phrase into its component characters—breath-resonance-life-motion, we can further appreciate that the artistic medium is not merely a passive, mimetic vehicle of the object under treatment, but also a generative source of life in motion.

There is a dialectic side of such a notion, however. In the ancient fable of Lord Ye, the "dragon lover," the Lord is so enthralled with the mysterious creature that he has dragon images inscribed and painted everywhere, from his garments to his home décor. But when the Dragon deity is finally summoned to descend to his abode, the Lord is paralyzed with terror by what he sees. The fable's moral is to be careful of what you wish for, but it speaks also to the mystical dynamism of artistic undertaking at its most engaged, however ironically—the contestation between techne and enchantment, and animation and animism.

Are animation artists of modern times descendants of Lord Ye? On the one hand, they strive to transform anything in lived and imagined experience into something lifelike or fantastic. On the other hand, they venture into the

2. Dictionary.com, "animation," 2012, https://www.dictionary.com/browse/animation.

world of objects, and the unknown, to invoke and encounter the dragon—be it identified with cosmic wonder or the digital sublime, the divine or the demonic. Sergei Eisenstein captured a century ago the gist of the animated body as "a rejection of once-and-forever allotted form, freedom from ossification, the ability to dynamically assume any form."[3] Eisenstein coined the term *plasmaticness* in the context of the motion picture, infusing it with a biopolitical hint. Historical hindsight tells us that the plasmatic implication of animation is not limited to cinematic production alone. Rather, it takes us to the enchanted domain of the numinous conjuration as much as the reenchanted domain of the cybernetic metamorphosis, such as 3D holograms for medical purposes and virtual reality (VR) films.

With these thoughts in mind, we turn to *Chinese Animation*. Inspired by the late Professor Yingjin Zhang's critical intervention that Chinese animation has entailed not a telos of historical development but instead "multiple lines of descent" through "parallel and parallax histories and trajectories," this volume stresses the multiplicity and heterogeneity that inform the encounters between creators and spectators in a variety of historical spaces and moments.[4] The volume is divided into five interrelated sections: junctures, gender, identities, digitality, and practices. "Junctures" foregrounds the way in which animation "absorbs, modifies, enhances, and destabilizes" established modes and genres, boundaries and disciplines.[5] From the combination of stop-motion and other cinematic tricks for creating special effects in early martial arts films to the emergence of massive multiplayer online role-playing games, animation spectators and players are continuously deterritorializing and reterritorializing their sensory and cognitive experience, something that drives home the kinetic core of animation. "Gender" focuses on animated expressions of gender to highlight the often-overlooked agencies of women and nonbinary gender identities, as symbolic figures or actual artists who have enhanced Chinese animation's powers of invention and imagination. "Digitality" takes up the question of digital animation and cinematic realism by examining 2D flash animation as special effects in live-action films and 3D CGI animation blockbusters that create a simulated reality with hyper realism.

3. Sergei Eisenstein, *Eisenstein on Disney*, ed. Jay Leyda , trans. Alan Upchurch (London: Methuen, 1988), 21.

4 See Yingjin Zhang's keynote essay included in this book, 14.

5 See the introduction in this book, 8.

I call attention to the section "Identities," which explores "Chineseness" as manifested or contested in animation from its inception to production and reception. Where is the "Chineseness" to be located? In the storyline (such as the adaptation of the *Journey to the West*), aesthetic effect (such as the ink-painting style), publicity strategy, or technological innovation? Although the question of national identity haunts almost all forms of medium articulations, it may be especially paradoxical in the case of animation because, as the editors posit, animation is by nature a genre that breaks bodily, technological, and other boundary lines. Indeed, what deserves equal if not more attention is the anthropocentric fixation that characterizes conventional animations, Chinese and non-Chinese alike. From the Wan Brothers' enterprise to Walt Disney's production, animation opens up as much as closes off the multiple relations between the human, nonhuman, and ahuman. The volume concludes with a line-up of essays by current practitioners of animation, whose visions and projects are leading Chinese animation to new horizons. Although their topics are too new to draw academic attention, they embody the spirit of animation as an amorphous force of creativity.

Daisy Yan Du, John A. Crespi, and Yiman Wang have accomplished an impressive project by featuring so many inspiring topics and scholars in one volume. Following their argument that animation points to multiple trajectories of media culture, one cannot help pondering what the next project may be. One possible direction may well be the historical relevance of animation to the experience we are undergoing now. Beyond the film industry around which most of the essays engage, we witness the unlikely linkages between biopolitics, animation, and everyday life. Looking back at the COVID-19 pandemic period in which the volume was produced, I think of cases suggestive of (unlikely) animation. Under the zero-tolerance policy, an extremely sophisticated "health code" was, like an arcade sniper game, designed to track down whoever transgressed the quarantine zones; robot dogs patrolled Shanghai lockdown as if actualizing the postsocialist, dystopic edition of *Toy Story*. More intriguingly, the lockdown law enforcers in their all-white uniforms were dubbed "Big White" by Chinese citizens, a sinister homage to Baymax from the Marvel series *Big Hero 6*, also nicknamed Big White by Chinese fans. Chinese civic life has never been so projected like an animation in the Gothic vein, nor has Chinese animation been so manipulated as to render Chinese life inanimate.

ACKNOWLEDGMENTS

Daisy Yan Du

Derived from the Inaugural Conference of the Association for Chinese Animation Studies (ACAS: https://acas.world/) held online in spring 2021, this book has been many years in the making. I would like to thank many colleagues, professionals, and friends who have supported this project along the way. The first person I must thank is Robert (Bob) M. Graham, former director of publications at the Harvard University Asia Center. During my stay as a Harvard-Yenching visiting scholar (2017–2018) in Cambridge, I became acquainted with Bob at a publication seminar held on the Harvard campus. In April 2018, when I told him that I planned to organize an international conference about Chinese animation and produce one or two edited books out of it, Bob was genuinely interested and offered his utmost support. Since then, we have kept in touch and exchanged numerous emails over the years. His generous support was not suspended during the pandemic, as I went to Cambridge during the summer and winter breaks and discussed with him for hours the progress and details of this book project. Bob walked this project through the most difficult years until he retired in the spring of 2022. Kristen Wanner then took over the project during the book proposal submission stage and offered her most professional support, which every author dreams of having. At that time, this project encountered some challenges resulting from our keynote speaker Professor Yingjin Zhang's untimely death. Kristen helped me navigate the copyright laws in dealing with this rare situation and offered constructive suggestions. In the spring of 2023, Qin Higley stepped in and oversaw the manuscript review and publication stage. She was extremely professional and punctual, always replying to my emails within twenty-four hours and answering my questions patiently, thoughtfully, and warmly. Without the three editors' dedication and hard work, this book could never have been published in such a timely manner.

After I left Harvard and returned to the Hong Kong University of Science and Technology (HKUST) in the spring of 2019, I discussed my envisioned conference with Kellee Tsai, dean of the School of Humanities and Social Science (SHSS) at my university, who, on hearing the idea for the first time, was even more excited than me. She immediately promised to fund the conference and assigned a secretary in her office to assist me. When more and more scholars approached me and expressed their desire to participate in the conference, I reached out to Andrew (Andy) Cohen, director of the HKUST Institute of Advanced Studies (IAS), for more funding. Andy simply asked how much extra funding I needed and wired the amount to my grant account within a few days. When the originally scheduled in-person conference (May 2020) was suspended by the pandemic, Kellee and Andy were more worried than I was and held meetings to discuss how to deal with the difficult situation. When we decided to postpone the conference by one year and move it online, Andy assigned a team of technicians and secretaries in his office to help me with the logistics. In addition to these two generous sponsors, I must thank Steven (Steve) Miles, head of the Division of Humanities at HKUST, for providing generous staff and financial support as well. I especially thank him for his efforts in securing the Hong Kong government funding (Job Creation Scheme) for me to hire a full-time research assistant for several years to help with the administrative and technical issues related to the ACAS conferences and this edited book. I can never say enough to thank Kellee, Andy, and Steve for their trust, generosity, and vision. They were the angels for the emerging field of Chinese animation studies, and I sincerely hope that this book truly lives up to their generous investment over the years.

The marathon ACAS Inaugural Conference was launched on Zoom between March 1 and May 12, 2021. We had nearly seventy speakers and 553 public registrants from thirty-two countries and regions. I must first acknowledge Liu Wenning's efforts in persuading the China Film Archive to screen its precious collection of early Chinese animated shorts at the conference. I thank our staff members and technicians who worked around the clock for this conference. Angi Law from the dean's office helped me navigate the complicated administrative system of my university and held in South Korea in June 2023, at which this ongoing book project was promoted to potential readers for the first time.

In June 2023, John, Yiman, and I co-organized a book publication workshop in honor of our keynote speaker Professor Yingjin Zhang (1957–2022). Professor Yingjin Zhang was one of the two keynote speakers at the ACAS Inaugural Conference in 2021. He submitted his rigorously researched and well-polished conference paper to me one month prior to the deadline. I was deeply impressed by his punctuality, reliability, and professionalism. The entire field of Chinese film studies was in distress after hearing the sad news of his untimely passing in June 2022. His celebrated book, *Chinese National Cinema* (Routledge, 2004), has become a textbook for undergraduate and graduate students, nurturing generations of young scholars interested in Chinese cinema. In that book, he did touch on Chinese animation, though very briefly. Perhaps it was no coincidence that his swan song, published posthumously in this edited volume, is about Chinese animation.

To support a pre-publication workshop for this book, Kellee provided the full funding requested in my budget. Andy provided us with his well-equipped conference room with a beautiful ocean view in the IAS building. To make this workshop well staffed, Steve sent his secretary Rita Chui to help me with the logistics, such as the reservation of conference and hotel rooms, meals, and commuting buses. Kellee dispatched Jenny Lim from her office to help me navigate the complicated financial system. I thank Rita and Jenny for working tirelessly for this workshop and will always appreciate their dedication and unconditional support. I must acknowledge the hard work of my research assistant Richard Li Fan, who worked on this project for several years. He diligently liaised with the contributors through numerous emails and helped with the preparation of PowerPoint slides and other technical tasks for the book publication workshop. He also assisted me in formatting and proofreading the manuscript. I hope by the time this book comes out, he will have realized his dream of emigrating to Canada.

I am indebted to my HKUST colleagues Jianmei Liu and Yan Lianke for their generous help in locating Professor Yingjin Zhang's widow, Xiao Su (Little Su). In February 2022, I lost contact with Professor Yingjin Zhang. I asked around but no one knew his whereabouts. He passed away that June, but the news of his passing was not publicized until November. After

Kristen advised me to seek permission from his family, I started a search around the world but to no avail. In January 2023, I told Jianmei about it during a casual conversation, and she assured me that she would be able to find Xiao Su. Jianmei asked the renowned writer Yan Lianke, Sin Wai Kin Professor of Chinese Culture at IAS, who had just helped Xiao Su with the publication of her widely circulated memorial blogs in mainland China. Through WeChat, Yan Lianke secured her written permission. I am very thankful to Xiao Su for her generous assistance. Although she chose to live a private and secluded life away from the limelight of academia, she still responded to my request enthusiastically and gave her permission quickly. She did not want to disclose her full name to the public, so I have used the name Xiao Su here.

I am grateful to David Der-wei Wang and Alexander Zahlten (Alex) for their unfailing support in contributing the foreword and afterword of this book. When I was preparing my book chapter about women animators' lyrical animation in the 1980s, I revisited David Der-wei Wang's book *The Lyrical in Epic Time: Modern Chinese Intellectuals and Artists Through the 1949 Crisis* (Columbia University Press, 2015) and realized that animation and literature were very close to each other. I wondered whether he had something to say about Chinese animation, so I invited him. To my surprise, he was very interested in the topic and enthusiastically completed his contribution on time. When I realized that no chapter dealt with Chinese and Japanese animation, I invited Alex to write an afterword to reflect on the topic. Alex delivered on his promise well before the deadline and offered his always unfailing support. In addition to the two special contributors, all other contributors also completed their chapters punctually. I thank them all for their professionalism and reliability. My special thanks go to Jie Li, who helped connect me with some potential contributors for this book.

The three anonymous reviewers read the manuscript carefully and provided us with constructive suggestions for further improvement. I thank them for their enthusiasm, compliments, and critical insights. I especially thank one of the reviewers for the page-by-page comments and corrections.

My thanks go to Chen Hailu for connecting me with the film producer Guan Minbo to seek the permission of our cover art. Hailu originally contributed a paper on *Goral Flying* (*Banling feidu*, 2025), the first CGI ink-painting animated feature film in greater China, to this edited book. Because the film was still in the making at the Shanghai Animation Film Studio, she was not allowed to disclose much information about it. She ended up withdrawing her paper and published a short essay about the film on the ACAS website instead. A film still from *Goral Flying* is the perfect cover art for this book because the film marks a new milestone for Chinese animation in the digital age. I also thank Hailu for designing the ACAS logo back in 2017, in which she used the concept of digital ink painting, combined with the interplay between images and words, to stand for Chinese animation. My sincere thanks also go to Guan Minbo for her efforts in securing the permission for our cover art from the Shanghai Animation Film Studio. I am grateful to Chang Guangxi, one of the directors of *Goral Flying*, for persuading the Shanghai Animation Film Studio to make an exception for me by providing the cover art for this book earlier than the originally scheduled time.

Last, I thank our copyeditor Helen Glenn Court and our indexer Steven Moore for their professional and timely work that helped speed up the publication process of this book.

The publication of this book was financially supported by the Research Grants Council of Hong Kong (Project Number: GRF 16601823), the Global China Center under SHSS, and the Book Publication Capacity Fund from the Division of Humanities, HKUST.

NOTE TO THE READER

This book uses the *pinyin* system. For scholars who mainly write and publish in English, we present their given names first and family names second. For those who mainly write and publish in Chinese or Japanese, we follow the Chinese and Japanese practices of presenting family names first and given names second.

To respect the linguistic and cultural differences in different regions and places, we let the authors decide to use either simplified or traditional Chinese characters in their chapters.

assisted me with the paperwork. Linus See, Tsz Chun Chan, and Eric Lin from IAS helped with the publicity and promotion of the conference and provided crucial administrative and technical support before, during, and after the conference. My research assistant Vincent Chao helped me with his meticulous attention to administrative issues, video editing, and paperwork. My PhD student Muyang Zhuang, who is now a tenure-track assistant professor at the College of Media and Arts of Tongji University (Shanghai), worked on the simultaneous translation in the chat room and impressed everyone with his accuracy, resourcefulness, and quick wit.

After I kicked off the conference, many colleagues approached me and expressed their interest in becoming involved with ACAS. I began to think about the expansion of ACAS, given the increasing visibility of Chinese animation studies in English-language academia. John A. Crespi and Yiman Wang became core members of ACAS in June 2021 and have brought new blood and dynamism to the field since then. I thank them for their unreserved trust when I initially approached them for an ACAS online database project in 2015. John firmly believed in what I was doing and immediately contributed an article to the ACAS website. That article was later revised into the introduction of his second monograph, *Manhua Modernity: Chinese Culture and the Pictorial Turn* (University of California Press, 2020). Yiman Wang contributed "The Animation that Deconstructs Itself—Liu Jian's *Piercing I* and *Have a Nice Day*," an essay she is now expanding into a bigger project. I thank them for working diligently as the associate editors of the ACAS website to acquire new contributions over the past few years, thus expanding the scope and diversifying the perspectives of the ACAS online database. More important, I extend my heartfelt thanks to them for their professional service in co-editing this book. We ran most of the editorial meetings online during the pandemic, gradually giving a coherent shape to this book, despite our disagreements and even arguments. John and Yiman read the papers carefully and offered invaluable suggestions for further improvement. I am sure that our authors benefited a lot from their feedback and have improved their writings significantly. I especially thank John for rendering our ideas in elegant yet objective language for the introduction. I also thank him for organizing "Defining the Paradigms: A Roundtable on the Emerging Fields of 'Chinese' Animation Studies and 'Chinese' Comics Studies" at the AAS-in-Asia conference multiplicities of Chinese animation. In doing so, this book defines Chinese animation studies as a new field that has emerged from the peripheries of modern Chinese literature and film studies on the one hand, and from the margins of Western and Japanese animation studies on the other.

How this field has materialized will look familiar to anyone who has followed the development of animation studies over the past several decades. From scattered essays in cinema studies in the 1990s to general histories of the art form in the early 2000s, and to increasingly specialized articles and monographs since the mid-2010s, Chinese animation studies has, like studies of American, European, and Japanese animation, emerged from, and in the shadow of, cinema studies. The first scholar to introduce Chinese animation to English-language readers was American filmmaker and film historian Jay Leyda, who touched occasionally on Chinese animation in the earliest book-length study in English of Chinese film, *Dianying: Electric Shadows*.[3] Through the 1980s and 1990s, Chinese film studies was itself a developing field, busy constructing its own histories and paradigms. In retrospect, the first essay on Chinese animation from that period, Marie-Claire Quiquemelle's account of the pioneering Wan brothers, thus seems fortunate to have found a place at the tail end of one of the first edited volumes on Chinese cinema in 1991.[4] Two years later, Mary Ann Farquhar's analysis of National Style (*minzu fengge* 民族风格) in Shanghai Animation Film Studio (SAFS) films was a breakthrough piece for its publication in *Animation Journal*, one of the earliest academic publications to focus exclusively on animation.[5] John Lent's 2001 edited volume *Animation in Asia and the Pacific* broadened the scope of Chinese animation with lively accounts of animation and animators not just in mainland China but in Taiwan, Hong Kong, and Singapore as well.[6]

Perhaps unsurprisingly given animation studies' position as a subfield within cinema studies, Chinese animation gained recognition through

3. Jay Leyda, *Dianying: An Account of Films and the Film Audience in China* (Cambridge, MA: MIT Press, 1972).

4. Quiquemelle, "The Wan Brothers."

5. Mary Ann Farquhar, "Monks and Monkey: A Study of 'National Style' in Chinese Animation," *Animation Journal* 1, no. 2 (1993): 5–27.

6. John A. Lent, ed., *Animation in Asia and the Pacific* (Bloomington: Indiana University Press, 2001).

the work of film scholars during the first fifteen years of the twenty-first century.[7] That state of affairs began to change in the mid-2010s due to a combination of factors: the expansion of animation studies in general, the greater accessibility of actual animation films through Internet video-streaming, and perhaps most importantly, the rapid development of both commercial and independent animation facilitated by digital technologies of animation production, as well as massive state investment in mainland China's domestic animation industry. In the wake of these changes, interest in Chinese animation accelerated. One landmark was a double special issue of the *Journal of Chinese Cinemas* in 2017. The contributions to that issue suggested a new diversity of scholarly innovations related to animation, from reconsiderations of the Wan brothers and SAFS to the interventions of Chinese animation in eco-cinema, cinephilia, and the postdigital.[8] Around the same time, scholarly monographs began to map out the historical and artistic breadth of Chinese animation in ever-greater detail. Rolf Giesen's book provides a comprehensive list of nearly one hundred years of works of animation.[9] Studies with sharper historical and analytical foci soon followed, from Sean Macdonald's perceptive

7. Yingjin Zhang, *Chinese National Cinema* (New York: Routledge, 2004); Stephanie Donald, *Little Friends: Children's Film and Media Culture in China* (Lanham, MD: Rowman & Littlefield, 2005); Paola Voci, *China on Video: Smaller-Screen Realities* (London: Taylor & Francis Group, 2010); Weihong Bao, *Fiery Cinema: The Emergence of an Affective Medium in China, 1915–1945* (Minneapolis: University of Minnesota Press, 2015); Jie Li, "A National Cinema for a Puppet State: The Manchurian Motion Picture Association," in *The Oxford Handbook of Chinese Cinemas*, ed. Carlos Rojas (New York: Oxford University Press, 2013), 79–97; Paola Voci, "DV and Animateur Cinema in China," in *DV-Made China: Digital Subjects and Social Transformations after Independent Film*, ed. Zhen Zhang (Honolulu: University of Hawai'i Press, 2015), 260–88; Daisy Yan Du, "The Dis/appearance of Animals in Animated Film during the Chinese Cultural Revolution, 1966–1976," *Positions: Asia Critique* 24, no. 2 (2016): 435–79; Paola Voci, "Para-animation in Practice and Theory: The Animateur, the Embodied Gesture and Enchantment," *Animation* 18, no. 1 (March 2023): 23–41 ; Daisy Yan Du, "The Manchukuo Film Association and Its Afterlives: Animated Filmmaking in Wartime and Postwar Peking," *Journal of Cinema and Media Studies* 63, no. 3 (Spring 2024): 119–42.

8. See *Journal of Chinese Cinemas* 11, nos. 2 & 3 (2017). The special issues were edited by Li Guo and Jinying Li.

9. Rolf Giesen, *Chinese Animation: A History and Filmography, 1922–2012* (Jefferson, NC: McFarland, 2015).

discussion of SAFS animation classics to Weihua Wu's account of the sociocultural redefinition of Chinese animation during the thirty years of the post–Cultural Revolution reform period and Daisy Yan Du's analysis of transnationalism and Chineseness from the 1940s to the 1970s.[10] The most recent book-length studies have focused on rapidly emerging phenomena in contemporary animation, such as Teri Silvio's theorization of performance and animation in twenty-first-century Taiwan knight-errant puppetry, the postsocialist media ecology that hosted independent animation in China, and mainstream animated feature films using computer-generated images (CGI) in China's marketized entertainment economy since 1995.[11] A defining moment within all this scholarly activity was the year 2015, which marked the establishment in Hong Kong of the Association for Chinese Animation Studies (ACAS), an organization created to foster intellectual community among the growing numbers of scholars, researchers, teachers, students, animators, and fans of Chinese animation around the world. The association's inaugural conference for scholars, held online in the spring of 2021, was the first academic conference in English devoted to Chinese animation. The best of the conference can be found in this edited volume.

10. Sean Macdonald, *Animation in China: History, Aesthetics, Media* (London: Routledge, 2016); Weihua Wu, *Chinese Animation, Creative Industries, and Digital Culture* (Abingdon, Oxon: Routledge, 2018); Wu's monograph was based on his PhD dissertation, "Animation in Postsocialist China: Visual Narrative, Modernity, and Digital Culture" (City University of Hong Kong, 2006), which is the first in English about Chinese animation; Daisy Yan Du, *Animated Encounters: Transnational Movements of Chinese Animation, 1940s–1970s* (Honolulu: University of Hawai'i Press, 2019); Du's monograph was derived from her PhD dissertation, "On the Move: The Trans/national Animated Film in 1940s–1970s China" (University of Wisconsin-Madison, May 2012), which is the second.

11. Teri Silvio, *Puppets, Gods, and Brands: Theorizing the Age of Animation from Taiwan*, (Honolulu: University of Hawai'i Press, 2019); Wenhai Zhou, *Chinese Independent Animation: Renegotiating Identity in Modern China* (Cham: Palgrave Macmillan, 2020); Shaopeng Chen, *The New Generation in Chinese Animation* (London: Bloomsbury Academic, 2022). Also of note are Winnie Fu, ed., *Frame after Frame* (Hong Kong: Hong Kong Film Archive, 2006) on Hong Kong animation and Daisy Yan Du, ed., *Chinese Animation and Socialism: From Animators' Perspectives* (Leiden: Brill, 2022), which comprises chapters written by animators rather than scholars. The translated, two-volume *History of Chinese Animation I & II* (London: Routledge, 2020) edited by Lijun Sun provides a panoramic historical overview similar to Giesen's *Chinese Animation*.

Any book of this sort, through processes of selection and arrangement, imparts a certain shape to its topic. With *Chinese Animation: Multiplicities in Motion*, we gesture toward a fluid dynamism akin to the medium of animation itself. A keyword in animation studies—*plasmaticness*—captures that idea well. In his admiring but ambivalent theorization of early Disney animation, Soviet filmmaker Sergei Eisenstein coined the term to denote the transformation, deformation, stretching, elongation, inflation, and deflation of animated bodies, characterized by "a rejection of once-and-forever allotted form, freedom from ossification, the ability to dynamically assume any form."[12] Eisenstein celebrated the rejection of rigid, realist forms as liberatory, and even revolutionary, for its potentials to break free from conventional perceptions and experiences of the world. An academic edited volume of articles is, of course, not the same thing as a jumping, jouncing, bending, bouncing Disney character. Yet plasmaticness is a helpful guiding metaphor for this book's goal of capturing the many potentials, both active and latent, set in motion by the emergence of Chinese animation studies.

Undeniably, the essays in this book build on the foundation of existing, and steadily growing, scholarship on Chinese animation studies. With the idea of the plasmatic, however, we draw attention not to verticality, building architectonically up from a base, but to notions of pliability and openness, to the need to stretch and deform certain guiding conventions. The most prominent convention to confront is the seemingly unavoidable act of presenting this book as Chinese animation. We are fully aware that using the word *Chinese* to refer to the variety of works discussed in this volume preempts other ways of constructing the field. As Thomas Lamarre has pointed out, the very phrase *Chinese animation* affects a geographical aggregation that oversimplifies the "migration of talents, international exhibition venues, modes of coproduction and co-investment, not to mention constant stylistic hybridization" that has decentered animation production among many disparate regions within, and beyond, the places conventionally regarded as being geographically or culturally Chinese.[13] The problem

12. Sergei Eisenstein, *Eisenstein on Disney*, ed. Jay Leyda, trans. Alan Upchurch (London: Methuen, 1988), 21.

13. Thomas Lamarre, "The Animation of China: An Interim Report," *Journal of Chinese Cinemas* 11, no. 2 (2017): 123–39, 125.

is compounded by the conventional, and grammatically unavoidable, use of prepositional phrases such as *animation in China*, which leads one to imagine a rigidly bounded place on the globe distinguished by a set of homogeneous Sinophonic, Sinographic, or Sino-cultural characteristics.[14]

Despite these formidable issues, using the words *China* and *Chinese* is a practical necessity that makes it possible to find this volume among countless others on related subjects. What we recommend, then, is that the nation-centric name of this book be regarded as an act of what Gayatri Spivak calls "strategic essentialism."[15] We provisionally use essentialist-sounding concepts like Chinese and China to posit Chinese animation as a discursively constructed constellation different from other national animations, thereby asserting the presence and visibility of Chinese animation in a field that has long been dominated by studies of American, European, and Japanese animations. In this sense, terms such as *Chinese animation* and *animation in China* may suggest a minority, if not victimized, position, despite their totalizing and hegemonic tendency to erase internal differences. Thus, on the one hand, the seemingly unitary identity implied by this book's title asserts in its own right a distinct perceptibility of Chinese animation in the field of world animation studies. At the same time, however, the dynamic multiplicity of essays gathered under this title collectively construct and deconstruct Chinese animation as a living and fluid constellation of creators, institutions, practices, and works that form an ever-shifting assemblage in decentered, dehierarchized, and globalized space, thus challenging the homogenizing tendencies of Chinese animation. As we see it, then, just as the art of animation confounds neat borders of arts, region, genre, and academic discipline, the field of Chinese animation studies, in the spirit of the plasmatic, is a field without fences.

In addition to challenging imagined spatial borders, this volume invites its readers to reconsider temporal borders, to think outside the boxes of historical periods and beyond the temporal lines extending through stories of origin. As Rita Felski, invoking Bruno Latour's actor-network

14. Ani Maitra and Rey Chow, "What's 'In'? Disaggregating Asia through New Media Actants," in *Routledge Handbook of New Media in Asia*, eds. Larissa Hjorth and Olivia Khoo (London: Routledge, 2015), 20.

15. Gayatri Chakravorty Spivak, "Subaltern Studies: Deconstructing Historiography," in *Other Worlds: Essays in Cultural Politics* (New York: Routledge, 2006), 270–304.

INTRODUCTION

Chinese Animation

A Statement of the Field

Daisy Yan Du, John A. Crespi, and Yiman Wang

This book arrives almost precisely a century after a screening of several American cartoons in a small Shanghai theater inspired the four Wan brothers—Laiming, Guchan, Chaochen, and Dihuan—to begin experimenting with animation in their tiny, cramped apartment using pencils, paper, a few lamps, and an old camera.[1] The brothers could not have known it at the time, but the passion they had for the new and seemingly magical art form was shared by creative contemporaries around the globe, from the Americas to Europe, the early Soviet Union, Japan, and India.[2] Chinese animation's global nature, inseparable from its localized character, has remained constant over the past hundred years. In the wake of geopolitical reconfigurations, technological innovations, and economic transformations, however, almost everything else has changed. The essays in this volume examine these transformations in the past, present, and future of Chinese animation. The authors do not tell one story, but instead adopt diverse methods to reflect on the artists, institutions, traditions, ideologies, technologies, and media that have over time formed, and continue to form, the

1. Marie-Claire Quiquemelle, "The Wan Brothers and Sixty Years of Animated Film in China," in *Perspectives on Chinese Cinema*, ed. Chris Berry (London: British Film Institute, 1991), 176.

2. Giannalberto Bendazzi, *Animation: A World History*, vol. 1 (Boca Raton, FL: CRC Press, 2016), 27–91. On early animation in India, see John A. Lent, "Ram Mohan and RM-USL: India's Change Agents of Animation," *Animation World Magazine* 3, no. 5 (August 1998), https://www.awn.com/mag/issue3.5/3.5pages/3.5lent.html.

theory, writes, "Time is not a tidy sequence of partitioned units, but a profusion of whirlpools and rapids, eddies and flows, in which objects, ideas, images, and texts from different moments swirl, tumble, and collide in ever-changing combinations and constellations."[16] That sentence, seeming almost to describe a work of experimental animation, speaks to the way we would like this volume to be read: as a guide to the alliances, attachments, diffusions, mimicries, and translations that pervade Chinese animated motifs, motions, genres, interfaces, and irruptions from Tang dynasty Mogao cave murals to *Kung Fu Hustle*.

How have we converted all these plasmatic multiplicities into the conventionally fixed form of an edited volume? The contributions resist being arrayed into any sequential history of Chinese animation, or being carved up by geographical regions to form some sort of imagined space of mainland China and other Chinese-speaking areas, or lining up obediently under a linguistically inspired header such as Sinophone animation.[17] Familiar and seemingly realist concepts of history, geography, and language are far too static, too prone to order and hierarchy, to capture the range of overt

16. Rita Felski, "Context Stinks!," *New Literary History* 42, no. 4 (Autumn 2011): 578.

17. We do not use Shu-mei Shih's term *Sinophone* animation because the term connotes resistance to mainland China. For better or worse, the animated films covered in our edited book are primarily set in or connected to mainland China, and it is impossible for us to erase its presence. We cannot use Sheldon Lu's term *Chinese-language* animation because many Chinese animated films include no languages at all but rely on images and music to deliver the themes and tell the stories. Additionally, some Chinese animated films were made by animators who do not speak Chinese languages. The rich diversity of the animated films presented in this book cannot be adequately addressed by the issue of language alone, so we do not want to emphasize the Chinese language. Alexander Zahlten attempts to resolve the issues brought on by phrases such as *Japanese animation* in the afterword of this book by introducing a new term, *animation associated with Japan*. We find it illuminating for the Chinese case, because all the animated films discussed in this volume are somehow associated with China. We cannot use "animation associated with China" for our book title because it is too long and does not function well for a book title. For the term *Sinophone*, see Shu-mei Shih, "The Concept of the Sinophone," *PMLA* 126, no. 3 (May 2011): 709–18. For similar ideas, see Rey Chow, "Introduction: On Chineseness as a Theoretical Problem," *boundary 2* 25, no. 3 (Autumn 1998): 1–24. For the debates between Sheldon Lu and Li Daoxin about the term *Chinese-language cinema*, see Shaoyi Sun, "Chinese-language Film or Chinese Cinema? Review of an Ongoing Debate in the Chinese Mainland," *Journal of Chinese Cinemas* 10, no. 1 (2016): 61–66.

and subtle relations threading throughout this book. The same goes for using other ready-to-hand subcategories, such as cinema and animation, stop-motion animation, early animation, socialist animation, digital animation, swordsman animation, and so on. The chapters indeed touch on all these important topics but the volume resists the urge to divide the field into animation types. That sort of division would wall off the multiple motions that make Chinese animation such a productively fluid field of study.

In recognition of all these multiplicities, the contributions to this book have been laid out in a manner that extends the vision of Professor Yingjin Zhang, the brilliant, generous, and admired scholar of Chinese film who gave one of the two keynote addresses at the 2021 ACAS Inaugural Conference, and who sadly and unexpectedly passed away in June 2022. In his address, Professor Zhang proposed an understanding of Chinese animation as media archaeology, an "alternative archive of Chinese film history" whose multiplicity, heterogeneity, and playful encounters with spectators in a variety of historical spaces and moments entail not a telos of development, but rather "multiple lines of descent." With Professor Zhang's vision in mind, we invite readers to approach the several sections of this book—junctures, gender, identities, digitality, and practices—as nodal points in a larger heterogeneous archive of Chinese animation. These themes, suggested by the essays themselves, emphasize how Chinese animation studies can shapeshift, freely aggregating, disaggregating, and reaggregating in ways that cut across a multiplicity of times, places, arts, genres, institutions, technologies, and industries. We also, in the concluding words of Professor Zhang's address, urge readers to "keep an open mind vis-à-vis Chinese animation, tracking parallel and parallax histories and trajectories, envisioning different futures, and revisiting forgotten pasts so as to better understand the present."[18]

By starting with the theme "Junctures," we foreground the futility of talking about animation apart from the many forms and genres of artistic practice that animation absorbs, modifies, enhances, and destabilizes. Put another way, we recognize the multiple instances of cross-mediation and remediation that give animation its defining heterogeneity. Here we begin with Panpan Yang's analysis of the co-emergence of animation and early Chinese cinema in her chapter "The Animation of Inanimate Objects in

18. See Yingjin Zhang's keynote essay in this book, 30.

Chinese Silent Cinema." By examining the role of stop-motion animation and other "tricks" applied to early Shanghai films of both fantasy and melodrama, Yang argues that animation helped create the conditions for an affective "enchanted space" that engaged the imaginations of China's early filmgoers. Of particular note, Yang finds Shanghai's martial arts films of the 1920s to be an important point of contact between cinema and animation. Such swordsman or knight-errant (*wuxia* 武侠) tales feature prominently in the Chinese popular entertainment tradition as well as in the development of Chinese animation practices. The next chapter, Jinying Li's "From Animation to Martial Arts: Toward the Transcendence of False Movements," brings the affinity between animation and cinematic tricks to the present by revealing resonances between the media-specific quality of animation and the conventions of the martial arts film from 1920s Shanghai to contemporary Hong Kong. With an eye to the prototypical Chinese superhero, Monkey King from the classic novel *Journey to the West*, Li points to the techniques by which animation and martial arts films both strive to transcend the moving image. Her exploration of the juncture between these two forms of action film brings new insight regarding the fundamental cinematic conundrum of using still images to generate movement.

The next two chapters in this section explore transmedial junctures in a key institutional locus for Chinese animation, namely the SAFS, where sponsorship by the socialist state facilitated a range of experimentation from the 1950s through the early 1990s. Linda Zhang's "'Toy Country': Playful Innovation in Socialist Chinese Puppet Animation" guides us through the pedagogy of world-building at the intersection of puppet animation and puppet craft in 1950s China. What Zhang discovers in this formative period is a resonance between the making of puppet animation films that narrate stories of playful, inventive, animated toys and the reinvention of puppets themselves as objects of ideologically constructive play. Where Linda Zhang explores the conjuncture of puppet animation and puppet making in the socialist 1950s, Shasha Liu takes on intermedial transformations in SAFS fine arts animation aimed at reinventing the animation industry after the Cultural Revolution. Liu performs a sensitively contextualized comparative analysis of two SAFS fine arts-style animations in the 1980s, *The Deer of Nine Colors* (*Jiuse lu* 九色鹿, 1981) and *Jiazi Saves the Deer* (*Jiazi jiulu* 夹子救鹿, 1985), both inspired by Dunhuang cave paintings. Her reading of these two films reveals the introduction of linear narrative and cinematic editing, the former induced by competition from *lianhuanhua* comic books, and the latter a response to competition from the global animation market.

The three essays in section 2, "Gender," highlight the often-overlooked agencies of women, either as symbolic figures or as actual artists, who have enhanced Chinese animation's powers of invention and imagination. Tim Shao-Hung Teng's chapter, "Psychic Grannies: Animation and Animism in Turn-of-the-Century Taiwan," offers an auto-ethnographically informed reading of the 1998 Taiwan feature animation *Grandma and Her Ghosts* (*Mofa ama* 魔法阿媽). Teng's analysis sets the tone for this section by delaminating the meanings embodied by the film's central character: a rural Taiwanese spirit medium, or "psychic granny." As a socially and politically peripheral figure possessing a certain occult power, this animated grandma's identity as a medium speaks to the power of the marginalized to disrupt and decenter the hegemonic claims of history, gender politics, geopolitics, and theories of media, much like the medium of animation itself. Women animators in the urban center of Shanghai are the topic of Daisy Yan Du's "Suspended Authorship: Women Animation Directors in Socialist China, 1940s–1980s," a meticulously researched account of the obscured contributions of SAFS female animation directors Chen Bo'er, Tang Cheng, Lin Wenxiao, and Hu Yihong. Working in a male-dominated field, yet one implicitly feminized by animation's subordination to the cinematic mainstream, Chen, Tang, Lin, and Hu challenged a state-owned, patriarchal system that suspended their claim to authorship. Their efforts, argues Du, opened the way for women independent animators to flourish in the 1990s and beyond. Picking up where Du leaves off, Paola Voci's chapter "When Animation Is *Accented* and *Gendered:* The Feminist Gestures of Women Animateurs" explores the growing visibility of contemporary female artists now transforming animation, and claiming their creative agency, through their work as independent artists. They do this, Voci argues, through creative practices that inhabit a liminal space of "light cultures," neither mainstream nor avant-garde, where their perspectives, gazes, voices, and corporeal presence are transforming the modalities of animation.

In section 3, "Identities," we have included essays that explore how changing animation technologies have in turn reshaped the ramifications of Chineseness. In a conscious contradiction to this volume's title, these essays thwart any simplistic idea of a distinctively Chinese animation. Indeed, the fundamental heterogeneity of animation as an artistic, technological, experimental, and globalized practice confounds assertions of essentialist cultural belonging, despite frequent claims to the contrary. Here we begin with Shannon Brownlee's essay on ink-painting animation, which asks the deceptively simple question, "What's in a Line?" Brownlee argues that even though ink-painting animation is typically viewed as quintessentially Chinese, it is in practice fraught with processes of diffusion across national borders, analogous to how a brush stroke of wet ink seeps across the surface of mulberry paper.

The next two chapters explore animation's construction of place in Taiwan and Hong Kong. Jasmine Yu-Hsing Chen's "Homemaking Allegory: Animating Taiwanese Local Memory in *The Little Sun*" traces the shift away from a China-centric imagination of homeland in Taiwan animation after the lifting of martial law in 1987. That shift was facilitated in part by the evolution of Taiwan's animation industry through the 1990s, when it developed beyond its role of outsourcing for U.S. and Japanese productions to produce original, self-branded animations. What Chen highlights is how the growth of localized production coincided with political liberalization to create an opportunity for animators to deploy their medium for reimagining Taiwanese identity. Chen's analysis of the television series *Little Sun* (*Xiao taiyang* 小太陽, 2010) thus examines how the allegory of homemaking in *Little Sun* recenters the identity of mainland immigrants in the local milieu of Taiwan. Jessica Chan's chapter "Animation as Action: The Old Master Q Animation Trilogy in Hong Kong" turns to comedy animation to explore questions of localized identity in the 1980s feature-length animations starring Hong Kong's most iconic cartoon character. These slapstick 2D films, Chan argues, not only exploit the fluid and plasmatic qualities of animation to reflect and construct a quintessential vision of Hong Kong's capitalist modernity in a moment of transition from colonial rule, but also remediate global cinematic pop culture icons from Bruce Lee to E.T. in a way that challenges the corporeal authenticity of live-action film.

Section 4, "Digitality," offers two perspectives on the encounter between digital animation and filmic realism. In "Animation as Agency in the Glistening City-Orb: Jia Zhangke's *The World*," Wendy Larson provides a multipronged analysis of the vividly irruptive fantasy sequences in Jia Zhangke's otherwise hyperrealist 2004 film *The World* (*Shijie* 世界). Against readings of the film that explain Jia's surreal flash animation as no more than a foil to his postsocialist critical realism, Larson argues that the film's visually jarring shifts between scenes of gray and gritty reality to transcendent digitized visions of color and flight represent not just the potential agency of the film's migrant worker characters, but also Jia's vision for overcoming the weighty conventions of cinematic realism. Where Larson examines digital animation's feeling of surreality vis-à-vis realist filmmaking, Yiman Wang engages with simulated reality through digital real feel. Wang's chapter, "When a Cat Flies: Futures of 3D Animation through *Cats and Peachtopia*," delves into a 2018 3D animation feature whose box office failure nearly bankrupted Light Chaser, the Chinese production company that sought to become China's Pixar. Wang examines *Cats and Peachtopia* (*Mao yu Taohuayuan* 猫与桃花源) using three disparate approaches to digital technology and algorithmic media production: the paradox of non-indexical real feel, the queer reading of Pixar animated films, and the new materialist critique of digital technology's geopolitical and environmental ramifications. Wang argues that *Cats and Peachtopia*'s commercial failure problematizes a priori unidirectional drive of futurism while inviting us to imagine multiple and equally viable heterogeneous futures.

The volume's fifth and final section gathers a set of practice-based research essays by current animators, whose visions are steering Chinese animation into a multiplicity of futures. Their topics, ranging from industrial to indie, are so new that they have yet to garner academic attention. Here the focus is on innovation and precarity in a fast-developing range of practices pushing against the boundaries of new technologies, the pressures of government regulation, the vagaries of entertainment markets, and the representation of multicultural societies. The first chapter, Jake Junjie Zhang's "The Path to Cinematic Immersion: Creating VR Animation in China," provides an insider's window into attempts to develop a cinematic language and end-user market for VR animation for the mass entertainment market. Isabel Galwey's "The Digital Turn in Hong Kong

Independent Animation" discusses the crucial role of digitality in independent animated filmmaking in Hong Kong, arguing that Hong Kong independent animation has been characterized by distinctive expressions of transmediality and nonnarrative attraction. The final chapter in this volume, Hannes Rall and Emma Harper's "Expanding Notions of Diasporic Chineseness: Toward a Singaporean Approach to VR," brings a practitioner's perspective to a recurring theme in this volume: animation's ongoing negotiation of traditional forms and modern media. Their essay reflects on and narrates how a culturally diverse team of Singaporean animators, academic researchers, and traditional performers collaborated to adapt the local Wayang Kulit tradition of shadow puppetry to the immersive experience of expanded animation.

This book concludes with Alexander Zahlten's consideration of Chinese animation studies' potential to offer a new beginning, to emerge as a field-in-formation that can unsettle long-standing, problematic patterns and assumptions resulting from the dominance of what one might call Japanimation. Zahlten's essay looks into a future that this edited volume hopes to shape. It is, of course, the goal of this volume to open the way toward new interventions into animation's present, past, and future. Although we have made *Chinese Animation: Multiplicities in Motion* as comprehensive as possible, it is of course by no means complete. Many subjects await further exploration, such as animated documentaries, animated special effects in live-action films, ethnographic animation, experimental animation, sound, music, and animation theory, to list a few. Nor should the field of Chinese animation studies be limited to Chinese-language or Han-centric points of view. Animation is nothing if not heterogeneous, and, as noted earlier, the Chineseness of Chinese animation is a porous and transmutable concept that needs to be stretched, squeezed, bent, bounced, and perhaps someday even tossed aside in favor of new analytical lexicons.

KEYNOTE ESSAY

Playful Dispositif and Remediation

Chinese Animation from the Perspective of Film History as Media Archaeology

Yingjin Zhang

Studies of Chinese animation have approached the topic from the methodologies of close reading, historical and art historical research, transnational studies, and animation and communication theories.[1] How, I ask in this chapter, can one approach Chinese animation from the perspective of film history as media archaeology? First, following Thomas Elsaesser, we understand that Chinese animation may encourage scholarship that departs from the time-honored teleological and organic models of historiography to trace multiple lines of descent rather than singular origins. In alternative parallel and parallax histories and trajectories, Chinese animation is intimately associated with several artistic genres and media while generating refreshing visual styles and forms, many of them touted for their national (*minzu* 民族) characteristics in official historiography, but subsequently judged as outdated in the wake of globalization.[2] Second, the concept of *dispositif*—involving materiality, bricolage, and assemblages—requires that we always examine the trio of medium, image, and spectator together in Chinese animation studies. The anticipation of the childlike curious spectator and fans of traditional visual and performing art forms explains particular types of national elements that dominated

1. This opening sentence was added by the editors for contextualization.

2. Thomas Elsaesser, *Film History as Media Archaeology: Tracking Digital Cinema* (Amsterdam: Amsterdam University Press, 2016).

VIDEO 1: A video recording of Professor Yingjin Zhang's keynote speech at the ACAS Inaugural Conference on March 1, 2021. To watch this video, scan the QR code with your mobile device or visit the ACAS YouTube channel: https://www.youtube.com/watch?v=GrClmeCz-TU.

Chinese animation in the socialist period of the 1950s to the 1980s. Third, in contemplating the what, when, and why of animation during the socialist period, we can better comprehend how the increasing importance of experience transformed animation into an encounter with what new technology would make possible. An investigation of media and technological innovations in Chinese animation history shows not so much definitive breaks from the past as consistent efforts at playful remediation, oftentimes generating simple delights of experiencing the familiar anew through the amalgamated artistic platform that is animation. Overall, Chinese animation represents a distinct transmedia synergy incorporating literature, theater, painting, music, and design, with its priorities shifting in different historical periods. Finally, precisely due to its inherent multiplicity and heterogeneity, Chinese animation does not conform to a single telos, despite relentless cases of historical exigency, ideological interpellation, and commercial restructuring from the 1940s onward. Chinese animation studies should therefore keep "a retrospective and prospective frame of mind at the same time" because, like cinema in general, animation is "still in permanent flux and becoming."[3]

3. Elsaesser, *Film History as Media Archaeology*, 94.

Insights from Film History as Media Archaeology

When suggesting the phrase "film history as media archaeology" in the late 1980s when early cinema had just begun to attract attention in film studies by challenging the dominant paradigms of textual criticism, Elsaesser foregrounded two key ideas of archaeology: first, the archive (the physical and virtual location of the documents, films, and objects that make up cinema's heritage), and second, the arché (origin, authority, governance, and so on).[4] In his elaboration, "The archive now shapes our view of the past more decisively than history, since the archive allows us at all times to revisit and thus to rewrite the past, to *reverse engineer our present*, and thus to fashion out of the archive also a different future."[5] Media archaeology, in this sense, aims to keep open the space for revisiting the past at multiple entry points, reassessing our present vis-à-vis alternative pasts, and reimaging a future different from what has been predetermined by the conventional models of teleological historiography.

Bringing Elsaesser's insight into animation studies, we may likewise envision Chinese animation as an *alternative archive* of Chinese film history that houses a variety of incompatible points of origin and authorities. Indeed, Chinese animation has long been alternative in Chinese film studies because it was perceived as consistently out of sync with Chinese film history in its habitual orientation to light-hearted entertainment and traditional values, and precisely due to its alterity relative to live-action fiction films, Chinese animation was rarely mentioned in standard Chinese film history before the 1990s.[6]

4. Elsaesser, *Film History as Media Archaeology*, 19, 56.

5. Elsaesser, *Film History as Media Archaeology*, 58.

6. As in other areas of Chinese film studies, histories and reference books on Chinese animation proliferated in the 2010s. See Bao Jigui 鲍济贵, *Zhongguo donghua dianying tongshi* 中国动画电影通史 (History of Chinese animation) (Beijing: Lianhuanhua chubanshe, 2010); Rolf Giesen, *Chinese Animation: A History and Filmography, 1922–2012* (Jefferson, NC: McFarland, 2015); John A. Lent and Ying Xu, "Chinese Animation Film: From Experimentation to Digitalization," in *Art, Politics, and Commerce in Chinese Cinema*, eds. Ying Zhu and Stanley Rosen (Hong Kong: Hong Kong University Press, 2010), 127–42; Sean Macdonald, *Animation in China: History, Aesthetics, Media* (New York: Routledge, 2016); Wang Liuyi 王六一, *Zhengtu: Zouxiang bainian de Zhongguo donghua* 征途：走向百年的中国动画 (March: Chinese animation enters new century), vols. 1–10 (Guizhou: Guizhou

Elsaesser frankly acknowledges the limits to our knowledge of film history. As he contends, history as archaeology "acknowledges that only a presumption of discontinuity . . . and of the fragment as lacuna . . . can give the present access to the past, which is always no more than *a past* (among many actual or possible historical 'nows'), since for the archaeologist, the past is made present to the present across nothing more than its relics and traces."[7] As typical of film historiography in general, disputes over many undocumented or not yet fully documented "origins" in Chinese cinema are numerous. In Chinese film history, *Battle of Dingjun Mountain* (*Dingjun shan* 定军山, 1905) has been accepted, albeit with a measure of uncertainty, as the first Chinese film production based on an existing Peking opera piece. Similarly, "Shu Zhendong Chinese Typewriter" (*Shu Zhendong huawen daziji* 舒振东华文打字机), an animated advertisement produced by twin brothers Wan Laiming 万籁鸣 (1899–1997) and Wan Guchan 万古蟾 (1899–1995) in 1922, has been considered one of the earliest Chinese animations,[8] thus making the Wan brothers the pioneers of the field.[9] In cases like these, what we have as verifiable documents of origin are print materials, not the actual live-action or animation works.

From the perspective of film history as media archaeology, we can stipulate that Chinese animation is a medium that contains what Elsaesser described as "relics and traces" from the past, and we therefore must admit that our understanding is necessarily limited by what has been found or rediscovered in different forms. It is through working with what we have at hand as fragmented evidence now that Elsaesser advocates for "the archaeology of possible futures and the perpetual presence of several pasts."[10] Methodologically, media archaeology reminds us to not only look forward but also look backward, as well as sideways, in exploring film history.

By emphasizing multidirectionality, heterogeneity, and variety, media archaeology further compels us to trace multiple lines of descent rather than

---

renmin chubanshe, 2012); Weihua Wu, *Chinese Animation, Creative Industries and Digital Culture* (Abingdon, Oxon: Routledge, 2018); Daisy Yan Du, *Animated Encounters: Transnational Movements of Chinese Animation* (Honolulu: University of Hawai'i Press, 2019).

7. Elsaesser, *Film History as Media Archaeology*, 99.

8. Giesen, *Chinese Animation*, 29.

9. John Lent and Ying Xu, "Chinese Animation Film."

10. Elsaesser, *Film History as Media Archaeology*, 99.

fixing definitive origins in film history. We would do better to extend our scope so as to account for parallel and parallax histories and trajectories that may be alternative to official historiography but are crucial to Chinese animation as an art form peculiarly associated with various artistic media and generative of refreshing audiovisual and performative styles and genres. However, before discussing examples of such styles and genres, we may briefly engage with dispositif, another key concept in film history as media archaeology.

Chinese Animation as Dispositif

Frank Kessler's extensive summary of theoretical deliberations on dispositif has been widely referenced in film history as media archaeology.[11] The original French meanings of *dispositif* denote "mechanism" and "ensemble of elements," and its English translations range from "apparatus," "device," and "procedure." Because the apparatus theory (as expounded by Leo Baudry and others) dominated film studies in the second half of the twentieth century, scholars have mostly opted to keep dispositif untranslated in English. Outside film studies, a number of eminent theorists have used dispositif in diverse conceptualizations, such as a totalizing field of forces (Giorgio Agamben); lines of flight (Gilles Deleuze and Félix Guattari); a heterogeneous ensemble consisting of discourses, institutions, and practices (Michel Foucault); and a space for different forms of performativity (Michel de Certeau). Within film studies, Tom Gunning has located different dispositifs, such as exhibitionist versus voyeuristic modes of presentation, or immersive fictional illusion versus playful rupture in the gaze at the camera. Among many insights that have come out of early cinema studies, cinema of attractions and aesthetics of astonishment both point to the indispensable participation of the audience, a consideration that has remained untheorized due to the previous obsession with ideal (or idealized) spectatorship. Expanding the concepts of dispositifs into a larger framework of cinematic practices, scholars have separately treated early cinema as a dispositif[12] in

11. See Errki Huhtamo and Jussi Parikka, eds., *Media Archaeology: Approaches, Applications, and Implications* (Berkeley: University of California Press, 2011); Jussi Parikka, *What Is Media Archaeology?* (London: Polity, 2012); Elsaesser, *Film History as Media Archaeology*.

12. Frank Kessler, "The Cinema of Attractions as Dispositif," in *The Cinema of Attractions Reloaded*, ed. Wanda Strauven (Amsterdam: Amsterdam University Press, 2007), 57–69.

film history in general and a trio of resonance, transparency, and agitation as distinctive dispositifs in Chinese film history in particular.[13]

For film history as media archaeology, Elsaesser offers this important definition: "a *dispositif* is a *dispositif* only when it entails a medium (a material support, most often a combination of technologies), an image (a representation, including a sound representation), and a spectator (liable to be solicited, subjectified, addressed by interpellation, or affectively and cognitively engaged)."[14] What is important here is the designation of the spectator as indispensable to the operation of a dispositif, which is never a mere medium or technology in and of itself, as if either medium or technology would have been miraculously self-sufficient to fully convey the significance of an image. The spectator, in other words, adds a crucial third dimension to a previous duo of a medium and an image. Elsaesser's tripartite conception of dispositif thus reminds us not to overcorrect the previous overemphasis on the image by proceeding to concentrate on the medium alone, because both the medium and the image are deployed and produced with the spectator in mind.

In Chinese animation, the spectator's preference was indeed a prominent factor in the creation of China's first feature-length animation film, *Princess Iron Fan* (*Tieshan gongzhu* 铁扇公主, 1941), directed by brothers Wan Laiming and Wan Guchan.[15] Although the Wan brothers had the ambition to compete with Hollywood animation, they did not opt for a wholesale borrowing from Walt Disney, not even after its global hit, *Snow White and the Seven Dwarfs* (1937), which had a successful theater run in Shanghai in 1938. Instead, the Wan brothers decided to draw from recognizable sources of Chinese elements in the design and execution of *Princess Iron Fan*: its narrative is based on the famous traditional Chinese novel, *Journey to the West* (*Xiyouji* 西游记), and its line drawing of charac-

13. Weihong Bao, *Fiery Cinema: The Emergence of an Affective Medium in China, 1915–1945* (Minneapolis: University of Minnesota Press, 2015).

14. Elsaesser, *Film History as Media Archaeology*, 113 (emphasis in the original).

15. Reportedly, the Wan Brothers assembled a team of more than one hundred artists and made more than twenty thousand drawings, a massive operation in wartime Shanghai. See Zhang Zhenhua 张振华, "Zhongguo tuohuangzhe: Wanshi shuangxiong de dongman yishu" 中国拓荒者——万氏双雄的动漫艺术 (Chinese pioneers: Wan brothers' animation arts), Sina.com, November 25, 2011, http://blog.sina.com.cn/s/blog_89bc0f1e010106gv.html.

ters may hail from a popular visual tradition in Chinese illustrated fiction (*xiuxiang xiaoshuo* 绣像小说). As early as 1936, Wan Laiming professed his orientation toward Chinese tradition in an article "Random Talks on Cartoons" (*Xianhua katong* 闲话卡通): "In order to acquire infinite vitality, China's animation must plant its roots deeply in the soil of its national tradition."[16] Many may consider this to be an authorial statement by Wan, but behind it is his consideration of a Chinese audience who would ultimately decide on the future orientation of Chinese animation.

At this juncture, we may revisit *Princess Iron Fan* as an archive and imagine its screenings in Japan-occupied Shanghai as a special experience for Chinese audiences of the early 1940s. *Princess Iron Fan* proved that animation could create a space for spectators to experience a delightful alternative to the dismal wartime exigence, to derive pleasure from a playful reconnection with traditional Chinese literature and art, and to regain their childlike mentality when everything else seemed overwhelmingly helpless and hopeless. In Shanghai as well as in overseas markets such as Singapore and Malaysia, the film achieved notable box office success. As a testimony to the efficacy of animation as dispositif, the presumption of the innocent childlike spectator in the experience of animation might have hoodwinked the Japanese censors when *Princess Iron Fan* had been given a theater run before it was quickly pulled from the market in Japan; still, the animation was believed to be "far more influential in wartime Japan than in wartime China."[17] This case demonstrated that animation "could pose a threat to the hegemony of adults and stage forms of childish mimicry that are playful, mischievous, recalcitrant, and subversive, beyond the control of adult authorities."[18] Although Daisy Yan Du has socialist animation in mind when she makes this observation, it applies to *Princess Iron Fan* as a special case of wartime animation.[19]

16. Zhang Zhenhua, "Zhongguo tuohuangzhe: Wanshi shuangxiong de dongman yishu."

17. Du, *Animated Encounters*, 19.

18. Du, *Animated Encounters*, 10.

19. Due to its playful dispositif, animation may have its own protective shield from overt ideological or political designation and interpretation. For this reason, grouping *Princess Iron Fan* among a group of "anti-Japanese propaganda films" produced by the Wan brothers may not be accurate to its historical context. See Li Guo and Jinying Li, "Animating Chinese Cinemas: A Preface," *Journal of Chinese Cinemas* 11, no. 2 (2017): 115–22.

Elsaesser considers cinema to be an effective dispositif to deliver "experience" to the spectator,[20] and he highlights film experience as an "encounter" intent on "addressing a spectator in his/her here-and-now."[21] Interestingly, Alan Cholodenko stakes a larger claim that "every encounter with film is an encounter with animation."[22] In Chinese film studies, Daisy Yan Du's monograph on Chinese animation was intentionally titled *Animated Encounters* (2019).[23] All these references to "encounter" presuppose the spectator, whose anticipated and manifested preferences for experience would shape the contours of the medium and the image of animation. Any encounter with animation, therefore, is enabled by dispositifs at various scales. As we shall see, as dispositif, Chinese animation has consistently pursued playful remediation, even in the otherwise repressive political climate of the socialist period.

Chinese Animation as Playful Remediation

Princess Iron Fan demonstrates that, in its early phase, Chinese animation already functioned as a playful dispositif that aimed to open up a range of potentials for remediation across arts, media, and technologies. True, playful dispositif may also characterize certain film subgenres, such as slapstick comedy and kung fu comedy, because they likewise anticipate the audience reaction and deliberately showcase cinematic devices within the diegesis in a way incompatible with the immersive illusion characteristic of classical cinema. Nonetheless, I would argue that, more than these cinematic subgenres, animation is a distinctive dispositif constantly looking for crossmediation and remediation.

In her study of Chinese animation of the socialist period, Yuanyuan Chen enumerates three traditional Chinese art forms that heavily influenced what she calls "classical Chinese animation."[24] First, classical Chinese

20. Elsaesser, *Film History as Media Archaeology*, 97.

21. Elsaesser, *Film History as Media Archaeology*, 132.

22. Alan Cholodenko, "The Animation of Cinema," *Semiotic Review of Books* 18, no. 2 (2008): 1–10.

23. Du, *Animated Encounters*.

24. Yuanyuan Chen, "Old or New Art? Rethinking Classical Chinese Animation," *Journal of Chinese Cinemas* 11, no. 2 (2017): 175–88.

literature provided a majority of narrative sources for Chinese animation to adopt and appropriate. Second, classical Chinese painting determined the familiar looks of Chinese animation in terms of lines, shapes, colors, and composition that would fit the ideological agenda of national styles during the socialist period. Third, traditional Chinese opera further interfaced with Chinese animation to generate recognizable facial designs, stylized bodily movements, symbolic martial arts routines, and rhythmic musical soundtracks. For example, in terms of design, sets, and colors, Wan Laiming specifically drew inspiration from Chinese traditions in visual and performative arts, such as landscape painting, architectural decorations, and operatic elements in the two-part *Uproar in Heaven* (*Danao tiangong* 大闹天宫, 1961, 1964). Wan Laiming also attempted to match operatic rhythms with camera shots, editing between scenes, and visual exaggeration to maximize humor, playfulness, and mischief in the character Monkey King. Compared with the nonchalant image of Monkey King in *Princess Iron Fan*, the adorable image of Monkey King in *Uproar in Heaven* exhibits features of traditional Chinese New Year painting (*nianhua* 年画), papercutting (*jianzhi* 剪纸), and operatic masks (*lianpu* 脸谱).[25]

Likewise, in other socialist animations, playfulness not only enhanced the refreshing experience of popular entertainment values for the audience but also encouraged the artists to play with technological innovation and explore new possibilities for crossmediation based on Chinese traditional arts and crafts. It was not a surprise that uniquely Chinese anima-

25. The figure of Monkey King in *Uproar in Heaven* was designed by the famous cartoon artist Zhang Guangyu 张光宇 (1900–1965), whose satirical illustrated series *The Cartoon Journey to the West* (*Xiyou manji* 西游漫记) was not published in book form until a decade later due to its criticism of Nationalist officials' wartime corruption and was instead exhibited to glowing reviews in Chongqing, Chengdu, and Hong Kong during 1945 and 1946. See Zhang Guangyu 张光宇, *Xiyou manji* 西游漫记 (The cartoon journey to the West) (Beijing: Renmin meishu chubanshe, 1958); Macdonald, *Animation in China*, 34–37; John A. Crespi, *Manhua Modernity: Chinese Culture and the Pictorial Turn* (Berkeley: University of California Press, 2020), 81–102. Whereas Zhang Guangyu's cartoon figures of Monkey King bear a much closer resemblance to Monkey King in *Uproar in Heaven* than Monkey King in *Princess Iron Fan*, his *Cartoon Journey to the West* is praised as "a sumptuous work, rich in comic invention, highly decorative, drawing its style not only from early Chinese art but also from that of Mexico and ancient Egypt." See Michael Sullivan, *Art and Artists of Twentieth-Century China* (Berkeley: University of California Press, 1996), 121.

tion forms, such as papercutting and ink painting (*shuimo* 水墨),[26] quickly emerged to satisfy audience curiosity as to what animation technologies could do, while keeping artistic innovation in line with the government's agenda of promoting traditional Chinese national styles and forms.[27] In the perspective of film history as media archaeology, we might regard each of these new animated crossmediation breakthroughs as new evidence of the potentiality of animation as dispositif. Indeed, as dispositif, new forms of papercutting and ink-painting animation foreground distinctive elements of materiality, bricolage, and assemblages of animation.

What deserves attention here is that Chinese animation artists almost always prioritized playfulness when they experimented with a new animation form.[28] The first papercutting animation, *Pigsy Eats Watermelon* (*Zhu Bajie chi xigua* 猪八戒吃西瓜, 1958), includes a precredit bricolage sequence in which two hands intrude into the screen, dexterously use a pair of scissors to make a papercutting head of Pigsy, and playfully assemble other moveable parts (a hat, a gown, and a watermelon) into a delightful figure of Pigsy. Similarly, the first ink-painting animation, *Little Tadpoles Look for Mama* (*Xiao kedou zhao mama* 小蝌蚪找妈妈, 1960), accentuates tiny black tadpoles' playful swimming actions against vast empty spaces (*liubai* 留白, as typical of composition in ink painting). Through a mechanism of childish identification guided by the easily comprehensible female voiceover narration, the tadpoles' innocence and persistence make their encounters with strangers who only partially resemble their mama (e.g., the goldfish with big eyes, the crab with a white belly, the turtle with four legs) ever so playful, wondrous, and ingenious.[29]

26. Helen Kang, "*Shui Mo Dong Hua*: The History and Development of Brush Painting Animation," *Animation Journal* 14 (2006): 63–75.

27. Mary Ann Farquhar, "Monks and Monkey: A Study of 'National Style' in Chinese Animation," *Animation Journal* 1, no. 2 (1993): 5–27; Jian Cui, "The Pursuit of a National Style of Chinese Animation," *Animation Journal* 14 (2006): 44–62.

28. In addition to papercutting and ink painting, new forms of socialist animation include paperfolding (*zhezhi* 折纸) and puppetry (*mu'ou* 木偶).

29. Other famous ink-painting animations of this period avoid voiceover narration and dialogue altogether and instead rely on music, sounds, and visual cues to express the characters' thoughts and emotions, thus paying tribute to traditional Chinese painting via its modern masters' recognizable subjects, for instance, Qi Baishi's 齐白石 (1864–1957) paint-

I understand playfulness as a kind of mindset, an artistic approach, or a mechanism that can enable animators to negotiate or play with the dominant ideology. Most Chinese animated films were created with a playful mindset. When needed or forced, animators could also produce politically serious films, albeit unwillingly, and the challenge for them is to use playfulness to successfully repackage serious matters, which is contingent on the negotiations between the animators and the dominant ideology. Playfulness therefore reserves the space of artistic freedom, resisting the government's top-down control of meaning.[30]

A Media Archaeological View of Chinese Socialist Animation

Chinese socialist animation provides a rich archive for crossmediality and remediation, but the fact that it fell out of favor since the 1990s after three decades of dominance in China illustrates how the history of Chinese animation does not follow a preset telos but instead goes through a tortuous route of innovation, frustration, and readjustment. Viewed from film history as media archaeology, Yuanyuan Chen's critical assessment of classical Chinese animation raises several questions. First, in terms of interpretation, Chen's statements such as Chinese artists "subordinated animation to the literary classics; over-prioritizing the techniques and conventions of traditional Chinese painting and opera inevitably tied animation to the orig-

ings of animals and flowers, or Li Keran's 李可染 (1907–1989) oxen as well as landscapes of mountains and rivers. See Panpan Yang, "Animating Landscape: Chinese Ink-and-Wash Animation, 1960–2013," *International Journal of Comic Art* 16, no. 2 (2014): 380–97. Chinese ink-painting animations also deliberately reconnected to the tradition of international silent cinema. Daisy Yan Du uses "the aesthetics of absence" to characterize ink-painting animation, suggesting that audiences appreciate this genre's invocation of silent cinema aesthetics on the one hand and the ideal world of Chinese literati (*wenren* 文人) painting on the other. The literati sentiments are perfectly embodied in *Feelings of Mountain and River* (*Shanshui qing* 山水情, 1988), a swan song to ink-painting animation. See Du, *Animated Encounters*, 131, 134.

30. This paragraph was added by the editors in line with the author's oral response to Daisy Yan Du's question about "playfulness and seriousness of Chinese animation" at the Inaugural Conference of the Association for Chinese Animation Studies.

inal masterpieces, and harmed its inherently cinematic nature"[31] are historically inaccurate and theoretically problematic. Similar to Chinese animation, fiction film in the West once relied on literature and theater to earn its legitimacy as the sixth art, especially in the classical cinema period and in genres such as heritage films. Besides, it is debatable whether the animation of any country has an "inherently cinematic nature." To cite a recent case of theorization, Thomas Lamarre differentiates between animetism and cinematism: whereas animetism is associated with "looking at the effects of speed laterally, sideways or crossways," cinematism prefers "the ballistic logistics of perception" and forever races along the trajectory of motion via new technology.[32] Rapid cuts with bombastic special effects, long takes, and long shots are equally cinematic, albeit working to please different kinds of audiences.

Second, in terms of periodization, Chen's tripartite division of post-1949 Chinese animation history into "three aesthetic phases" of classical, modern, and postmodern, "influenced, in chronological order, by traditional Chinese culture, by Western modernist art and literature and most recently by post-modernism,"[33] reveals an exclusive reliance on teleological historiography and has resulted in problematic assertions. Take a look at Chen's two assertions: "Chinese ink-painting animation keeps repeating the old-fashioned stories, out of step with the times on the theme";[34] relying on traditional arts "overshadowed the destiny of classical Chinese animation and precipitated its foreseeable decline due to its falling behind the times."[35] Chen's conception of the times is teleological in that it implies that newer is better. Besides, who set the destiny or telos of Chinese animation, classical or not? Who foresaw the reputed decline of socialist animation after the 1980s? Are modern and postmodern universal measurements on the progression of the times in history in sync across the globe?

Third, in terms of film history, Chen's conclusion that, because of its alleged overreliance on "other established art forms, classical Chinese animation arguably is a dependent rather than a free independent art,

31. Chen, "Old or New Art," 185.

32. Thomas Lamarre, *The Anime Machine: A Media History of Animation* (Minneapolis: University of Minnesota Press, 2009), 5–6.

33. Chen, "Old or New Art," 186.

34. Chen, "Old or New Art," 182.

35. Chen, "Old or New Art," 185.

which partly leads to its short-lived success and flourish,"[36] invites further contestation. For one thing, thirty years is a rather long period for any kind of success. For another, animation has hardly ever been a free independent art because, from the outset, it was produced technologically via dispositif at various scales as an interdependent, crossmedia artistic platform that conscientiously appropriated elements of literature, theater, painting, and performance, just as cinema was never a free, independent art unrelated to other established art forms. Again, film history as media archaeology reminds us that judging from a fixed vantage point of destiny and retroactively integrating certain relics and traces of the past into a coherent narrative of historical progress may miss important insights from alternative parallel and parallax views that intentionally resist or ignore this teleological mode of historiography.

Lamarre thus comments on Yuanyuan Chen's assessment, "We might look at classical Chinese animation from both sides, both deterritorializing and reterritorializing processes, without condemning or redeeming it."[37] In my view, Chinese animation of the socialist period is deterritorializing because it intentionally interfaced and integrated itself with traditional Chinese art forms and animation technology; it is reterritorializing in its effort to invent uniquely Chinese animation features and genres to distinguish itself from Hollywood, European, and Japanese animations. Historically speaking, both processes were already visible in the early 1940s with *Princess Iron Fan*, which grounded itself in Chinese traditions and foreshadowed the state-sanctioned national styles in socialist animation. By negotiating between crossmedia innovation and ideological compliance, Chinese socialist animation certainly has its redeeming qualities; after all, it was reputedly praised as the "Chinese school" of animation in world cinema for its distinct looks.[38] Nonetheless, retrospectively condemning it for falling behind the times and losing its market appeal in the 1990s and afterward revalidates the teleological model of historiography and resorts to the box office as a principal measurement of the new times to come.

36. Chen, "Old or New Art," 185.

37. Thomas Lamarre, "The Animation of China: An Interim Report," *Journal of Chinese Cinemas* 11, no. 2 (2017): 123–39.

38. Yin Yan 尹岩, "Donghua dianying zhong de Zhongguo xuepai" 动画电影中的中国学派 (The Chinese school of animation), in *Dangdai dianying* 当代电影 (Contemporary cinema), 6 (1988): 71–79; Du, *Animated Encounters*, 14.

Playful Remediation of Chinese Animation in the Digital Age

During the three decades from the 1990s to the 2010s, Chinese animation went through a prolonged downtime as it reengaged the new world of animation technologies, forms, and styles made accessible through China's reconnection with the outside world.[39] Interestingly, the Chinese government first discontinued state subsidies in animation in the 1990s, plunging it from the peak of spectacular success to a state of mere survival; in the new century, the state gradually began to reinvest in animation, but this time as part of larger crossmedia, multisector, cultural creative industries (publishing, film, television, internet, advertising, design, and gaming).[40] In this radical transition period of adaptation to frequently renewed animation technologies (flash animation, stop-motion animation, CGI animation), new styles, new audiences, and new markets, Chinese feature-length animation experienced ups and downs. Its occasional successes included *Lotus Lantern* (*Baolian deng* 宝莲灯, 1999), which combined "the commercial formula of Disney cartoons with the narrative and characters of a traditional folk story."[41]

By the 2010s, Chinese animation managed to move up in box office rankings and become a serious contender to live-action films in the Chinese market. *Monkey King: The Hero Is Back* (*Xiyouji zhi dasheng guilai* 西游记

39. Du, *Animated Encounters*, 181–85. The title of this section was added by the editors. The original title was "Conclusion."

40. The body of scholarship on Chinese cinema (including animation) as part of larger creative industries and as a state-sponsored project of soft power is growing. See, for instance, Michael Keane, *Creative Industries in China: Art, Design and Media* (London: Polity, 2013); Xiaying Xu and Tony Schirato, "Chinese Creative Industries, Soft Power and Censorship: The Case of Animation," *Communication, Politics & Culture* 48, no. 2 (2015): 24–43; Shaopeng Chen, "Industrial Transformation in Chinese Animation Cinema (1995–2015)," *New Cinemas: Journal of Contemporary Film* 15, no. 2 (2017): 157–74; Paola Voci and Hui Luo, eds., *Screening China's Soft Power* (New York: Routledge, 2018).

41. Guo and Li, "Animating Chinese Cinemas," 118. *Lotus Lantern* received RMB 12 million in investment and scored RMB 25 million at box office. See Bilibili, "Dianying zui TOP" 电影最TOP (Top films), episode 132: "Cong Wukong dao Nezha, yikouqi kanwan guochan donghua fazhan shi" 从悟空到哪吒, 一口气看完国产动画发展史 (From Monkey King to Nezha: The history of Chinese animation watched in one sitting), September 4, 2019, Bilibili.com, https://www.bilibili.com/video/av66591838.

之大圣归来, 2015) is a popular 3D animation film that earned RMB 956 million at the box office. Hailed as a "phenomenal film" (*xianxiang ji yingpian* 现象级影片), it took eight years to produce and won several major awards in China, including the Golden Rooster in 2015 and the Huabiao Prize in 2016. The next phenomenal animation, *Nezha* (*Nezha zhi motong jiangshi* 哪吒之魔童降世, 2019) set a record of RMB 5 billion at the box office and became number one top-grossing film in 2019, beating number two, *The Wandering Earth* (*Liulang diqiu* 流浪地球, 2019), a blockbuster disaster film based on Liu Cixin's 刘慈欣 world-famous, award-winning science fiction saga.

What is significant in these two recent box office successes of animation features is their persistent recourse to traditional Chinese literature, painting, and music, although their respective portrayals of Monkey King and Nezha differ radically from the same legendary figures in socialist animations, *Uproar in Heaven* and *Nezha Conquers the Dragon King* (*Nezha naohai* 哪吒闹海, 1979), the latter being the first CinemaScope animation in China. Admittedly, archetypal protagonists and familiar narratives only touch the surface of similarities between socialist and contemporary animations in China, but it is important to observe that the new generation of Chinese animation artists no longer pursue either exclusively Chinese artistic traditions or exclusively new fashions in international styles. Instead, they have appropriated and incorporated diverse resources in their playful, yet innovative audiovisual design, narrative modification, and nuanced characterization that boast of elements traceable not only to Hollywood animation and Japanese anime but also to live-action films, computer games, and the like. In this regard, contemporary Chinese animation can be reconceptualized as what Lamarre attributes to a Japanese anime series or film, "the nodal point in a *transmedial network* that entails proliferating series of narrative and non-narrative forms across media interfaces and platforms, such as the computer, television, movie theater, and cell phone."[42]

The playful remediation of Chinese animation from the analog to the digital age over the past few decades invokes the concept of sedimentation in media archaeology. As Jussi Parikka points out, "Media archaeology sees media cultures as sedimented and layered, a fold of time and materi-

42. Lamarre, *The Anime Machine*, xiv.

ality where the past might be suddenly discovered anew."[43] For the playful remediation of Monkey King and Nezha, most audiences are probably not aware of the rich layers of sedimentation, but this is exactly what media archaeologists could explore. That is the beauty of our scholarship. The new versions of Monkey King and Nezha depart drastically from the early cel animation versions, so we cannot simply use the influence paradigm to approach remediation. The animators may be aware of the layers of sedimentation, which may be invisible to the new generation of viewers. The older generation of viewers who have watched both cel and digital versions may also notice the layers of sedimentation. Thus playful remediation of the animated films may also suggest the remediation of spectators.[44]

To expand my contemplation of Chinese animation as a playful dispositif and remediation in the digital age, I cite one example of a transmedial network that falls outside the purview of commercial operations. Paola Voci coins the term *animateur cinema* to refer to a particular type of amateur animation—a short digital work that is shared online for free, played on small screen, and often dwells on light reality. Animateur cinema is noninstitutional, noncommercial, nonconformist, alternative, and even subversive in its pursuit of a liminal cultural space in contemporary China. It is experimental (like avant-garde cinema), exhibitionist (like early cinema), but nonetheless creative in its engagement with genre mixing, thematic recoding, and relentless humor, pastiche, and parody. Its playful manipulation of existing audiovisual and narrative resources intensifies the viewer's awareness of the medium and encourages a new understanding of the image. One of Voci's examples, *Holding One's Hand* (*Shouxia liuqing* 手下留情, 2004), is an award-winning college student work that accentuates the dexterity of human hands in projecting shadows of animal shapes. This work pays homage to a long tradition of shadow play (*yingxi* 影戏) in China and subtly references the ink-painting animation of the socialist period.[45] In such a simple encounter with animation, the spectator

43. Parikka, *What Is Media Archaeology?*, 3.

44. This paragraph was added by the editors in line with the author's oral response to Thomas Lamarre's question about the issue of sedimentation and the audience's awareness of the rich layers of sedimentation at the Inaugural Conference of the Association for Chinese Animation Studies.

45. Ideas of shadow play and handmade cinema are further developed in Paola Voci,

simultaneously sees magical images and the media that make magic work. Moreover, the human hand has been reinstated in its materiality as part of digital dispositifs that enable the production, circulation, and appreciation of the animateur short.

Conclusion

From noncommercial animateur cinema that offers delightful moments of encounter to blockbuster sagas of legendary heroes that guarantee the viewer an exhilarating experience of gorgeous scenes, fantastic stories, and spectacular actions, Chinese animation has gone a long way in reinventing itself, remarkably retaining its distinctive features of playful remediation, and persistently reinvigorating its bricolage of dispositifs at various scales. Just as it is not feasible to expect, in retrospect, that *Princess Iron Fan* would anticipate the exact look, address, and narrative of *Monkey King: The Hero Is Back*, it is unnecessary—and impossible—to use either *Monkey King: The Hero Is Back* or *Nezha* as a prospective norm to chart the destiny of Chinese animation in the future. Film history as media archaeology urges us to keep an open mind vis-à-vis Chinese animation, tracking parallel and parallax histories and trajectories, envisioning different futures, and revisiting forgotten pasts so as to better understand the present.

"Electric Shadows Reloaded: The Post-Digital Animateur, Shadow Play and Handmade Cinema," *Journal of Chinese Cinemas* 11, no. 3 (2017): 192–209.

SECTION ONE

Junctures

ONE

The Animation of Inanimate Objects in Chinese Silent Cinema

Panpan Yang

The dream of animation here is equally the terror caused by animation . . . for such movement would only cause the obliteration of the subject—the inhuman spectacle of a dream no longer in need of its dreamer.

—Susan Stewart[1]

If any technical predecessor of animation need be identified, it would certainly be the stop-motion substitution technique.

—Donald Crafton[2]

When animation as a category in motion pictures did not yet exist, its technical predecessors largely coincided with a history of the supernatural in silent cinema, weaving in and out of it. In tracing the early days—if not the origin myth—of American animation, for instance, one cannot eschew *The Haunted Hotel* (1907), which was a huge success in the United States and Europe alike. In this five-hundred-foot Vitagraph picture, a traveler spends a night at a mysterious inn. After being served food and drink, he looks at what is on the table, astonished. In the following close-up, presumably from his point of view, a bottle of wine moves by

1. Susan Stewart, *On Longing: Narratives of the Miniature, the Gigantic, the Souvenir, the Collection* (Durham, NC: Duke University Press, 1993), 172.

2. Donald Crafton, *Before Mickey: The Animated Film, 1898–1928* (Chicago: University of Chicago Press, 1993), 9.

itself, as does a loaf of bread. A knife slices the bread.[3] A teapot pours tea. Sugar tongs drop two lumps of sugar into the teacup. A spoon stirs the tea. In this sequence, all these inanimate objects move seemingly automatically, as if manipulated by an invisible ghost.

For audiences that more or less know how this trick sequence is made, the ghost or spirit here is not the goblin hiding itself in the kettle but mainly the technique we now call stop-motion animation: objects are physically moved or manipulated in very small increments between individually photographed frames so that they will appear to be moving on their own when the series of frames is played rapidly. If our understanding of a ghost can be "taken both literally and metaphorically as the animation of something dead and lifeless,"[4] a ghost is probably the most powerful metaphor for object animation, the subgenre of stop-motion animation that enlivens inanimate objects.

What if the ghost appears or reappears in a different cultural context? This chapter traces the moments of animation of inanimate objects in so-called live-action Chinese films in the silent era. I show that the animation of inanimate, everyday objects in Chinese silent cinemas can be achieved by using the stop-motion technique, wires, or combined methods. The stop-motion technique in particular forges a vantage point to respond to the marginalization of Chinese animation in theoretical discourses. To arrive at this reading, the chapter relies on nonextant, extant, and partially extant Chinese films, print materials, and film and media theories. In doing so, the chapter offers an alternative route to a more complex and nuanced understanding of the early history of Chinese animation, which is not all about animated cartoons and which cannot be complete without an understanding of photography.

An Empty Dream or the "Trick" Beginning

In the history of Chinese cinema, *An Empty Dream* (*Qing xu meng* 清虚梦, 1922), a three-reel trick picture directed by Ren Pengnian and photo-

3. A knife moving on its own accord also appears in *Le Rêve des Marmitons* (1908).

4. Judith Zeitlin, "The Ghosts of Things," in *Fantômes dans l'Extrême-Orient d'hier et d'aujourd'hui*, vol. 1 (Paris: Presses de l'Inalco, 2017), 205–21.

graphed by Liao Enshou, can be said to be a counterpoint or correlate to Blackton's *The Haunted Hotel*. *An Empty Dream* was adapted from "The Taoist of Mount Lao" (*Laoshan daoshi* 崂山道士) in Pu Songling's 蒲松龄 (1640–1715) *Strange Tales from a Chinese Studio* (*Liaozhai zhiyi* 聊斋志异),[5] in which a fervent admirer of Daoism heads to Mount Lao with the hope of learning Daoist tricks but ends up returning home because he could not bear the hardship of life as a disciple. No print of the film survives. But the possible interplay between Daoist tricks in the diegesis and camera tricks in the film production seems to have contributed to the film's success. A June 27, 1922, advertisement in the *Shenbao* (申报) newspaper referred to *An Empty Dream* as "an unprecedented trick picture" (*huanshu yingpian* 幻术影片) and praised it for "exhausting what cinematography could do."[6] This advertisement even included a list of the most astonishing tricks in the film: "A Daoist master suddenly appears in the sky. A broken jar restores its shape. A paper-cut moon gives out a bright light. Wine and meat come into sight on an empty plate. A magic trick summons the fairy maiden Chang E. A mantra allows you to walk through the wall."[7] Here, the notion of the trick becomes a site of encounter between the Chinese classical tale and the modern medium of film, as it takes shape in the confrontation between the world that Pu Songling conjures up—one thick with ghosts, fox-spirits, and fairy maidens—and the ghosts in the machine. The confrontation itself was a novelty at that time and therefore newsworthy.

An Empty Dream was a product of the Commercial Press, which had been publishing books since 1897 but also produced films as one of its sideline enterprises between 1917 and 1927. In a 1957 article, "My Memory of the Film Department of The Commercial Press," Yang Xiaozhong 杨小仲, who worked there as a scriptwriter and director during the first half of the 1920s, recalls that "there were some special effects in *An Empty Dream*, such as a broken jar that restores its shape, a person walking through the

5. Pu Songling 蒲松龄 (1640–1715), *Liaozhai zhiyi* 聊斋志异 (Strange tales from a Chinese studio), facsimile reprint of the author's manuscript, Beijing, 1955. For an English translation, see Pu Songling, *Strange Tales from a Chinese Studio*, trans. John Minford (London: Penguin, 2006).

6. *Shenbao* 申报 (Shun pao), June 27, 1922.

7. *Shenbao*, June 27, 1922.

wall, and objects walking by themselves. That was quite popular at that time."[8] Yang, however, does not offer a word about technical details. A similar yet not identical account can be found in Zhong Dafeng's highly influential article "On Shadow Play." Citing Yang's memoir, Zhong notes, "*An Empty Dream* was shot in 1922. It used special effects cinematography, such as a broken jar that restores its shape (reverse motion), a person walking through the wall (stop trick or double exposure), and objects walking by themselves (stop-motion technique)."[9] This description sounds reasonable, but the words in parentheses are likely Zhong's speculations. If there is indeed a trick scene in which objects appears to walk automatically in *An Empty Dream*, it remains uncertain whether this can be said to be an early example of stop-motion animation. Think, for instance, of the table scene in *The Haunted Hotel*: the animation of the wine bottle, the loaf of bread, the knife, the sugar tongs, and the spoon were indeed achieved via the technique of stop-motion substitution, but wires—the old technique of the stage magician—were used to create the effect of tea pouring itself out. As audiences watched the scene, "the sharpest, most attentive eye was unable to detect any wire,"[10] but the filmmakers had to use wires because liquids could not be manipulated frame by frame. Is it possible that wires were used in the production of *An Empty Dream* to create the special effect of "objects walking by themselves"? Is it true that something had been "tricked" before shooting? Can it be that, similar to *The Haunted Hotel*, *An Empty Dream* had combined cinematography experiments with the magic theater methods of behind-the-scenes manipulation?

All these possibilities resist the simplified solution as such: first was *An Empty Dream* and only then could the history of Chinese stop-motion animation begin. Instead, the trick beginning, if not to say its mystery, is exactly part of the charm of the maze of history. As Jane Gaines beautifully puts it in "First Fictions," here we are forced to move beyond an invest-

8. Yang Xiaozhong 杨小仲, "Yi Shangwu yinshuguan dianyingbu" 忆商务印书馆电影部 (My memory of the film department of the Commercial Press), *Zhonguo dianying* 中国电影 (Chinese film), no. 1 (1957): 80.

9. Zhong Dafeng 钟大丰, "Lun yingxi" 论影戏 (On shadow play), *Beijing dianying xueyuan xuebao* 北京电影学院学报 (Journal of the Beijing Film Academy), no. 2 (1985): 65.

10. Crafton, *Before Mickey*, 16.

ment with a singular, inaugural moment to "a fascination with the problem of where, how, and whether to begin."[11] Recall that neither stop-motion animation (*dingge donghua* 定格动画) nor special effects (*texiao* 特效) existed in Chinese-language discourse in the 1920s. Here the thicket of problems becomes tangled, involving not only the affinities between animation, special effects, and the ephemeral "trick picture" genre but also the instability of industry labels and critical vocabularies.

Shadow Play or The Trick's on Us

A closer examination of what was then referred to as trick pictures is in order. A bilingual article with trick pictures in its title, published in *English Magazine* (*Yingwen zazhi* 英文杂志) in 1923, is not necessarily about cinematic special effects but instead about how to cast strong shadows of a goat, a swan, a pipe, and a priest by manipulating one's hands between a lamp and a sheet of white paper—what is often called *shou yingxi* (手影戏, hand shadow play) or *deng yingxi* (灯影戏, lamp shadow play).[12] This brings to mind, again, Zhong Dafeng's essay "On Shadow Play," in which he reminds us that shadow play (*yingxi* 影戏)—from its miniature form of hand shadow play to shadow puppet theater—had long existed as a popular form of entertainment when cinema came to China. According to Zhong, from the late nineteenth century to the 1930s, shadow play was the most common appellation for cinema in Chinese.[13]

Revisiting the notion of shadow play in the context of animation studies, Paola Voci observes the striking similarities between the antiquated tradition of shadow play performance and German film director Lotte Reiniger's silhouette animated films, the most well-known of which is *Die Abenteuer des Prinzen Achmed* (*The Adventures of Prince Achmed*, 1926).[14] Voci does not, however, move one more step toward articulating the question that might twist our understanding of the early Chinese name for

11. Jane M. Gaines, "First Fictions," *Signs* 30, no. 1 (Autumn 2004): 1294.

12. *Yingwen zazhi* 英文杂志 (English magazine) 9, no. 2 (1923): 200.

13. Zhong Dafeng, "Lun yingxi," 54.

14. Paola Voci, "Electric Shadows Reloaded: The Post-Digital Animateur, Shadow Play and Handmade Cinema," *Journal of Chinese Cinemas* 1, no. 3 (2017): 119–203.

cinema: isn't it more proper, or at least more intuitive, to consider (hand) shadow play as proto-animation than as proto-cinema? The hand (*shou* 手) is of course crucial to *shou yingxi*, yet shadow play can be conducted behind the sheet or screen so that the hands of the imagemaker are seen as shadows. Crystallized in the reinvented concept of shadow play as proto-animation is a mode of imagemaking that simultaneously privileges and conceals the presence of the hand. This mode of production is situated at the intersection of a highly restricted space, like a sheet of white paper on a wall or a table, and the temporality of the cinema of attractions: "now you see it, now you don't."[15] This was here, now it's gone.

Even more unsettling is the concept of play in shadow play: in English and Chinese alike, play (*xi* 戏) can mean drama or to perform or put into effect, especially as a jest or deception—that is, a trick. Writing in the mid-1980s, Zhong Dafeng and Chen Xihe retroactively salvaged a statement from Hou Yao's 1926 *A Method of Shadow Play Scriptwriting* (*Yingxi juben zuofa* 影戏剧本作法)—"shadow play is one kind of play [drama]"—to theorize about what could be potentially claimed as a distinct Chinese ontology of cinema, one that emphasized narratives, actions, and structures.[16] What they conveniently (and perhaps intentionally) left out was the second meaning of play, with which I am more concerned: tricks, attractions, and sensations, all embedded in the semantic transformation of *shadow play—cinema—animation—trick pictures*.

The trick of stopping the camera (*tingpai* 停拍) provides a conceptual playing field in this regard. A 1931 article, "Common Knowledge of Making Trick Films," unlocked the secret of "making one object suddenly

15. Tom Gunning, "'Now You See It, Now You Don't': The Temporality of the Cinema of Attractions," *Velvet Light Trap* 32 (Fall 1993): 3–12.

16. See Hou Yao 侯曜, *Yingxi juben zuofa* 影戏剧本作法 (A method of shadow play scriptwriting) (Shanghai: Taidong shuju, 1926); Zhong Dafeng, "Lun yingxi"; Zhong Dafeng 钟大丰, "'Yingxi' lilun suyuan" '影戏' 理论溯源 (Tracing the history of shadow play theory), *Dangdai dianying* 当代电影 (Contemporary cinema), no. 3 (1986): 75–80; Chen Xihe 陈犀禾, "Zhongguo dianying meixue de zairenshi" 中国电影美学的再认识 (Rethinking Chinese film aesthetic), *Dangdai dianying* 当代电影 (Contemporary cinema), no. 1 (1986): 82–90. For a provocative revisiting of shadow play theory, see Victor Fan, *Cinema Approaching Reality: Locating Chinese Film Theory* (Minneapolis: University of Minnesota Press, 2015), 17–42.

(dis)appear" or "having a lifeless object walking or flying itself."[17] The former is what we now call the stop trick or substitution splice; the latter is what we now call the stop-motion technique or stop-motion animation. In a Méliès-like, almost simplified fashion, the writer emphasized stopping the camera as the trick for the two cases; the difference between the two was said to be one of degree rather than of kind—stopping the camera once or many times.[18] If there is something special about the trick of "having a lifeless object walking or flying itself," it has to do with the dimension of time. The trick on us is not that something happens in one moment, in the twinkling of an eye, but that lifeless objects are moving in time. It affects duration.

In addition, it is extremely telling that this early account of how to make stop-motion animation was published in *Photography Pictorial* (*Sheying huabao* 摄影画报), a publication of the China Photography Association founded by Lin Zecang in 1925. Entailed here is the possibility of overturning a majority of classical film theorists' habitual understanding that sees animation as drawing pictures, as something irrelevant to photography, hence irrelevant to film theories. For many classical film theorists, to define what cinema is, we need to first define what photography is. Animation, or drawing pictures as they might call it, is therefore eclipsed in their theoretical discourses. The important anthology *Animating Film Theory*, edited by Karen Beckman, marks the relatively recent, collaborative, corrective effort of engaging animation with theories of film.[19] My emphasis here is not just that animation could wrap itself in the cloak of photography discourse, but that,

17. Chen Mingche 陈明彻, "Shezhi huanshu yingpian zhi changshi (xu)" 摄制幻术影片之常识(续) (Common knowledge of making tricks, part two), *Sheying huabao* 摄影画报 (Photography pictorial) 7, no. 306 (1931): 7. For the first half of the article, see Chen Mingche, "Shezhi huanshu yingpian zhi changshi (weiwan)" 摄制幻术影片之常识 (未完) (Common knowledge of making tricks, part one), *Sheying huabao* 摄影画报 (Photography pictorial) 7, no. 305 (1931): 7.

18. Colin Williamson has pointed out that "the quick change . . . is related on a technical level to stop motion animation." My approach of special effects as animation is indebted to Williamson. See Colin Williamson, *Hidden in Plain Sight: An Archaeology of Magic and the Cinema* (New Brunswick, NJ: Rutgers University Press, 2015), 113.

19. See Karen Beckman, ed., *Animating Film Theory* (Durham, NC: Duke University Press, 2014).

in the Chinese historical context, a species of animation was indeed recognized as photography, as a genre of photography that is not realistic photography. The early history of animation in a different cultural context forcefully challenges the habitual yet one-sided understanding that resulted in animation's marginalization in film theory, an understanding that was formulated in a mostly Euro-American tradition of film studies. A historically contextualized theoretical inquiry, I contend, gestures toward a convincing argument in favor of animation's being a complement to photography, rather than a limited case or an irrelevant exception. In a sense, the intimate relation between animation and photography is made visible by the juxtaposition of this very account of stop-motion animation and the illustrated advertisement of the Agfa family travel cinecamera on the same page (fig. 1.1).

A 1937 article titled "Cinematography Tricks" offered a rather different description of what it called *tingpai* (stopping the camera): "First, shoot two persons fighting with each other on a cliff. Show the face of one person who is about to fall off the cliff. Stop the camera. Then, in a long shot, shoot a dummy in the same clothes falling off the cliff. Stop the camera again. Finally, shoot a close-up of the pretend dead person under the cliff."[20] What is described here is the combination of pro-filmic substitution (a dummy) and matching on action. The author also notes that this solution is applicable to difficult or dangerous situations. The use of a dummy aims to be an imperceptible trick: if the trick is well done (that is, the dummy is well made, and the camera is careful to film it at a certain distance and from certain angles), the viewer will not be able to notice the substitution of the dummy.[21] For audiences today, the commonly used editing technique of matching on action will not be considered a trick. This example leads us to think about the historical dimension of a trick: every trick, device, or technology might experience a process of becoming part of the habitual. In a sense, a trick proves itself to be a significant one by being forgotten. To examine a trick as it once was, therefore, is to create a counter-experience;

20. Shu Yan 舒湮, "Sheying qiaoshu" 摄影巧术 (Cinematography tricks), *Wanying* 万影 (Ten thousand films) 6 (1937): 29–30.

21. For Christian Metz's seminal discussion of imperceptible *trucage*, see Christian Metz, "'Trucage' and the Film," trans. Françoise Meltzer, *Critical Inquiry* 3, no. 4 (Summer 1977): 663–64.

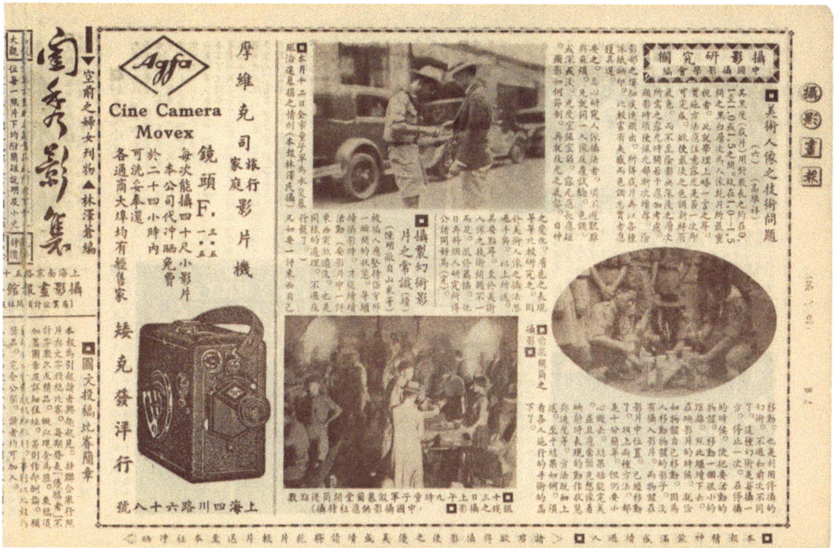

FIGURE 1.1. The juxtaposition of an early account of stop-motion animation and a Movex camera advertisement, *Sheying huabao* 7, no. 306 (1931). Courtesy of Shanghai Library.

we must reimagine the excitement that it once stirred up, or in Tom Gunning's words, "try to recapture a quality it has lost."[22]

Reexamining the once-new editing technique, the trick lies less in stopping the camera than in splicing the shots—that is, juxtaposing any two points in space to suggest a relationship between them. Even if the component shots were filmed in different locations, audiences would still assume a spatial whole. If the trick is exploited to its limit, cinema can construct an imaginary space, one that cannot be labeled as here or there in the world that we inhabit and phenomenally access through our senses. The question of splicing also allows us to think afresh about the trick of stopping the camera as mentioned in the *Photography Pictorial* article. In contrast to the term used here, the trick of *tingpai* actually lies less in stopping the camera

22. Tom Gunning, "Re-Newing Old Technologies: Astonishment, Second Nature, and the Uncanny in Technology from the Previous Turn-of-the-Century," in *Rethinking Media Change: The Aesthetics of Transition*, eds. David Thorburn and Henry Jenkins (Cambridge, MA: MIT Press, 2013), 39.

than in splicing the frames in a way that is almost literally seamless, in contrast to matching-on-action editing, or, more broadly put, continuity editing, which can be referred to as seamless editing only metaphorically.[23] The trick of splicing the frames (or stop-motion) aims to be invisible yet perceptible:[24] it is something hidden inside, something that showcases cinema's capacity of astonishing the senses, something that audiences could not see but nonetheless could sense, recognize, and delight in. Shall we say that editing can happen within one shot or that, for stop-motion animation, a frame qualifies as a shot? The most basic terminologies we use to talk about film are less stable than we think, and animation constantly throws the most basic terminologies into question.

A Pair of Boots Walking

Another example of the animation of inanimate objects comes from *Kan the Great Knight-Errant* (*Daxia Gan Fengchi* 大侠甘凤池, 1928), the partially extant martial arts film directed by Yang Xiaozhong. Having left the film department of the Commercial Press in 1926 and run the short-lived Guoguang Film Company for less than a year, Yang joined the Great Wall Film Company in 1927 and directed *Kan the Great Knight-Errant* in his second year there.

In one extant fragment of the film, a swordsman sneaks into the house of an evil medicine dealer. Exquisitely designed sandalwood furniture and a corner of a window with auspicious (*jixiang* 吉祥) coin patterns in the background frame the room. Equally exquisite are the swordsman's unique martial arts costume, exaggerated cap, and white boots with black stripes. Wan Guchan, who was later hailed as the forefather of Chinese animation, worked for a significant period of his time at the Great Wall Film Company as a set and costume designer for *Kan the Great Knight-Errant* and two other feature films.

In this fragment, the swordsman bends over to look at his boots, at the

23. My inspiration again comes from Tom Gunning, "'Primitive' Cinema: A Frame-up? Or the Trick's on Us," *Cinema Journal* 28, no. 2 (Winter 1989): 3–12.

24. For Metz's distinction of visible trucage, invisible trucage, and imperceptible trucage, see Metz, "'Trucage' and the Film," 665.

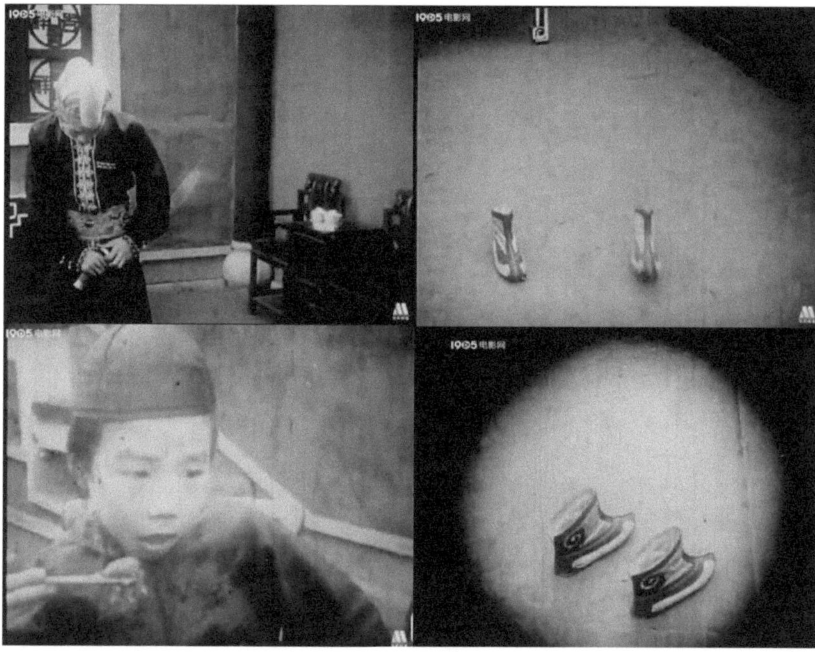

FIGURE 1.2. A pair of boots walking itself, in *Kan the Great Knight-Errant* (1928).

moment off screen, as if coming up with an idea. In the twinkling of an eye, his body becomes invisible. In the next shot, the audience sees only his boots, still framed by the furniture, from a slightly higher angle. The not-so-well-matched cut between the two shots creates a sense of artificiality. We see the boots walking toward us, step by step, until going off screen. Then we are shown a close-up of the shocked expression of Little Tiger Kan, the son of Kan the Great Knight-Errant, who is about to put food into his mouth, but now can no longer move his chopsticks. The subsequent shot cuts back to the pair of boots marching without human feet inside, in a closer view (fig. 1.2). The use of vignetting and the restricted field of view of the last shot forcefully holds the audience's attention at the center of the image: the boots "tattling" on their absent owner. The extant fragment ends here.

As the boots are walking, at some moments they do not touch the ground. This detail reveals that this scene was more likely created using wires rather than stop-motion animation. Erasing the wires was a relatively mature technique in the late 1920s Chinese film industry. In *The*

Burning of the Red Lotus Temple (*Huoshao Hongliansi* 火烧红莲寺, 1928–1931), for example, steel wires were used in the filming process of dangerous scenes, yet they were invisible to audiences. In the film developing process, the wires on a certain frame can be erased by masking certain areas of the frame to selectively control which areas are exposed. Alternatively, another shot with an identical backdrop and without wires can be filmed. The image with wires overlaps with the image without wires when a third image is to be exposed.

The lack of a complete print poses a challenge to understanding the position of the segment in the film's narrative. The film was loosely based on *Kan the Great Knight-Errant in Jiangnan*, a bestseller during the huge boom of martial arts fiction in the early 1920s. The extant part of *Kan the Great Knight-Errant*, approximately twenty-three minutes, is not so much about the hero in the film's title as about his two children, Little Tiger Kan and Little Butterfly Kan. In fact, Kan the Great Knight-Errant, "whose self-imposed function was to fight the unkind rich and help the poor," never appears in the extant segment.[25] Yet that only part of the film survived does not prevent a close reading of the trick scene. I do not have substantial evidence to prove that the jump cut, between the medium shot of the swordsman who becomes invisible and the next shot of the walking boots, was not an amateurish mistake, but it seems significant that in the first shot, the pair of boots is off screen. Because of this, audiences are held in suspension between incompatible explanatory options. Did the bodyguard use the magic of the invisible body (*yinshen shu* 隐身术)? Or maybe the pair of boots is taking on a life of its own? Because only a fragment of the trick scene survives, the fantastic lingers rather than being settled psychologically in the end. Here I am evoking the notion of the fantastic as Tzvetan Todorov outlined it: "In a world which is indeed our world, the one we know, a world without devils, sylphides, or vampires, there occurs an event which cannot be explained by the laws of this same familiar world."[26] Fantasy is by no means the antonym of reality; instead, the two are entangled. Along these lines, we can explain why it is import-

25. "Daxia Gan Fengchi: Changcheng chupian" 大侠甘凤池: 长城出片 (*Kan the Great Knight-Errant*: A Great Wall production), *Xin yinxing* 新银星 (New silver star) 1 (1928): 43.

26. Tzvetan Todorov, *The Fantastic: A Structural Approach to a Literary Genre*, trans. Richard Howard (Cleveland, OH: Case Western Reserve University Press, 1973), 25.

ant for the sandalwood furniture and the corner of the window with the auspicious coin patterns to be included in the frame: they need to be there to demonstrate that it is the same familiar world.

Special Effects of the Martial Arts-Magic Spirit Craze

Special effects, such as stop-motion tricks and multiple exposure, were "a hallmark of the martial arts-magic spirit craze of 1928–32."[27] Another kind of special effect well noticed in this genre was called "flying swords in white light" (*feijian baiguang* 飞剑白光), records of which can be found in fragments or print materials of *Kan the Great Knight-Errant*, *The Burning of the Red Lotus Temple*, and a large corpus of other films of the craze—or as Lu Hongshi puts it, in "almost every film" of the craze.[28] This stunt is achieved using a combination of drawn animation and live-action footage (fig. 1.3).[29]

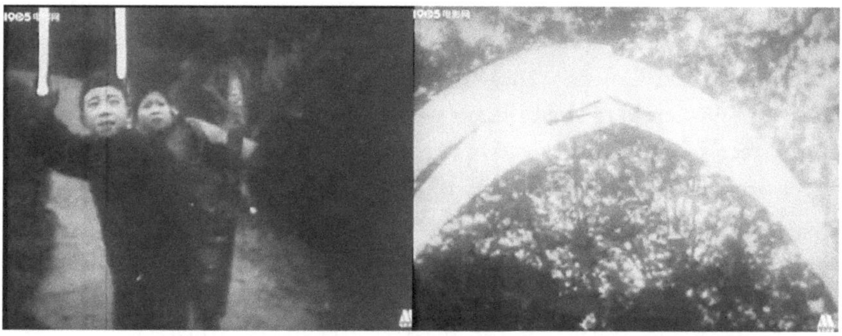

FIGURE 1.3. Flying swords in white light, in *Kan the Great Knight-Errant* (1928).

27. Judith Zeitlin, "Operatic Ghosts on Screen," *Opera Quarterly* 26, no. 2–3 (Summer 2010): 230. See also Zhen Zhang, *An Amorous History of the Silver Screen: Shanghai Cinema, 1896–1937* (Chicago: University of Chicago Press, 2005), 199–243.

28. Lu Hongshi 陆弘石, *Zhongguo dianying: Miaoshu yu chanshi* 中国电影：描述与阐释 (Chinese cinema: Description and interpretation) (Beijing: Zhongguo dianying chubanshe, 2002), 111. Multiple exposure and "flying swords in white light" are two examples of visible trucage, according to Metz's categories. See Metz, "'Trucage' and the Film," 665.

29. For a discussion on the affinity between animation and martial arts films, see Jinying Li's "From Animation to Martial Arts: Toward the Transcendence of False Movements," chapter 2 in this volume.

My interest here is not so much in providing a list of special effects in martial arts-magic spirit films as in thinking about how the term *special effects*, albeit coined later, serves as a useful paradigm for studying cinematic tricks. First, in regard to the notion of special: the special power of a trick must go beyond surprising audiences because it does not fade after multiple viewings; it persists, so to speak, as described in the article "Common Knowledge of Making Trick Films" from *Photography Pictorial*. For example, the experience of watching a pair of boots walking by itself, again and again is almost a delightful craziness, one that touches, stings, and delights the viewer. Second, regarding effects: the term implies an audience, without which any effects are only floating, empty words. This line of thought is therefore bound up with the question of reception. According to *Shenbao* reports, when *Kan the Great Knight-Errant* premiered in Shanghai Grand Theater on May 24, 1928, the upper and lower floors were crowded with nearly one thousand audience members.[30] In September 1928, it was shown in New Allan Grand Theater on Haining Road in Shanghai, and audiences rushed to the movie house despite the heavy rain. The three-day run was extended to a six-day run.[31] Film distributors and theater owners from New York, Chicago, and Singapore soon booked prints of *Kan the Great Knight-Errant*.[32] The brilliant use of special effects contributed to the film's effectiveness, or its affective density, as demonstrated by these newspaper reports. At the intersection of the two lines of inquiry, the problem of special effects becomes that of special affects.

To better account for the impacts of special effects (the animation of inanimate objects, flying swords in white light, and so on) on audiences in the historical context of the martial arts-magic spirit craze (1928–1932), a dialectic of enchantment and disenchantment must be brought into the limelight. For audiences at that time, the viewing experience (of a film of this genre) was the process of being drawn into an enchanted space, one that often promised sensual and spiritual fulfillment. We are not unfamiliar with highly suspicious anecdotes that audiences burned incense to worship the gods in martial arts magic-spirit films or that,

30. *Shenbao*, May 24, 28, 1928.

31. *Shenbao*, September 18, 1928.

32. *Shenbao*, October 27, 1928, March 1, 1929.

after watching the films, they found their way to Mount Emei in search of immortals. Even filmmakers were enchanted by what they created, with some placing a niche in the film set to display the statue of a god.[33] It might not be coincidence that the aforementioned article from *Photography Pictorial* was published in 1931, the year that marked the official ban on many films of the craze as part of the Nationalist government's anti-superstition campaign.[34] To some extent, articles unlocking secrets of film tricks function as the breaking of enchantment. If we do not adopt the assumption of a naïve audience that took whatever appeared on the screen as real, it could even be argued that a paradox was at work in the film viewing experience: disenchantment through enchantment.[35] In other words, it was films of this genre that largely demystified magic and spirit by showing them to audiences as cinematic tricks; the lesson of disenchantment is taught in the space of enchantment.

A String of Pearls Dancing

An exact example of the stop-motion trick can be found in *The Pearl Necklace* (*Yichuan zhenzhu* 一串珍珠, 1926), directed by Li Zeyuan and written by Hou Yao. My analysis of *The Pearl Necklace* is built mainly on Zhen Zhang's fascinating reading of it, but also pushes some of her insights into a different direction.[36]

33. See, for instance, Lu Hongshi, *Zhongguo dianying: Miaoshu yu chanshi*, 112.

34. For a historical contextualization of the ban, see Zhen Zhang, *An Amorous History*, 235.

35. Speaking of disenchantment through enchantment, I have in mind *Dream of the Red Chamber* (*Hong lou meng* aka *Shitou ji*), an eighteenth-century novel generally acknowledged to be the pinnacle of Chinese vernacular fiction. The hero, Baoyu, has a dream in chapter 5 that the Goddess of Disenchantment tells him that the purpose of his dream visit is "disenchantment through enchantment." For one edition of the novel, see Cao Xueqin 曹雪芹, *Shitou ji* 石头记 (The story of the stone) (Nanjing: Yilin chubanshe, 2017). For a nuanced reading, see Li Wai-Yee, *Enchantment and Disenchantment: Love and Illusion in Chinese Literature* (Princeton, NJ: Princeton University Press, 1993).

36. See Zhen Zhang, *An Amorous History*, 151–98. Daisy Yan Du also addresses the use of stop-motion animation, which forms part of what she describes as early Chinese animation's "symbiotic relationship with live-action film." See Daisy Yan Du, *Animated*

The script of *The Pearl Necklace* transplanted Maupassant's 1884 short story "La Parure" to the setting of urban Shanghai. Two days before the film's premiere at the Embassy Theater on January 21, 1926, an article in the *Shenbao* newspaper introduced the film as "a baby whose mother had a romantic relationship with Maupassant."[37] Not surprisingly, Hou's script replaced the diamond necklace in Maupassant's story with a string of pearls, a motif that cross-references a wealth of allusions in Chinese classical poetry and vernacular tales (fig. 1.4). Fittingly, the first bilingual title card right after the film's credits addressed its audiences with "Don't you know? Don't you know? A string of pearls is equal to a million rings of sorrow." Almost a flash-forward, this title card then prefigures the sentimental melodrama: "If a woman drags herself down the road of vanity, her husband will be her victim surely."

As prefigured here, after the borrowed pearl necklace has been lost and her husband has gone to jail, Xiuzhen (the equivalent to the Madame Mathilde Loisel character in the short story) has to mend clothes for a living. The long, lonely night of sewing in her shabby bedroom is intercut with shots of her husband in prison and graphically adorned, bilingual title cards. The haunting and return of memory—her one night of radiance at the fancy Lantern Festival party that reoccurs in a flashback—pain her. In her point-of-view shot, the threads and buttons on the table dissolve into the pearl necklace, which has cost her and her husband any chance for future happiness. The dissolve here functions as a liminal device that throws the audiences into an enchanted space. The pearl necklace dances in circles, metamorphosing into the shape of the two gigantic Chinese ideographs *huo huan* (祸患), accompanied with an English translation in the form of the nondiegetic intertitle, "Misfortune." It expresses the intention of communicating the message of misfortune to the viewer. That said, the pearl necklace not only comes to life but also assumes the role of a narrative commentator (fig. 1.4). The necklace eventually dissolves back into the shape of threads and buttons.

Zhen Zhang has pointed out "the round shape of pearls (and the string,

---

Encounters: Transnational Movements of Chinese Animation, 1940s–1970s (Honolulu: University of Hawai'i Press, 2019), 37–38.

37. *Shenbao*, January 19, 21, 1926.

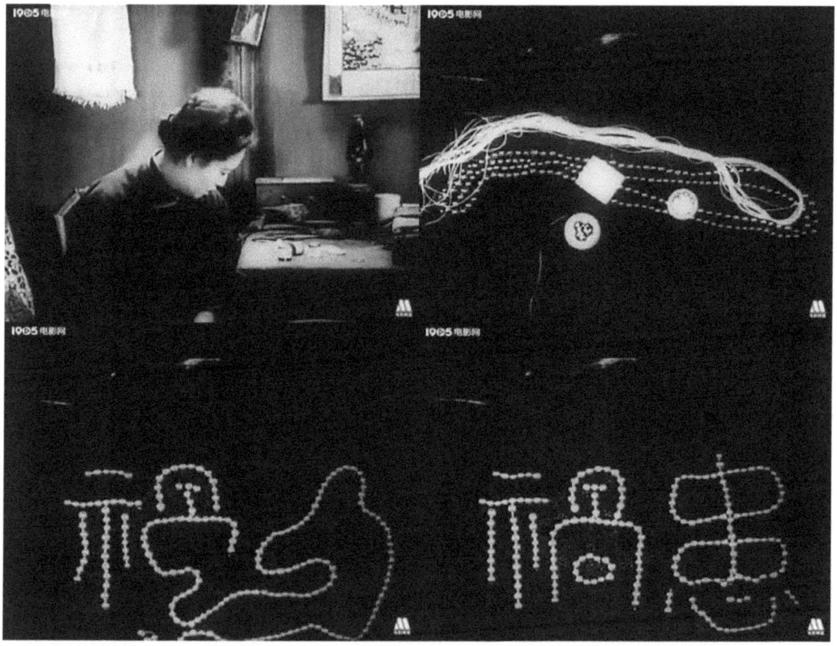

FIGURE 1.4. A stop-motion trick sequence, in *The Pearl Necklace* (1926).

or *chuan* 串) and their literary association with tears" and has commented on how the lyrical title card preceding the flashback—"My Tears must stop, for every drop / Hinders needles and thread"—summons Xiuzhen's memory of the fateful pearl necklace.[38] My argument, however, does not end with a cinematic revivification of literary allusions linking pearls and teardrops. I believe something more interesting is at work in the stop-motion trick sequence: the string of pearls here is a stunt performer who is employed to take the teardrops' place in doing what teardrops are not capable of—that is, being moved and manipulated between frames. Similar to the boots in *Kan the Great Knight-Errant*, the string of pearls gains a kind of anti-anthropocentric life.

38. Zhen Zhang, *An Amorous History*, 172, 175.

A View of a/the World

Using the sequence of the dancing pearl necklace as an example, I hope to unpack the theoretical entanglements surrounding stop-motion animation, which occupies a precarious position between animation and live-action cinema. Some of classical film theory's key writings (by Bazin, Kracauer, Panofsky, and others), most of which derived the nature of cinema from the ontology of the photographic image, have made animation seemingly irrelevant. In this regard, Stanley Cavell perhaps offers the most famous (or infamous) statement: defining movies "as successions of automatic world projections," he once declared, "[animated] cartoons are *not* movies."[39] Cavell's distinction between painting and still photography, between a presentation and a transcription, could be transplanted to make an unequivocal argument about the ontological divide between animated cartoon and live-action movie. Like a painting, an animated cartoon is a representation that "emphasizes the identity of its subject, hence it may be called a likeness"; like a photograph, a live-action movie "emphasizes the existence of its subject, recording it, hence it may be called a transcription."[40] Interpreting Cavell's highly succinct conclusion that "a painting *is* a world; a photograph is *of* the world,"[41] we might say, just as succinctly, that a cartoon *is* a world; a movie is *of* the world.

This distinction, however, is rather shaky, given the diversity of photographic and pictorial practices. Suzanne Buchan, for one, has invoked it to question it. Writing about puppet animation, she has noticed that this region of animation "represents a different 'world' for the spectator . . . something between 'a world' . . . and 'the world.'"[42] For Buchan, the crucial point is that, watching puppet animation, audiences can understand that the space does exist "outside the cinematic experience, albeit in minia-

39. Stanley Cavell, *The World Viewed: Reflections on the Ontology of Film* (Cambridge, MA: Harvard University Press, 1979), 168.

40. Cavell, "What Photography Calls Thinking," in *Cavell on Film*, ed. William Rothman (Albany: State University of New York Press, 2005), 118.

41. Cavell, *The World Viewed*, 24.

42. Suzanne Buchan, "The Animated Spectator: Watching the Quay Brothers' 'Worlds,'" in *Animated Worlds*, ed. Suzanne Buchan (Bloomington: Indiana University Press, 2007), 15–38.

ture"[43]—to put it more broadly, space provides a conceptual framework through which we understand the world. This is a persuasive claim worth probing further.

First, the stop-motion animation sequence in *The Pearl Necklace*, for instance, does not deal with puppets. Instead, the heroine is a string of pearls, one that can be of the same scale of a pearl necklace we wear in everyday life. The space the audience can infer beyond the frame is not a miniature set, but the same set in which its adjacent live-action shots were filmed: a shabby bedroom. If puppet animation partly satisfies the spectator's "spatial hunger"[44] (to borrow animator Art Clokey's term), the stop-motion trick sequence in *The Pearl Necklace* satisfies it completely: it is the same sense of moving through space, in the same world that does not have to reduce its scale.

Second, to avoid equivocality in stating "something between 'a world' and 'the world,'" we need to think about a stop-motion trick's relation to the world in two steps: the liminal spatial unit of a frame and the sequence (or shot) as a whole. Each frame of the stop-motion sequence is a photograph, a view of the world. We have no doubt about this. In a film like *The Pearl Necklace*, which contains both live-action and stop-motion sequences, a frame from the live-action sequence and a frame from the stop-motion sequence might share a view of the same world. Yet, for Cavell, photography's relation to the world is also a conviction. Movies, like still photography, might help us regain our conviction of the world by removing our subjectivity in the task of transcription and presenting to us a world past.[45] Stop-motion animation fits well into Cavell's definition of movies as "successions of automatic world projections,"[46] but the sequence as a whole cannot declare or convince us of a past existence. To explain this paradox, scrutiny of the intricate relations of movement, time, and space in the realm of stop-motion animation is needed.

43. Buchan, "The Animated Spectator."

44. Art Clokey, "Trimensional Animation" (unpublished typescript, 1977).

45. Cavell, "What Photography Calls Thinking," 124.

46. Cavell, *The World Viewed*, 72.

Movement, Time, and Space

If cinema far surpasses photography in its potential to produce a strong impression of reality, at least some credit should be given to cinematic movement. For Metz, the strong impression of reality that motion enhances is, first of all, a sense of immediacy, presence, and evocation.[47] Movement created by animation, however, has a tendency to substitute physical laws with imagination. It can, as Gunning writes, "endow otherwise 'impossible' motion and transformations with the immediacy of perception that Metz claims movement entails."[48] In the realm of stop-motion animation, in which a knife slices bread by itself and a necklace dances on its own, the movement injects the impression of the fantastic, the ghostly, or the impossible into the individual frames that could have spoken for the real. Viewing a live-action movie, audiences find themselves simultaneously experiencing a past tense ("That was happening," or, as Cavell might call it, a world past) and a present tense that movement entails ("This is happening"). In stop-motion animation, the vividness of movement might still evoke a sense of presence, a feeling that all the strange things are happening. However, other than on the level of fictional film narrative, audiences would not perceive such a stop-motion animation sequence in the past tense. It is not an event past, not a duration past.

Another way to explain why stop-motion animation fails to declare a past existence is to say that time is manipulated in its production. The work of the camera operator in live-action film production, in a certain sense, is to record or transfigure an existence that is becoming past while being filmed. It is a task toward the past. On the contrary, when it comes to the work of the animator—in this case that of *The Pearl Necklace*'s still camera operator Chen Peilin—putting frames into motion is by no means a form of reproduction, but more or less an invention, one that might be even out of the animator's control. It is a task toward the future. In the *Shenbao* newspaper, an enthusiastic reviewer praised Chen Peilin's cinema-

47. Christian Metz, "On the Impression of Reality in the Cinema," in *Film Language: A Semiotics of the Cinema*, trans. Michael Taylor (New York: Oxford University Press, 1974), 315.

48. Tom Gunning, "Moving Away from the Index: Cinema and the Impression of Reality," *A Journal of Feminist Cultural Studies* 18, no. 1 (2007): 46.

tography: "All the tricks are really magical, especially the scene in which a string of pearls morphs into 'Misfortune.'"[49] The reviewer's response again demonstrates that what we now see as stop-motion animation was then considered part of the camera operator's toolbox.

Considering the job of animator (or camera operator) as a game with time underlines a sense of contingency in stop-animation production: contingency ineluctably emerges in the production mode of manipulation and control. Between frames, the animator might move the object to the left or right on a whim. A frame—a photograph—can be duplicated and thus become two or three frames when the animator is a bit lazy or tries to be economical. The resulting appearance of a stop-motion animation might even surprise its animator. If that happens, it is partly because another naughty animator called Time has played a role in the creation. For Roland Barthes, a photograph's punctum is often, if we speak of form, a detail, an object, that makes the viewer pensive. Barthes's example is a pearl necklace, which he had seen worn by someone in his own family, in Ver der Zee's photograph.[50] Ultimately, a photograph's punctum, according to Barthes, is an understanding of time: the "lacerating emphasis" of "that-has-been."[51] If there is something that we may call the punctum of the stop-motion trick sequence in *The Pearl Necklace*, it is the punctum simultaneously of form and of intensity. If I am allowed to formulate it in a fashion similar to Barthes, I would say that the stop-motion trick's punctum has to do with its temporal vertigo: between a frame and a sequence, or between "that has been," "that will be," and "that is happening now."

As we have shown, in *The Haunted Hotel, Kan the Great Knight-Errant,* and *The Pearl Necklace,* their trick sequences in which an inanimate object comes to life were created by different methods and technologies. They are all sequences full of animation, vivacity, and liveliness. Strictly speaking, stop-motion animation techniques were used in *The Pearl Necklace* and part of *The Haunted Hotel,* but not in *Kan the Great Knight-Errant.* It may be striking that for *The Haunted Hotel* and *The Pearl Necklace* alike, the stop-motion animation sequence does not exist in the same space-time

49. *Shenbao,* January 21, 1926.

50. Roland Barthes, *Camera Lucida: Reflections on Photography,* trans. Richard Howard (New York: Hill & McGraw, 1981), 53.

51. Barthes, *Camera Lucida,* 77, 96.

continuum as its adjacent live-action sequences. As is evident in all the three examples, the act of looking, signaled by a point-of-view structure, might be employed to weave these trick sequences into the photography-based, lifelike universe, thus naturalizing the special effect. The device of point of view, as we understand it today, is a competent assistant in creating the illusion of spatial continuity. This also amounts to saying that the trick sequence is sutured into the diegetic time through editing. However, a stop-motion animation sequence in live-action cinema foregrounds an "immiscible"[52] zone where time derails: it is simultaneously in and out of the flow of diegetic time. The enchanted temporality of the stop-motion animation sequence cannot be entirely translated into the diegetic flow. Instead, it anticipates a moment when time diverts itself from its intended course.

Furthermore, a sequence created using the stop-motion technique helps conceive and define *enchanted space*,[53] a concept that ties together many threads woven through this chapter. The concept of an enchanted space does not simply mean the backdrop of a stop-motion shot, nor does it refer to the set design. Rather, it denotes a dynamic spatial and perceptual network comprised of objects, selected elements of the set, lighting, special effects, impossible motion, derailed time, and audiences. Compared with time, which "possesses no sensory medium of its own" and has to "anchor itself to any suitable perceptual embodiment," space is more privileged in visual studies as it "is directly embodied in the visual world."[54] Even when I say "time derails," as if there were forking paths of time, a spatial metaphor is inevitable. With audiences as a crucial component of an enchanted space, I seek to acknowledge that "the world of film," is "a mode of experience," a "mechanism by which anything reaches the screen and, on reaching it,

52. I borrow the word *immiscible* from Bliss Cua Lim, *Translating Time: Cinema, the Fantastic, and Temporal Critique* (Durham, NC: Duke University Press, 2009), 32.

53. In formulating the concept of enchanted space, I am indebted to Wu Hung, especially his definition of feminine space. See, for example, Hung Wu, "Beyond Stereotypes: The Twelve Beauties in Qing Court Art and the *Dream of the Red Chamber*," in *Writing Women in Late Imperial China*, eds. Ellen Widmer and Kang-I Sun Chang (Palo Alto, CA: Stanford University Press, 1996), 306–65.

54. Rudolf Arnheim, "A Stricture on Space and Time." *Critical Inquiry* 4, no. 4 (1978): 653.

affects us,"[55] without making "the/a world" the site and vortex of multiple and irreconcilable meanings.

The Effortfulness of Being

Now permit me to dwell, for one more moment on the stop-motion animation sequence in *The Pearl Necklace*. The jerky quality of the pearl necklace's stop-motion dance makes the interstices between frames tangible. The labor and difficulty of making stop-motion animation becomes visible. The cores of the apparatuses of live-action movement and stop-motion movement are in fact similar: what we tend to recognize as a single, continuous movement is achieved through a process based on intermittent, discontinuous motion. The difference is that whereas live-action movement, with the aid of the persistence of our vision, always pretends to be effortless, stop-motion movement willingly acknowledges the paradox, and more importantly, acknowledges the production process as effortful. In other words, stop-motion animation provides an intensified form of the apparatus of cinematic movement. It is in this sense that Jennifer Barker calls stop-motion animation "cinema *par excellence*."[56] The poetics of stop-motion animation, to borrow Vivian Sobchack's expression, is ultimately about "the incredible effortfulness of being."[57]

Think back, in the meshes of your memory, to the midnight hours when you suddenly wake up, hear your own intermittent heartbeats, somewhat out of joint, and come to realize how effortful life is. To some extent, the intermittent, jerky, imperfect stop-motion movement spells out "our lived-body's 'comprehension' of effortfulness, of fatigue, of being 'worn out' or 'used up,' of being physically marked (if not scarred) by life."[58] In doing so,

55. Dudley Andrew, *Concepts in Film Theory* (New York: Oxford University Press, 1984), 40.

56. Jennifer M. Barker, *The Tactile Eye: Touch and the Cinematic Experience* (Berkeley: University of California Press, 2009), 136.

57. Vivian Sobchack, "Animation and Automation, or, the Incredible Effortfulness of Being," *Screen* 50, no. 4 (Winter 2009): 375–91.

58. Vivian Sobchack, "Stop + Motion: On Animation, Inertia, and Innervation" (paper presented at *Kracauer Lectures in Film and Media Theory*, December 5, 2015).

it animates us. In this regard, one graphically adorned title card earlier in the nightly sewing is extremely telling:

> With fingers weary and worn,
> With eyelids heavy and red,
> Stitch, Stitch, Stitch,
> In poverty, hunger, and dirt.

The bilingual title card was again a product of cross-cultural conjunction, translating selected lines from "The Song of the Shirt," a poem written by Thomas Hood in 1843, into the classical Chinese poetic fashion. With calligraphy by Li Rudi and drawing by Zhang Tiren, the title cards in *The Pearl Necklace* were carefully and beautifully done in a manner unmatched in most Chinese silent films. The graphic elements of some of these art titles are not related to the diegetic world of the film, but others, including the one I mention here, are obviously visual interpretations of the diegesis. A little drawing of a woman mending clothes—a printed cartoon version of Xiuzhen—appears in the upper-right corner of the frame. The drawing soon comes into life in the next (live-action) shot, transcending the boundary between stillness and motion as well as the ontological divide of printed cartoon and live-action cinema. The narrative gist of this sequence—life is effortful, or even painful—coincides with the feeling that the intermittent, jerky, imperfect stop-motion movement evokes in us, not only affectively but also corporeally. The stop-motion sequence serves the narrative when it is simultaneously a resistance: because of the effortfulness of life, we, like Xiuzhen, are in need of a reverie, a hallucination, or an interruption of the repetitive, homogenous, disenchanted hours of work.

The word *fingers* in the intertitle is key to our understanding of stop-motion animation's punctum. Jennifer Barker, among others, has elaborated on stop-motion animation as "a haptic art form, one that address itself first and foremost to the fingertips, provoking our desire to touch, caress, squeeze, and scrape the images before us."[59] I would add that very often it is literally more *touching* when what gets animated are body-related objects (such as a pair of boots or a pearl necklace) which serve as part of

59. Barker, *The Tactile Eye*, 137.

our extended body and constantly touch our skin. Indeed, the "moving" image of the pearl necklace is beckoning to our fingertips. Its texture and materiality, as well as the personal, intimate, bodily, and even painful memory that it carries, make it even more so. Not surprising at all, ending the nightly sewing sequence is a reaction shot of Xiuzhen, who does exactly what audiences are seduced to do, want to do, but could not actually accomplish: she grasps the objects on the table with her fingers.

Conclusion

With a structure that resembles a string of pearls, this chapter weaves together three case studies from Chinese silent cinemas to show that everyday objects can be enlivened through the stop-motion technique or other means. It further explores the moments film tricks affected audiences in a space of enchantment. While disturbing the conventional historical narrative surrounding the so-called first trick film in Chinese film history, this chapter demonstrates that in the Chinese historical context, this species of stop-motion animation, was indeed understood as part and parcel of trick photography. As the marginalized part of Chinese film history enters theoretical discourse, we are empowered to challenge, rethink, or even overturn the dominant attitude in classical film theories in the Western tradition that conceptualizes animation as something irrelevant to photography and to photography-based theories of cinema. When Chinese animation is no longer film theory's forgotten land,[60] we discover that Chinese animation suggests a rethinking of space in a global context.

60. Again, I take inspiration from Karen Beckman, who vividly describes animation as "the land that film theory forgot, or rejected." See Karen Beckman, "Film Theory's Animated Map," *Framework* 56, no. 2 (Fall 2015): 472.

TWO

From Animation to Martial Arts

Toward the Transcendence of False Movements

Jinying Li

One of the genre signatures of martial arts cinema is its stunning feature of spectacular movements that break physical rules and exceed bodily limits, which in many cases can appear to be quite cartoonish. For instance, Stephen Chow's *Kung Fu Hustle* (*Gong fu* 功夫, 2004), a film widely claimed to be a significant homage to martial arts cinema with extensive references and allusions to its genre history and conventions, features highly exaggerated and comical action sequences that resemble Disney cartoons more than King Hu's martial arts classics. The film's extensive use of animation styles suggests a deeply rooted connection between martial arts cinema and animation, and the connection can be quite hilarious, as in the case of *Kung Fu Hustle*.

In fact, animation (*donghua pian* 动画片) and martial arts films (*wuxia pian* 武侠片) have demonstrated a close affinity with each other in the history of Chinese cinema. As Weihong Bao observes in her historical study of the emergence of affective media in China, these two popular forms of moving images overlap "historically and conceptually" in the development of China's vernacular version of technologically mediated modern senses.[1] The martial arts films frequently rely on various animation techniques such as stop-motion and computer-generated imagery (CGI) to create stunning special effects in spectacular fighting scenes. Chinese animations

1. Weihong Bao, *Fiery Cinema: The Emergence of an Affective Medium in China, 1915–1945* (Minneapolis: University of Minnesota Press, 2015), 363.

often take their narrative and visual references from the genre conventions of martial arts, featuring fighting warriors and heroic fantasies in exotic sceneries in animated imagery. More important, both Chinese animation and martial arts cinema have constantly been endorsed by the nationalist discourse claiming cultural heritage. Notions such as the National Style (*minzu fengge* 民族风格) in describing Chinese animations and folk traditions (*minjian chuantong* 民间传统) in characterizing martial arts films distinctively brand these two forms as essentialized cultural markers of Chineseness, suggesting their shared historical legacy in addressing certain crises and anxieties in national identity. Despite such close affinities, these two connected forms of moving images have rarely been examined together in studies of Chinese cinema.

This essay provides an analytical mapping of the historical and aesthetical overlaps between animation and martial arts cinema. My purpose is to explore different modalities of generating modern movements in both Chinese animations and martial arts films and to demonstrate that both animation and martial arts emerged and developed in Chinese history as powerful vehicles to negotiate with competing conceptualizations of movement in shaping a vernacular perception of space, time, physicality, and vitality vis-à-vis the violent force of modernity. These historical questions also lead to the theoretical examination of how cinema grapples with its inherent challenge to endow "dead" images with movement that appear to be "alive." The first part of the essay maps the historical conjunctures between animation and martial arts cinema through their shared roots in shadow play, their mutual mythological anchor in the figure of Monkey King, as well as the central role of the Wan brothers in the historical development of the techniques, forms, and conventions of both Chinese animations and martial arts films. Such historical conjunctures also underline the closely related aesthetic connections between these two cinematic forms due to their shared techniques and technologies in generating moving images. The second part of the essay thus focuses on these shared technical characteristics and demonstrates the aesthetic affinity between animation and martial arts cinema, particularly in the ways in which they strive to embellish the intensity, physicality, and vitality of bodily motion. With these technical concerns at the center of their production, these two forms of moving images tackle the question of movement as an intrinsic problem of cinema, which is what Henri Bergson describes as the fundamental falsehood of cinematic movement.[2] The *false movement* generated by the cinematic machine, which is abstract, mechanical, and homogenous, is taken as an intrinsic problem in the techno-aesthetic conditions of moving images, a problem that both animation and martial arts cinema struggle to overcome through their shared techniques such as mickey-mousing sound effects, plasmatic physics, and extreme verticality.

Toward a Vernacular History of the Movement-Image: Martial Arts, Animation, and Shadow Play

Let's begin with the historical moment in the late Qing period when the question of bodily movement suddenly became a national problem in China, which led Tan Sitong, a famous intellectual and reformer, to advocate for strengthening the nation with physical movement and bodybuilding.[3] In the late nineteenth century, the waning Qing dynasty was struggling with both the external onslaught from Western imperialism and the internal turmoil from local rebels. The disastrous loss in the Sino-Japanese War of 1895 further intensified the strong sense of national shame and crisis. This gave rise to a popular discourse that identified the national problem in the supposed weakness of the Chinese body—the so-called Sick Man of East Asia. At the center of this crisis is the problem of movement, in that it was believed that the weakness of the Chinese body was due to the lack of movement. Tan Sitong "saw direct connections between a society's 'dynamism' or 'love of movement' and the status of that nation on the world stage."[4] Explaining the Western hegemony in their love of movement (*dong* 动) and China's fall in its passivity (*jing* 静), Tan advocated the need "to

2. Henri Bergson, *Creative Evolution*, trans. Arthur Mitchell (New York: H. Holt, 1911), 272–370.

3. About this history, see Andrew D. Morris, *Marrow of the Nation: A History of Sport and Physical Culture in Republican China* (Berkeley: University of California Press, 2004).

4. Andrew Morris, "'To Make the Four Hundred Million Move': The Late Qing Dynasty Origins of Modern Chinese Sport and Physical Culture," *Comparative Studies in Society and History* 42, no. 4 (October 2000): 880.

make the four hundred million move."[5] The notion of movement here is not simply referring to the motion of a physical body, but is also allegorically associated with the movement of national uprising and progression. To "make the four hundred million move," modern physical culture was brought to urban China, along with the introduction of the concept of *tiyu* 体育 (physical education, literally body cultivation) as an ideological symbol of "status, masculinity, and nationalism."[6] The question of how a body should move thus became the center of a nationalist project that conflated bodybuilding with nation-building.

It is in this historical context that martial arts were reinvented as a vernacular form of modern sports. As Weihong Bao rightly observed, the popularization of martial arts in early modern China directly resulted from the rise of a strong physical culture as a nationalist modernization agenda. Martial arts were thus remade from the supposed backward tradition to the progressive technologization, "shaking off feudal and superstitious trapping" and being reshaped "into a modern institution."[7] Techniques from Western sports such as gymnastics, soccer, and tennis were incorporated into the physical training, and various modern media technologies such as photography, film, and the gramophone were also used for a "scientific approach to martial arts."[8] In other words, martial arts as we know it today is largely a modern reinvention, a result of the technologization of body and movement as part of a nationalist project of bodybuilding designed to address the crisis of national identity by tapping into the anxiety of physical bodies, particularly the male ones.

In the same historical context, another folk culture of movement also flourished in China vis-à-vis the introduction of modern technological motion. That was shadow play, an indigenous form of moving images that combines puppet performance with screen projection, in which the flat cutout figures (the shadow puppets) are maneuvered against projected light so that their shadows are animated on screen. Shadow play has been widely claimed to be the origin, or a precursor, of Chinese cinema, not least because cinema, when introduced to China, was also called shadow

5. Morris, "To Make the Four Hundred Million Move."

6. Morris, "To Make the Four Hundred Million Move," 877.

7. Bao, *Fiery Cinema*, 55.

8. Bao, *Fiery Cinema*, 55.

play (*yingxi* 影戏) until it was renamed electric shadow (*dianying* 电影) in the 1930s.[9] Because of such historical and conceptual overlaps between these two kinds of shadow plays, the term has become the focus of debates on the genealogy and ontology of Chinese cinema. The notion of shadow play, according to Chinese historians, prioritizes play (*xi* 戏) over shadow (*ying* 影), which anchors the genealogical and ontological root of Chinese cinema to theatrical traditions.[10] Such an emphasis on theatricality is at odds with Western film theories that often associate cinema's ontology with photography.[11]

The theoretical debate between the theatrical and the photographic, however, overlooks the third possibility in understanding the historical forms of shadow play in the genealogy of cinema—that is, the animated. Shadow play, after all, is a form of puppet animation, and its key attraction is to animate, that is, to give life to an inanimate object by making it move so that the shadows of those leather-made objects would be able to play. In other words, to have a play, the shadow has to be animated by puppetry movement first. Therefore, rather than with theatricality or photography, I align shadow play with animation, which is to say that the genealogical paradigms of Chinese cinema are not only shadow (photography) and play (theater), but also animation. Indeed, animation, which is literally translated in Chinese as moving pictures (*donghua* 动画), has increasingly been claimed as the very foundation of cinema. As Cholodenko says, "all film, film as such, is a form of animation."[12] Therefore, to theorize and historicize Chinese cinema, its conceptual and genealogical relationship with shadow play needs to be reexamined through the lens of animation.

In fact, Chinese animation and shadow play have informed and influ-

9. Zhen Zhang, *An Amorous History of the Silver Screen: Shanghai Cinema, 1896–1937* (Chicago: University of Chicago Press, 2006), 89–117.

10. See Zhong Dafeng 钟大丰, "Lun yingxi" 论影戏 (On shadow play), *Beijing dianying xueyuan xuebao* 北京电影学院学报 (Journal of the Beijing Film Academy), no. 2 (1985): 54–92; Zhong Dafeng 钟大丰, "'Yingxi' lilun suyuan" "影戏"理论溯源 (Tracing the history of the shadow play theory), *Dangdai dianying* 当代电影 (Contemporary cinema), 3 (1986): 75–80.

11. André Bazin, "The Ontology of the Photographic Image," in *What Is Cinema?* Vol. I, trans. Hugh Gray (Berkeley: University of California Press, 2004), 9–16.

12. Alan Cholodenko, "'First Principles' of Animation," in *Animating Film Theory*, ed. Karen Beckman (Durham, NC: Duke University Press, 2014), 98.

enced each other both historically and aesthetically. The first Chinese animated feature film, *Princess Iron Fan* (*Tieshan gongzhu* 铁扇公主, 1941), demonstrates visual styles that resemble shadow play, especially in action sequences that emphasize surface-oriented lateral motions. From the 1950s to the 1980s, in the so-called golden era of Chinese animation, the graphic styles of shadow play were displayed or referred to by numerous animations, including *Mr. Dongguo and the Wolf* (*Dongguo xiansheng he lang* 东郭先生和狼, 1955), *The Wagging Wolf* (*Hui yao weiba de lang* 会摇尾巴的狼, 1955), *Pigsy Eats Watermelon* (*Zhu bajie chi xigua* 猪八戒吃西瓜, 1958), and *Zhang Fei Examines the Melon* (*Zhang Fei shengua* 张飞审瓜, 1980). The experimentation and production of shadow-play-like moving images in Chinese animations gave rise to a stylistic category called shadow play animation (*piying donghua* 皮影动画), suggesting a close historical and aesthetic kinship between these two forms. When Chinese animation entered the digital era, shadow play continued to be a popular resource for stylistic inspiration, its visual styles often simulated using computer-generated images. The legacy of shadow play has been so widely celebrated in Chinese animation that a popular 3D-animated feature film, *Monkey King: The Hero Is Back* (*Xiyouji zhi dasheng guilai* 西游记之大圣归来, 2015), specifically features a computer-generated sequence of shadow play at the beginning of the film as homage.[13]

Emphasizing animated motion, shadow play is also akin to the martial arts in developing the vernacular forms of modern movements. Relying on martial arts stories as narrative sources, the most spectacular moments in shadow play performances are often the fighting scenes, which are marked by an intense sense of speed, force, and dynamics, generating a powerful sensation of movement through the puppeteer's maneuvers. Compared with other forms of theatrical plays, shadow play is more appealing to children precisely because it has a much faster pace and features more action than dialogue. Thus the skill of a shadow play puppeteer, like that of a well-trained martial artist, is often demonstrated by the speed and precision of maneuver in generating the dynamics, force, and intensity of spectacular movements. Such enjoyment and admiration of mobility, velocity, and energy are also the cultural trope and aesthetic signature of vernacular

13. About the legacy of shadow play in Chinese animation, see Jason McGrath, "Suppositionality, Virtuality, and Chinese Cinema," *boundary 2* 49, no.1 (February 2022): 263–92.

modernity, when the increasing entanglement between body and machines in China's early modern era gave rise to new sensations and perceptions that were to be articulated and negotiated in locally situated cultural forms such as martial arts, shadow play, and the newly emergent Chinese animation.[14]

The Wan Brothers

Associating shadow play with animation and martial arts, I want to point out that the notion of play (*xi* 戏) here does not simply refer to theatrical plays (*xiju* 戏剧), but also means playfulness and gameplay (*youxi* 游戏), which are often associated with the joy of movement. It is this emphasis on playful movement that drew Wan Laiming, a founding figure of Chinese animation, to the enchanting culture of shadow play in his childhood. Wan and his brothers are widely regarded as the founding figures whose early pioneer works mark the beginning of Chinese animation. According to Wan's autobiography, both play (*wan* 玩) and movement (*dong* 动) played a defining role in cultivating the brothers' life-long interest in and devotion to animation. When they were children, the brothers loved to play with almost anything that moved. In Wan's own account, he wrote, "Ever since I was young, I was interested in movement. I always enjoyed watching things that move, always enjoyed playing with small animals, catching butterflies and other creatures."[15] Among the things that move, the Wan brothers were particularly enchanted by shadow play, a form of moving images they enjoyed so much that they created their own home-made shadow play performances. Such an early interest in playing with movement led the brothers to artistic experimentations and innovations in animation in their adulthood.

The Wan brothers began to make animated short films in the 1920s. They made more than twenty animated shorts for numerous studios in that early period. One that survives is a Mickey Mouse–like cartoon they made for the live-action film *Scenes of City Life* (*Dushi fengguang* 都市风

14. On vernacular modernity in China, see Zhang, *An Amorous History*.

15. Wan Laiming 万籁鸣 and Wan Guohun 万国魂, *Wo yu Sun Wukong* 我与孙悟空 (Monkey King and me) (Taiyuan: Beiyue wenyi, 1986), 6; quoted in Sean Macdonald, *Animation in China: History, Aesthetics, Media* (New York: Routledge, 2015), 16.

光, 1935), a film within the film that functions as a mediated reflection of the fast-paced modern urban life infused with exaggerated movements and body transformations. What stands out in this short cartoon is the use of squash-and-stretch technique for metamorphic body transformations, which make the animated caricatures appear to be elastic and malleable, an effect celebrated by Eisenstein as *plasmaticness*.[16] Another characteristic is the use of music as sound effect to synchronize with the tempo and trajectory of animated movement, a common strategy in animation production known as mickey-mousing. Both of these are standard techniques developed by the Disney studio in the 1930s that were later widely incorporated by both Chinese animation and martial arts cinema. The prevalence of such animation techniques in martial arts cinema (as I further demonstrate in detail later in the chapter) not only underlines their shared technological conditions, but also highlights the central role of the Wan brothers in the development of these two forms of moving images in Chinese film history, because it was likely through the Wan brothers, who had been experimenting with squash-and-stretch and mickey-mousing in their early animation works, that these techniques were introduced to both Chinese animation and martial arts films.

Indeed, the Wan brothers were not only the pioneers of animation but also the foundational figures in the development of martial arts cinemas as a popular genre that combines vernacular folk traditions with modern film technologies. While experimenting with short animations, the Wan brothers worked on art design and special effects for numerous live-action films throughout their early career from the 1920s to the 1940s. One of the films they worked on is *The Burning of the Red Lotus Temple* (*Huoshao Hongliansi* 火烧红蓮寺, 1928), whose phenomenal success launched the whole genre of the so-called martial arts-magic spirit films (*wuxia shenguai pian* 武侠神怪片). Exemplifying the hybridity and ambiguity of vernacular modernism, the early martial arts-magic spirit films successfully blur the boundary between magic and science, between folk ethos and technological wonders, between vernacular fantasies and modern aspirations.[17] Although the genre was overwhelmingly criticized by the contemporary

16. Sergei Eisenstein, *Eisenstein on Disney*, ed. Jay Leyda, trans. Alan Upchurch (London: Methuen, 1988).

17. See Zhen Zhang, *An Amorous History*, 199–243.

Chinese government as backward, superstitious, and nonscientific, it was actually the genre that most extensively relied on cutting-edge film technologies, including animation techniques such as hand-drawn graphics, stop-motion, and animated metamorphosis, to create the special effects for the spectacles of fantastic movements and magical transformations (e.g., hovering swords, flying warriors, and changing bodies). Therefore, it is hardly surprising that the Wan brothers' animation skills thrived in this popular genre's early historical development, because both animation and martial arts films flourish in the fertile interplay between the technological and the fantastic for generating the sensation of movement.

Not only did early martial arts films extensively use animation techniques, but the genre's narrative and visual styles also had tremendous influence on the aesthetic formation of Chinese animation, especially in the animation works by the Wan brothers. In 1941, when the genre of martial arts-magic spirit films had been banned by the Republican government, the Wan brothers made China's first animated feature film, *Princess Iron Fan*. This film demonstrates close affinity and similarity with early martial arts films in its narrative, styles, and character design. Adapted from the classical fantasy novel *Journey to the West* (*Xiyouji* 西游记) centered on the mythical figure of Monkey King, which had been one of the most popular literary sources for early martial arts-magic spirit films, *Princess Iron Fan* features an abundance of flying figures, spectacular actions, thrilling combats, stunning swordfights, and magical transformations, all of which are the signature attractions of the martial arts genre (fig. 2.1). The outbreak of the Sino-Japan war in the late 1930s also provided a fertile historical background for the remediated revival of the historical legacy of martial arts in the form of animation as a nationalist modern project. *Princess Iron Fan*, featuring the heroic fighting scenes of Monkey King defeating evil demons in animated spectacles, was hailed upon its release as a patriotic film inspiring people's resistance against the Japanese invasion.[18] This nationalist project in the genre form of martial arts waned after the war.

After the foundation of the People's Republic of China in 1949, the socialist government ruled by the Chinese Communist Party largely banned the martial arts genre in literature, cinema, and comic books, lead-

18. See Bao, *Fiery Cinema*, 359–74.

FIGURE 2.1. Animated martial arts actions, in *Princess Iron Fan* (1941).

ing to the genre's almost complete disappearance from mainland China for decades until its revival in the 1990s. But the legacy of martial arts cinema survived in animated imagery and continued to influence the development of Chinese animation in its golden era from the 1950s to the 1980s. Animation, as the media form of the "unrealistic," provided an enclave for the fantastic and magical elements of martial arts cinema to survive against the doctrine of socialist realism that otherwise eradicated the genre from Chinese cinema of the socialist era.

In the early 1960s, the Wan brothers directed another feature animation, *Uproar in Heaven* (*Danao tiangong* 大闹天宫, 1961, 1964), a film widely celebrated as the pinnacle of artistic achievement in Chinese animation. As the film's title suggests, its key theme and attraction is *nao* 闹—uproar, disturbance, and chaos—the kinetic energy and sensational intensity of which are animated through the spectacles of movement and transformation. These animated spectacles in *Uproar in Heaven*, not surprisingly, resemble the early martial arts films in their tempo, choreography, background design, sound effects, and even camera angles. The film features extensive fighting sequences with martial arts actions that are animated with the dynamic motion of the plasmatic figures (fig. 2.2).

FIGURE 2.2. Animated martial arts actions, in *Uproar in Heaven* (1961, 1964).

In fact, both *Princess Iron Fan* and *Uproar in Heaven*, the two most famous animation films in Chinese history, can be described as animated martial arts cinema. *Princess Iron Fan* was even advertised as such—"an animated martial arts-magic spirit film" (*donghua wuxia shenguai pian* 动画武侠神怪片)—when it was released in the 1940s. As the foundational figures in the historical formations of both Chinese animation and martial arts cinema, the Wan brothers, through their pioneer works across these two forms, discovered and fortified the nexuses between animation and martial arts in their shared technical formulas such as squash-and-stretch and mickey-mousing, their common historical legacy of addressing the national crisis through spectacular bodily movement, as well as their mutual cultural inspiration from the mythology of Monkey King in *Journey to the West*.

Monkey King

Like *Princess Iron Fan, Uproar in Heaven* is based on the novel *Journey to the West* and centers on the mythical figure of Monkey King. Sean Macdonald, in his groundbreaking study of Chinese animation history, argues that the "Monkey King *is* animation in China," because the literary and graphic figuration of Monkey King was intertwined with the figura-

FIGURE 2.3. Monkey King in Hong Kong martial arts cinema, in *Princess Iron Fan* (1966).

tion of the medium of animation in China.[19] I would push the argument a step further and argue that Monkey King is also martial arts cinema in China. Marked by his dynamic energy, rebellious aspirations, supreme magical power, and unbeatable martial skills, Monkey King is, by and large, an archetypal martial arts hero. This mythical figure embodies and foreshadows the cultural fantasy of a folk hero with grassroots aspiration who fights against injustice and oppression with combat skills and physical strength, a fantasy that gave rise to the popular imagination of martial arts as a transmedia genre in literature and cinema.

Therefore, it is not accidental that the cinematic imagination of this heroic character of Monkey King was a key element that paved the foundation of martial arts cinema throughout the genre's history. When the early genre form of martial arts-magic spirit films was first established between 1927 and 1931, a great number of these films were cinematic adaptations of *Journey to the West*, featuring the heroic figure of Monkey King, including a live-action version of *Princess Iron Fan*. Although the genre was banned in mainland China after 1949, its cinematic legacy was subsequently revived and thrived in postwar Hong Kong. Stories from *Journey to the West*, especially those centered on Monkey King, formed the backbone of the newly

19. Macdonald, *Animation in China*.

flourishing martial arts films in postwar Hong Kong, a most popular genre with transnational appeals that quickly became the signature of Hong Kong cinema (fig. 2.3). From the 1950s to the 1980s, more than thirty Hong Kong martial arts films were adapted from or related with the stories of *Journey to the West*. Among them, the most famous ones are the five films released by Shaw Brothers: *The Monkey Goes West* (1966), *Princess Iron Fan* (1966), *Cave of the Silken Web* (1967), *The Land of Many Perfumes* (1968), and *The Fantastic Magic Baby* (1975). The last of these was directed by Chang Cheh, one of the most famous martial arts filmmakers. Beyond these adaptations, the legendary figure of Monkey King was also incorporated into fictional modern settings in action films such as *The Monkey in Hong Kong* (*Sun Wukong danao Xianggang* 孙悟空大闹香港, 1969) and *The Monkey Comes Again* (*Sun Wukong zainao Xianggang* 孙悟空再闹香港, 1971). The mythical imagination of Monkey King was very much at the cultural center of Hong Kong martial arts cinema.

The Wan brothers' temporary stay in Hong Kong from 1947 to 1956, where they worked as art directors to escape the civil war, also contributed to the local revival of martial arts films that reanimated the lives and stories of Monkey King in Hong Kong cinema. The Wan brothers' excursion in Hong Kong, though not particularly productive or eventful, had a significant impact on the Hong Kong film industry by introducing animation techniques to local filmmakers and artists.[20] One of them is King Hu, who began his career working as assistant to the Wan brothers and later became a world-famous filmmaker, a foundational figure for the establishment of the new school martial arts cinema (*xinpai wuxia pian* 新派武侠片). King Hu was very interested in animation and had tried to make an animated feature film in the 1980s, albeit unsuccessfully. Hu's passion in animation was carried on by a younger generation of filmmakers, who, under his stylistic influence, put forward what came to be known as the Hong Kong New Wave. One of these is Tsui Hark, whose strong emphasis on special effects, spectacular actions, and excessive mise-en-scène, which all became part of his signature style, decisively returns martial arts cinema to its original roots in animated magical spirit. In 1987, Tsui Hark directed

20. About the Wan brothers' work and influence in Hong Kong cinema, see Daisy Yan Du, "Suspended Animation: The Wan Brothers and the (In)Animate Mainland-Hong Kong Encounter, 1947–1956," *Journal of Chinese Cinemas* 11, no. 2 (2017): 140–58.

one of the most canonic films of Hong King New Wave, *A Chinese Ghost Story* (*Qiannü youhun* 倩女幽魂). Combining martial arts with magical spirit, the film features extensive use of stop-motion animation in its spectacular fighting scenes. This martial arts film was so popular that it quickly spread into a multimedia franchise that includes an animated feature film produced by Tsui ten years later.

Tsui Hark, as well as a group of Hong Kong filmmakers working in the martial arts genre, were the key players in the recent revival of Monkey King imagination in both Chinese animation and martial arts cinema. Tsui Hark directed the latest installment of Stephen Chow's film series *Journey to the West* (2013, 2017), which launched a cycle of Monkey King frenzy in Chinese cinema of the twenty-first century. Notable martial arts films in this cycle include the tremendously popular *Monkey King* series, *The Monkey King* (*Xiyouji zhi danao tiangong* 西游记之大闹天宫, 2014), *The Monkey King 2* (*Xiyouji zhi Sun Wukong sanda Baigujing* 西游记之三打白骨精, 2016), and *The Monkey King 3* (*Xiyouji nü'er guo* 西游记女儿国, 2018), all of which were directed by Hong Kong filmmaker Cheang Pou-soi. Other examples include such box-office hits as *A Chinese Odyssey: Part Three* (*Dahua xiyou 3* 大话西游三, 2016) and *Wu Kong* (*Wukong zhuan* 悟空传, 2017), both of which were also directed by Hong Kong filmmakers. In this Monkey King cycle there emerged one of the most commercially successful films in Chinese animation—*Monkey King: The Hero Is Back*, a 3D computer animation that on its release was the highest-grossing animated film in China. With the rapid growth and commercial success of Chinese film market, China's rising film industry was eager to create its homegrown superhero blockbusters with "Chinese characteristics." The fantastic figure of Monkey King provides the key ingredients: the cultural legacy of folk mythology and national styles in Chinese animation that are forever emblematized in *Uproar in Heaven*, as well as the history of vernacular modernism in martial arts cinema that is marked by the transversal between folk imaginations and technological advancements, between national pride and global aspirations. The transmedia imaginary of Monkey King thus anchors the most profound historical conjuncture between Chinese animation and martial arts cinema.

Aesthetic Modes: Toward the Transcendence of False Movements

The historical entanglements between Chinese animation and martial arts cinema reveal the deeply rooted affinities of these two cinematic forms in their shared technicality and aesthetics, which, I argue, underline the fundamental crisis in cinematic motion that both animation and martial arts genre have to struggle with as their central problem. The key issue is how moving images tackle the inherent tension and ambivalence between movement and image in what Deleuze calls "the movement-image." It is not simply the image that moves, but also images that present and think of themselves as movement. Situated at the dialectic tension between motion and stillness, the moving images have to address movement as their material foundation as well as intrinsic problem. In the words of Deleuze, "It was necessary, at any cost, to overcome this duality of image and movement, of consciousness and thing."[21] This duality, or the ambivalence, has to be dealt with as cinema's inherent crisis. This crisis is especially critical for animation and martial arts films because they are almost all about spectacular movements in cinematic images as a foundational feature that takes priority over narrative or realism: we watch a cartoon or a martial arts film to be amused by the lively energy of a cartoon caricature or the fighting feats of a kung fu hero, regardless of the stories or realistic claims (or lack thereof). It is therefore difficult for animation or martial arts films to resort to storytelling or photographic realism to conceal or disavow the crisis of the movement-image. Relying on the marvelous or comical movements as the key attraction of their cultural forms, animation and martial arts cinema have to grapple with the problematic duality of image and movement up front. And they found similar solutions, which are manifested in their shared techniques: mickey-mousing effects, plasmatic physicality, and extreme verticality.

21. Gilles Deleuze, *Cinema 1: The Movement-Image*, trans. Hugh Tomlinson and Barbara Habberjam (Minneapolis: University of Minnesota Press, 1986), 56.

The Mickey-Mousing Effects

In animations as well as martial arts films, the music soundtrack is strongly relied on to create artificial synchronization with the dynamic movements. We observe the extensive use of such soundtracks to enhance the intensity of movements through "pseudo-synchronization" in both animated films such as the Wan brothers' *Uproar in Heaven* and martial arts films such as King Hu's *Dragon Inn* (*Longmen kezhan* 龙门客栈, 1967). In such soundtracks, the musical trajectory coincides with the visual motion trajectory (rising, falling, jumping, zigzagging, and the like), and the instrumental punctuations in music function as sound effects to be synchronized with the actions in moving images, creating what Phillip Brothy calls "symbiotic fusion" between audio musical flow and visual graphic motion, which mobilizes the temporal dynamics and intensifies the physical energy of those spectacular movements.[22] Such a strategy of synchronizing the rhythm and trajectory between sound and image, as I mentioned earlier, is a common practice in animation production called mickey-mousing because it was first developed in the Disney studio's Mickey Mouse cartoons. The mickey-mousing effect is primarily achieved by the isomorphic and iconic uses of music's rhythm, volume, tone, and timbre to symbolically match the shapes and motions of animated images.[23] The isomorphism between the audio trajectory and the visual motion creates kinetic energy with a strong sense of being "concrete, realistic, cannie."[24]

For Disney, the sound, especially the music, possesses something that animation never has, which is "an organic life" of its own.[25] Such a sense of liveliness in sound, according to Michel Chion, owes to the eye's relative inertia compared to the ear's alertness in identifying motion. Therefore, cartoons without sound "tend to telescope, they do not impress themselves

22. Philip Brophy, "Animation of Sound," in *Movie Music, The Film Reader*, ed. Kay Dickinson (New York: Routledge, 2002), 133–42.

23. Scott Curtis, "The Sound of Early Warner Bros. Cartoons," in *Sound Theory, Sound Practice*, ed. Rick Altman (New York: Routledge, 1992), 201–202.

24. Michel Chion, *Audio-Vision: Sound on Screen*, ed. and trans. Claudia Gorbman (New York: Columbia University Press, 1994), 122.

25. Frank Thomas and Ollie Johnston, *Disney Animation: The Illusion of Life* (New York: Abbeville Press, 1981).

well in the mind, they go by too fast. . . . Sounds help to imprint rapid visual sensations into memory."[26] We probably can say the same thing about martial arts cinema, which also largely relies on sound effects to "imprint rapid visual sensations" of movement. That is the reason Disney was so obsessed with music and mickey-mousing. Through the symbiotic fusion between sound and image, Disney animation effectively synthesized a powerful brand of "illusion of life."

Although we may criticize the ideological implication in Disney's naturalizing view of the sound-image relationship, his recognition of the vital force—"an intrinsic life"—in sound explains the persistent and widespread use of mickey-mousing effects in both Chinese animation and martial arts cinema. The graphic imagery of those cartoon figures and action heroes is not just animated by the cinematic apparatus that projects twenty-four frames per second, but is also animated and energized by the rhythm and tempo of the musical soundtrack. It feels as if those figures are not simply moving themselves, but being moved by something—a physical energy, a dynamic flow, or a vital life force, that mobilizes the entire visual universe and gives it a vibrancy of life through the "organic life" of audio soundwaves. This is what Philip Brothy calls "acoustical physics," which is the effect of sound in creating the perceptual affect of speed, motion, force, and energy.[27] This vital force in sound, which had been discovered by Disney animation at the very beginning of sound cinema, is also one of the most powerful ingredients in manufacturing the dynamic motion in martial art cinema.

Plasmatic Physicality

The metamorphic aesthetic of animation is famously celebrated by Sergei Eisenstein as *plasmaticness*, "a rejection of once-and-forever allotted form, freedom from ossification, the ability to dynamically assume any form."[28] For Eisenstein, the best example of animated plasmaticness is Disney cartoons' signature technique called squash-and-stretch, which renders animated bodies with exaggerated elasticity, as if they were bouncing balls made of rubber. To achieve this effect of squash-and-stretch in animated motion,

26. Chion, *Audio-Vision*, 122.

27. Brophy, "Animation of Sound."

28. Eisenstein, *Eisenstein on Disney*, 21.

however, the sense of physical elasticity has to be generated not only by spatial distortion but also by temporal distortion. The motion is to be animated with a varying speed: a bouncing ball moves faster as it approaches or leaves the ground and slower as it approaches the maximum position. Such a structure of timing is called slow-in and slow-out, one of the twelve principles of animation developed by the Disney studio's in-house technical manual. This timing schema with varying speeds, according to Disney animators, would create a more "organic" movement—"a very spirited result" — rather than the movement with a uniform velocity that feels "mechanical."[29]

The principle of slow-in and slow-out, in fact, has not only been adopted by Chinese animation, as in the case of the Wan brothers' early animation for the film *Scenes of City Life* (1935) discussed earlier, but has also been widely practiced in martial arts cinema, especially in the Hong Kong action films popularized globally since the 1980s by the canonic works of such filmmakers as Tsui Hark, Ching Siu-tung, and Yuen Woo-ping. The fighting sequences in these films often use cranked camera speed or ramping speed in post-production editing to create varying velocities in movement to intensify the dynamics and perceptual impacts of the actions. Tsui Hark's *A Chinese Ghost Story* (1987), for instance, extensively features spectacular movements with varying speeds of slow-in and slow-out to create a dynamic effect of plasmatic physicality to enhance the perceptual intensity of the fighting scenes. This technique is so popular in the martial arts genre that it has almost become a cliché in action movies from China to Hollywood, especially after the exaggerated and excessive use of this technique in *The Matrix* (1999).

Emphasizing the use of common animation techniques such as mickey-mousing, squash-and-stretch, and slow-in and slow-out in martial arts films, I do not simply argue that martial arts cinema borrowed or learned those techniques from Disney. Instead, I emphasize that both animation and martial arts films are dealing with the same crisis and problem and thus find strikingly similar solutions. They try to address the inherent questions of vitality (how to make bodily motion appear more alive through mickey-mousing) and physicality (how to intensify physical strength through squash-and-stretch, slow-in and slow-out) in the duality of the movement-image, which in itself has neither the sense of life nor physical impact. It seems that both animation and martial arts films realized, from the very

29. Thomas and Johnston, *Disney Animation*.

beginning, that the mere cinematic apparatus is not adequate to produce images as movements. Something else is needed, something more excessive, more remarkable (e.g., sound or plasmaticness), to enhance the perceptual feeling of movement. In other words, cinematic movement, the movement of people and things generated by sequential projection, which is the medium foundation of cinema, is "incapable of being satisfied within the limits set by the primitive conditions," and it demands additional "emancipation."[30] But what is wrong with the primitive conditions of cinematic motion? Why is there a problem at the first place? Where does it come from?

In *Cinema 1*, Deleuze begins his exploration of the so-called movement-image with Bergson's critique of cinema. For Bergson, the cinematographic movement generated in the apparatus is fundamentally a false one—it is abstract, mechanical, homogenous, uniform, and imperceptible. Deleuze argues that Bergson's critique should only be targeted at the first level of the cinematic movement, the level of a closed set of moving parts. However, there are also the second and the third levels, correlating with Bergson's second and third theses of movement—the level of movement of translation between the parts and the whole, and the level of duration of a changing whole. The circulation between these three levels constitutes the movement-image, which can overcome the problem of false movement by supplementing it with the additional levels of relation and duration in the forms of film editing and narration. But the question remains: is there a possibility that cinema's primitive condition—the very first level of the mechanical moving parts—can address its own problem, overcome its own falsehood?

For Bergson, false movements are constituted by two kinds of elements: formal transcendental elements (poses) that operate as privileged instants (e.g., dance), and immanent material elements (sections or snapshots) that operate as any-instant-whatevers (e.g., cinema).[31] Animation and martial arts, however, are operating somewhere in between. As the techniques of squash–stretch and slow-in-slow-out suggest, certain moments in animation and martial arts are more remarkable than others. They are often called poses, extremes, or key frames. Therefore, animation is often created in a process called pose-to-pose, with animators designing only the key poses and less skilled laborers drawing the in-betweens. In martial arts cinema, actions are also designed mostly through poses. Thus animation and martial arts cinema

30. Deleuze, *Cinema 1*, 25.

31. Bergson, *Creative Evolution*.

produce transcendental forms of poses (privileged instants) through the very mechanism of snapshots (any-instant-whatevers), dialectically crossing the boundary between the ideas and the materials, between the essential and the immanent. This ambiguity between the privileged instants of timeless poses and the any-instant-whatevers of film frames points to a possibility for the cinematic movement to transcend the binary of its inherent falsehood. That potentiality and aspiration to transcend the cinematic movement's own falsehood are often explicitly visualized (or, we may say, confessed) by the recurrent embrace of extreme verticality as one of the most popular visual motifs in both animation and martial arts cinema.

Extreme Verticality

In her groundbreaking study of the aesthetics of spectacle in digital cinemas, Kristen Whissel raised the notion of *new verticality* to describe how digital technologies brought a new spatial configuration to cinema that emphasizes vertical movement to an excessive degree: the fantastic fights or breathtaking falls of film bodies that seem to defy the physical laws of gravity.[32] According to Whissel, this new verticality "often functions emblematically to represent an abstract quality or 'state of thing.'" And, as a result, it "functions allegorically to give dynamic, hyperkinetic expression to power and the individual's relation to it."[33] It is not clear how "new" this vertical imagination actually is, given that the spectacle of vertical movements had been a key attraction of martial arts cinema and animations since the beginning. In animation, the exaggerated vertical motion in the sudden fall or rise of a cartoon figure, which is often featured as a comic gag, is the central element in what Scott Bukatman calls cartoon physics, a set of unnatural laws of an alternative universe whereby "momentum trumps inertia, gravity is a sometime thing."[34] In martial arts cinema, ranging from King Hu's *A Touch of Zen* (*Xianü* 侠女, 1971) to Ang Lee's *Crouching Tiger*

32. Kristen Whissel, *Spectacular Digital Effects: CGI and Contemporary Cinema* (Durham, NC: Duke University Press, 2014), 21–58.

33. Whissel, *Spectacular Digital Effects*, 22.

34. Scott Bukatman, "Pertaining to Cartoon Physics: Or, the Cartoon Cat in the Machine," in *Animating Film Theory*, ed. Karen Beckman (Durham, NC: Duke University Press, 2014), 303.

Hidden Dragon (*Wohu canglong* 卧虎藏龙, 2000), the mode of extreme verticality is one of the stylistic signatures of the genre, and the stunning vertical movement of those flying warriors, hovering arrows, and dancing swords are often the most memorable moments in our collective amazement with these spectacular films. In fact, the stylistic feature of excessive vertical motion is so closely associated with the genre of martial arts that Whissel's key examples of new verticality in digital cinema are no other than the famous martial arts films *Crouching Tiger Hidden Dragon* and *Hero* (*Yingxiong* 英雄, 2002).

Although the aesthetic mode of extreme vertical movement may not be entirely new, the emblematized articulation of powerful force, as Whissel rightly observes, is certainly evident in the overt obsession with verticality in both Chinese animation and martial arts cinema. In the Wan brothers' animation films *Princess Iron Fan* (1941) and *Uproar in Heaven* (1964), spectacular vertical movements are featured in fighting scenes to intensify the climactic battle between the mighty heroism of Monkey King and the overwhelming power of the oppressive force, be it the deadly army of Bull Demon King in *Princess* or the heavenly troops of Jade Emperor in *Uproar*. Like the dramatic vertical fall at the end of *Crouching Tiger Hidden Dragon* (which Whissel discusses in detail in her book), the extreme verticality of Monkey King's fights in the Wan brothers' animations can also be read as a "dynamic, hyperkinetic expression" of the historical and political allegories of powerful forces and their impacts on individuals—Japanese invasion in the 1940s and China's authoritarian regime in the 1960s.

But I argue that the forces at stake here are not necessarily the external ones such as the political power of the state or the historical force of the war. What animation and martial arts cinema are struggling with is the internal force of the medium itself. It is the machinic power of cinema's own apparatus. What this spectacular verticality mobilizes is a cinematic spirit that seeks to transcend its own technological machine—a vital spirit that is struggling with a mechanical "false" movement that gives rise to its very spiritual life, like martial arts cinema that is constantly tapping into the genre's magical spirit to tackle the fantastic and unexplainable bodily motion that breaks the physical laws of Newtonian mechanics. This vital spirit, which is expressed in the aesthetic forces of mickey-mousing sound effects, plasmatic physics, and extreme vertical motion, is the core of Bukatman's notion of cartoon physics, for it provides "a freedom from traditional causality, freedom from natural laws."[35] It is thus a transcendental spirit, and both Chinese animation and martial arts cinema provide a fertile cultural ground for this spirit to prevail and to transcend both the external forces (of historical or political powers) and the internal ones (of cinematic apparatus). In other words, what makes animation and martial arts cinema uniquely powerful and appealing is their shared technical and aesthetic focus on mickey-mousing, plasmaticness, and verticality, all of which address and transcend cinema's technological uncanny. These aesthetic conjectures between animation and martial arts, which all hinge on various ways to enhance the vital sprit of movement against the physical law of mechanics, not only allow "a reimagining of the body and its relation to the world,"[36] but also call for a recalibration of the cinematic medium and its inherent falsehood.

Conclusion

I conclude this chapter by coming back to *Kung Fu Hustle*, a film celebrated as a well-received homage to the genre history and conventions of martial arts cinema. Like many martial arts films, *Kung Fu Hustle* is stylistically akin to animation (as I mentioned at the beginning), which is particularly marked by its stunning staging of spectacular vertical movements. One of the most dramatic iterations of such extreme verticality occurs at the film's climax, when the hero, seemingly enlightened by a Buddha (in the shape of a cloud), was finally able to defeat the enemy by using a spectacular move with vertical trajectory called the Buddhist Palm (fig. 2.4). However, this marvelous martial arts skill, the Buddhist Palm, had been claimed to be completely false throughout most of the film's narrative. When the hero first tried to learn it in his childhood, the kung fu manual he bought was a fake one. In fact, the question of whether martial arts is a fraud is one of the central themes, as well as a running gag, in the entire movie. However, the spectacular vertical movement at the end of film is not so much to confirm the truthfulness of martial arts as to transcend its claimed falsehood. The movement may be false—after all, it is constructed with computer-generated special effects—but the force, energy, vitality, and spirit can be

35. Bukatman, "Pertaining to Cartoon Physics," 311.

36. Bukatman, "Pertaining to Cartoon Physics," 304.

FIGURE 2.4. The cartoon physics of extreme verticality, in *Kung Fu Hustle* (2004).

felt genuinely, which is especially significant considering that the film takes the genre of martial arts as an allegory of a national-local identity to reconfigure a historiography of transnational cinemas and to reimagine a geopolitical space of post-1997 Hong Kong in the context of globalization. If the historical junctions between Chinese animation and martial arts cinema lie in their shared struggle with the external force of global modernity and its relationship with the vernacular, then the aesthetic nexuses between these two forms hinge on their shared struggle with the intrinsic falsehood of the modem machine and its iteration in cinematic movements.

THREE

Toy Country

Playful Innovation in Socialist Chinese Puppet Animation

LINDA C. ZHANG

During the early socialist era in the People's Republic of China (PRC), animation produced at the Animation Division of Shanghai Film Studio (before it became the Shanghai Animation Film Studio later in 1957) was especially diverse in form and content. The period from the 1950s and early 1960s was highly experimental: animators sought to incorporate elements from Chinese folk literature, opera, and myths into animation, especially within the emerging, popular medium of puppet animation.[1] Puppet animation during the socialist era in China has received historical attention from both English and Chinese scholarship, much of it focused on specific animators and their filmographies as well as the studio history and its engagement with Eastern European puppet animation. Scholars including Teri Silvio, Noboru Tomonari, Yiman Wang, and Suzanne Buchan have also broken critical ground in examining puppet and stop-motion animation and its intersections with performance, television, experimental film, and folk religion across different time periods and cultural contexts.[2] Panpan Yang's chapter in this volume (chapter 1), "The

1. Sean Macdonald, "Jin Xi: Master of Puppet Animation," *Journal of Chinese Cinemas* 11, no. 2 (2017): 160–61.

2. Teri Silvio, *Puppets, Gods, and Brands: Theorizing the Age of Animation from Taiwan* (Honolulu: University of Hawai'i Press, 2019); Noboru Tomonari, "Marionettes No Longer: Politics in the Early Puppet Animation of Kawamoto Kihachirō," in *Routledge Handbook*

Animation of Inanimate Objects in Chinese Silent Cinema," has expanded our theoretical understanding of stop-motion animation through the lens of trick photography in early live-action cinema in China. But thus far, as Sean Macdonald has argued and worked to remedy through translations of filmmaker writing, puppet animation from socialist China has not yet found its footing in critical theory or analysis.[3]

To address this lacuna, this chapter takes two analytical tracks. First, I investigate the relationships between puppets, toys, machines, and children across various iterations of socialist puppet animation from the early 1950s to the early 1960s in China. In my analysis, I find that in early PRC puppet animation films, toys frequently enact technologically mediated creative labor. Within the narrative worlds of these films, puppet toys promote strong social responsibility and citizenship while engineering creative solutions, to the point that they start manufacturing new toys or new production methods and paving the way toward their own technological revolution. Puppets, toys—and by proxy, children—become the inventors and innovators creating new worlds and nations on blank screens.

Second, this chapter considers how the aesthetics of toys intersects with ideas from childhood education to define the specificity of puppet animation as both medium and genre. Marc Steinberg has written about the toy as a mass medium, and toys as part of a greater *media mix*, as a way to put Henry Jenkins's idea of media convergence in conversation with Japanese cross-media serialization, character merchandising, and entertainment franchises.[4] This study also proposes that the toy serves as a mass medium—not merely for entertainment, but also for a pedagogical project informed by the shifting goals of animation in the PRC. As puppet animation film modeled the creative labor of building a new nation, behind

of Japanese Cinema, eds. Joanne Bernardi and Shota T. Ogawa (London: Routledge, 2020), 231–46; Yiman Wang, "The Mortal Animal and the Techno-Animated Life—Chen Qiang's Experimental Zooetic Animation Trilogy, Cut Off," *Journal of Chinese Cinemas* 11, no. 3 (2017): 210–26; Suzanne Buchan, *The Quay Brothers* (Minneapolis: University of Minnesota Press, 2011).

3. Macdonald, "Jin Xi," 161.

4. Marc Steinberg, *Anime's Media Mix: Franchising Toys and Characters in Japan*, (Minneapolis: University of Minnesota Press, 2012), xv, 89.

the scenes, PRC filmmakers also sought to define and build the legacy of puppet animation. In China, the Animation Division of Shanghai Film Studio and, after 1957, the Shanghai Animation Film Studio drew on folk puppetry in its puppet animation, sending filmmakers to visit master puppeteers in regional areas to learn the craft of puppet design, storytelling, and other stage techniques to adapt to the screen.[5] Animators—particularly Yu Zheguang 虞哲光 (1906–1991), a prolific puppet designer for the studio—bridged puppet animation, children's education, and pedagogy in their work.

Through Yu Zheguang's work, the history of puppet animation film can be reread as the transformation of a traditional folk art into technologically modernized media for children. Chinese film critics and filmmakers such as Yu Zheguang sought to distinguish puppet animation from puppet theater, live-action film, and hand-drawn cel animation. Central to their discussions were terms such as the puppet (*mu'ou* 木偶) and puppet animation (*mu'ou pian* 木偶片), as well as the ideas of puppet aesthetic (*ou'wei* 偶味) and toys (*wanju* 玩具).[6] In the animated films, puppets and toys modeled the labor of building a nation through the activities of childhood play; meanwhile, these elements of childhood play were increasingly embedded within the definition of puppet animation, setting it apart from other forms of revolutionary art and animation.

5. Lü Heng 吕衡, "Mu'ou pian zuozhe de yici xuexi" 木偶片作者的一次学习 (Puppet animators go to learn), *Dazhong dianying* 大众电影 (Popular movies), 3 (1957): 28; He Yi 贺宜, "Wei ertong dianying shiye fazhan er nuli—kan mu'oupian *Xiaoxiao yingxiong* ji qita" 为儿童电影事业的发展而努力—看木偶片《小小英雄》及其他 (Working for the development of the children's movie industry—watching the puppet animation *Little Hero* and other films), *Dazhong dianying* 大众电影 (Popular movies) 22 (1954): 12–15; Yue Lu 岳路, "Mu'ou pian shi zenyang paishe de?" 木偶片是怎样拍摄的 (How the puppet animation was made), *Dazhong dianying* 大众电影 (Popular movies) 5 (1957): 31.

6. Teri Silvio's work brings critical understanding to the concept of the *ang-a* (in Holo) or *ou* 偶 (in Mandarin). Silvio's approach to *ang-a* considers animation more broadly between the intersections of Taiwanese folk religious practice, puppet theater tradition, contemporary animation production, as well as fan cosplay. See Silvio, *Puppets, Gods, and Brands*, 56.

Dreams, Inventions, and Innovation in Socialist Puppet Animation

One of the PRC's earliest stop-motion, puppet animation films, *The Dream of Xiaomei* (*Xiaomei de meng* 小梅的梦, 1954) directed by Jin Xi 靳夕 (1919–1997), used a striking double-exposure method to combine both live-action film and stop-motion animation. Although such techniques had already been used by many film studios in China both before and after 1949 to introduce animated sequences or unique visual effects in largely live-action movies, their use in *The Dream of Xiaomei* was celebrated by its filmmakers as a technological triumph, giving on-screen time to both living and puppet actors, allowing them to interact together on screen for eight scenes of the film.[7] Starting with *The Dream of Xiaomei*, I trace a succession of puppet animation films that transition from the metaphoric dreams of inventions to feats of engineering and mechanical production. I find that in doing so, these films celebrated and reflected on technological progress and national building.

In *The Dream of Xiaomei*, the interaction is between the titular character, a young girl named Xiaomei, and her toy puppets, who teach her a central moral lesson about taking on social responsibility and contributing to a budding nation. The film itself similarly provides a pedagogical vision of technological innovation looking toward the future of the PRC as a nation. At the beginning of the film, Xiaomei damages her new toys, which she had purchased from a New Year's puppet theater show. After falling asleep in frustration, she starts dreaming about their coming alive and repairing each other by inventively using straws, hoses, basins, and brushes from Xiaomei's room.[8] In the midst of the toys' collective harmony, Xiaomei wakes

7. Jin Xi 靳夕, "Women gongzuo zai mu'ou zhi jia" 我们工作在木偶之家 (We work at the puppet's home), *Dazhong dianying* 大众电影 (Popular movies), 3 (1955): 12–13. In this article, the director of the film describes the puppets as if they were actors on break in their dressing room, preparing for their roles in movies such as *The Dream of Xiaomei* and *Little Hero*. The article then transitions into emphasizing the amount of labor used in the double-exposure method that allowed cooperation between both living and puppet actors.

8. The original name of *The Dream of Xiaomei* was *Toy Encounter* (*Wanju de zaoyu* 玩具的遭遇), highlighting the initially negative relationship between the titular character and the toys in the film. Cao Di 曹迪, *Zhongguo dingge donghua* 中国定格动画 (Chinese stop-motion animation) (Beijing: Communication University of China Press, 2018), 245.

FIGURE 3.1. The gate of "Toy Country" is complete, in *The Dream of Xiaomei* (1954).

up. Pleased by the sight, she joins them in building a new town and town gate (fig. 3.1), marked with a sign reading Toy Country (*wanju guo* 玩具国). The celebration of this new "nation" commences with the toys singing and marching through the gate, finally arranging themselves to write a final message for Xiaomei to read: "Cherish your toys" (*aihu wanju* 爱护玩具). By the end of the film, Xiaomei has acquired the building blocks of learning how to construct, and become an ideal member of, this new society.

Only a few years after *The Dream of Xiaomei* (1954) was released, the 1958 short color animation *Little Inventors* (*Xiao faming jia* 小发明家) directed by Chen Zhenghong 陈正鸿 (1927–2018) came out, presenting a story in animated form that resembled a sequel to *The Dream of Xiaomei* both in puppet design and in narrative spirit. Notably, the double-exposure method was not used for *Little Inventors;* the film was entirely set in the country of the puppet toys. The filmic world of *Little Inventors* is a bright and colorful landscape that looks to be made of children's toy blocks. The puppet characters are designed in the style of dolls or animal figures. Unlike *The Dream of Xiaomei, Little Inventors* favors a full immersion into

FIGURE 3.2. The class meets, in *Little Inventors* (1958).

the toy world. *Little Inventors* seemingly inherited the energetic attitude in *The Dream of Xiaomei* toward building and contributing to a new society; however, the former is more focused on portraying the process of inventing solutions through the self-sufficiency of the toys themselves.

The film is about a group of students—designed to resemble stuffed animals and toys—who have trouble getting to class on time every day. Their school, located at the top of a mountain and across a valley, presents a near-impossible commute. After hearing their complaints and sympathizing with them, their teacher (portrayed by an elephant puppet), encourages them to use their wits to solve problems by writing the motto "Use your brains, find a way!" (*dong naojin, zhao qiaomen* 动脑筋，找窍门) on the blackboard (fig. 3.2).

One of the students, Xiao Linzi, comes home and ponders how to solve the issue of crossing the mountain gorge. After sketching and modeling various solutions, she decides, with the encouragement of another classmate, to set up a wind-powered system of cables and gondolas that the students can use to cross the gorge. With her class, Xiao Linzi starts the project and makes various improvements to the model. They incorporate the mechanisms of a windmill, and later, a bicycle, to make the gondola move more quickly. At the film's conclusion, Xiao Linzi and her classmates celebrate together by riding the gondolas before finally starting their new class on time.

Little Inventors shows the toy characters solving problems by observing their immediate surroundings (including the playground) and incorporating mechanisms from everyday objects or everyday sights (windmills, bikes) into the solution. The teacher specifically encourages his students to innovate and design new machines. In response to one of the students, a bird who wishes for a pair of wings for each of its classmates, the teacher responds, "It's wonderful to imagine the possibilities, but you'll need a machine to make it happen." The focus on innovative problem-solving using technology to create a new reality is clear in *Little Inventors*.

If *The Dream of Xiaomei* (1954) and *Little Inventors* (1958) displayed a progression of toys finding creative solutions to build up their communities, then the 1960 stop-motion animation film *The Innovators* (*Gexin mi* 革新迷) visualized the next step of that movement, where the puppet characters actualize their dreams through mass production—creating more toys in their own modernized factory (fig. 3.3). In depicting the technological reproduction of toys as both play and creative labor, *The Innovators* self-reflexively reproduces the form and aesthetics of puppet toys and of puppet animation.

The short twenty-minute film produced by Shanghai Animation Film Studio and directed by Jin Xi presents the story of how a young worker revolutionized his workplace—a factory for plastic toys—by inventing new methods of automation. After a grueling day at the factory with his fellow workers straining to produce toy ducks by manual labor, the main character, Xiao Wang, announces his plan to try a "technological revolution" that he hopes will inspire his colleagues to work overtime to create new designs for automation in their toy factory. Although Xiao Wang at first faces resistance from his colleagues and even his parents, eventually he gets everyone to work together, gather ideas and materials, and create an automated assembly line by the end of the film.

What allows the toy factory to revolutionize itself, in the end, is the outside-the-box thinking whereby Xiao Wang and his father gather

FIGURE 3.3. A color spread on "Animations Reflecting the Technological Revolution" from an issue of *Dazhong dianying* 大众电影 (Popular movies) in 1960. Courtesy of the C. V. Starr East Asian Library, University of California, Berkeley.

inspiration from everyday items. Both father and son take ideas from household items, such as a noodle strainer or parts of a bed frame, to add to the factory's automation blueprint. Additionally, they both run off in excitement to draw new plans after encounters with various items at the neighborhood playground, including a spinning roundabout, a seesaw, and even a paddle ball set. Together, parent and child are drawn into the fervor to mechanize the functions of their factory production and to revolutionize the boundaries between community and factory, work and play.

Work and play are inseparable in *The Innovators*, largely because of their displacement onto the articulation of Chinese nationalism and socialist nation-building. Not only do playground mechanics and toys inspire and improve the production line of the newly revolutionized toy factory, but the very management of the assembly line also includes many robots in the shape of toy animals. At the conclusion of the film, we see Xiao Wang's dreams and inspirations come to life as rabbit-, elephant-, and giraffe-shaped automatons maintain the flow of the production line, producing row after row of plastic toy ducks. The newly produced toy ducks, then, seem to allegorically stand in for success in building the socialist nation. Not just in *The Innovators,* but also in *Little Inventors* and *The Dream of Xiaomei,* play serves as training for children to become socialist subjects—and toys are never just toys.

Puppet Aesthetic and Nation-Building

The Innovators, Little Inventors, and *The Dream of Xiaomei* sought to modernize puppet animation, aligning the technological potential of puppet and stop-motion animation with the nation-building effort in the PRC. In creating a new reality out of toys, these films succeeded in looking toward the future and the possibilities of tomorrow. Beyond the films themselves, PRC animators and film critics also wrote critical texts theorizing the artistic medium by looking further into the past rather than just toward the future. These essays connected Chinese puppet animation to traditional forms of Chinese folk puppet theater as a way to legitimize the medium's national heritage. The arguments in these essays reflect multiple efforts to define the specificity of puppet animation as a medium. I examine these discussions here, finding certain conflicts between their rhetoric and the films themselves as a reflection of the challenges in defining puppet animation during the early PRC period. I argue that although the puppet aesthetic (*ou'wei*) was part of puppet animation's claim to national heritage and medium specificity during the 1980s, the idea of a puppet aesthetic stemmed from earlier discussions of how puppet animation could educate, teach, and help form future socialist subjects in China. In turn, we may need to reexamine Chinese puppet animation as not just an example of cultural heritage, but also a medium that was inventively working with modern theories of education.

The process of defining puppet animation was a root-seeking, nation-building effort in the 1950s. In the years surrounding the release of *The Dream of Xiaomei,* the Shanghai Animation Film Studio filmmakers working on puppet animation consciously drew on folk traditions of wooden and shadow puppetry, sometimes conducting fieldwork of their own, such as traveling to Guangxi to observe the folk traditions of the Dao minority, or in another case, traveling specifically to observe master puppeteers and their practices at a major puppet animation conference held in Xi'an on November 25, 1957.[9] This conscious appeal to national heritage—modern puppet animation evolving from folk puppet theater—stemmed from an analogous claim made between puppet theater and animation in Eastern Europe. The Animation Division of the Shanghai Film Studio worked to build stronger relationships, particularly with the Czechoslovakian animation industry—an international leader in puppet animation film and a particularly important model for animators from not just the Eastern bloc but also East Asia.[10]

Chinese animators, like their Czech counterparts, sought to base puppet animation on folk puppetry to build a stronger sense of cultural nationalism. During this period, the early Cold War era, Chinese and Czech animators felt the cultural authority of the Soviet Union and in turn tried to develop a sense of National Style that could counter the hegemonic Soviet cultural presence. For puppet animators in both China and Czechoslovakia, the world of toys offered folk traditions that contributed to a renewed sense of cultural nationalism.[11] As Cathleen Giustino has argued, puppets and toys were especially important for representing folk traditions that could distinguish Czechoslovakia on the world stage.[12]

Theoretical and historical writing on puppet animation in China, however, seemed to only flourish in the field starting in the late 1970s and the early 1980s.[13] During this time, Chinese animation was showered with

9. Lü Heng, "Mu'ou pian zuozhe de yici xuexi" 12.

10. Notable Czech animation director Jirí Trnka (1912–1969) mentored animators from East Asia such as Kawamoto Kihachirō (1925–2010). See Tomonari, "Marionettes no longer," 240. Puppet animation director Jin Xi wrote several essays about the artistic practice and diversity of subject matter in Trnka's films. See Sean Macdonald, "Artifice, Fantasy, and Exaggeration: The Boundless Limitations of Puppets," *Journal of Cinema and Media Studies* 59, no. 3 (2020): 117.

11. Tomonari has also argued that a similar propaganda strategy was employed by the Japanese Communist Party during the Cold War, and that puppet plays have been associated with leftist-leaning nationalism in Japan. See Tomonari, "Marionettes No Longer," 237.

12. Cathleen M. Giustino, "Toys, Ideology, and the Avant-Garde in Socialist Czechoslovakia before 1968," in *Childhood by Design*, ed. Megan Brandow-Faller (New York: Bloomsbury Publishing, 2018), 173.

13. Although animators and critics such as Jin Xi, Lü Heng, and Qiao Yu wrote about

a renewal of international attention and film awards following the recuperation of animators and films after the Cultural Revolution, as well as increased screenings of films around the globe, including feature films such as the 1979 *Nezha Conquers the Dragon King* (*Nezha naohai* 哪吒闹海) and the 1978 complete release of *Uproar in Heaven* (*Danao tiangong* 大闹天宫). With a perspective of a renewed industry, animators and film critics sought to expand the cultural legitimacy for Chinese animation produced since the beginning of the PRC, culminating in anthologies such as *Research and Production of Fine Arts Film* (*Meishu dianying chuangzuo yanjiu* 美术电影创作研究), first published in 1981. From this collection, I examine essays on puppet animation, in which the animators, artists, and other critics aimed to both theorize and historicize puppet animation as its own form, genre, and even medium. Much of this literature also sought to delineate a particular puppet aesthetic that was both a unique animation style as well as an essential characteristic of regional Chinese folk craft and puppet theater.

In describing a puppet aesthetic, these writers revealed a desire to create something realistic enough to engage its audience, but not so realistic that it would too closely resemble live-action movies. For example, in a 1984 essay titled "On the Art Design of Puppet Animation," the artist (and erstwhile animation film poster designer) Jin Baisong 金柏松 (1944–) compared puppet actors with live actors, noting some significant limitations to the actors of the puppet kind:

> The truth, as those who have been in the art of puppetry have known for a while, is that puppet actors have a lot of limitations and shortcomings. For instance, the puppet always has a "wooden aesthetic" to it—it cannot have any tears dripping from its eyes, nor can it have subtle expressions. However, with these limitations, therein lie its strengths. Artists can use their techniques to create a "puppet aesthetic" just through the shapes of these types of wooden heads. Even though they don't have subtle expressions, they can use actions that real people cannot use. Furthermore, they are not limited

---

puppet animation in the 1950s, these publications focused on introducing the technology or the process of shooting puppet animation and stop-motion animation films. Notably, however, Jin Xi published essays on theories of puppet animation in the late 1950s and the early 1960s.

> by the weather or environment. . . . Artists should use these strengths to break new artistic ground.[14]

In discussing how to transform a more negative feeling of the wooden aesthetic to something full of potential—the puppet aesthetic—Jin referred to the complications created by using multiple heads that were switched on and off the puppet actors between individual shots to show changes in expression, as well as the various techniques developed to show puppet actors crying through the stop-motion filmmaking process. Jin argued that those difficulties created opportunities for the puppet animation film to find new types of artistic space—in other words, a medium specificity and a certain departure from realism that were unique to puppet animation films.

Although Jin Baisong did not specify what that puppet aesthetic comprised, he did make sure to give negative examples of puppet animation from the Cultural Revolution era that disregarded what makes puppet animation unique. Jin found that they presented a particular issue of becoming too uncannily realistic, writing, "the unique qualities of puppetry were eliminated in the period of 'model operas'—it was a huge mistake in the leadership to try to pursue the idea of 'making them similar to real people,' creating headaches for everyone."[15] With a similar sentiment, director Jin Xi also wrote in "Three Topics on Animation Film" that puppet animation should not try to imitate people:

> Puppet animation is not able to accurately express people's physiological characteristics and the various physical phenomena of their substantive movements. Thus, we should use the unique methods that puppet animation possesses to express them. If we inflexibly try our utmost to make it do

14. Jin Baisong 金柏松, "Tan mu'ou pian meigong" 谈木偶片美工 (On the art design of puppet animation), in *Meishu dianying chuangzuo yanjiu* 美术电影创作研究 (Research and production of fine arts film), ed. Ministry of Culture, Film Bureau "Film and News" editorial office, and China Film Press domestic film editorial office (Beijing: Zhongguo dianying chubanshe, 1984), 48.

15. Jin Baisong, "Tan mu'ou pian de meigong," 50.

> something that it is not competent at, . . . we will eventually even lose the concrete, unique things of our own.[16]

What emerged from Jin Baisong's and Jin Xi's writing was a sense of puppet animation's unique relationship with reality. Attempting cinematic or physiological realism would cost puppet animation film something dear.

According to the animation film director, Cheng Zhongyue 程中岳, one of the unique and specific elements to puppet animation film lay in the movements of the characters themselves. Without careful thought and design, Cheng warned, puppet animations would lose their charm, color, and power in telling a story. Agreeing with Jin Baisong and Jin Xi that movements should not try to imitate human actions, Cheng proposed that puppet movements should focus on maximum efficiency by using exaggerated and comical movements to create character types:

> The subtle movements of puppets are not that many; rather they are few and delicate. . . . The key to puppet movements is to resonate with the different unique looks, to grasp and find the details in the character's movements during the performance, and to design the typical movements—to create exaggerated yet coherent movements.[17]

In addition to describing the relation between motion and character, Cheng also focuses on the debate over whether puppet characters in animation should move their mouths consistently to the dialogue. Cheng's argument is that puppet animation—an innately surrealist art—required finding balance between imitating life and breaking new ground:

> Here, I think of the great artist Qi Baishi 齐白石 (1864–1957) and what he said about painting: "Subtlety is found in between like and unlike." . . . I believe that when puppets are talking, the mouths can move but should not move too much in case their movements are not similar to people's. A more

16. Jin Xi 靳夕, "Meishu pian chuangzuo santi" 美术片创作三题 (Three topics on animation film), in *Meishu dianying chuangzuo yanjiu*, 45.

17. Cheng Zhongyue 程中岳, "Mu'ou pian dongzuo biaoyan yishu sanlun" 木偶片动作表演艺术散论 (An essay on the art of puppet movements and performance), in *Meishu dianying chuangzuo yanjiu*, 69.

> naturalistic performance would destroy the beauty and surrealist magic of the puppet art. On the other hand, if the mouth doesn't move at all, it wouldn't adequately support the reality of life. In summary, designing the puppet characters and their subtle movement requires a holistic conception. Their mouths should move only until there is a benefit. They should move enough to have artistic aesthetic, especially to have a true feeling of life. But it should also exceed life itself (*gaoyu shenghuo* 高于生活) to become a true artistic creation.[18]

To "exceed life itself," as Cheng puts it, seems to be exactly the point of finding something unique in puppet animation. It can neither be lifelike nor too uncanny, but must fall somewhere between reality and unreality. For Cheng, this puppet aesthetic is not subtle enough to be realistic and therefore must rely on caricature-like movements to create a new style. But in doing so, puppet animation communicates vitality and lifelikeness using techniques that are in fact independent of realist depictions of the body, speech, gesture, and movement. Such techniques not only embody Cheng's puppet aesthetic, but also make up the growing core of a new artistic medium.

Cheng Zhongyue drew inspiration not only from painting but also from poetry and Peking opera, insisting on cross-fertilization across media that draws upon various forms and stylizations to create a new aesthetic.[19] Following this line of thought, Cheng also argued that puppet animation should draw from other arts as well as from life and nature. In doing so, puppet animation would be better able to convey a sense of puppet aesthetic:

> Drawing on the sense of rhythm from puppet stage performance can deepen the feeling of "puppet aesthetic" (*ou'wei* 偶味) in the movement of the puppet, allowing the image of the puppet on the silver screen to appear more

18. Cheng, "Mu'ou pian dongzuo biaoyan yishu sanlun," 70.

19. For example, Cheng Zhongyue referred to the movement of striking a pose (*liang xiang* 亮相) in the Peking Opera as an example of a technique that puppet animation performance could draw upon, particularly in its use of exaggeration and succinctness in conveying personality and mannerisms of the characters. The classics said that to "study poetry, you need to train outside of poetry." See Cheng, "Mu'ou pian dongzuo biaoyan yishu sanlun," 70.

> vividly, more accurately, and more moving. The classic painters advocated for "creating from the outside" in order to "find the origin of the heart."[20]

Here Cheng argues for drawing inspiration from highly stylized artistic forms, such as in classical painting—debatably among the least lifelike areas of art. Like Jin Xi, Cheng Zhongyue was also concerned with defining the puppet aesthetic and puppet animation as a fine arts medium. This writing provides a new lens for considering different forms of experimentation in puppet animation: such as its toy-like design, methods used in "exceeding life," strategies for creating exaggerated movements on screen, as well as applications for use in children's education.

This historical discussion mostly from the 1980s, on the topic of the puppet aesthetic, reflects multiple efforts to define puppet animation against other artistic media. But the focus on the puppet aesthetic eclipsed other elements integral to puppet animation film, including ideas from children's education such as the usage of toys as educational models. I turn to the background of one particular puppet animator and designer who worked on puppet animation at the Shanghai studio: Yu Zheguang. As an animator, writer, and educator, Yu Zheguang experimented with different forms of puppet arts, providing a germane example of how puppet animation relied on a pedagogical view of toys as learning tools.

The Production of Toys at Home

Yu Zheguang is a point of focus because of his background in puppet theater, and because he saw puppet animation as a form that was endlessly useful for a young demographic of children during their early education. In his activities as a filmmaker, educator, and children's book writer, Yu also demonstrated how puppetry could engage various forms of media simultaneously. In his publications, he actively traced the genealogy of the form to a longer, traditional history of puppet theater and shadow puppet theater, seeking to adapt the strengths of the older artistic media to the new medium of puppet animation. Last, Yu Zheguang transported the

20. Cheng, "Mu'ou pian dongzuo biaoyan yishu sanlun," 70.

puppet play from the stage and screen to a mobile, portable object that could be reproduced at home in the form of paper-folding craft books and children's puppetry script manuals. Puppetry was a mobile, tangible, reproducible form that could be used for teaching.

Through Yu Zheguang's work, the history of puppet animation film can be reread as the transformation of traditional folk art to technologically modernized media for children. His career can serve as a nexus of ideas for how the puppet toy could operate across various forms of Chinese socialist media—from folk theater to the animation screen and further toward craft manuals and children's books. Here, I argue that Yu's work allows us a way to conceive of the puppet aesthetic beyond a question of traditional and cultural heritage, but also toward the question of how to teach the processes of production and labor. For Yu, what was unique about the puppet aesthetic in animation was both its ability to model behavior and creative solutions for children, and its capacity to be reproduced as home projects of toy-making and theater production beyond the screen.

Just as Xiao Wang in *The Innovators* was passionate about starting a technological revolution in his factory—a factory that produced toys—Yu Zheguang also was very focused on the materiality of puppet toys, having devoted much of his career to designing and creating puppets. In 1955, Yu even founded a small puppet-making workshop in Shanghai—known as The Puppet Home (*mu'ou zhijia* 木偶之家) that produced puppets for use in primary and preschool puppet plays.[21] We might interpret the character of Xiao Wang in *The Innovators* as an expression of Yu's commitment to continuous innovation in toy factories at home or at school, in rural and urban areas, across various media and their expressions on the page, on the stage, and on the screen. When working in animation, Yu's first major assignment in the Shanghai studio after he joined in 1950 was character design for classic puppet animation films such as *The Dream of Xiaomei, A Careless Plump Boy, A Little Hero,* as well as *The Magic Paintbrush*. Only later, in the mid-1950s, did Yu transition to directing puppet animations such as *Mr. Dongguo, Hunting Story,* and *Plump Sister-in-Law Returns Home*.[22]

21. Cao Di, *Zhongguo dingge donghua*, 240.

22. Cao Maotang 曹懋唐, "Yu Zheguang 虞哲光," in *Zhongguo dianyingjia liezhuan* no. 6 中国电影家列传第6集 (Biographies of China's filmmakers, vol. 6), ed. Chinese History Research Bureau (Beijing: Zhongguo dianying chubanshe, 1986), 499.

Yu Zheguang's puppet design achievements aside, records of his work characterize him first as a lifelong educator who sought to integrate pedagogy into his animation. In the 1930s, Yu studied and worked with prominent teachers and education reformers such as Zhang Zonglin and Chen Heqin.[23] Chen, an official within the Shanghai Public Education Bureau who had been trained in child psychology, mentored Yu and collaborated with him to create new puppet theater material at conferences for children's education and science education.[24] At the Shanghai Animation Film Studio, Yu Zheguang was known as the animator most focused on developing puppet animation through toy design and children's education.[25] Yu was also credited as the innovator of paper-folding puppet animation—much like puppet animation except that the puppets are crafted out of folded paper. As Li, Shu, and Cao Maotang describe in their respective biographies of Yu Zheguang, he hoped to create a new genre of film and performance that would appeal particularly to preschoolers through its materiality—paper and string constructed into familiar shapes (triangles, tubes, squares)—and its form of animal toy puppets.[26] Paper-folding puppet animation delighted simply because it was playful. Origami-like animals, with tails shaped like accordions, could revolve, expand, and contract just like a piece of paper come to life.

Yu was deeply interested in the art of puppet theater: prior to joining the studio, he designed and wrote educational puppet theater plays, and later at the animation studio, he directed documentary films about both traditional and educational puppet performance.[27] Yu's later publications, in fact, indicate that he was interested in giving teachers, children, and families a way to produce their own plays by themselves both at home and

23. Cao Di, *Zhongguo dingge donghua*, 234.

24. Cao Di, *Zhongguo dingge donghua*, 234.

25. Cao Maotang, "Yu Zheguang," 496–501; Li Baozhuan 李保传 and Shu Xiaping 束霞平, *Zhongguo donghua dianying dashi* 中国动画电影大师 (The masters of Chinese animated films) (Beijing: Communication University of China Press, 2012), 29.

26. Cao Maotang, "Yu Zheguang," 500; Li Baozhuan and Shu Xiaping, *Zhongguo donghua dianying dashi*, 29, 31–32.

27. These include the 1962 documentaries of traditional puppet theater, *Daming County* (*Daming fu* 大名府) and *Performance in a Hand* (*Zhang zhong xi* 掌中戏), and the 1958 film *For the Children* (*Weile haizi men* 为了孩子们).

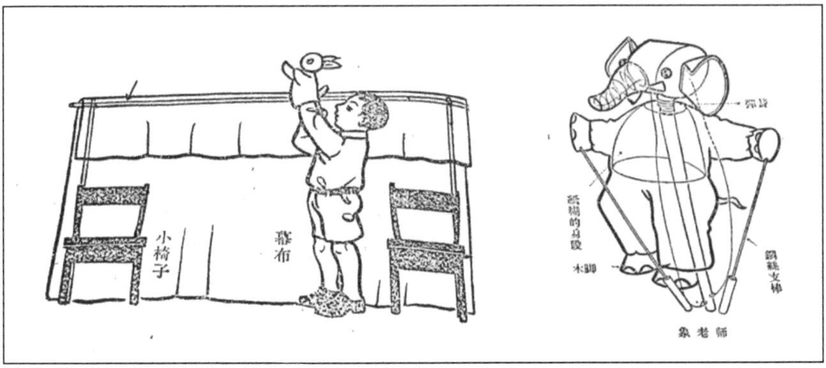

FIGURE 3.4. A diagram of a puppet stage in *Little Red's New Clothes* (1956) and a diagram of a puppet design in *Little Rabbit Plants Beans* (1950).

in the classroom. Since the early 1930s and well into the 1950s, Yu published children's craftbooks that featured large, simple images with bold outlines that could be easily traced or cut out.[28] In *Paper Folding for Children*, for example, Yu included images of children watching films, holding meetings on the Great Leap Forward, and celebrating the PRC's October National Holiday. These images, in turn, could be colored in, cut out, and folded into paper dolls and puppets with preset backgrounds and settings. Yu also included scripts in detailed playbooks, including the 1956 Shanghai Culture Press publication *Little Red's New Clothes* (*Xiaohong de xin yifu* 小红的新衣服) and the 1950 Commercial Press book *Little Rabbit Plants Beans* (*Xiaotu zhongdou* 小兔种豆). Yu included instructions not just on making puppets, but also on how to construct makeshift puppet theaters and how to manipulate puppets in a performance (fig. 3.4). The children on Yu's pages were imagined as not just spectators, but also as budding actors, puppeteers, and future educators themselves.

Yu Zheguang's activity as a writer displayed his deep investment in the history and the future of puppet theater, as well as its contemporary

28. Titles include *Children's Toys* (*Ertong wanju gong* 儿童玩具工, 1931), *Little Home Models* (*Xiao jiating moxing* 小家庭模型, 1935), *Little Animal Models* (*Xiao dongwu moxing* 小动物模型, 1935), and *Paper Folding for Children* (*Ertong zhigong* 儿童纸工, 1958). Quite a few of these works were published in the 1930s, which also suggests the popularity of the genre prior to the socialist period and its longevity in print culture.

transformation into puppet animation. While Yu was working on puppet animation films at the Shanghai Animation Film Studio, in 1957 and 1958 he also published *The Art of Puppet Theater* (*Mu'ouxi yishu* 木偶戏艺术) and *The Art of Shadow Puppet Theater* (*Pi'yingxi yishu* 皮影戏艺术) with the Shanghai Culture Press.

In *The Art of Puppet Theater*, Yu Zheguang proposed his particular vision of puppet theater, one that would continue the folk traditions of the past but at the same time embody the new ideals of the socialist present and future. In his introduction, titled "The Educational Value of Puppet Theater," Yu presented puppet theater not only as a folk theater tradition, but also as a tool that could be developed for educating children. He wrote that because puppet theater had always been created for the laboring masses, it had not been developed as a fine art but was considered instead to be only a minor branch of theater. In the new era, however, Yu proposed that puppetry be used as a dissemination tool because of its unique ability to attract young children, increase their general knowledge, and "raise their moral characters." "Now," Yu Zheguang wrote, "we can see the value of education that puppet theater in particular, among various forms of drama, can provide." That value, in his argument, came from a particular allure to be found in puppet theater's unique mix of humor, satire, childish simplicity, and exaggeration in movement, form, script, and performance. Furthermore, its unique quality was the expansion of the idea of the toy: "Puppets have always had unique and humorous appearances incorporating intensely vivid childishness along with a certain pure allure. At the same time, puppets are basically toys—so we can say that puppetry has expanded the function of the toy itself."[29] To expand on Yu's proposal, puppets had already extended the previously limited understandings of the function of the toy itself. The toy was not only a plaything for children; it was also a promotional and educational tool because of its power to draw in its target audience and its ability to reach children.

Behind this understanding of the puppet's allure lay Yu Zheguang's particular logic about how children relate to seeing characters, particularly animals, in a puppet play. Animal characters for adults may seem unrealistic, Yu argued, but for children, animal characters even in puppet form

29. Yu Zheguang 虞哲光, *Mu'ou xi yishu* 木偶戏艺术 (The art of puppet theater) (Shanghai: Shanghai Culture Press, 1957), 2.

appear to be real people and models of behavior. Yu proposed that children readily accept animals as people and are particularly susceptible to copying what they see on the stage.[30] Furthermore, Yu found that puppet theater as a performance genre lends itself to children's acceptance of the story as something true and close to their hearts, to the extent that they relate emotionally to the characters as well.[31] Because of this, it was logical to use animal puppets to promote moral education or other messages to young audiences.

One of the contradictions within Yu's writing lies in the balance between the allure of animal puppets and a desire to not stray too far from reality. Using animals as substitutes for people may have made the story more interesting to the audience, but Yu also warned against overusing fantasy elements: "As for the content for children's plays, we must take care to avoid too many fantasy elements that lead to more questions from children. If this becomes too severe, this will harm children. That is why we must also not use horror elements in scenes either."[32] What, then, was the ideal balance that Yu sought in puppetry? By way of an answer, he wrote that puppetry should provide stories that resonate with children's lives and teach them important lessons of life:

> Puppetry needs to describe the conflicts and problems of the children's own lives, and to describe stories that they enjoy. The stories need to be relaxing and happy, the themes need to be clear, and the dialogue needs to be childlike. The movements can be accompanied by music to make a dance; doing so will increase the appeal of the scene; for adults, puppetry should criticize the corrupt and ugly parts of life, sing the praises of new life and health, and use strong satire as well as deep morals to imbue the stories with positive educational value.[33]

For Yu Zheguang, then, puppetry should not surpass the boundaries of realism to the extent that young audiences would forget that puppets are toys, and in that regard, merely a substitute for human beings. The toy is

30. Yu Zheguang, *The Art of Puppet Theater*, 24.
31. Yu Zheguang, *The Art of Puppet Theater*, 27.
32. Yu Zheguang, *The Art of Puppet Theater*, 24.
33. Yu Zheguang, *The Art of Puppet Theater*, 22.

only a temporary replacement, even a transitional object in the Winnicottian sense, and never a complete substitute for a human character. Instead, puppets help convey conflicts so that children can begin working toward their own understanding of how to grow into society.

Conclusion: Dreaming of Toys

I return here to *The Dream of Xiaomei* to revisit the question of human presence in puppet animation films. In the 1955 issue of *Popular Movies*, the playwright and poet Qiao Yu reviewed *The Dream of Xiaomei* in a piece titled "A Fairytale Movie with Rich Imagination," commenting on how Xiaomei watched the construction of Toy Country. At first, Qiao Yu found Xiaomei was surprised and envious of the toys, but was eventually brought into a marvelous world that stimulated her intellectual curiosity. In effect, Xiaomei became a proxy for the reaction of children who viewed the film:

> This little fairytale world is full of passion for labor and the wisdom of creation. The film movingly and actively expresses this, and in such an innocent and interesting way. . . . There are many ingenious elements that resonate with the hearts of children. Therefore, the film can naturally draw its targeted audience into the film to educate and stimulate their minds. Without a doubt, this film will have a large influence on children; it will be well-received by them. When mothers bring their children to see the movie, the children will receive, among other beneficial messages, one that they won't entirely understand yet of "Cherishing your toys."[34]

In describing the film's didactic and beneficial influence on children, Qiao Yu's reading of *The Dream of Xiaomei* suggests that the toys modeled accountability for Xiaomei through the construct of Toy Country.

In Qiao Yu's review, if cherishing your toys could be understood as cherishing your fellow citizens, then we could understand Xiaomei's toys as models of not only individual responsibility, but also socialist citizenship

34. Qiao Yu 乔羽, "Yibu youzhe fengfu xiangxiang de tonghuapian *Xiaomei de meng*" 一部有着丰富想象的童话片《小梅的梦》(A fairytale movie with rich imagination: *The dream of Xiaomei*), *Dazhong dianying* 大众电影 (Popular movies), 3 (1955): 11.

contributing to collective labor. *The Dream of Xiaomei* teaches Xiaomei (and viewers of the film) through counterexamples. In one—a scene in the middle of *The Dream of Xiaomei*—the wooden puppet boy takes a toy plane for a spin around the room and, seeing a beautiful landscape painting on the wall, flies closer until he enters the painting, to the shock of the other toys. Taken in by this world so removed from the broken toys in Xiaomei's room, the boy forgets his urgent task. The traditional landscape painting is suddenly transformed into a seductive vision of a place both out of time and irrelevant to the socialist present. It is only when a toy bird flies over and reminds the puppet boy of his task that he is shaken out of his daydream and away from this deviation. Turning back from his wrong turn, the boy heads back to the present, where the labor of rebuilding toys—or the socialist work of rebuilding the Chinese nation—awaits him back in Xiaomei's room. The boy and the citizens of Toy Country are then later joined by Xiaomei herself. Following the spirit of Yu Zheguang's puppet education, then, the wooden puppet boy's path of coming back to build Toy Country was an analogous lesson for Xiaomei's initial behavior, her growth and developing subjectivity, and her contributions to a burgeoning nation.

If *The Dream of Xiaomei* signals an example of socialist citizenship, it also previews what could be considered socialist animation. Puppet animation as a medium—in its particular relationship with movement, rhythm, embodiment, and filming technology—depended on the creative labor of the animators. Although made invisible by the film technology of stop-motion, the laborious process of creation that brought life to toys and puppets was reflected by the parallel labor performed by the puppets within the film. Within *The Dream of Xiaomei, Little Inventors,* and *The Innovators,* that same creative labor became even more evident as the puppet toys also built, created, and gave life to the world around them. *The Dream of Xiaomei* and its puppet animation successors—on the screen—actualized the educational and technological promise of puppet animation that Yu Zheguang worked toward while also fulfilling the potential of a puppet aesthetic that animators and artists such as Cheng Zhongyue, Jin Xi, and Jin Baisong sought to find within the film medium.

FOUR

Adapting Dunhuang in a Transitional Period

Negotiated Intermediality in *The Deer of Nine Colors* and *Jiazi Saves the Deer*

Shasha Liu

Since its emergence, animation has negotiated with other media. Under the theme of junctures, previous chapters discuss the intermedia encounters involving animation, cinema, and craft in the Chinese context. This chapter focuses on the entanglement between fine arts and cinema by considering the titling of animation as fine arts film (*meishu dianying* 美术电影) in China, beginning in the mid-twentieth century and spanning several decades. However, animations produced during the Cultural Revolution (1966–1976) were primarily politically oriented and lacked media specificity. After those tumultuous years, Chinese animators and critics reviewed approaches to production and endeavored to rebuild the industry. These continuous discussions and efforts are well represented in the 1989 article "A Child Without a Mama: The Ontology of Fine Arts Films," where the Chinese animation scholar Nie Xinru analyzes animation from a media perspective by identifying its possible origins.[1] Further, he outlines the changing relationship between Chinese animation productions and other media in the previous decade, marking a shift from a material-based

1. Nie Xinru 聂欣如, "Meiyou mama de haizi: Meishu dianying benti lun" 没有妈妈的孩子——美术电影本体论 (A child without a mama: The ontology of fine arts film) *Dangdai dianying* 当代电影 (Contemporary cinema) 5 (1989), republished in *Zhongguo dianying nian jian* 中国电影年鉴 (China film annals) (1990): 124–27.

theory (*cailiao lun* 材料论) of Chinese animation, which distinguished itself from film by referencing various fine arts mediums, to animations emphasizing cinematic methods (*dianying shouduan* 电影手段) that were produced starting from the mid-1980s. Among the animations Nie lists to substantiate this shift are *The Deer of Nine Colors* (*Jiuse lu* 九色鹿, 1981), which in referencing mural paintings is an example of the material-based school of animation, and *Jiazi Saves the Deer* (*Jiazi jiulu* 夹子救鹿, 1985), which represents the cinematic pursuit in late-1980s Chinese animation by interweaving fine arts and cinematic methods, such as cinematic shots. Nie's use of these two animations as examples is quite interesting, but more intriguing is the heated debate on the media specificity of animation in the late 1980s, in which his analysis participated.

Using Nie's discussions as a point of departure, this chapter compares *The Deer of Nine Colors* and *Jiazi Saves the Deer*, both of which narrate specific Buddhist Jataka stories found in mural paintings in the Dunhuang caves, an ancient Buddhist archeological site along the Silk Road at Dunhuang, China, and famous for Buddhist artifacts constructed between the fourth and fourteenth centuries.[2] Scholars have identified references to visual and narrative elements of Dunhuang murals in *The Deer of Nine Colors*.[3] These discussions, however, are limited to investiga-

2. *Deer Girl* (*Lunü* 鹿女, 1993) also adapts a specific Dunhuang mural. I do not discuss this animation, however, because the two I do study here better represent the transition in Chinese animation that Nie pinpoints. Furthermore, my research indicates that the first animation that refers to Dunhuang art is *The Conceited General* (*Jiao'ao de jiangjun* 骄傲的将军, 1956). See Shasha Liu, "Zooming in on the Animated Background: Mediated Dunhuang Murals with Design in *the Conceited General*," *Journal of Chinese Cinemas* 15, no. 1 (2021): 22–38.

3. Shao Yuan 邵媛, "Donghuapian *Jiuse lu* yu Dunhuang bihua *Luwang bensheng tu* yishu fengge qianxi" 动画片《九色鹿》与敦煌壁画《鹿王本生图》艺术风格浅析 (Analyzing the artistic styles of the animation of *The Deer of Nine Colors* and the Dunhuang mural of the *Jataka Story of the Deer King*), *Dianying wenxue* 电影文学 (Film literature) 9 (2013): 54–55; Zhou Lixin 周立新 and Yang Wenting 杨文婷, "Qianxi donghuapian '*Jiuse lu*' de yishu tese" 浅析动画片《九色鹿》的艺术特色 (Analyzing the artistic features of the animation of *The Deer of Nine Colors*), *Jiangxi keji shifan daxue xuebao* 江西科技师范大学学报 (Journal of Jiangxi Normal University of Science and Technology) 5 (2010): 118–20; Ding Peng 丁鹏, "Dunhuang bihua de donghua chuangzuo yanjiu: Yi donghuapian *Jiuse lu* wei li" 敦煌壁画的动画创作研究——以动画片九色鹿为例 (A study of

tions of references to ancient Chinese art traditions as part of a National Style (*minzu fengge* 民族风格), a common focus of early Chinese animation studies.[4] Although more recent studies of Chinese animation strive to look beyond the nationalization features to consider, for instance, transnational interactions with Japanese animation or the influence of Western Modernist art, they rarely investigate the ideological undercurrents that inform the shifts in Chinese animation.[5] Furthermore, animation studies scholars have analyzed the relationship between animation and cinema in the Western context by tracing the emergence of animation as an independent field since the 1990s, when the digital turn in film productions associated cinema with animation.[6] Chinese approaches to animation in the 1980s, however, illustrate an opposite movement, wherein animation was associated with cinema. This non-Western case of Chinese animation thus facilitates a more complex understanding of the relationship between these two media, animation and cinema, in a global context.

In comparing these two Dunhuang animations, this chapter argues that the varied production approaches, as pointed out by Nie Xinru, coincide with intermedial debates in Chinese animation in the years following the

animation composition based on the wall paintings from Dunhuang: With reference to the *Nine Colored Deer*), *Dunhuang xue* 敦煌学 (Dunhuang research) 33 (2017): 1–16.

4. On National Style, see Mary Ann Farquhar, "Monks and Monkey: A Study of National Style in Chinese Animation," *Animation Journal* 1, no. 2 (1993): 4–27; Helen Kang, "*Shui Mo Dong Hua*: The History and Development of Brush Painting Animation." *Animation Journal* 14 (2006): 63–74; Jian Cui, "The Pursuit of a National Style of Chinese Animation," *Animation Journal* 14 (2006): 44–62; Weihua Wu, "Catachresis 1 and Metaphor in Theorizing Chinese Animation," in *Chinese Animation, Creative Industries, and Digital Culture* (London: Routledge, 2017), 11–44.

5. Yuanyuan Chen, "The Rebel of the Chinese School: Modernist Expression in A Da's Late Animations," *Modernism / Modernity* 22, no. 1 (2015): 81–104; Daisy Yan Du, *Animated Encounters: Transnational Movements of Chinese Animation*, 1940s–1970s (Honolulu: University of Hawai'i Press, 2019).

6. See Karen Beckman, ed., *Animating Film Theory* (Durham, NC: Duke University Press, 2014). This volume's discussion of animation and cinema include Herve Joubert-Laurencin, "André Martin, Inventor of Animation Cinema: Prolegomena for a History of Terms," trans. Lucy Swanson, 85–97; Alan Cholodenko, "'First Principles' of Animation," 98–110; Suzanne Buchan, "Animation, in Theory," 111–31.

Cultural Revolution.[7] Negotiating approaches in animation productions, *The Deer of Nine Colors* uses animation as a branch of fine arts (*meishu* 美术), whereas *Jiazi Saves the Deer* recreates a Buddhist Jataka story by emphasizing more cinematic methods. In addition, the production of these two animations was intertwined with picture books (*lianhuanhua* 连环画), which further testifies to Chinese animators' struggles with linear storytelling and their efforts to differentiate mural paintings from animated images.[8] By unpacking the intermediality of these cultural productions, this chapter aims to highlight the complicated conceptual change of animation as a medium in China.

From Fine Arts to Cinematic Methods

In the late 1970s and early 1980s, animation's media specificity reemerged as a vital issue for Chinese animators and critics first in criticism of animations produced during the tumultuous years of the Cultural Revolution (1966–1976). Critics pointed out that Chinese animations produced during that period, which focused on class struggle, lacked media specificity because the Gang of Four criticized media specificity as associated with capitalism.[9] The realistic (*xieshi* 写实) look in animations of the late 1960s and early 1970s, as Daisy Yan Du suggests,[10] could be viewed as a manifestation of the lack of media specificity: animations produced during the Cultural Revolution were usually stories adapted from actual events to carry political meanings and tended to depict figures with life-like features.[11] In the late 1970s, Chinese animations returned to imagined

7. For detailed discussions of existing approaches to intermediality, see Gabriele Rippl, *Handbook of Intermediality: Literature-Image-Sound-Music* (Berlin: De Gruyter, 2015), 47–58.

8. I borrow "picture books" here to facilitate the understanding of *lianhuanhua*, a translation by Lin Su-Hsing and Julia F. Andrews in David Pong, ed., *Encyclopedia of Modern China*, vol. 1 (Detroit, MI: Charles Scribner's Sons / Gale, Cengage Learning, 2009), 317–18.

9. Zhang Boqing 章柏青, "Mantan meishu dianying" 漫谈美术电影 (Discussing fine arts films), *Dianying pingjie* 电影评介 (Movie review) Z1 (1979): 2–3.

10. Daisy Yan Du discusses the promotion of realism in animation productions during the Cultural Revolution in *Animated Encounters*, 157–59.

11. *Trial Voyage* (*Shihang* 试航, 1976) is a representative example. For details of this

depictions, such as the cartoonish illustrations in *One Night in the Art Gallery* (*Hualang yiye* 画廊一夜, 1978), produced by the Shanghai Animation Film Studio immediately after the Cultural Revolution. In 1979, one year after *One Night*'s release, a newspaper article titled "The Last Name of Fine Arts Films Should be 'Fine Arts'" argued for the significance of fine arts in Chinese animation productions.[12] Chinese animators and critics restated that animation's specific characteristic, distinguishing it from live-action films, should be exaggeration (*kuazhang* 夸张).[13] And although *One Night* adapted actual events, consistent with animation productions during the Cultural Revolution, it added an imaginative dimension to the story to differentiate itself from the previous realistic style.[14] Thus the late

---

animation, see Chu Zheng 初征, "Meishu dianying geming de xin chengguo: Caise meishupian *Shihang* guanhou" 美术电影革命的新成果——彩色美术片《试航》观后 (The new achievement of fine arts films: Review of color fine arts film *Trial Voyage*), *Renmin ribao* 人民日报 (People's daily), June 9, 1976: 3.

12. "Meishu dianying yingdang xing 'mei'" 美术电影应当姓'美' (The last name of fine arts film should be "fine arts"), *Wenhui bao* 文汇报 (Wenhui daily), March 22, 1979.

13. Chu Zheng, "Meishu dianying," 3. Song Lin 松林, "Mantan meishu dianying juben de tedian" 漫谈美术电影剧本的特点 (Discussing the features of fine arts film scripts), *Dianying xinzuo* 电影新作 (New films) 2 (1979): 79–81. The release of *One Night in the Art Gallery* also prompted another argument: that the last name of fine arts films should be "children." See "Meishu dianying shouxian ying xing 'er': Wenxue dianying gongzuozhe taolun fuwu duixiang deng wenti" 美术电影首先应姓"儿": 文学电影工作者讨论服务对象等问题 (The last name of fine arts film should be "children": Discussing audiences and other issues by artists in the fields of film and literature), *Jiefang ribao* 解放日报 (Jiefang daily), February 10, 1982. According to Wang Liuyi 王六一, ed., *Zhengtu: Zouxiang bainian de Zhongguo donghua*, vol. 3, *Zhongguo donghua shi*, 征途: 走向百年的中国动画 卷3 (March: Chinese animation enters a new century, vol. 3) (Beijing: Sanchen yingku yinxiang chubanshe, 2012), 22. These two viewpoints had not been formally debated, but were discussed at the same time in a meeting. See Wu Lun 伍伦, "Meishu dianying chuangzuo suixiang 美术电影创作随想 (Discussion on fine arts film productions), *Dianying yishu* 电影艺术 (Film art) 6 (1984): 43.

14. The event in the animation refers to the black painting exhibitions during the Cultural Revolution. For details of the black painting exhibitions, see Julia F. Andrews, "The Black Painting Exhibitions," in *Painters and Politics in the People's Republic of China, 1949–1979* (Berkeley: University of California Press, 1994), 368–76. For related secondary sources on attacking black paintings, see "Wenge houqi de 'pi heihua' yundong" 文革后期的"批黑画"运动 (The campaign of "attacking black paintings" in the later period of

1970s witnessed a return to the emphasis on fine arts and an exaggerated style of depiction.

Nevertheless, the cultural and economic contexts of the late 1970s and early 1980s marked an ideological shift discernable in Chinese animators' dissatisfaction with fine arts approaches. On the one hand, this dissatisfaction derived from their encounters with worldwide animation productions at international animation festivals,[15] where they were exposed to various painting genres and new techniques used in foreign animations.[16] By contrast, Chinese animations, dominated by the pursuit of the National Style and reference to traditional art forms, seemed outdated.[17] On the other hand, the labor-intensive and time-consuming production mode associated with fine arts seemed to be at odds with the new marketing strategy, which was changing from a production mode based on a government-regulated quota for the film industry to a market-oriented mode catering to the television industry.[18] The time- and labor-intensive production of short animations based on traditional art forms simply could not keep pace with the production requirements of a television industry now competing with imported Japanese and Hollywood animations.

---

the Cultural Revolution), *Dangshi bolan* 党史博览 (Party history expo) no. 9 (2004): 27; Hou Dechang 侯德昌, "1974 nian Beijing pi 'heihua' shijian" 1974 年北京批"黑画"事件 (Attacking "black paintings" in 1974 in Beijing), *Shiji* 世纪 (Century) (2017): 16–17.

15. "35 nian lai Zhongguo meishupian huo guoji dianyingjie jiang yilan biao" 35 年来中国美术片获国际电影节奖一览表 (List of international film festival awards received by Chinese animations in the last 35 years), *Dangdai dianying* 当代电影 (Popular movies) no. 2 (1984): 159–60.

16. Zhang Songlin 张松林, Xu Jingda 徐景达, and Zhou Keqin 周克勤, "Cong Sagelebu guilai" 从萨格勒布归来 (Coming back from Zagreb), *Dianying tongxun* 电影通讯 (Film report) 9 (1982): 33.

17. Lü Lü 吕律, "Duihua: Zhongguo donghua dianying de kunhuo he jietuo" 对话：中国动画电影的困惑和解脱 (Dialogue: Dilemma and resolution of Chinese animated film), *Dianying yishu* 电影艺术 (Film art) 11 (1989): 33; Wang Yongjun 王永钧, "Woguo meishupian xianzhuang jianping" 我国美术片现状简评 (A short review of the current status of our fine arts films), *Dianying pingjie* 电影评介 (Movie review) 6 (1989): 12–13.

18. Zhang Huilin 张慧临, *20 Shiji Zhongguo donghua yishu shi* 20世纪中国动画艺术史 (The history of Chinese animated film in the twentieth century) (Xi'an: Shanxi renmin meishu chubanshe, 2002), 135.

In this context, the media specificity of animation emerges not just as an aesthetic issue stemming from an ideological shift in the period following the Cultural Revolution but also as one that materially affects Chinese animators' ability to compete in the Chinese global animation market. Chinese animation productions in the 1980s, responding to this market, emphasized cinematic methods, eclipsing the post–Cultural Revolution emphasis on fine arts. According to Song Lin, the cinematic approach—including the construction of main themes, the depiction of figural movements, and the organization of a cohesive plot—was brought up in a meeting attended by animation directors in 1982.[19] The pursuit of cinematic methods was further represented by the slogan "nationalization, modernization, animating and cinematic representation" (*minzu hua* 民族化, *xiandai hua* 现代化, *donghua hua* 动画化, *dianying hua* 电影化), which was claimed in the production of *Monkey King Conquers the Demon* (*Jinhou xiangyao* 金猴降妖, 1985), one of the major feature films in Chinese animation history.[20]

In their emphasis on cinematic methods and interest in animation from a media perspective, Chinese animators seemed to find allies in worldwide animation productions. In 1988, a short review introduced Norman McLaren, a Scottish Canadian animator (1914–1987), by briefly discussing his adoption of various cinematic techniques in his animations.[21] Titled "The Charm of Technology," the review emphasized the significance of cinematic techniques. One year later, another article, titled "Dialogue: Dilemma and Resolution of Chinese Animated Film," recounts Norman McLaren's well-known definition of animation: "Animation is not the art of drawings that move but the art of movements that are drawn."[22] The

19. Song Lin 松林, "Meishupian yao quanmian tigao yishu zhiliang" 美术片要全面提高艺术质量 (The artistic quality of fine arts films must be improved in all respects), *Dianying tongxun* 电影通讯 (Film report) 9 (1984): 38, 41–42.

20. Wang Liuyi, *Zhengtu: Zouxiang bainian*, 194.

21. Li Yan 李燕, "Jishu shouduan de meili" 技术手段的魅力 (The charm of technology), *Dianying yishu* 电影艺术 (Film art) 5 (1988): 29.

22. Lü Lü, "Duihua: Zhongguo donghua," 35; Georges Sifianos, "The Definition of Animation: A Letter from Noman McLaren," *Animation Journal* 3, no. 2 (Spring 1995): 62–66. For the origin of McLaren's statement, see Maureen Furniss, *Art in Motion: Animation Aesthetic* (Eastleigh, UK: John Libbey, 2007), 5.

article restates the vital role of cinematic techniques in animation, challenging traditional animation approaches, emphasizing drawing and narrative, and regarding photography as a recording tool alone. Chinese animation, mainly relying on formal representations predetermined by their references to traditional art forms, seemed ready to benefit from this modern technique-oriented approach.

This chapter examines *The Deer of Nine Colors* and *Jiazi Saves a Deer* as works that demonstrate the change in Chinese animation productions in the 1980s, when animators negotiated a transition from a post–Cultural Revolution revival of the fine arts approach to a more plot-driven cinematic approach.

The Deer of Nine Colors: The Pursuit of Fine Arts

The Deer of Nine Colors is widely regarded as the best-known animation adapted from Dunhuang art. It is based on a mural in Mogao Cave 257 and retells a Buddhist Jataka story about a magical nine-colored deer. As the painting relates, the deer rescues a drowning man from a river who eventually reaches an imperial palace and leads a royal deer hunt. Released in 1981, the animation closely refers to the Dunhuang art tradition but retells the story by adding several plot elements. In contrast with the national-style perspective often applied in Chinese animation studies, the discussion below analyzes references to Dunhuang art to point out Chinese animators' perception of animation from a medium perspective.

The fine arts approach is first indicated in *The Deer of Nine Colors'* reference to practices in Dunhuang art exhibitions in the 1950s, which showcased the detailed presentation of geographic and panoramic views of the site. The animation starts with a geographic view, a handscroll map lit by the well-known gilt bronze human-shaped lamp from the Han dynasty (*Changxin gongdeng* 长信宫灯). The lamp illuminates Dunhuang and the Mogao Grottoes, situating them as an oasis on the map. The camera then moves to the upper right corner of the scene to show seven Chinese characters on a black background: *The Panoramic View of Dunhuang Caves* (*Dunhuang Mogao ku quantu* 敦煌莫高窟全图). A dim panoramic view of the site is further obscured by a textual description of the site on screen.

Although the map and panoramic view might be interpreted as the animators' endeavor to deliver educational information, it also reflects popular practices for displaying Dunhuang in art exhibitions in the mid-twentieth century, when the animator Qian Jiajun 钱家骏 (1916–2011) first attempted to produce *The Deer of Nine Colors* as early as 1958.[23] A map and a horizontal layout of the site's facade are among materials from 1948 and 1951 Dunhuang exhibitions. For example, an article in *Xinjiang Daily* about the 1948 exhibition states that a map in the exhibition entrance indicates the geographic location of Dunhuang and, clearly referring to a visual source, described the horizontal layout of the caves.[24] Similarly, the 1951 exhibition catalog lists two maps: *The Panoramic View of the Mogao Grottoes* (*Mogao ku quanjing* 莫高窟全景) and *Geographic Locations of the Mogao Grottoes* (*Mogao ku weizhi tu* 莫高窟位置图).[25] Although no images are listed in these two textual sources, two maps are included in

23. "1958 nian de meishupian" 1958年的美术片 (Animations in 1958), *Zhongguo dianying* 中国电影 (Chinese films) 6 (1958): 31. According to Pu Jiaxiang 浦稼祥, the halt in the production was due to the Literature and Art Rectification Movement 文艺整风运动 of the mid-1950s. See Pu Jiaxiang, *Donghua chuangzuo qishilu* 动画创作启示录 (Revelation on animation creation) (Beijing: Beijing lianhe chuban gongsi, 2014), 44. Similarly, Li Zhen 李镇 states that the halt in the 1958 production was due to the slogan proposed by Kang Sheng 康生, "Pull out the white flags on the silver screen" 拔掉银幕上的白旗. See Li Zhen, "Ta zi huazhong lai: Xiangei yuanxing de Qian Jiajun xiansheng" 他自画中来——献给远行的钱家骏先生 (He is from paintings: To commemorate Mr. Qian Jiajun), *Dangdai dianying* 当代电影 (Contemporary cinema) 11 (2011): 38. However, another article mentions that Qian Jiajun's 1957 animation *The Gigantic Turnip* (*Ba luobo* 拔萝卜) was criticized for capitalist tendencies. See "Shangying chuangzuo ganbu zhanlan da bianlun" 上影创作干部展览大辩论 (Discussions by producers from the Shanghai Film Studio), *Wenhui bao* 文汇报 (Wenhui daily), January 4, 1958. Although no textual materials criticize this particular animation, it could be supposed that the plot, which centers on the failure to pull out a giant turnip, did not accord with the political climate in China at that time. Thus one could speculate that the halt in the production of *The Deer of Nine Colors* was related to the investigation of Qian Jiajun resulting from criticism of *The Gigantic Turnip.*

24. "Dunhuang yizhan guanhou" 敦煌艺展观后 (After visiting the Dunhuang exhibition), *Xinjiang ribao* 新疆日报 (Xinjiang daily), November 10, 1948.

25. Dunhuang wenwu yanjiu suo 敦煌文物研究所编, ed., *Dunhuang wenwu zhanlan mulu* 敦煌文物展览目录 (Catalog of the exhibition of Dunhuang artifacts) (Beijing: Zhongyang zhengfu wenhuabu wenwuju, 1951), 8–9.

a book, *The Art of Mogao Grottoes at Dunhuang* (*Dunhuang Mogao ku yishu* 敦煌莫高窟艺术), published in 1957 and written by Pan Jiezi 潘絜兹 (1915–2002), a Chinese artist who worked as an assistant researcher at the Dunhuang Academy in 1945.[26] The images are quite similar to those in the animation. Because Pan Jiezi was the animation scriptwriter, Qian Jiajun might have consulted him about including these two maps to provide specific information about Dunhuang. In any event, the panoramic and geographic depictions of Dunhuang in *The Deer of Nine Colors* are consistent with the promotion of fine arts in the field of animation during the early 1980s.

The fine arts approach is also represented in the animation's close reference to the Dunhuang tradition through a vivid architectural animation of Cave 257, showing the mural's location to emphasize the animation's association with the site. This realistic depiction is shown at both the beginning and end of the animation. At the beginning, following the shots of the two maps and the textual description of Dunhuang, the animation displays the facade of the cave. The exterior wall is decorated with four representative figures: Kashyapa and Ananda on the right and left sides of the cave entrance, respectively, and two apsaras flying above. The cave's location is indicated by the numerals 257 above the entrance and indirectly hinted at by the architectural surroundings, specifically, the painted wooden structure on the right side of the cave entrance and the cement rail in front of the cave. Zooming in, the animation reveals the cave's interior. The central pillar present in the actual cave architecture is removed from the scene so that the featured mural is presented directly as the camera enters the cave. Although the animators altered the original wall paintings—for instance, replacing original murals with the thousand-Buddha pattern on top of the mural or adding the profile of a Buddhist sculpture on the left side of the cave entrance—they depict the featured mural in its actual location at the bottom of the west wall. Next, the animation's title, *Jiuse lu*, is displayed with the mural painting as the background, and the animation's association with the Dunhuang mural is stressed with a line displayed under the title that reads "adapted from the Dunhuang mural, the Jataka story of the Deer King." The animation ends

26. Pan Jiezi 潘絜兹, *Dunhuang Mogao ku yishu* 敦煌莫高窟艺术 (The art of Mogao grottoes at Dunhuang), reprint (Shanghai: Shanghai renmin chubanshe, 1981), 2–5.

with the camera zooming out from the deer to the cave's facade, matching the shot from the beginning but then pulling back further to reveal more of the location: a gigantic cave facade, with Cave 257 on the second tier, where it is in fact located.

Additionally, the fine arts references in *The Deer of Nine Colors* are in part the result of the participation of fine arts graduates in the animation's production. The production crew of *The Deer of Nine Colors* included the set designer Feng Jiannan 冯健男 (1940–), who was a graduate of the oil painting department at Nanjing Art Academy and joined the Shanghai Animation Film Studio in 1964. The attention paid to the original mural's materiality could be viewed as another aspect resulting from Feng's fine arts education. The moving images in celluloid animations typically included two types of paintings, settings and figures. Usually figures are painted on celluloid, and settings are drawn on paper. In this animation, the deer and its inverted image, with depictions of waves in the water and other minor decorative elements, are painted on celluloid. In contrast, the major set with a laterite background and the bluish lake are painted on paper. Because of this production procedure, the display of materiality of murals in *The Deer of Nine Colors* is mainly represented by settings. Feng Jiannan stated that, at the suggestion of the character designer Hu Yongkai 胡永凯 (1945–), he adopted *gaoli* paper (高丽纸) to better represent the texture of mural paintings. According to Feng, *gaoli* paper balances the properties of raw rice paper (*shengxuan* 生宣), which absorbs water well, and ripe rice paper (*shuxuan* 熟宣), which does not do so as well. Moreover, it could be painted on both sides using either thick or thin colors. Because of the durability and thickness of this particular kind of paper, Feng could use multiple techniques to paint the set design. Sometimes he would apply several layers of colors to one side of the paper.[27] Other times, he would apply colors on the front side of the paper and add other colors on its backside, which creates depth and imitates the aging quality of murals (fig. 4.1). Applying colors on both sides is a painting technique used in *gongbi zhongcai* 工笔重彩, a genre in traditional Chinese painting in which layered mineral colors are applied to silk. Feng's painting techniques implicitly reference those of traditional Chinese painting, but his

27. Feng Jiannan, interview with the author, Shanghai, May 2, 2017.

FIGURE 4.1. A deer walking in the forest, in *The Deer of Nine Colors* (1981).

depiction of the material characteristics of the Dunhuang murals comes from his oil painting background.[28] The *gaoli* paper's durability helps the layered colors attain the visual effect of the original mural. Moreover, the paper's texture, visible through the lighter colors, also mimics the mural surface's materiality. Chinese animators' fine arts educational backgrounds thus brought an emphasis on fine arts painting techniques to the production process.

Finally, the pursuit of fine arts in animation is also manifested in its use of such imaginative approaches as exaggeration and ahistorical modification, popular again after the Cultural Revolution. The imaginative approach is indicated by modified figural depictions, which in displaying a Han-domi-

28. Feng Jiannan 冯健男, "Cong changjing sheji tan donghuapian *Jiuse lu* de dansheng: Mianhuai Qian Jiajun xiansheng" 从场景设计谈动画片《九色鹿》的诞生——缅怀钱家骏先生 (Discussing *The Deer of Nine Colors* by focusing on the set design: To commemorate Mr. Qian Jiajun), *Nanjing yishu xueyuan xuebao (meishu yu sheji ban)* 南京艺术学院学报 (美术与设计版) (Journal of Nanjing Arts Institute [Fine Arts & Design]) 6 (2011): 139.

nated kingdom attests to the political context in twentieth-century China. More specifically, when the troupe of merchants, appearing in a Middle Eastern facial and clothing style, arrive at the palace, they meet with the king, a figure adapted from a mural painting on the east wall in Cave 220 at the Mogao Grottoes. The Northern Wei style of the slim-bodied figure in the original mural is replaced by a Tang-style imperial figure with a tall and bulky body and Han Chinese facial features. Similarly, the depiction of the queen showcases the same artistic style. Except for her slender body shape, which differs from plump-bodied females in Tang dynasty art, both facial decoration and headdress are in a Tang style. In terms of the choice of painting style, Feng Jiannan explains that the mural's original representations are too simplified to please audiences, and the mural paintings in the Tang dynasty are too complicated to be adapted for animation.[29] As a result, Feng adds, animators have chosen the Northern Wei style as a basis and then made specific alterations based on the Sui and Tang murals.[30] The depictions of the king and queen could be considered examples of this practice. However, this representation implies a Han-dominated kingdom in Dunhuang, which is an imagination of history shared by the public.

As discussed, *The Deer of Nine Colors* displays the fine arts' emphasis on Chinese animations in the early 1980s. Nevertheless, these efforts were not encouraged. In 1982, one year after the animation's release, the director of the Shanghai Animation Film Studio Te Wei 特伟 (1915–2010) stated his criticism of some Chinese animations, including *The Deer of Nine Colors*:

> *The Deer of Nine Colors* adapts Dunhuang art, which, it must be said, gives it a unique look as well as a certain basis in terms of theme and story. As an animated film, however, it falls short in a number of ways. The theme not only lacks depth, but is also weakly mastered. The characters lack personality. The kindness of the main character, the Deer of Nine Colors, is quite ordinary and thus unable to engage the audience. Interpersonal relationships, such as between the king and queen, are not constructed properly. The plot development lacks fluency such that the dramatic climax falls flat. Also, the movements are drawn in an oversimplified manner. Consequently,

29. Feng Jiannan, "Cong changjing sheji tan donghuapian," 138.
30. Feng Jiannan, "Cong changjing sheji tan donghuapian," 138.

> the film is of poor quality. Aside from the Dunhuang colors, there is not much for viewers to appreciate.[31]

Clearly, the approach used by the animation crew of *The Deer of Nine Colors* did not meet the new standards, despite its post–Cultural Revolution reintroduction of fine arts. By analyzing the animation's retelling in *lianhuanhua* 连环画 form, the following section presents Chinese animators' struggle to generate cohesive plots.

The Intervention of *Lianhuanhua*

Both *The Deer of Nine Colors* and *Jiazi Saves the Deer* indicate animators' negotiations of the intermediality between animation and *lianhuanhua*. In the Dunhuang mural, the story is not represented linearly: it displays the saving of the drowning man by the deer on the left; the encounter of the deer, the king, and his royal troupe in the middle; and the drowning man informing the king and the royal court about the deer on the right. In contrast to the mural's nonlinear visual representation, the animation recounts a linear story by adding plot elements to make the story more fulfilling. Adapted from the animation, the *lianhuanhua* version of *The Deer of Nine Colors* renders the original rectangular-shaped frames as still images printed in a book. However, the *lianhuanhua* strengthens linear storytelling by reorganizing the scenes from the animation. As shown (tab. 4.1), the *lianhuanhua* shifts the scene of the deer rescuing the drowning man from before to after the merchants' reception by the king.

This reorganization of the plot indicates a dissatisfaction with the animation's storytelling, echoing Te Wei's criticism. From another perspective, this

31. Te Wei 特伟, "Meishu dianying yao geng shang yicenglou" 美术电影要更上一层楼 (Fine arts film should attain a further step up), *Dianying yishu* 电影艺术 (Film art) 6 (1982): 14. Part of the article is reprinted in another article: Te Wei 特伟, "Meishu dianying chuangzuo fangtan" 美术电影创作放谈 (Discussions on fine arts film productions), in *Meishu dianying chuangzuo yanjiu* 美术电影创作研究 (Research and production of fine arts film), ed. Editorial Office for Film Newsletters of the Film Bureau, T. M. O. C. & Editorial Office for the Domestic Film of the Chinese Film Press (Beijing: Zhongguo dianying chubanshe, 1984), 1–11.

Table 4.1. Negotiations of Intermediality

	Major Scenes in *The Deer of Nine Colors*	**Major Plots in the *lianhuanhua***
1	The deer saves the merchants in the desert.	The deer saves the merchants in the desert.
2	The deer rescues the drowning man.	The merchants are received by the king in the palace.
3	The merchants are received by the king in the palace.	The deer rescues the drowning man.
4	The drowning man informs the royal court about the deer and the subsequent hunting.	The drowning man informs the royal court about the deer and the subsequent hunting.
5	The encounter between the king and the deer in the hunt.	The encounter between the king and the deer in the hunt.

also implies the distinct media specificities of animation and *lianhuanhua*. In *lianhuanhua*, the images would be tightly linked together to facilitate the story development and ease readers' understanding in the reading process. Placing the scene in which the drowning man first appears immediately before the scene in which the drowning man reports the deer's existence to the royal court helps readers link the plot points together. These configurations with linear storytelling show Chinese animators' struggle to recount the Dunhuang story. More importantly, the plot's reordering indicates the role of *lianhuanhua* in forming the narrative.

With the promotion of *lianhuanhua* in the 1980s and early 1990s, Dunhuang mural paintings were selected as examples to prove that the *lianhuanhua* form of visual representation was practiced in traditional Chinese art.[32] According to this view, Dunhuang murals are perceived as "linked mural paintings" (*lianhuan bihua* 连环壁画). Relative to *The Deer of Nine Colors*, the intervention of *lianhuanhua* in *Jiazi Saves the Deer* further assists the formation of linear storytelling in the animation.

32. Li Song 李松, "Lianhuanhua zatan" 连环画杂谈 (Discussions of *lianhuanhua*), *Meishu yanjiu* 美术研究 (Art research) 2 (1980): 11. However, *lianhuanhua* only emerged as a new artistic genre in Republican China. See Shen Kuiyi, "Comics, Picture Books, and Cartoonists in Republican China," *Inks: Cartoon and Comic Art Studies* 4 (1997): 2–16; Julia F. Andrews, "Literature in Line: Picture Stories in the People's Republic of China," *Inks: Cartoon and Comic Art Studies* 4 (1997): 17–32.

Jiazi Saves the Deer: Seeking Cinematic Methods

The animation for *Jiazi Saves the Deer* is based on a *lianhuanhua*, which features Jiazi, a child living in the mountains with his elderly parents. Jiazi dies after disguising himself as a deer to save wild animals during a royal hunt, but eventually comes back to life with the assistance of the animals' magical powers. The book was painted by Liu Jude 刘巨德 (1946–), a graduate of Tsinghua University who majored in graphic design. In 1984, Liu's book won the first prize in a national competition of fine arts books, which eventually led to its adaptation as an animation by the Shanghai Animation Film Studio.

Liu's *lianhuanhua* is inspired by mural paintings depicting the Buddhist Jataka story of Shanzi (睒子) in Dunhuang, such as Cave 299, one of eight murals in the Mogao Grottoes based on Samaka Jataka. Similar to the mural of *The Deer of Nine Colors*, the Cave 299 mural is also in a nonlinear format, with the royal hunting scene on the left, the meeting between the king and Shanzi's parents on the right, and Shanzi's resurrection as well as his reunion with his parents in the center.[33] Replacing the mural's unusual narrative structure, the book presents scenes in a linear order, with a consistent painting style and numbers to indicate the sequence of images and events. The book further embraces a linear mode of storytelling by omitting the meeting between the royal troupe and Shanzi's parents as depicted in the mural painting, replacing it with interactions between Shanzi and the animals. Moreover, the original Buddhist Jataka story, *Shanzi bensheng* 睒子本生, is retitled *Jiazi jiulu* 夹子救鹿.[34] The retitling eases the reception and lays the foundation for an animated adaptation which, like the

33. Higashiyama Kengo points out that eight murals in Dunhuang depict the Samaka Jataka, seven in the Mogao Grottoes and one in the Western Thousand Buddhas Caves. Higashiyama also suggests that all of the depictions are in a horizontal multiscene format and usually highlight the narrative climax in the middle of the murals. See Higashiyama Kengo 东山健吾, "Dunhuang shiku bensheng gushihua de xingshi: Yi *Shanzi bensheng tu* wei zhongxin" 敦煌石窟本生故事画的形式——以睒子本生图为中心 (The forms of Jataka stories illustrated in Dunhuang grottoes: Focusing on the illustrations to Samaka Jataka), trans. Li Mei 李梅, ed. Zhao Shengliang 赵声良, *Dunhuang yanjiu* 敦煌研究 (Dunhuang research) 126, no. 2 (2011): 1–11.

34. In the *lianhuanhua*, Shanzi was renamed Jiazi, most likely because the *shan* character is relatively obscure and would be hard for the target audience, children, to read.

lianhuanhua, would be aimed at children. Additionally, whereas the mural invokes a spiritual power, the magical power that restores Jiazi to life in the *lianhuanhua* comes from the animals. This modification also enhances the storytelling by strengthening the book's central theme.

The intervention of *lianhuanhua* between mural and animation facilitates the animation's linear narration. However, adapting from *lianhuanhua* to animation is not always a smooth process. In 1997, Qian Yunda, a Chinese animator at the Shanghai Animation Film Studio, recounted an unsuccessful adaptation of *lianhuanhua* to animation and elaborates on the difference between images in animation and *lianhuanhua*:

> Differing from individual artworks, *lianhuanhua* comprises multiple coherent images. However, each painting's contents are usually the most representative movements in relatively still spaces. . . . In contrast, animation has to represent the process of movements with multiple images. Otherwise, it (the figure) will not move. Also, other than movement, animation must use montage, which puts together separate shots and sounds to compose an artwork.[35]

This article implies that creating animation based on *lianhuanhua* was a common practice, and it also highlights the two characteristics of animation that distinguish it from *lianhuanhua*: movement and montage.

The animation of *Jiazi Saves the Deer* illustrates these two characteristics. First, Liu Jude stated that he had to compose different versions of Jiazi, including the front, profile, and back views, all of which would be necessary to transform the still images into moving ones. Moreover, the animators had to draw all the different physical movements that appear in the animation. Second, in contrast to the separate images in the *lianhuanhua*, the animation images have been linked through montage. For instance, the transition between images in the *lianhuanhua* is mainly achieved through page sequencing, the figures' appearances, and the accompanying narrative text. However, the animation uses frame transitions to advance the storyline from scene to scene. The transformation from one frame to another is what moves the plot of the story forward.

35. Qian Yunda 钱运达, "Donghua yu lianhuanhua" 动画与连环画 (Animation and lianhuanhua), *Dianying xinzuo* 电影新作 (New films) 4 (1997): 56–57.

FIGURE 4.2. An old lady holding a newborn, in *Jiazi Saves the Deer* (1985).

The adaption of *Jiazi Saves the Deer* from *lianhuanhua* into animation also demonstrates the move away from fine arts animation through its use of cinematic methods, an approach that resonates with new perceptions of the medium of animation. The animation starts with a scene that imitates a film viewing experience in a theater. The audience is led into the story by a voice-over, introducing the birth of Jiazi. After moving the camera from the upper to the lower part of the screen and then panning to the right, the photographer of this animation zooms in to display a house with a light shining through a window. Later, the screen presents only the lighted window, through which the viewer sees a grey-haired lady holding a newborn (fig. 4.2). This scene imitates a film viewing experience in a theater by leaving dark space around the lighted screen. Conversely, in *The Deer of Nine Colors,* cinematic presentation comes into play at the beginning and end of the animation when depicting the original Dunhuang cave art. For example, at the end of the animation, the animators zoom out from the deer in the mural to the exterior of Cave 257, and then to a wide-angle shot of the grottoes. In contrast to how *The Deer of the Nine Colors* explicitly links itself to the Dunhuang cave mural, *Jiazi Saves the Deer* moves away from any association with fine arts practice to stress its association with cinema.

Additionally, *Jiazi Saves the Deer* deploys various cinematic methods, such as multiple high-angle shots, to convey the figures' emotional develop-

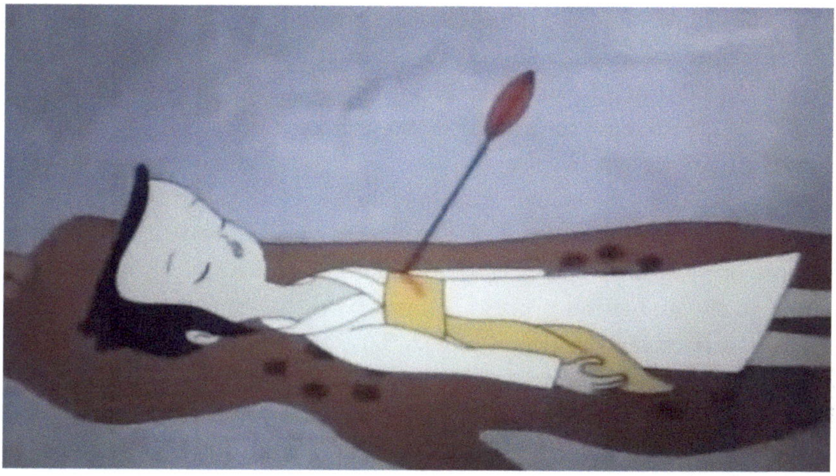

FIGURE 4.3. Jiazi lying on the ground with an arrow piercing his belly, in *Jiazi Saves the Deer* (1985).

FIGURE 4.4. Jiazi lying on the ground in the forest, in *Jiazi Saves the Deer* (1985).

ment. For instance, in the scene in which Jiazi dies disguised as a deer, the animation first shows a close-up of Jiazi lying on the ground; the camera then slowly moves away to display Jiazi, surrounded by the forest, from a high-angle perspective (figs. 4.3, 4.4). The animation conveys a sense of sorrow for Jiazi's death by shifting from a close-up to a high-angle view. In contrast, characterization in *The Deer of Nine Colors* is attained by depicting interactions. For example, after the scene where the royal court learns about the deer, the drowning man's moral character is implied by the darkening of his skin and is further addressed through his several comical interactions with a donkey. In transposing the donkey, initially painted in the drowning scene on the mural, to the hunting scene in the animation, the animators intentionally add plot elements, including the drowning man's several attempts to ride the donkey and the donkey's running away after the man drowns in the end.

In addition to their adaptation of *lianhuanhua* and use of cinematic methods, the animators' cinematic perspective is also evident in their use of prescoring, which makes certain visual art choices dependent on the sound in the animation process. Animators at the time typically created sound to match images; however, *Jiazi Saves the Deer* featured prescoring. For instance, in one scene, *Jiazi* is playing the flute while dancing with animals in the forest. Each shot in the scene corresponds with a specific section of the music, such that the music predetermines the movement of the imagery.[36] Hence, if the *lianhuanhua* first minimizes the influence of Dunhuang art on the structure, content, and look of the story, and the cinematic methods further diminish fine arts' influence, then the prescoring weakens the role of visualizations.

Conclusion

In comparing *The Deer of Nine Colors* and *Jiazi Saves the Deer*, this chapter discusses the varied adaptations of Dunhuang murals in the transitional period of Chinese animation production in the 1980s. Resonating with concurrent discussions of animation from a media perspective, the former animation emphasizes fine arts and strives to create an animation with a distinctive Dunhuang style, while the latter adopts various cinematic methods to associate animation with cinema. In mediating fine arts and cinema, the production of these two animations was intertwined with *lianhuanhua*, which further testifies to Chinese animators' struggles with linear storytelling and their efforts to differentiate mural paintings from animated images. The shift of emphasis from fine arts to cinematic methods in Chinese animation could be interpreted as a result of Chinese animators' reflection

36. Yan Dingxian 严定宪 and Lin Wenxiao 林文肖, *Donghua daoyan chuangzuo* 动画导演创作 (Animation directors' productions) (Beijing: Zhongguo haiyang chubanshe, 2015), 53–54.

on their medium after the Cultural Revolution. However, the shift also points to emerging struggles that Chinese animators had to confront. In again promoting fine arts, Chinese animators sought to embark on another prosperous period; however, in the 1980s, with the increasing dialogue with worldwide animations and changes in the domestic animation industry, the fine arts approach could no longer meet cultural and artistic expectations. Although current research points out that reference to prestigious ancient art forms in classical Chinese animation hindered the development of Chinese animation, this chapter suggests that Chinese animators did strive to experiment with new ways to adapt art traditions in contemporary times.[37] *The Deer of Nine Colors* and *Jiazi Saves the Deer*, as two cases, exemplify these animators' efforts to make the change.

37. Yuanyuan Chen, "Old or New Art: Rethinking Classical Chinese Animation," *Journal of Chinese Cinemas* 11, no. 2 (2017): 175–88.

SECTION TWO

Gender

FIVE

Psychic Grannies

Animation and Animism in Turn-of-the-Century Taiwan

TIM SHAO-HUNG TENG

For many Taiwanese, especially those growing up around the turn of the millennium, *Grandma and Her Ghosts* (*Mofa ama* 魔法阿媽, 1998) is a film they hold fond memories of to this day. With rich references to folk religion cultures, the animated feature dramatizes the enchanted encounter of an urban child and his estranged grandmother, whose profession as a shamaness in a suburban neighborhood leads the grandson on to ever stranger and more daring adventures (fig. 5.1). The resonance created by this family melodrama, which perfectly blends the paranormal and the everyday, revolves around the psychic grandmother. The decision to feature an elder character obviously goes against popular taste given over to Japanese and American productions, wherein princesses, teenage girls, and cute animals reign supreme. Yet the grandmother, "a frightful apparition with ferocious eyes and crinkly skin the color of dried-up tangerines," proves more than able to command audience attention.[1] In addition to her formidable superpowers, what also endear her to the audience are her quirky but ultimately loving personality, her down-to-earthness that readily evokes one's own family members, and, not least, her lively speech, inimitably dubbed in Taiwanese by the late actress Wen Ying, herself an icon of Taiwan's film and television scene of recent decades.

1. Ken Eisner, "Grandma and Her Ghosts," *Variety*, November 1, 1998, https://variety.com/1998/film/reviews/grandma-and-her-ghosts-1200456141.

FIGURE 5.1. The psychic grandmother and her grandson, Dou Dou, in *Grandma and Her Ghosts* (1998). Courtesy of Ricefilm International Co. Ltd.

Regarded by critics then and now as "a milestone of Taiwanese animation," *Grandma and Her Ghosts* (*Grandma*) was infamously snubbed at the 1998 Golden Horse Awards.[2] It was expecting to win the Best Animation Award, but the jury decided to grant the prize to neither of the two nominees. As later revealed, members of the jury worried that awarding the film would mean "promoting superstition" and "encouraging feudal superstitious thoughts." During their discussion, one jury member suggested, "Should we promote this film, soon there will be many Sung Chi-li's.[3] It is full of the strange, the powerful, the disorderly, and the spiritual (*guaili luanshen* 怪力亂神); these are not mythology but outright superstition."[4] Another chimed in, "The main spectators of animated films should be chil-

2. Wen Tien Hsiang 聞天祥, "Taiwan donghua de lichengbei" 台灣動畫的里程碑 (The milestone of Taiwanese animation), in *Mofa ama: Wo ba ama bian katong le* 魔法阿媽: 我把阿媽變卡通了 (*Grandma and Her Ghosts*: I turned grandma into a cartoon), ed. Rice Film International Co. (Taipei: Rye Field, 1999), 197–203.

3. Sung Chi-li is a famous Taiwanese geomancer and cult leader who made constant media appearances in the 1990s and early 2000s.

4. "Jin 20 nian de jingdian! Bei Jinmajiang beipan de *Mofa ama*" 近20年的經典! 被金馬獎背叛的"魔法阿媽" (A classic for nearly 20 years! *Mofa ama*, the film betrayed by the Golden Horse Awards), *PTT Bulletin Board System*, August 30, 2016, https://www.ptt.cc/bbs/movie/M.1472510602.A.A47.html.

dren under two years of age. . . . The shamans and ghosts in the film will surely have negative impacts on them."[5] Not surprisingly, these curiously self-assured views soon solicited pushback from film workers and fans alike. Some ridiculed that the "ghost island" (*guidao* 鬼島)—a nickname for Taiwan christened by acerbic netizens—was indeed full of superstitious people like the jury members, who nonetheless advocated striking down superstition. Others wondered if according to their standard, the witch, the Seven Dwarfs, and Snow White kissed awake by the prince were really rational and scientific enough.[6]

The Golden Horse jury's worry appears uncalled for today considering especially the global success of *Coco* (2017). Like *Grandma*, the Mexican animated blockbuster is set during the festival of the dead and is no less haunted by ghosts hailing from folk religion. Yet the jury's concerns also raised critical questions as to what themes are deemed proper for animation, and what kind of spectatorial effect the medium is best at invoking. Also intriguingly, why did a film like *Grandma* emerge in turn-of-the-millenium Taiwan in animated form? To address these questions, this chapter considers animation alongside the concept of animism, whose wide application and rich implications have inspired discussions across disciplines including anthropology and religious studies, literature and art history, and film and media studies. Through the juxtaposition of animation and animism, the chapter ponders why the encounter between animation and religion is indeed an apt one that speaks to the time and space of the film's production.

Using *Grandma* as a guide, I first sketch out various manifestations of ghosts in folk religious beliefs through the lens of animism. In referencing theories of animation and animism proposed by anthropologists, I engage concepts that lie at the core of animist worldviews, such as kinship, relationality, and the environment, to delineate a distinct mode of sociality found in the film. I then shift the focus to the psychic granny, known in Mandarin as *shenpo* 神婆, whose versatile career can be parsed in different registers as an ethnographic figure, an animating medium, a

5. "Jinma pingshen yingdai gongbu, bufen yanlun feiyi suosi" 金馬評審影帶公布，部分言論匪夷所思 (Golden Horse jury videotapes published, some comments are mind-boggling), *Lianhe bao* 聯合報 (United daily), December 14, 1998, 26.

6. "Jin 20 nian de jingdian!"

set of cultural techniques, and a media theorist.[7] To these explications, I supply anecdotes from the life and work of my own grandmother, whose profession as a shamaness in rural Taiwan sheds light on female mediumship as a site-specific and community-oriented media practice. Grandma's mediumistic career, I suggest, invites conversations with and reflections upon key topics raised in media studies today. Across historic, ethnographic, and theoretical accounts, the many psychic grannies that animate life and media in Taiwan constitute a fertile meeting ground where animation and religion, by a mutual investment in animism, stage their felicitous encounter.

Fantastic Ghosts and Where to Find Them

Taiwan at the turn of the millennium was haunted by ghosts. This is best evidenced by the ghostly presences pervading literary and cinematic imaginations around the period. In literature, novelists such as Li Ang 李昂 and Song Zelai 宋澤萊 are often singled out for their pioneering work in magical realism that marks a departure from these authors' realist careers. In his endorsement of Li Ang, David Der-wei Wang likens the writer to "a pen-brandishing and ink-splashing shamaness, beckoning us into a twisted and ghostly world infused with bewitching sublimity."[8] Indeed, in her *Visible Ghosts* (*Kandejian de gui* 看得見的鬼, 2004), Li assumes the role of a medium that transports us into a realm populated by vengeful spirits. Each of the five stories features a female ghost who dies an unjust death, prompting her to return to the human world to settle with the evildoers. These explicitly gendered tales mark the site of patriarchal violence where the violated can assert their voice only through a return of the repressed. The ghostly furnishes an allegorical lens through which to make sense of the many political issues facing Taiwan: its history of layered colonialism, unredressed political massacres, bureaucratic corrup-

7. Psychic granny would also be a closer translation of the film's Chinese title, which means magical grandma.

8. These words can be found on the back cover of Li Ang's novel *Beigang xianglu renren cha: Dai zhencaodai de mogui xilie* 北港香爐人人插：戴貞操帶的魔鬼系列 (Beigang incense burner of lust: The devil with a chastity belt series) (Taipei: Rye Field, 1997).

tion, and setbacks suffered by feminist movements. The liminal experience between the surreal and the real as articulated in these extraordinary stories emerged in a timely manner when, in 2000, the nation underwent a historically unprecedented transfer of power as the Nationalist Party was defeated in the year's presidential election by the native opposition party.

In film, ghosts assume numerous guises in works typically associated with the second wave of Taiwan New Cinema, including *Connection by Fate* (*Chaoji gongmin* 超級公民, 1998), *What Time Is It There?* (*Ni nabian jidian* 你那邊幾點, 2001), and *Goodbye, Dragon Inn* (*Bu san* 不散, 2003). Through the trope of the ghost, these films probe the disintegration of the nuclear family and further atomization of individuals, the marginalization of queer and aboriginal identities, and the disappearance of old Taipei in the thick of the modernization project. Displaying a haunting and melancholic charm, the ghost in these films finds embodiment in the deceased father, cruising queers, exploited aborigines, and the alienated city of Taipei itself.[9] Although belonging to this haunted scene in turn-of-the-century film and literature, the ghosts in *Grandma* derive their unique hauntology independently of their contemporaries. The film's approach to these amiable and cutified ghosts gestures toward the *yōkai* 妖怪 (strange apparition) tradition in Japanese manga and anime culture.[10] Its plotline, for instance, shares some similarities with the manga series *Hanada shōnen shi* (花田少年史, 1993–1995), whose highly popular cartoon version aired in Taiwan in the mid-2000s. *Hanada* centers around a young boy who acquires the ability of clairvoyance after suffering a head injury. Although initially terrified by ghosts, he overcomes the fear, befriends a gang of ghostly buddies, and helps bring their unfinished business to closure.

9. For an analysis of these films, see Lin Wenchi, "Taiwan dianying zhong de shijimo Taibei" 台灣電影中的世紀末台北 (Taipei at the end of the century in Taiwan cinema), in *2004 Taibeixue guoji xueshu yantaohui lunwenji* 2004 台北學國際學術研討會論文集 (Collected essays from the 2004 International Conference on Taipei Studies), ed. Liao Hsien-Hao and Lin Chiu-Fan (Taipei: Taibei wenhua ju, 2006), 113–26.

10. For an illuminating account of the *yōkai* culture in manga and anime, see Michael Dylan Foster's books, *Pandemonium and Parade: Japanese Monsters and the Culture of Yōkai* (Berkeley: University of California Press, 2008), 160–203; *The Book of Yōkai: Mysterious Creatures of Japanese Folklore* (Berkeley: University of California Press, 2010), 61–73.

In addition to a common narrative premise, both *Grandma* and *Hanada* share indelible links to the Taiwanese language and culture. With the Taiwanese grandmother at the narrative center, a substantial part of the dialogue in *Grandma* is delivered in her native language. *Hanada* came with both Mandarin and Taiwanese dubs, but it was the latter that enjoyed wide popularity throughout its airtime. Thus both the film and television series tap into the robust cultural energies found in the local language, itself saturated with expressions borrowed from the folk religion. *Hanada* is often credited for popularizing the Taiwanese term *mô-sîn-á* 魔神仔—roughly equivalent to ghosts but especially akin to goblins, elves, or fairies in Western folklore—which became broadly used in everyday language. *Mô-sîn-á* has ambiguous origins still debated among historians, linguists, and anthropologists. A fascinating case study in etymology, *mô-sîn-á* suggests possible origins from various sources, from the Daoist ghost *bû-siông* 無常, who ushers the dead into the underworld, to the state of listlessness and delirium (*bô-sîn* 無神) triggered by the grim reaper, who leads one astray and drains one's soul away; from the monstrous creatures hiding in the mountains, *mô-sîn* 魍神 to those that "whip away" one's spirit, *bong-sîn* 摸神; from the Dutch word for shadow and ghost (*schim*) to the badger-like creature in Japanese folk legends (*mujina*).[11] The term contains in itself a rich array of transcultural references embedded within Taiwan's layered colonial histories. Ever shapeshifting in language and image, *mô-sîn-á* also befits animation's penchant for metamorphosis and plasticity—qualities that Sergei Eisenstein christened *the plasmatic*, characterized by him as a "rejection of once and forever allotted form, freedom from ossification, the ability to dynamically assume any form."[12]

As the anthropologist of religion Lin Mei-Rong reminds us, although people usually use *mô-sîn-á* and ghost interchangeably as if they meant the same thing, *mô-sîn-á* should in fact be distinguished from ghosts in terms of appearance, origination, and the locations they are often found. In essence, Lin notes, *mô-sîn-á* designates species of mountain sprites and water demons (*shanjing shuiguai* 山精水怪). In local Taiwanese accounts,

11. Lin Mei-Rong and Li Chia-Kai, *Mô-sîn-á de renleixue xiangxiang* 魔神仔的人類學想像 (The anthropological imagination of *mô-sîn-á*) (Taipei: Wunan, 2014), 10–13.

12. Sergei Eisenstein, *Eisenstein on Disney*, ed. Jay Leyda, trans. Alan Upchurch (London: Methuen, 1988), 21.

a *mô-sîn-á* appears short and tiny, sometimes looking like a child and at other times showing up in the guise of a woman; it has the power to bewitch and beguile, putting one under its malicious spell and thereby making one lost in the mountains or drowned in waters.[13] Not so much resembling the phantom-looking ghost, which is what humans are expected to become after death, *mô-sîn-á* appears earthbound and concretely embodied. Its creaturely appearance ties it to specific geographical locales and suggests a proximity to animals and the animalistic. In between ghosts, goblins, and gods, *mô-sîn-á* traverses an uncertain ontological ground encompassing both ill-intentioned demons as well as the spirit of animals, mountains, trees, rocks, water, and so forth. Distilling recurring motifs from *mô-sîn-á* folktales, Lin discerns traces of humans' pre-civilizational settlement in the jungles.[14] Following Lin's insight, I see these traces as pointing toward residual connections with ancient animist beliefs, whose presence nonetheless obtains in many modern-day practices. Because of its affinities to nature as well as rich implications for human-environment interaction, *mô-sîn-á* folklore, as one author puts it, displays an "environmental thinking and geographical conception" on the one hand, and the formation of an "animist actor network" on the other.[15] Identifying a *mô-sîn-á*, one often also evokes a concrete milieu in which it is embedded.

Along his adventure, the young protagonist Dou Dou in *Grandma* acquires the ability to see paranormal beings, in turn developing special bonds with a few *mô-sîn-á* friends. Distinguished from the dark, transparent, and anonymous ghosts often arriving in numbers, these *mô-sîn-á* characters appear fully fleshed, further endowed with distinct personalities

13. Lin Mei-Rong 林美容, *Taiwan guizaigu: Cong minsu kanjian Taiwanren de mingjie xiangxiang* 台灣鬼仔古：從民俗看見台灣人的冥界想像 (Taiwan ghost stories: Taiwanese imagination of the underworld in folk traditions) (Taipei: Yuexiong, 2017), 1.

14. Wang Yizhen 王怡蓁, "*Mô-sîn-á*, guigushi, kanjian renmen de beihuan lihe" 魔神仔，鬼故事，看見人們的悲歡離合 (Seeing people's joy and sorrow, parting and reunion in *mô-sîn-á* and ghost stories), *Yan zhi you wu* 研之有悟 (Researchyowu), July 13, 2018, https://research.sinica.edu.tw/lin-mei-rong-folklore-mosina-ghost-taiwan.

15. Liang Ting-Yu 梁廷毓, "Lun 'jingguai' yu '*mô-sîn-á*' chuanwen zhong de shengtai siwei yu shenti jiexian" 論"精怪"與"魔神仔"傳聞中的生態思維與身體界限 (A study of the ecological thinking and body limits in elf and *mô-sîn-á* folklore), *Taiwan wenxue yanjiu xuebao* 台灣文學研究學報 (Journal of Taiwan literary studies) 31 (2020): 53–72, 59, 68.

and individuality. They are tied to specific milieus that call attention to the film's setting in Keelung, a major port city in northeastern Taiwan. An enormous whale that died from being stranded on the beach indexes the oceanic environment. A squashed snake, a roadkill victim, alludes to the transport infrastructure built for commuting between the port and the capital city (at the end of the film, the snake comically dies a second death, this time run over by Dou Dou's mother driving the family from the city to Grandma's). Kuro, Grandma's black cat later possessed by a fugitive evil spirit, is associated with the discarded shipyard originally constructed for transporting and storing coal during the Japanese colonial era. Although it would be a bit of a stretch to maintain, which some critics do, that the film shows an awareness of environmental damage through these *mô-sîn-á* characters, there is indeed some indication of the ecological dimension inherent in the film's dramatized human–nonhuman relations that this chapter wishes to explore. To better qualify these relations, which I characterize as animistic, I bring together anthropological theories, religious practices, and animation depictions to conjure forth an animated vision—an ecopolitical insight and a novel way of observing the world—that the film trains its protagonists and spectators alike to acquire.

The Animated Vision

In her study of animation culture in twenty-first-century Taiwan, cultural anthropologist Teri Silvio argues that as we entered the new century, we have also transitioned from the age of performance to that of animation. This is evidenced not only by the ubiquity of cartoon characters in everyday life in East Asia and beyond, but also by the pervasive animated mascots, vinyl figurines, plush toys, and brand logos owned by various businesses ranging from banks, life insurance companies, national postal service, convenience stores, to, indeed, temples and other venues of religious worship.[16] Animation, in other words, has turned into a driving force of corporatized social relations shaped largely within the service industry. Silvio's insight lies in her contention that animation is not merely a cultural

16. Teri Silvio, *Puppets, Gods, and Brands: Theorizing the Age of Animation from Taiwan* (Honolulu: Hawai'i University Press, 2019), 39.

phenomenon of the digital age, but more importantly, can be formulated as a method by which to understand contemporary social relations straddling larger categories of nature and technology, the local and the global, real and virtual, human and nonhuman. If the age of performance focused a great deal on self-identity and self-expression through repeated embodiment and mimesis (what Silvio terms "the construction of social selves"), animation allows an engagement with the nonhuman through acts of "creation, perception, and interaction" (what she terms "the construction of social others").[17] This reorientation develops in tandem with new questions alongside emergent disciplines in the first decades of the millennium. Emerging across the humanities and social sciences, these questions and topics include human–nonhuman relations and environmental justice, artificial intelligence and new materialism, indigeneity and animism.[18] As a medium germane to these topics and fields, animation in the age of animation doubles as a site where a host of nonhuman characters including animals, toys, cyborgs, machines, monsters, and ghosts acquire heightened visibility, allowing novel imaginations of an ecology humans share with their more-than-human others.

To better qualify animation vis-à-vis performance, Silvio defines the act of animation as the "*projection* of qualities perceived as human . . . outside the self and into the sensory environment through acts of creation, perception, and interaction." This she sets in contrast to performance's "*introjection* of qualities from exterior models and the expression of those qualities through the medium of the body" (emphasis added).[19] Such a definition of animation, however, tends to assume an original site of subject position, which projects its perceptual content defined as human onto an external object defined as nonhuman. This projectionism unwittingly sets up a dichotomy between self and other, subject and object, human and nonhuman along a unidirectional axis designating here and there, with the subject remaining the presupposed point of reference. Because many of Silvio's case studies involve not just the animation of puppets and figurines but also animist interactions with them, they gesture toward the entwinement of and ultimate slippage between animation and animism, both characterized by an

17. Silvio, *Puppets, Gods, and Brands*, 18–19.

18. Silvio, *Puppets, Gods, and Brands*, 36.

19. Silvio, *Puppets, Gods, and Brands*, 18–19.

investment of vitality or life force in nonhuman beings. Methodologically grounded in anthropology, Silvio's innovative framework stands to benefit from a cross-referencing of key concepts raised in so-called new animism studies emerging within the field.

Gathering momentum around the same time that the paradigm shift from performance to animation delineated by Silvio took place, new animism launched at the turn of the millennium a revisionist study of animist worldviews found in non-Western, nonmodernist tribal societies. Pushing back against an evolutionist evaluation of animist cultures by the preceding generations of anthropologists, scholars such as Nurit Bird-David, Tim Ingold, Eduardo Viveiros de Castro, and Philippe Descola attempted to retheorize these cultures' inherent ways of perceiving and interacting with the environment, where nuanced modes of engagement eschew rigid bifurcations between subject and object, nature and culture, human and animal.[20] Descola, for instance, famously constructs a fourfold model of ontology, where he defines animism as "a continuity of souls and a discontinuity of bodies."[21] According to this formulation, when an observer encounters an animated being, she would recognize it as having a similar interiority but a different physicality. Basing her observations in the Nayaka hunter-gatherer societies in South India, Bird-David for her part proposes a "relational epistemology," where hunter-gatherers "do not dichotomize other beings vis-à-vis themselves but regard them, while differentiated, as nested within each other."[22] This relational mode draws on a specific notion of personhood attributed to humans and nonhumans alike, resulting in a perception of *we-ness* populated by numerous human persons, animal persons, stone persons, hill persons, wind persons, and so forth. Instead of invoking the notion of the bounded individual, person-

20. See, for example, Nurit Bird-David, "'Animism' Revisited: Personhood, Environment, and Relational Epistemology," *Current Anthropology* 40, no. S1 (1999): S67–91; Tim Ingold, *The Perception of the Environment: Essays on Livelihood, Dwelling and Skill* (London: Routledge, 2000); Eduardo Viveiros de Castro, "Cosmological Deixis and Amerindian Perspectivism," *Journal of the Royal Anthropological Institute* 4 (1998): 469–88; Philippe Descola, *Beyond Nature and Culture*, trans. Janet Lloyd (Chicago: University of Chicago Press: 2013).

21. Philippe Descola, "Beyond Nature and Culture," in *The Handbook of Contemporary Animism*, ed. Graham Harvey (London: Routledge, 2014), 79.

22. Bird-David, "'Animism' Revisited," S73.

hood entails an understanding of the *dividual*—a term Bird-David borrowed from Marilyn Strathern in her study of Melanesian cultures—as divisible and transformable into larger or smaller units of relations. If dividual is defined as "a person constitutive of relations," its verb, to "dividuate," means to be reflexively attentive to the relations formed around dividual persons: "When I individuate a human being I am conscious of her 'in herself'; when I dividuate her I am conscious of how she relates with me."[23] In perceiving a person as "one whom we share with" rather than one who is, the process of dividuation prioritizes relationality, which precedes the terms being related.

Seen in this light, the dichotomized, unidirectional projection assumed in Silvio's model of animation can be reoriented as nested relations constitutive of many back-and-forth recognitions between mutually engaging persons without holding fast to a presupposed subject content.[24] These multivalent interactions and reciprocal engagements are themselves evidenced in Silvio's case study of the animation of folk religion deities in the form of vinyl figurines, where collectors animate but are in turn animated—in the sense of feeling comforted, buoyed, healed, and revitalized—by the figurines.[25] Echoing Bird-David's relational epistemology, Silvio notes how some of her interviewees attribute their special ties with the figurines to "relational destiny," her apt translation of the untranslatable Chinese term *yuanfen* 緣分.[26]

Bird-David further observes that in Nayaka culture, people commonly dividuate each other as kin and relatives. In everyday interaction, they address each other by kinship terms regardless of the existence of blood relations, across species boundaries. Relations in their understanding are defined more via recurring social practices such as sharing and visiting than by descent or genealogy. In her recent writings, Bird-David gave up altogether the analytical concept of personhood for its "common associations with a static, interior identity."[27] Instead, she proposes "relatives" as an "a-priori plural" and geographically bounded concept that is humbler in

23. Bird-David, "'Animism' Revisited," S72.

24. Bird-David, "'Animism' Revisited," S73.

25. See Silvio, *Puppets, Gods, and Brands*, chap. 3.

26. Silvio, *Puppets, Gods, and Brands*, 112–16.

27. Isabel Laack, "The New Animism and Its Challenges to the Study of Religion," *Method and Theory in the Study of Religion* 32 (2020): 123.

scale but equally able to assemble humans and nonhumans, who in living together or having dealings with each other in a delimited locale constitute each other as relatable.[28] Devoid of connotations of consanguinity, the language of relatives adopted by the Nayaka people can also be found in the traditional view of ghosts in Taiwan. There, ghosts who are not bound by familial ties—that is, who are not properly venerated or remembered by their offspring, otherwise known as lonesome spirits and stray ghosts (*guhun yegui* 孤魂野鬼)—are given the alias good brothers (*hó-hiann-tī* 好兄弟). Although the term is used euphemistically to avoid addressing ghosts explicitly, it also functions as a speech act, on whose invocation humans are bound ethically to certain social obligations toward its addressees. During the Ghost Month, for example, when the spirits of the dead are set free from the underworld, it is incumbent on humans to feast the wandering *hó-hiann-tī* ghosts and to host a variety of rituals—releasing water lanterns, organizing pole-climbing competitions, conducting praying ceremonies—to help usher them into the world of reincarnation.[29]

Set during the Ghost Month, *Grandma* dramatizes this imperative of "making kin" in animist societies, of entering into a relational field so that its human protagonists can dividuate with the wandering spirits, be they a *hó-hiann-tī* or a *mô-sîn-á*. By way of Silvio's and Bird-David's theorization of animation and animism, one can also discern the fundamental differences setting apart *Coco* and *Grandma*, both of which portray ghostly encounters during the festival of the dead from the perspective of a boy despite the distinct practices and worldviews implied in each context. Whereas in *Coco*, young Miguel is assisted by the ghosts of his family members to reconstruct the family's genealogy, in *Grandma*, Dou Dou develops horizontal lines of dividuation with lost and lonesome spirits he chances upon in his vicinity. If *Coco* is charged with an impulse to track down the family's patriarchal origin so as to ascertain its protagonist's raison-d'être, *Grandma*, in the absence of a fatherly figure, fabricates a relational web of

28. Nurit Bird-David, "Persons or Relatives? Animistic Scales of Practice and Imagination," in *Rethinking Relations and Animism: Personhood and Materiality*, eds. Miguel Astor-Aguilera and Graham Harvey (Abingdon, UK: Routledge, 2018), 25–34.

29. For a detailed account of these rituals, see Lin Fu-shih 林富士, *Guhun yu guixiong de shijie: Bei Taiwan de ligui xinyang* 孤魂與鬼雄的世界：北台灣的厲鬼信仰 (The world of lonesome spirits and ghost heroes: Religious beliefs of malicious spirits in northern Taiwan) (Taipei: Xinbeishi wenhua ju, 1995), 178–99.

dividual persons—enfolding humans, animals, and spirits—through the mediumship of the psychic granny. Released two decades after *Grandma*, *Coco* nonetheless fits Silvio's performance paradigm better for its earnest exploration of self-identity through repeated staging of Miguel's musical talent. *Grandma*, on the other hand, animates relations both familial and nonfamilial; in approaching the nonfamilial through the familial while redefining the familial as replete with the nonfamilial, the film introduces themes of animism into the emergent paradigm of animation.

Returning to fin-de-siècle Taiwan, one finds that a dominant theme in film at this historical moment is the dissolution of sociofamilial ties against the gloomy backdrop of global capitalism. Take Tsai Ming-liang 蔡明亮, the filmmaker known for his fondness for ghosts and who used to apprentice under Wang Shau-Di 王小棣, the director of *Grandma*. In Tsai's feature films made around the turn of the millennium, including *The River* (*Heliu* 河流, 1997), *The Hole* (*Dong* 洞, 1998), *What Time Is It There?* and *Goodbye, Dragon Inn*, scholars detect an "uncomfortable stripping away of forms of sociality" that especially takes the heteronormative nuclear family as a target of relentless deconstruction.[30] In these films, the household is a bare placeholder of defunct familial relations that approximates, in the words of Rey Chow, an "archaeological find, its members being the walking exhibits of a collective order that has survived in the form of ruins."[31] Even a film such as Edward Yang's 楊德昌 *Yi Yi* (一一, 2000), which features a tight-knit family across three generations, poignantly follows each of its members' gradual isolation and alienation. From the outset, *Grandma* echoes its contemporaries in depicting a scenario of family dissonance: Dou Dou is raised in a single-parent family; his father, working abroad, has rarely been around; his mother has fallen out with her mother since marrying a man her mother doesn't approve of; Dou Dou is therefore estranged from Grandma, whom he detests in their first encounter—urged by the possessed Kuro, he even plans to sell Grandma to a recycle peddler. Yet against this modernist premise of alienated and commodified social relations, the film soon settles into a different mode, wherein kinship ties proliferate and thrive on the underlying scenario of voided sociality. In

30. Jean Ma, *Melancholy Drift: Marking Time in Chinese Cinema* (Hong Kong: Hong Kong University Press, 2010), 106.

31. Rey Chow, *Sentimental Fabulations, Contemporary Chinese Films: Attachment in the Age of Global Visibility* (New York: Columbia University Press, 2007), 188.

bonding vertically with Grandma and relating horizontally to other human, animal, and ghost relatives, Dou Dou's dividuation unleashes a potential that remains untapped in contemporary New Cinema works. Arguably, it is the medium of animation, with its animistic proclivity, that fosters a fertile ground where kinship relations abound. To dividuate, Dou Dou acquires what I call an animated vision that mirrors animation's method of enlivening nonhuman characters.

Halfway into the film, Dou Dou learns that if he gathers Grandma's tears and applies them to his eyes, he will be able to see the paranormal beings only Grandma and their neighbor Ah-Min, a kindhearted teenage boy, can see. Situated near the narrative center, Dou Dou's acquisition of clairvoyance ushers into the second half of the film a fantastic world teeming with nonhuman persons. With their penchant for transformation and supernatural skills, these nonhuman persons constitute a site where animation's medium specificity—associated with the elastic, plastic, and plasmatic—is most vividly showcased. These include the whale mentioned earlier, who laboriously trains with Ah-Min to learn how to walk on its tail. Just as it is about to stumble, it miraculously soars into the sky, floating and gliding with ease and elegance. These flying scenes call to mind what Thomas Lamarre calls animetism in his discussion of Miyazaki Hayao's films, in which protagonists share an inclination to fly, float, and glide, special skills that echo the motion of sliding planes in open compositing animation.[32] There is also the snake, nicknamed Flatty, whose squashed but springy body, shaped as such due to a road accident, embodies the squash-and-stretch technique of animation. Shy little girl Apple appears with a doll, which talks on behalf of its owner. Because Apple is frightened by Niutou 牛頭 and Mamian 馬面, the ox-headed and horse-faced demons in charge of bringing the dead to the underworld, by the end of the film, the two couriers from hell appear in cutified miniature form to escort Apple (fig. 5.2). In addition to many other anonymous stray ghosts that take on numerous guises—best represented by the bedeviled Kuro, who devours fellow ghosts and grows incredibly large, as well as the starved spirits whose forms morph as they gorge on the feast prepared for them—the film flourishes in a stylistic display of phantasmatic plasmaticity, exhibiting animation's affinity with shapeshifting things (fig. 5.3).

32. Thomas Lamarre, *The Anime Machine: A Media Theory of Animation* (Minneapolis: University of Minnesota Press, 2009), 3–100.

FIGURE 5.2. The ox-headed and horse-faced demons appear in cutified miniature form to escort Apple, in *Grandma and Her Ghosts* (1998). Courtesy of Ricefilm International Co. Ltd.

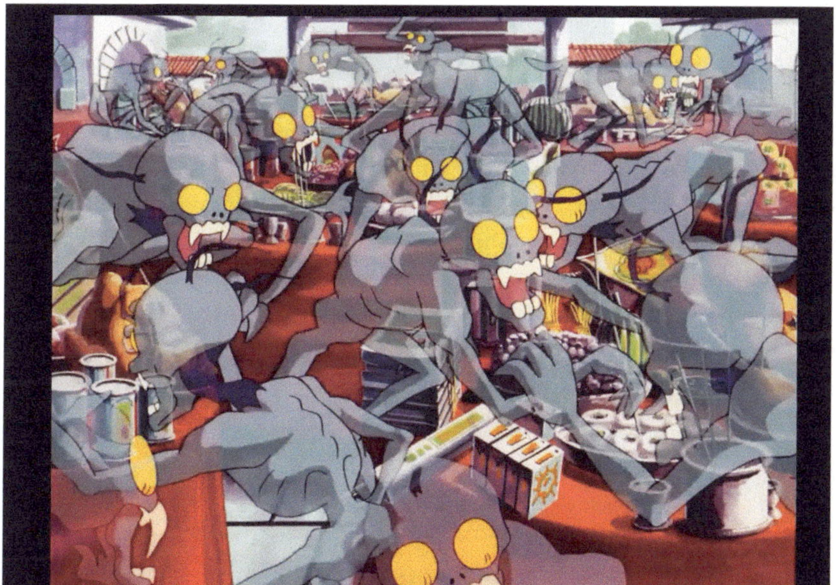

FIGURE 5.3. Masses of ghosts feast during the Ghost Festival, in *Grandma and Her Ghosts* (1998). Courtesy of Ricefilm International Co. Ltd.

In Lamarre's discussion, he contrasts Miyazaki's animetism with what he calls cinematism. If cinematism entails speedy movements into depth endowed with a self-centric *ballistic vision*, animetism responds by creating a different body suspended between sky and earth as if between layers of the animated image, at once open to and grounded in the technological world.[33] Open compositing, in other words, "allows for a vision of less violent and hierarchical interaction between self and environment, the human and the nonhuman."[34] Dou Dou's animated vision is in concert with this animetic worldview introduced by open compositing, the method the animators of *Grandma* adopted.[35] This vision not only enables its possessor to see the unseeable spirits left out in the interstices between worlds, but also encourages the seer to cultivate a relationship with them. When Dou Dou asks Ah-Min about his ability to see his whale friend, Ah-Min replies that it is a fate he embraces, "since I'm able to see, I must also be able to help." As Ah-Min speaks, we see that Dou Dou takes out the bottle containing Grandma's tears and contemplates it. As instructed by Kuro, once he collects three drops of Grandma's tears, he will be able to sell her away. Ah-Min's words, however, suggest a different strategy that puts these tears to an alternate use: if applying them means gaining the ability to see the unseeable beings, this vision comes with a binding condition that requires the seer to also see the demands made by these beings. Indeed, in the film as in real religious practices, ghost persons often act more like subjects who pose a demand to which humans must take care to respond: the whale wishes to learn to walk; the girl needs assistance in overcoming her fear of Niutou and Mamian; Flatty implores Dou Dou to help it grab food at the Ghost Festival, because its tiny body cannot possibly compete with other aggressive ghosts. As Grandma's tears equip Dou Dou with a fresh pair of eyes, the purpose of these tears shifts from the original "transacting away" to an ethical "including in," "bonding with," and "answering to." In other words, Dou Dou's animated vision does not

33. Lamarre, *The Anime Machine*, 73–75.

34. Silvio, *Puppets, Gods, and Brands*, 41.

35. For a quick glimpse of the film's production process, see the interview with the animator Mai Renjie in Huang Po-ta, "Xingsu *Mofa ama* de Mai Renjie" 形塑"魔法阿媽"的麥人杰 (Mai Renjie, who shapes *Grandma and Her Ghosts*), in *Mofa ama: Wo ba ama bian katong le*, 149–58.

merely visualize the ghosts as representable entities; more importantly, it animates the relations sustained between him and the ghosts. Seeing is hence seeing not just the human, animal, and ghost persons per se, but also the relations that implicate the viewer within. Whereas the ballistic vision, which Lamarre invokes via Paul Virilio, signals the intensification of perspectivalism that further entrenches the subject–object dichotomy, Dou Dou's animated vision sees by way of ecology, ascribing subjectivity and energies to the seen while forming mutual relations that assist in each other's flourishing.

Like the scale-sensitive view Bird-David proposes in her discussion of animist relatives, in *Grandma*, the boundaries within which human and nonhuman persons dividuate one another are fairly limited. This is evidenced in the final showdown scene with Kuro. Having been incapacitated by Kuro in an accident, the hospitalized Grandma swaps bodies with her pet dog Shiro and arrives in the form of the dog to help Dou Dou and Ah-Min defeat Kuro. Grandma asks Dou Dou to draw a circle on the ground in hopes of confining Kuro within the sphere of her spell. However, this act of marking the boundary does not so much hem Kuro in—it soon proves futile because the demon easily breaks free—as it marks the limits for those identified as relatives regarding where their kinship dividuation stops. If the animist ecology forged by Dou Dou's animated vision nurtures the bonds with fellow dividual persons, the delimiting circle turns this ethical openness into a moral enclosure, distinguishing malicious demons from benign *mô-sîn-á* so as to preempt the former's entrance into the contact zone, the zone of relationality. In so doing, *hó-hiann-tī* as good brothers is interpreted in a moralistic vein—good or *hó* here means benevolent, conducive, or advantageous rather than the neutral connotations of proximity and a high degree of relatability. Crucially, at the borders of the contact zone, it is the psychic granny who functions as a gatekeeper of dividual relations, which at her behest fold back on themselves to form a homogenous world defined in terms of the benevolent kin. As well as introducing the possibilities of dividuating with nonhuman persons, her mediumship hence also calls attention to the limits of such encounters. Grandma's psychic mediumship, in other words, marks its own limits.

Psychic Grannies, Media Theorists

Insofar as it opens up a contact zone while drawing that zone into enclosure, the mediumistic career of the psychic granny functions like a double-edged sword with high sociopolitical stakes. The relations formed by way of the animated vision promise an encounter with and inclusion of nonhuman persons capable of reorienting kinship relations, in turn redefining what it means to be family. Yet, ultimately, the narrative arc of *Grandma* is most intent on tracing the increasing attachment of Dou Dou to Grandma. They are then joined by Dou Dou's parents to make for a traditional happy ending. In the final reunion scene, three generations gather in the same frame. With the father back in the picture, Mother reconciled with Grandma, and the Ghost Month drawing to a close, the haunted kinship relations give way to the norm of blood relatives. With her commanding power as a narrative engine, the psychic granny thus straddles two types of narrative operations, namely, the animational and the performative. On the one hand, she spins a centrifugal relational web forging ties with the animated others; on the other, her mediumship gears toward a centripetal movement that essentializes the consanguineous family, thereby reinstating its social normativity.

In many ways, this dual operation of the psychic granny is vividly present in my personal family history. As the matriarch of a family extending four generations, my grandmother, who assumed the profession of a shamaness in the late 1970s, continues to define what it means to be family for us.[36] Here I turn to an ethnographic mode of writing to draw out some connections between the film and the practice of my grandmother, both

36. In Taiwan, the number of shamans grew rapidly in the mid- and late 1980s. As anthropologist Hu Tai-li's study shows, this history has much to do with the sudden popularity of a form of lottery called *dajiale* 大家樂 around the same period. The *dajiale* craze prompted buyers to seek winning numbers from gods, ghosts, and even objects like stones and trees. Naturally, these buyers turned to shamans and priests for inspiration. See Hu Tai-li 胡台麗, "Shen, gui yu dutu: 'Dajiale' duxi fanying zhi minsu xinyang" 神, 鬼與賭徒: "大家樂" 賭戲反映之民俗信仰 (Gods, ghosts, and gamblers: Folk religion as reflected in the "Dajiale" gambling), in *Dierjie guoji hanxue huiyi lunwenji: Minsu yu wenhua zu* 第二屆國際漢學會議論文集: 民俗與文化組 (Collected essays from the Second International Conference on Sinology: Volume of ethnology and culture) (Taipei: Academia Sinica, 1989), 125–78.

of which are rooted in the fertile soil of folk religious culture. Called a *tâng-ki* 童乩 in Taiwanese, a shaman or spirit medium is known for a variety of skills including healing, divination, exorcism, communication with the dead, and channeling divine messages.[37] The profession of a *tâng-ki* is rather male-dominant, and so my grandmother's experience warrants some consideration.[38] In presenting the psychic granny as a close family member, my goal is to show the life and work of a rural shamaness beyond cartoon fictionalization, to approach her experience and techniques, aesthetics and politics, as historically grounded, and, through her technical operation embedded in a mytho-religious system, to grapple with the theoretical potential such a figure might have in store for film and media scholars. In weaving history with theory, personal anecdotes with academic accounts, I aim to conceptualize the psychic granny as embodying many roles, such as an ethnographic figure, an animating medium, a set of cultural techniques, and—because of her ability to mobilize and reorient media theories around her—a media theorist.

As an animating medium, Grandma's recent (summer 2021) encounter with a stray cat is worth some remarks. Merely a few months old, the kitten was abandoned by her mother somewhere near Grandma's. Out of survival instinct, the kitten ingeniously found her way to Grandma's backyard and had sheltered there since. In the first few phone calls with Grandma that summer, we heard the kitten's faint meowing in the background and asked Grandma about it. Grandma sounded annoyed, expressing her wish to get rid of the kitten because, in folk belief, cats are deemed ominous—often associated with the *yin* energy, prone to be possessed by malicious spirits, rumored to own several lives as expressed in the idiom *jiuming guaimao* 九命怪貓 (strange cat with nine lives). (As should be obvious, these occultic associations are the main source for featuring the bewitched Kuro as an antagonist in *Grandma*.) A few weeks later, however, we learned that the

37. For an etymological tracing of the term *tâng-ki* in addition to what the role of a *tâng-ki* entails, see Lin Fu-shih, *Guhun yu guixiong de shijie*, 159–78.

38. For a discussion of shamanism in China from a gender perspective, see Mayfair Yang, "Shamanism and Spirit Possession in Chinese Modernity: Some Preliminary Reflections on a Gendered Religiosity of the Body," *Review of Religion and Chinese Society* 2 (2015): 51–86. See also Davide Torri and Sophie Roche, eds., *The Shamaness in Asia: Gender, Religion and the State* (New York: Routledge, 2021).

kitten, now given the name Manni (transliteration of Money), had been adopted by Grandma. What changed her mind? According to Grandma, it was all because of a dream. In it, she saw Manni walking toward her with golden, shimmering feet. It soon dawned upon Grandma that Manni was a reincarnation of Hu Yeh 虎爺, a lower-ranking Daoist deity who resembles a tiger and whose icon is often placed underneath an altar. Believed to be sent to accompany and guard Grandma, Manni therefore stayed as kin, a relative in the sense of being in proximity, coliving, and interdependent, animated by the spirit of a deity.

At other times, Grandma assumes the role of a more traditional matriarch, dictating family business according to her will. This she often does during her consultation sessions. In these sessions, Grandma performs what is known as *lóh-tuânn* 落壇 (descending to the altar), where she presides over the altar and lets herself be possessed by the family deity, answering questions from family members and other worshippers on behalf of the deity. It is on these occasions that Grandma, speaking in trance as an authoritative immortal while surrounded by puffs of incense smoke, gives admonitions that seem to accord with her own wishes—telling one of her sons-in-law not to sell a family house; advising an uncle and his wife to bear another child after two consecutive daughters, as this time a boy was guaranteed (and it indeed was); or asking me to prioritize producing progeny for the family rather than burying my head in books all day. In trying to instruct us on domestic affairs, Grandma shifts from the animational to a more performative mode of mediumship. Here, Grandma's performance recalls what anthropologist Maurice Godelier once called the ventriloquist's dummy in his study of kinship structures. As ventriloquist's dummies, kinship members go about practicing and settling family matters—such as marriage, reproduction, and inheritance—that appropriate initially non-kinship-specific contents from larger socioeconomic, political, and religious structures. In Grandma's case, her consultations constitute a primary locus where social norms such as a patriarchal notion of gender become attached to, reproduced, and sedimented as family relations.[39] One may hence compare Grandma's mediumship not with a vacuous vessel channeling god's messages, but with a semi-subject

39. Maurice Godelier, *The Metamorphoses of Kinship*, trans. Nora Scott (New York: Verso, 2011).

who in surreptitiously voicing herself becomes someone else's dummy twice. Ultimately it is the heteropatriarchal norm that speaks via family deity via Grandma.

Seen in this light, the practice of the psychic granny, in addition to being animational and performative, is also political. This political dimension of female spirit mediumship has attracted some attention from a cultural studies perspective across Eastern and Western contexts, which celebrates the subversive potential of female mediumship. In his classic study of female mediums in nineteenth-century American spiritualism, for instance, Jeffrey Sconce notes how female mediums "in a state of mediumistic trance . . . were able to comment on a variety of contemporary social issues of concern to women, including marital equality, reproductive rights, and universal suffrage."[40] This view echoes I. M. Lewis's earlier account of how spirit possession staged by women expresses forms of protestation in male-dominated societies.[41] Based on her fieldwork in Wenzhou, China, Mayfair Yang further calls attention to the shamaness's body. As Yang observes, compared with the male shamanic bodies that endure through a long history of control and censure in modern China, the female ones are relatively sheltered from direct discipline by the state in either political or economic registers. This niche occupancy of the domestic abode renders their bodies more sensitive, suggestible, and susceptible to ancestor and divine callings.[42] As I have recounted, Grandma's spirit mediumship is conformist rather than transgressive relative to the status quo. Her body does not so much shelter from the outside world as it actively partakes in worldly fluctuations: she can usually be found sitting in front of the altar in her house with doors wide open, welcoming those in need of her service. To get at the political dimension of Grandma's mediumship, I therefore suggest that gender per se, because of its complicity with the patriarchal sociofamilial system, might not be the most productive site of interrogation. Instead, I turn to techniques—especially their cosmological attributes manifest in embodied gender terms—as a more promising entry point.

40. Jeffrey Sconce, *Haunted Media: Electronic Presence from Telegraphy to Television* (Durham, NC: Duke University Press, 2000), 12.

41. I. M. Lewis, *Ecstatic Religion: A Study of Shamanism and Spirit Possession* (London: Routledge, 2003).

42. Yang, "Shamanism and Spirit Possession."

Rather than a domestically ensconced individual, Grandma acts more like a composite of techniques employed to hold a family and community together: children who have trouble sleeping or wail for no reason—believed to have a piece of their soul scared away by unclean things—are brought to her for a *siu-kiann* 收驚 (putting away scare) session in order to bring back and assuage the wayward piece; some followers come for talismans to hang in vehicles, tuck under pillows, or place on children's desks for protection and blessing; others wish to communicate with their dearly departed. On each of these occasions, Grandma can be spotted with some kind of tools, further highlighting her technical presence—waving a handful of incense sticks, casting moon blocks, wielding a writing brush, or reading messages from a cup of rice grains. Annually, residents of Grandma's rural town attend a series of rituals lasting from day to night to celebrate the family deity's birthday. On this day, she would perform what a *tâng-ki* is best known for: shaking and wobbling violently in a state of trance, Grandma would self-lacerate with a variety of weapons including a sword, a mace, a sawtooth spear, and more (fig. 5.4). Perhaps psychic grannies bear an ontological relationship with their tools: as historian of religion Liu Jih-wann notes, inherent in the name *tâng-ki* is the character *ki* 乩 that means the tools and techniques of divination.[43] These techniques, another historian of religion Lin Fu-shih reminds us, cannot be viewed separately from techne or artistic creation—music, dance, medicine, astrology, divination—thought to have originated from and coevolved with shamanism in ancient Chinese civilization.[44]

With her close tie to techniques and techne, the psychic granny provides a unique perspective on a central topic discussed among contemporary film and media theorists. Much of the discussion revolves around the question of technology, of how an alternative relation to it can foster a future free of bifurcations imposed by Western philosophy between culture and nature, human and nonhuman, exploiter and exploited.[45] Among the

43. Quoted in Lin Fu-shih, *Guhun yu guixiong de shijie*, 160.

44. Lin Fu-shih, *Guhun yu guixiong de shijie*, 165.

45. A foundational text to which this group of work often refers is Martin Heidegger, "The Question Concerning Technology," in *The Question Concerning Technology and Other Essays*, trans. W. Lovitt (New York: Garland, 1977), 3–35. See also Bernard Stiegler, *Technics and Time, 1: The Fault of Epimetheus*, trans. Richard Beardsworth and George Collins (Stanford, CA: Stanford University Press, 1998).

FIGURE 5.4. Grandma performs self-laceration during an annual celebration of the family deity's birthday. Photo by the author.

scholars writing on this topic, Yuk Hui proposes the concept of *cosmotechnics* that aims to unearth the rich cosmological system behind the historical development of technics. Technics, as Hui illustrates, never develops in a void: "Scientific and technical thinking emerges under cosmological conditions that are expressed in the relations between humans and their milieus."[46] Just as milieu varies, so one needs to adopt a milieu-specific understanding of technics that refutes its pretense of universal applicability.[47] As scholars have shown, instances of cosmotechnics can be gleaned from the view of the body as mapped onto cosmology in Chinese medicine; the Amazonian hunter-gatherer's perception of the environment; the

46. Yuk Hui, *The Question Concerning Technology: An Essay in Cosmotechnics* (Falmouth, UK: Urbanomic, 2016), 18.

47. I borrow the term milieu-specific from Melody Jue, who elaborates on the concept in the introduction to her *Wild Blue Media: Thinking Through Seawater* (Durham, NC: Duke University Press, 2020).

"co-naturality between human network and natural geography" found in media infrastructures such as the television antenna; and the entanglement of urban architecture, climate, and feng shui in East Asia.[48] Grandma's technics, too, are attuned to a cosmological order that informs much of her practice. In instructing us to face our furniture in certain directions so as not to disrupt the circulation of *qi*, or to adopt a vegetarian diet according to the lunar calendar as dictated by Buddhist precepts and principles of Chinese medicine, Grandma shows how much she and her fellow shamans, priests, and geomancers learn to adjust their daily behavior to the resonance between self and world, thereby coproducing a moral cosmology.

Paralleling the rethinking of technology and cosmology in media studies in recent years is a resurgence of interest in mythology in the humanities. Scholars turn to mythological figures and their worldviews in hopes of excavating alternative modes of thinking to dominant discourses of gender, ethics, media technology, and the Anthropocene. Yet be it Judith Butler's Antigone or Bruno Latour's Gaia, Donna Haraway's Medusa or Alexander Galloway's Hermes, Iris, and the Furies, the newly nominated mortals and immortals point rather inadequately to a single origin in Greek mythology as if it had a universal purchase.[49] In the context of film studies' institutional

48. Gilbert Simondon quoted in Hui, *The Question Concerning Technology*, 22. Hui draws on Simondon's example of the television antenna to illustrate the notion of cosmotechnics. For the case of Chinese medicine, see Shigehisa Kuriyama, "The Imagination of the Body and the History of Embodied Experience: The Case of Chinese Views of the Viscera," in *The Imagination of the Body and the History of Bodily Experience*, ed. Shigehisa Kuriyama (Kyoto: International Research Center for Japanese Studies, 2001), 17–29; for the case of the Amazonian hunter-gatherer, see Tim Ingold, "Hunting and Gathering as Ways of Perceiving the Environment," in *Redefining Nature: Ecology, Culture, and Domestication*, ed. Roy Ellen and Katsuyoshi Fukui (Oxford: Berg, 1996), 40–60; for a discussion of feng shui and urban architecture in Hong Kong, see Yuriko Furuhata, "Of Dragons and Geoengineering: Rethinking Elemental Media," *Media+Environment* 1, no. 1 (2019), https://doi.org/10.1525/001c.10797.

49. A similar critique was advanced by Yuriko Furuhata, who points out the inadequate appropriation of Gaia (James Lovelock and Latour) and Medusa (Haraway) to account for global climate change. See Yuriko Furuhata, "*Weathering with You*: Mythical Time and the Paradox of the Anthropocene," *Representations* 157 (2022): 68–89. For another critique of the monolingualization of referential frameworks in environmental humanities, see Kathleen D. Morris, "Provincializing the Anthropocene: Eurocentrism in the Earth System," in *At*

transition into media studies, one scholar once complained to me that just as film studies finally launched an earnest exploration of regional cinema, joined propitiously by a heteroglossia of articulations from women's cinema to queer cinema, from Black cinema to Indigenous and disability studies, it got hurled back to a monolithic framework of Greek mythology popularized by the work of new media theorists. I do not necessarily endorse this view—after all, regional film studies' sectarian tendency to specialize in cultures "of one's own" should accommodate media studies' agenda to address the urgent problems of structural discrimination and mass surveillance, ecological crisis, and species extinction, all of which require a trans-regional perspective. Yet in thinking with the psychic granny, I also see the value in arguing that even the more universal concerns of media theory can benefit from a scale-sensitive understanding of the way mediation works, how it entwines with local cosmologies, following Grandma's small-scale, community-based practices.

For its adeptness at creating enchanted worlds, animation is a medium fit for constructing a cosmotechnic worldview presented in humble groundedness. It is, furthermore, the female medium of these animated worlds who embodies an ethical relationship between technics and cosmology, often mediated by milieu-specific myths, folktales, or religious beliefs. Appreciating how Sheeta in *Castle in the Sky* (*Tenkū no shiro Rapyuta* 天空の城ラピュタ, 1986) articulates a different, freer relationship to the technology of flight, Lamarre maintains that the girl "embodies the technological condition, affords salvation or releasement, and appears as the new god or new paradigm to give constancy to a new understanding, a new way

Nature's Edge: The Global Present and Long-Term History, ed. Gunnel Cederlöf and Mahesh Rangarajan (New Delhi: Oxford University Press, 2019), 2–14. For Greek mythology-inspired theorizations, see Judith Butler, *Antigone's Claim: Kinship between Life and Death* (New York: Columbia University Press, 2010); Bruno Latour, *Facing Gaia: Eight Lectures on the New Climate Regime*, trans. Catherine Porter (Cambridge: Polity, 2017); Donna Haraway, "Staying with the Trouble: Anthropocene, Capitalocene, Chthulucene," in *Anthropocene or Capitalocene? Nature, History, and the Crisis of Capitalism*, ed. Jason W. Moore (Oakland, CA: PM Press, 2016), 34–76; Alexander R. Galloway, "Love of the Middle," in *Excommunication: Three Inquiries in Media and Mediation*, by Alexander R. Galloway, Eugene Thacker, and McKenzie Wark (Chicago: University of Chicago Press, 2013), 25–76. See also Claudia Breger, "Gods, German Scholars, and the Gift of Greece: Friedrich Kittler's Philhellenic Fantasies," *Theory, Culture & Society* 23, nos. 7–8 (2006): 111–34.

of living with technology, a new rootedness."[50] In a way, Miyazaki's heroines from Nausicaä to Sheeta, from Kiki to Princess Mononoke, who constantly inhabit an animist world, all promise this "new god," "new paradigm," "new understanding," "new way of living with technology," "new rootedness." They are further joined by young Mazu 媽祖, the Chinese sea goddess, whose legendary life full of fantastical encounters with the sea is recounted in the Taiwanese animated film *Mazu* (*Hai zhi chuanshuo: Mazu* 海之傳說: 媽祖, 2007); the eponymous protagonist immersed in the Polynesian oceanic environment alive with mythical elements in *Moana* (2016); and the Shintō-inspired weather maiden who brings sunshine to the rain-drenched city in Shinkai Makoto's *Weathering with You* (*Tenki no ko* 天気の子, 2019).

Insofar as Lamarre repeatedly emphasizes the quality of the new, which he ascribes to Miyazaki's girl protagonists, psychic granny appears an ill fit in animation's pantheon of female mediums. Her mediumship, however, is a no less delicate matter that draws the old and the new into a dialectical circuit, further highlighting at its core the question of generational transformation. In recent decades, psychic granny's techniques have become obsolete, gradually replaced by a younger generation of spirit mediums boasting more "hygienic" methods without engaging blood and violent trance.[51] Paralleling psychic granny's displacement is the industrial phasing out of cel animation, the technique that breathes life into her cinematic avatar. Yet on their way to obsolescence, these outmoded techniques also turn into new forms of mnemotechnics, where generational and transgenerational memories can be inscribed. On its twenty-third anniversary, *Grandma* was rereleased to wide acclaim following a 4K digital restoration. One keyword constantly appearing in media coverage was transgenerational, describing how the film shaped collective memory for audiences across generations.[52] The film itself deals with the intergener-

50. Lamarre, *The Anime Machine*, 84.

51. For a study of the paradigm shift in spirit mediumship from shamanism to "spirit communication," see Lin Mei-Rong 林美容, "Cong jitong dao tonglingren: Yu shenling goutong meijie de dianfan zhuanyi" 從乩童到通靈人：與神靈溝通媒介的典範轉移 (From *chi-tong* to *tong-ling-ren*: A paradigm shift in the medium of communication with deities), *Ciji daxue renwen shehui kexue xuekan* 慈濟大學人文社會科學學刊 (Tzu Chi University journal of the humanities and social science) 16 (2014): 1–26.

52. See, for example, "Wang Shau-Di: Kuashidai de gongtong huiyi, ta de mingzi shi 'a

ational dynamic based on the story of the scriptwriter's mother and her grandson; it resonates with many audience members' experiences with their grandparents; now these grown-up audiences bring their young ones to reexperience the film. Beyond blood relations, one film preservationist, who has grown reliant on computer vision for detecting signs of damage and decay, shares how restoring a cel animation film like *Grandma* requires manual checkup frame by frame, leading him to appreciate the intricate craft embodied by the previous generation of animators.[53] Much like Grandma in her role of taking care of Dou Dou in the film, she also forms a system of care—cultivating attention, experience, and knowledge—for her audiences spanning generations. Thus the psychic granny draws her spectators into what Bernard Stiegler in his work on generation and care calls long-circuit transindividuation, which I see as echoing animism's mutually invested process of dividuation.[54] Spinning transgenerational long circuits that forestall short-circuit cooptation by mass media, the stories of the psychic granny catalyze the emergence of relived memories, sustained attention, and an ethics of care—care for family histories, for the shamans and their sociocultural legacies, for the prospects of local animation industry.[55] Constitutive of a host of familial and nonfamilial relations enlivened by memories and endowed with a vital life, psychic granny thus marks the locus where animation and animism finally converge.

---

ma'!" 王小棣: 跨世代的共同回憶, 她的名字是"阿媽" (Shau-Di Wang: Transgenerational collective memory, her name is "Grandma"), *Gongmin baoju* 公民報橘 (CitiOrange), November 9, 2021, https://buzzorange.com/citiorange/2021/11/09/magic-grandmom-4k.

53. See the interview with director Shau-Di Wang and a preservationist: Taiwan Film and Audiovisual Institute, *Episode 1: Mofa ama chongfan dayinmu la!!! Ft. Wang Shau-Di daoyan* 魔法阿嬤重返大銀幕啦!!! Ft.王小棣 導演 (Psychic granny returns to the big screen!!! Feat. Director Shau-Di Wang), November 21, 2021, YouTube video, 44:12, https://www.youtube.com/watch?v=7V-z_qwUr4o.

54. Bernard Stiegler, *Taking Care of Youth and the Generations*, trans. Stephen Barker (Stanford, CA: Stanford University Press, 2010). See also Bernard Stiegler and Irit Rogoff, "Transindividuation," *e-flux* 14 (2010): 1–6.

55. For example, the PTS documentary series *Zhuge zaomeng* 逐格造夢 (Pursuing dreams frame by frame, 2010) traces the history of Taiwan's animation industry from the 1970s into the new century. In their interviews in the series, Shau-Di Wang and scriptwriter Huang Li-ming comment on the many dilemmas facing the industry.

SIX

Suspended Authorship

Women Animation Directors in Socialist China, 1940s–1980s

Daisy Yan Du

How has gender affected the trajectory of film history, especially when it comes to authorship? How and to what extent can a gender analysis of film and film history enhance our knowledge of both? These questions have inspired heated debates in film studies. However, two major gaps exist in these discussions: they unanimously consider adults as the intended audience of cinematic texts while neglecting children, and they focus on live-action films without addressing other mediums such as animation. If we draw attention to animation that targets children as its intended audience, can we shed new light on the debates about gender and authorship?

In this chapter, I reexamine the authorship and gender question by focusing on Chinese socialist animation, which I loosely define as the predigital cel or stop-motion animations handmade by veteran animators between the late 1940s and 1980s. I include the 1980s because the collective socialist mode of animated filmmaking continued at the state-owned Shanghai Animation Film Studio (SAFS) until the studio was officially forced by the state to enter the free market in 1995. By analyzing socialist animation classics that targeted child audiences, I hope to provide a new point of view on debates about female authorship as well as on female aesthetics and perspectives. It is difficult to detect a distinct female aesthetics or perspective in socialist animated films directed or codirected by women animators, but this does not mean that Chinese women animators lacked a female consciousness à la Western feminist theories, nor is this lack an inadequacy or weakness. These films must be analyzed in context by considering the films' intended audience (children) and the socialist mode of animated filmmaking. Working on animated films for children limited women animators' ability to explore more audacious topics related to women specifically, such as female sexualities and desires. Women animators were also constrained by working at a time when gender differences were theoretically subordinate to class differences in the state-controlled animation industry. It was very difficult for women animators to articulate an alternative female perspective. As a result, female authorship, and even authorship itself, was suspended in socialist animated filmmaking based on collectivism and the assembly line of production. Although a distinct female aesthetics-perspective did not appear until the rise of independent animation in the 1990s (see Paola Voci's "feminist gestures" of women animateurs in chapter 7), socialist women animators' tireless efforts to make a difference in Chinese animation history must be acknowledged, precisely because their individual labor and creativities were often subsumed under collective authorship. The differences they made within the state-controlled animation industry, though not always gender-specific, are adequate to call them socialist cine-feminists, defined as women practitioners making innovations, exploring alternative paths, and even challenging the established mainstream conventions symbolically coded as authoritative, masculine, and patriarchal.

Female Authorship, Aesthetics, and Perspectives

Western feminist film criticism is characterized by oppositional or counter thinking, often against a patriarchal mainstream.[1] Claire Johnston, for instance, redefined women's cinema as a confrontational counter-cinema

1. For an overview of this debate in feminist film studies, see Lucy Fischer, "Pre/Texts: An Introduction," *Shot/Countershot: Film Tradition and Women's Cinema* (Princeton: Princeton University Press, 1989), 3–31; Alison Butler, *Women's Cinema: The Contested Screen* (London: Wallflower, 2002), 1–23; Judith Mayne, "Female Authorship Reconsidered," in *The Woman at the Keyhole* (Bloomington: Indiana University Press, 1990), 89–123.

tasked with a mission to undermine the dominant male discourse.[2] In a similar vein, Laura Mulvey advocated for a feminist "new language of desire" in opposition to the male-centered mainstream mode of cinematic representation. She rejected the possibility for feminists to work within the mainstream and advocated instead for feminist avant-garde aesthetics based on negation, which is radically different from the male-centered mainstream aesthetics.[3]

An important revision of the concept of counter-cinema is the theory of minor cinema. Alison Butler regards women's cinema as *minor cinema*, a term inspired by Gilles Deleuze and Félix Guattari's concept of *minor literature*, which refers to the literature written in the major language by minority authors. By entering the mainstream, minor literature can finally achieve its subversive goals against the center. The notion of minor cinema thus legitimizes women filmmakers to work within the mainstream male-centered film industry where, like Trojan horses, they use the mainstream language to deconstruct the center from within. In other words, they simultaneously work within and against the patriarchal mainstream.

The same issue has informed Chinese cinema studies. Dai Jinhua argues that the history of Chinese live-action cinema has almost no female cinematic tradition. Although women have made films since the early 1980s, most of them look like films made by men and lack any distinct female aesthetics, style, perspective, or subjectivity, let alone a feminist consciousness. Women as a category of gender and sexual difference were invisible in the history of Chinese cinema.[4] Along the same line, Shuqin Cui, Ann Kaplan, Louisa Wei, and Zhen Zhang all argue that the history of Chinese cinema lacked a female tradition and women filmmakers were often marginalized by their male counterparts.[5] Women filmmakers, espe-

2. Claire Johnston, "Women's Cinema as Counter-Cinema," in *Notes on Women's Cinema*, ed. Claire Johnston (London: Society for Education in Film and Television, 1973), 24–31.

3. Laura Mulvey, "Film, Feminism and the Avant-Garde," in *Women Writing and Writing about Women*, ed. Mary Jacobus (London: Barnes & Noble Books, 1979), 177–95.

4. Dai Jinhua, "Invisible Women: Contemporary Chinese Cinema and Women's Film," *Positions* 3, no. 1 (1995): 274.

5. Shuqin Cui, *Women through the Lens: Gender and Nation in a Century of Chinese Cinema* (Honolulu: University of Hawai'i Press, 2003); Ann Kaplan, "Problematizing Cross-Cultural Analysis: The Case of Women in the Recent Chinese Cinema," *Wide Angle*

cially socialist ones, had to hide their gender and sexual identity to join the male-centered mainstream film production, often at the cost of losing the female self. Many critics concur that during the socialist decades there was no real women's cinema. Under socialism, feminist concerns about gender and sexual differences were eclipsed by class differences.

However, in her studies of socialist women directors such as Wang Ping and Dong Kena, Lingzhen Wang insists that a true women's cinema did exist in socialist China. She acknowledges the interdependent relationship between feminism and socialism and regards these women directors as both feminists and socialists. Wang argues against the Western concept of counter-cinema by maintaining that socialist women's cinema must work within the male-centered official discourse of the state and must be understood in relation to larger institutional, political, sociohistorical, and cultural forces. These socialist women directors' films, although produced within the mainstream state system, did criticize male centrism and articulate a female and feminist perspective.[6] This view is echoed by Zheng Wang, who argues that socialist feminists could still articulate feminist concerns and fight against patriarchy while working at the center of a male-dominated filmmaking system controlled by the authoritarian state.[7]

These debates boil down to the central issue of sameness and difference. Some women filmmakers, especially those working in the mainstream film industry, made films like men and did not leave their gender marks, whereas others accentuated their female perspective and made their films different from those created by men. At first, critics welcomed the former, because it meant gender equality between women and men as women were assimilated into the masculine paradigm, albeit at the cost of losing the female self. Recent feminist critics have generally praised the latter kind of film

---

11, no. 2 (January 1989): 40–50; Louisa Wei, "Women's Trajectories in Chinese and Japanese Cinemas: A Chronological Overview," in *Dekalog: On East Asian Filmmakers*, ed. Kate Taylor (London: Wallflower, 2011), 13–44; Zhen Zhang, *Women Filmmakers in Sinophone World Cinema* (Amsterdam: Amsterdam University Press, 2023).

6. Lingzhen Wang, "Wang Ping and Women's Cinema in Socialist China: Institutional Practice, Feminist Cultures, and Embedded Authorship," *Signs: Journal of Women in Culture and Society* 40, no. 3 (2015): 589–622.

7. Zheng Wang, *Finding Women in the State: A Socialist Feminist Revolution in the People's Republic* (Oakland: University of California Press, 2017).

while trying to detect a possible female perspective hidden in women's films accused of belonging to the male mainstream. They think that it is necessary for films made by women to have a distinct female subjectivity, style, and consciousness. Such an approach, however, often leads to the reassertion of essentialist ideas such as feminine emotions and interiority and therefore carries the risk of reducing women's cinema to an isolated gender enclave, thus further marginalizing women's films and validating the male standard. Also, overemphasizing the single correlation between the biological sex of filmmakers and their subsequent gender perspective in films is suggestive of biological determinism, neglecting other factors that may have shaped their films. Both arguments (i.e., women filmmakers are the same as or different from men) have reinforced the male standard by recognizing it as *the* standard. But what happens if we change the standard to female?

Female Standard and Suspended Authorship in Socialist Animation

Unlike live-action filmmaking, animated filmmaking in socialist China was not a mainstream industry. Because of its double marginality, that is, a marginalized art form for children, animation was often dubbed as "kids' stuff" (*xiao erke* 小儿科), which made some artists, especially male artists, reluctant to join the SAFS because to be an animator meant to be marginalized.[8] It is no exaggeration to say that socialist animated filmmaking was always already infantilized and feminized. At the SAFS, most of the staff were women. Although women directors were rare, women made up around one-third of key animators, half of the in-betweeners, and 80 to 90 percent of the inkers and painters. In total, women made up more than half of the entire staff.[9] Undoubtedly women performed most of the labor and formed the foundation of the studio. Male animators were feminized and infantilized crossdressers, usurping an inherently feminine and childish art form.

8. Daisy Yan Du, *Animated Encounters: Transnational Movements of Chinese Animation, 1940s–1970s* (Honolulu: University of Hawai'i Press, 2019), 8–13.

9. Percentage numbers are based on my interviews in Shanghai with Duan Xiaoxuan about women animators on July 18, 2017, and with Lin Wenxiao on July 17, 2017.

Dai Jinhua once lamented that it was difficult for women directors to articulate a distinctly female perspective because a cameraman with a male vision was often in charge of cinematography.[10] In socialist animation, however, cinematography had long been controlled by a powerful camerawoman named Duan Xiaoxuan 段孝萱 (1934–), who was the head of the Technology Department of SAFS and played a dominant role in animation cinematography between the 1950s and 1980s. If we follow Dai's argument, the feminization of animation cinematography and technology would have made it difficult for male directors to express a male perspective, thus creating a female standard in socialist animated filmmaking.

A distinct female perspective seems rare in socialist animation because, in most cases, animators dealt with subject matter such as animals and children in a fantastic manner. Animals and children were often degendered and desexualized, or they were not perceived in the same gendered and sexualized way as adult human characters. Because these films targeted children, animators had to downplay, if not completely erase, gender and sexualities in the films. In socialist China, when gender erasure and desexualization became a trend even for adults in everyday life and fictional representations (live-action films, posters, paintings), how could socialist animators portray gendered and sexualized perspectives and address issues specific to the female body in their films for children?

Under the circumstances of socialist filmmaking, even the concept of authorship could be put in quotation marks. Socialist animated filmmaking was a collective enterprise, involving directors, cinematographers, character designers, scriptwriters, key animators, in-betweeners, inkers, painters, voice actors, and composers, both men and women. It is difficult to argue for authorship or directorship in film, unlike for a book or painting, given its collaborative nature. Berys Gaut, for instance, argues that "films we must acknowledge to have multiple authors."[11] Socialist animated filmmaking was even more meticulously collaborative than live-action films. Each frame was collectively drawn by a group of animators, photographed, and then animated frame by frame. Ian Condry therefore argues

10. Dai Jinhua, "Invisible Women," 274.

11. Berys Gaut, "Film Authorship and Collaboration," in *Film Theory and Philosophy*, ed. Richard Allen and Murray Smith, 149–72 (Oxford: Oxford University Press, 1997), 150.

that the global success of anime is because of its "collaborative creativity."[12] Such collaborative creativity was even more reinforced by authoritarian politics and centralized state control in socialist animated filmmaking. Due to its collective nature, authorship was often suspended, and directors' names were erased in many animated films at that time. Films such as the first ink-painting animation, *Little Tadpoles Look for Mama* (*Xiao kedou zhao mama* 小蝌蚪找妈妈, 1960), for instance, used "collectively created" (*jiti biandao* 集体编导 or *jiti chuangzuo* 集体创作) to refer to its director.[13] Wan Laiming 万籁鸣, the director of *Uproar in Heaven*, also stated humbly that the film was created collectively by the entire crew.[14]

Although it is difficult to assert authorship in socialist animated filmmaking, let alone one with a distinct female perspective, this phenomenon has much more nuance and must be understood in the context of socialist animated filmmaking. The following sections revolve around socialist women animation directors and analyze their films from a gender-fluid rather than a gender-predetermined perspective.

Female Tradition: Women Directors and Coauthorship under High Socialism

The first animation director in socialist China was, in fact, a woman named Chen Bo'er 陈波儿 (1907–1951). Chen started her career as an active leftist actress and played the female protagonist in the well-known live-action film *The Plunder of Peach and Plum* (*Taoli jie* 桃李劫, 1934). Under her leadership, the Film Bureau Performing Arts Institute of the Central Ministry of Culture was established in 1950 as the first film university in socialist China, which in 1953 became the Beijing Film Academy. In 1946, she was appointed Communist Party secretary of the Northeast Film Studio and began to

12. Ian Condry, *The Soul of Anime: Collaborative Creativity and Japan's Media Success Story* (Durham, NC: Duke University Press, 2013), 2.

13. Du, *Animated Encounters*, 7–8.

14. Zhang Guanhong 张关鸿, "*Danao tiangong* chushi qianhou: Fang donghuapian yishujia Wan Laiming" 《大闹天宫》出世前后：访动画片艺术家万籁鸣 (The birth of *Uproar in Heaven*: An interview with animator Wan Laiming), *Wenhui bao* 文汇报 (Wenhui daily), November 12, 1961.

make animated films with Mochinaga Tadahito and others. In 1947, they made *The Dream to Be an Emperor* (*Huangdi meng* 皇帝梦, 1947), the first animated film produced in socialist China. Chen Bo'er worked as director and script writer, and Mochinaga Tadahito oversaw animation.

Given Chen's history of promoting strong women images in live-action cinema, it comes as no surprise that she used a powerful and masculinized female voiceover for the animated film. As Zheng Wang explains, as early as the 1930s, Chen Bo'er published numerous political essays advocating for national salvation and women's liberation. In these essays, Chen used masculine language and assumed a male voice, making it very difficult for readers to locate the author's gender identity.[15] As a political satire criticizing the collaboration between George Marshall and Chiang Kai-shek, the animated film looks masculine and has no female characters, though a female voiceover narrates the story. As in most documentaries, extradiegetic voiceovers are often male, symbolizing truth, power, and authority on the discourse level.[16] Voiceover thus assumes a higher and even more powerful position than images in the diegesis. The use of a female voiceover here, probably the voice of Chen Bo'er herself, hints at a socialist feminist stance: women can participate in and even control the masculine political discourse. That stance is all the more significant in that the first voice in the history of Chinese socialist animation was female.

As the only animated film made by Chen Bo'er, *The Dream to Be an Emperor* does not reflect a distinct female subjectivity per se, although Chen Bo'er can be called a socialist feminist. Chen Bo'er would have directed more animated films had she not died, too young, in 1951. That a woman became the first animation director in socialist China gestures toward the intimate kinship between women and animation, a femininized and infantilized minor art form at that time. Chen Bo'er planted the first seeds of female tradition in socialist animation. Had it not been for her untimely death, would she later become the president of SAFS to lead the development of Chinese animation in place of Te Wei 特伟?

15. Zheng Wang, *Finding Women in the State*, 148–63.

16. Bill Nichols, *Introduction to Documentary* (Bloomington: Indiana University Press, 2017); Mary Ann Doane, "The Voice in the Cinema: The Articulation of Body and Space," *Yale French Studies* 60 (1980): 33–50; Kaja Silverman, *The Acoustic Mirror: The Female Voice in Psychoanalysis and Cinema* (Bloomington: Indiana University Press, 1988).

Chen Bo'er was probably the first to propose the idea of a national style in socialist China. When she was directing *The Dream to Be an Emperor*, she advocated that the film should look Chinese by using traditional Chinese arts. She and her colleagues therefore used the form of Peking opera and invited an artist to perform the actions so that animators could reproduce his movements in the animated film. The discourse of the National Style has often been credited to Te Wei, who advocated using traditional Chinese arts, literature, and culture to articulate a distinct Chinese identity in animated films in the late 1950s and early 1960s. It was undoubtedly Te Wei who institutionalized the discourse, but in the late 1940s, a woman animator had already envisioned the future direction of socialist animation.

Tang Cheng 唐澄 (1919–1986) was the best-known woman animation director succeeding Chen Bo'er. Different from Chen, Tang had been trained in traditional Chinese painting since childhood, even studying at the Shanghai Academy of Fine Arts. In March 1950 she joined the Animation Division of the Shanghai Film Studio, which became SAFS in 1957. Because of her solid training in traditional Chinese painting, Tang Cheng started her animation career as an in-betweener, drawing intermediate images and movements between key frames designed by key animators. She learned quickly and was promoted to the position of key animator in 1952. In the late 1950s, Tang Cheng started to direct animated shorts, but her name as a director was frequently suspended in the name of "collectively created."[17]

During the socialist years, Tang Cheng codirected quite a few films with male directors, *Uproar in Heaven* (*Danao tiangong* 大闹天宫, 1961, 1964) being the most well known. It includes two episodes—both feature-length. Wan Laiming (1900–1997), the forefather of Chinese animation, has been widely recognized as the director of this film, overshadowing Tang Cheng who codirected. According to my interviews with Duan Xiaoxuan, who worked closely with Wan Laiming and Tang Cheng for several decades, Tang Cheng carried out the concrete and detailed directorial work in the capacity of an executive director while Wan Laiming oversaw the overall designs. In the credit sequence of the original film, Wan Laiming's name

17. Duan Xiaoxuan, interview, Shanghai, July 18, 2017.

was foregrounded as the director of the film and Tang Cheng was credited as the assistant director, her name appearing much later. In 2012, when SAFS was adapting the film into the 3D version, it listed Wan Laiming and Tang Cheng together equally as directors.[18]

Tang Cheng never directed an animated film solely on her own. She always codirected with male colleagues throughout her career. She codirected *Heroic Little Sisters of the Grassland* (*Caoyuan yingxiong xiao jiemei* 草原英雄小姐妹, 1964) with a male director named Qian Yunda 钱运达 (1928–), in which they presented strong girl heroes just as Chen Bo'er did. For this film, she was credited as the second director.

During the height of the Cultural Revolution, Tang Cheng began to take a leading role by working as the first director with a male counterpart named Wu Qiang 邬强. Together, they codirected a film titled *The Night of the Flooding Tide* (*Da chaoxun zhi ye* 大潮汛之夜, 1975), featuring the class struggle between heroic children and saboteurs who try to damage the first ship built by some villagers after 1949. In 1982, Tang Cheng and Wu Qiang worked again as directors for the ink-painting animated film *The Deer's Bell* (*Lu ling* 鹿铃), the third such film in Chinese animation history. This was Tang Cheng's last film. She fell ill and passed away in 1986. In this film, Tang Cheng and Wu Qiang portrayed a softer image of girls, which, however, is not predetermined by the gender identities of the directors because both the female and male directors had a role to play. Gender was suspended in this collaborative and androgynous authorship.

Rather than dismissing coauthorship as the exploitation and even victimization of women animators, we should take the sociohistorical background into account. At that time, it was a common practice for a junior director to work closely with a senior director for mentoring purposes. With this method, the studio trained and promoted many talented young directors at a time when the studio was short of animation directors, especially women directors.[19] Coauthorship opened the door for women animators to become independent directors in the future. Through coauthorship, women directors like Tang Cheng made a difference by asserting female presence in the male-dominated directorship at SAFS.

18. Duan Xiaoxuan, interview.

19. Duan Xiaoxuan, interview.

The Inward Turn: Women Directors and Lyrical Animation in the 1980s

It was not until the early 1980s that women animation directors began to direct films independently, a shift that coincided with a grand exploration of stylistic, aesthetic, and thematic innovations of animated filmmaking at SAFS, in which women animators played a leading role. Amid the exposure to international arts in the early 1980s, many Chinese animators realized that the tradition of National Style and socialist realism could no longer meet the diverse demands of 1980s audiences. Innovations were thus imperative. Dai Tielang 戴铁郎, a male director, was unsatisfied with the predominance of traditional Chinese folklore and legends in Chinese animation and innovated the trend of science fiction animated filmmaking. A Da 阿达, another male director, departed from socialist realism by espousing a minimalist, modernist, and even experimental style in animated filmmaking. His filmmaking philosophy was later enthusiastically promoted by a woman animator Hu Yihong 胡依红 in her own search of a new animation language. Lin Wenxiao 林文肖, the first woman animator who directed films independently in the 1980s, tried to channel Chinese animation inward by focusing on emotions and lyricism, rather than on hilarious actions and movements. It is tempting to attribute the inward turn to the gender identity of Lin Wenxiao, as women are often associated with emotions and men with actions. However, gender alone is not sufficient to explain the phenomenon.

Lin Wenxiao (1935–2023) was the most active and accomplished woman director of the 1980s (fig. 6.1). She joined the Animation Department (founded in 1950) at the Suzhou Fine Arts Academy (Suzhou meizhuan 苏州美专) in 1951 and later transferred to the Film Bureau Performing Arts Institute, soon to be renamed the Beijing Film Academy, in 1952. Upon graduation, she joined the Animation Division of the Shanghai Film Studio in 1953, where she started her animation career as an inker and was gradually promoted to animation designer, key animator, and director. During the socialist years, she worked as a key animator for *Little Tadpoles Look for Mama* (ink-painting animation), *Uproar in Heaven* (cel animation), *The Herd Boy's Flute* (*Mudi* 牧笛, ink-painting animation, 1963), *Nezha Conquers the Dragon King* (*Nezha naohai* 哪吒闹海, cel animation,

FIGURE 6.1. Lin Wenxiao and her husband Yan Dingxian (1936–2022), at the Conference Lodge of Hong Kong University of Science and Technology. Photo by the author on April 29, 2017.

1979), among others. Like Tang Cheng, Lin Wenxiao started by codirecting animated films with senior male directors. In 1978, she worked as the second director with A Da on the film *One Night in the Art Gallery* (*Hualang yiye* 画廊一夜, 1978), which criticizes the coercion of arts during the Cultural Revolution.

Lin Wenxiao debuted as an independent director for *Snow Boy* (*Xue haizi* 雪孩子, cel animation) in 1980. Featuring a boy made of snow who sacrifices his life to save a boy rabbit caught in fire, *Snow Boy* was a big hit, moving many Chinese children to tears in the 1980s. In 2017, the story was included in the textbook for the second grade of elementary school students in mainland China. Like *One Night in the Art Gallery*, *Snow Boy* was also made as a subtle response to the Cultural Revolution (fig. 6.2). According to Lin Wenxiao, although some children did not experience the Cultural Revolution, their childish innocence, kindness, purity, and loveliness had been contaminated. When she saw several naughty children abusing a homeless kitten to death, she tried to stop them but failed. Lin Wenxiao realized that children lacked the concept of love and sympathy for others. When she read the script of *Snow Boy*, she was immediately touched and decided to adapt it

FIGURE 6.2. Snow Boy and Boy Rabbit playing together, in *The Snow Boy* (1980).

into an animated film. She therefore set the guiding principles for the tone of this film as rich in childish delight, vivid and lively, and lyrical and touching (*fuyou ertong qingqu, shengdong huopo, shuqing ganren* 富有儿童情趣, 生动活泼, 抒情感人).[20] This animated short has been widely applauded for its lyricism, emotional expression, and subtlety.

The gender identity of the director may have played a role in defining the overall lyrical tone of this film. The film is feminine and childlike in its portrayal of a fairytale world and cute rabbits. Because women are conventionally associated with emotions, sentimentality, compassion, and maternal love, it is easy to attribute the lyrical style of this film to the gender identity of the female director.

Such a lyrical tone, however, was written and preset by the film scriptwriter, a man named Ji Hong 嵇鸿, a professional writer for children's literature. He wrote this fairy tale when he saw snowfall in Shanghai in the winter of 1979. During the Cultural Revolution, fairy tales and

20. Lin Wenxiao 林文肖, "Zai xinling zhong boxia yike meide zhongzi" 在心灵中播下一颗美的种子 (Planting a good seed in the heart), *Meishu dianying chuangzuo yanjiu* 美术电影创作研究 (Research and production of fine arts film) (Beijing: Zhongguo dianying chubanshe, 1984), 159.

talking animals were banned.[21] When Ji Hong tried to publish *Snow Boy*, it was rejected because the editors did not understand fairy tales. When he submitted *Snow Boy* to SAFS to be considered as a film script, a staff member asked, "How can an inanimate snow boy move around?" Te Wei, then president of the studio, praised it and approved it as a film script. However, no animation directors wanted to use it. Because all the scenes of snow are white and dull, it would be difficult for animators to draw and shoot the film, they thought, and the audiences would not like it.[22] Perhaps it was no coincidence that a female director found a rapport with this film script. The feminine and childish qualities of the story may have touched Lin Wenxiao's heart, especially given that she was a mother herself. Writing a story about maternal love, childish friendship, and self-sacrifice, the male writer Ji Hong was feminized and infantilized, assuming a marginalized position in the literary circle. Unsatisfied with how children's literature and film have long been trivialized as "kids' stuff," Ji Hong began to write novels and essays for adults in the late 1980s and early 1990s.[23] His change of career bespeaks the very feminization, infantilization, and marginalization of artists working on children's arts.

Where Ji Hong set the lyrical tone of the film, the female director foregrounded its potentials. The script incorporated three acts demonstrating the Snow Boy's kind heart and willingness to help others before the climactic fire scene. He helps a little pine tree regain its shape by removing the heavy snow on its branches; he catches a squirrel falling from a tree and saves its life; he covers a frozen bird with leaves to keep it warm. These action-packed details were diluted in the film. Instead, Lin Wenxiao and her team added two skiing sequences accompanied by lyrical music and songs. The first sequence takes place after Mother Rabbit's departure. Boy Rabbit takes Snow Boy to the fields to ski together. The music is light and lovely, suggesting a happy mood and the blossoming friendship of the two.

21. Du, *Animated Encounters*, 152–80.

22. Ji Hong 嵇鸿, "Kanke: Ji *Xue haizi* he tade luansheng jiejie *Ni guniang*" 坎坷：记《雪孩子》和他的孪生姐姐《泥姑娘》 (Hardships: On *Snow Boy* and its twin sister *Mud Girl*), *Yishu jie* 艺术界 (Art circle) no. 1 (1994): 40–42.

23. Ji Hong 嵇鸿, "*Xue haizi* chuangzuo de qianhou" 《雪孩子》创作的前后 (The birth of *Snow Boy*), *Xiaoxue yuwen jiaoxue* 小学语文教学 (Elementary school Chinese education) 6 (2006), 29–30; Ji Hong, "Kanke," 40–42.

It also paves the way for the climax of the film when Snow Boy saves his dear friend from a fire. The second sequence happens after Boy Rabbit goes home to sleep. Snow Boy skis alone in the forest, accompanied by lyrical music and a theme song sung by Zhu Fengbo 朱逢博, a famous female soprano at the time. Long takes and slow camera movements reinforce the lyrical mood. Children's play and pleasure in snow are thus foregrounded, and the three "good deeds" are pushed to the background. As Lin Wenxiao has noted, the lyricism of the film was built through collective efforts.[24] Jin Fuzai 金复载, a male musician, composed the music and the lyrics for the theme songs. The music adds an auditory dimension to the lyricism of the film.

Lyricism existed in Chinese animated filmmaking prior to 1980, in films such as *Peacock Princess* (*Kongque gongzhu* 孔雀公主, 1963) and *The Herd Boy's Flute*, but it was not until the 1980s that animators, represented by Lin Wenxiao, started to systematically theorize lyricism as an important approach to animated filmmaking. Lin Wenxiao continued to explore lyricism after the success of *The Snow Boy*. In 1985, she codirected *Jiazi Saves the Deer* (*Jiazi jiulu* 夹子救鹿) with Chang Guangxi 常光希 as the second director. Later, in 1986, they published an essay titled "The Exploration of the Lyrical Style in Animation." At that time, animation was viewed as suitable for portraying exaggerated and distorted characters, surprising comic moments, as well as magical, adventurous, and action-packed narratives. According to senior male director Wang Shuchen 王树忱: "It is difficult to portray interior psychological activities and subtle emotions and feelings in animation. We often adopt the method of 'single line and flat color' to portray characters, so it is easier to depict the exaggerated and the funny stuff but quite difficult to portray genuine emotions."[25] Lin and Chang challenged this accepted wisdom by arguing that animation is equally suited to portraying implicit and restrained emotions, simple and elegant images, and beautiful and touching music, with slow, stable, and smooth rhythm.[26] They tried to push animation from the exterior-oriented actions,

24. Lin Wenxiao, "Zai xinling zhong boxia yike meide zhongzi," 161.

25. Wang Shuchen 王树忱, "*Nezha naohai* de juben gaibian he yinmu tixian" 《哪吒闹海》的剧本改编和银幕体现 (The script adaption and screen representation of *Nezha Conquers the Dragon King*), *Dianying* 电影 (Movie) 4 (1979): 35.

26. Lin Wenxiao 林文肖 and Chang Guangxi 常光希, "Donghuapian shuqing fengge

movements, and narratives to the interior dimensions of emotions, mood, and atmosphere, thus opening new possibilities for Chinese animation.

In *Jiazi Saves the Deer*, for instance, the characters do not exhibit any plasmatic movements, body deformations, or transformations, nor do they display strong and exaggerated facial expressions. When Jiazi witnesses the sudden death of a mother deer, rather than rendering him with strong facial expressions, the animators downplayed the movement and let him just lift his eyes in a restrained manner. The king is always portrayed in profile and back views, with only one close-up of parts of his face when he draws his bow to kill the deer. He always appears in semi-darkness through cinematographic and lighting effects. The animals are not anthropomorphized but are instead presented as natural creatures. To keep the lyrical and peaceful atmosphere, neither the human nor animal characters speak. The pace of the entire film in general is very gentle and slow, except for the sequence of the king's hunting. To underscore the lyricism of the film, the plot is not complicated, nor are its conflicts too intense. The film's lyricism is further enhanced by the prescored music. The male musician Jin Fuzai composed the music for the entire film first, after reading the storyboard. In line with the lyrical music, the animators then designed the character movements. The colors and artistic styles of the film, designed by male artist Liu Jude 刘巨德, are simple, elegant, and peaceful, once again commensurate with the film's lyrical tone.[27]

Given that women are often associated with subtle emotions, feelings, sentimentality, as well as the natural world, perhaps it was not a coincidence that a woman director spearheaded the systematic exploration and theorization of lyricism in Chinese animated filmmaking in the 1980s. In this sense, lyricism has parallels to femininity. David Der-wei Wang argues that lyricism, a "poetics of selfhood," was often taken up to critique the grand narratives of the epic time in post-1949 China and beyond.[28] Lyricism therefore implies an alternative and even dissident position that is effeminate and marginal. Although Lin did not explicitly challenge the authoritative

---

de tansuo" 动画片抒情风格的探索 (On the lyrical style of animation), *Dianying* 电影 (Movie), 12 (1986): 18.

27. Lin and Chang, "Donghuapian shuqing fengge de tansuo," 18–20.

28. David Der-wei Wang, *The Lyrical in Epic Time: Modern Chinese Intellectuals and Artists Through the 1949 Crisis* (New York: Columbia University Press, 2015), viiii–x.

conventions at SAFS, her theorization and practice of lyricism already attested to her alterity, making her a cine-feminist against the patriarchal mainstream.

Suspended Animation as a Feminist Counter Animation in the 1980s

In addition to Lin Wenxiao, another woman animator was making breakthroughs in the early 1980s. Hu Yihong graduated from the Animation Department of Beijing Film Academy in 1978 and joined the SAFS in the early 1980s. In early 1983, she published an essay in *Film Art*, articulating her theorization of Chinese animation styles. According to her, many animated films produced by SAFS still followed the realistic and full-animation style of Disney's *Snow White* (1937), which was outdated. She regards "expressiveness" (*xieyi* 写意), which is for her the major characteristic of traditional Chinese aesthetics, as the medium-specificity of Chinese animation. To illustrate her ideas, she compares *Uproar in Heaven* with *Three Monks* (*Sange heshang* 三个和尚, 1980), an animated short directed by a male animator A Da. Whereas *Uproar in Heaven* follows the realistic style of Disney features, *Three Monks* is more expressive and functions as a true exemplar of Chinese animation. Hu believes that the expressiveness of *Three Monks* represents the future direction of Chinese animation, for it won numerous awards at international film festivals, a successful example of Chinese animation merging with the global trend of modern art represented by the Zagreb School.[29]

In 1984, Hu Yihong published another bold article in *Film Art*, advocating her theory of counter animation, which proposes a minimalist and experimental style against the realist tradition of the SAFS. Her case study was *The Song of Drawings* (*Hua de ge* 画的歌, 1981), directed by A Da. *The Song of Drawings* is a combination of documentary and animation. It documents peasants' drawings in Jinshan 金山, Shanghai. In a traditional documentary, the live-action camera would show a drawing by zooming in and zooming out from certain angles. In this film, A Da used the animation

29. Hu Yihong 胡依红, "Donghuapian de shenmei tezheng" 动画片的审美特征 (The aesthetic features of animated film), *Dianying yishu* 电影艺术 (Film art) 2 (1983): 48–51.

language of stop-motion to document the drawings. For instance, to show the movement of a duck flapping its wings, A Da located two ducks in the drawings with their wings pointing in opposite directions. He then shot them frame by frame to generate the animated illusion of movement. For Hu, *The Song of Drawings* looks like a "de-animated film," but it is a new kind of animated film in the making. It is close to the animated shorts made by the Zagreb School, which moved away from the escapism of Disney and bravely confronted modern realities. Disney features, Hu suggests, are outdated and need to be enshrined in museums. Although Hu sets up Disney features as her straw man, she is alluding to the National Style and socialist realism, with *Uproar in Heaven*, long cherished at SAFS, as a prime example.[30]

Hu's article provoked controversy in the animation community. Qian Yunda and Ma Kexuan 马克宣—senior male animators at SAFS and staunch practitioners of the National Style—soon published a rebuttal in *Film Art* in 1985. They argue that A Da's *The Song of Drawings* is a documentary, not an animated film, so it is not appropriate for Hu Yihong to cite it as representative of the future direction of Chinese animation. They contend that only a few scenes are animated with the stop-motion technique, like the duck flapping its wings, and that most of the scenes juxtapose the shots strategically to create the illusion of movement. Such technique is not animation, but a kind of cinematic montage in live-action filmmaking. The film, they conclude, makes breakthroughs in documentary language, not in animation.[31]

Hu Yihong never addressed their questions but continued to assert her viewpoints elsewhere. In a book chapter, "The Possibility of Animation Innovation," published in 1985, Hu continued to celebrate cinematic montage as a new animation language. Her case study was *The Butterfly Spring* (*Hudie quan* 蝴蝶泉, 1983), an animated short directed again by

30. Hu Yihong 胡依红, "Cong *Hua de ge* kan donghua yuyan de tupo" 从《画的歌》看动画语言的突破 (On the innovation of animation language from *The Song of Drawings*), *Dianying yishu* 电影艺术 (Film art) 6 (1984): 44–46.

31. Qian Yunda 钱运达 and Ma Kexuan 马克宣, "*Hua de ge* yu donghua dianying guannian: Yu Hu Yihong tongzhi shangque" 《画的歌》与动画电影观念: 与胡依红同志商榷 (*The Song of Drawings* and animation language: A discussion with Comrade Hu Yihong), *Dianying yishu* 电影艺术 (Film art) 6 (1985): 28–32.

A Da. Based on an ethnic Bai legend, the film begins with a live-action footage of the Butterfly Spring in Yunnan, followed by an animated love story illustrating its origin. A Da downplayed animation and movement while highlighting the importance of cinematography, editing, and music. Through editing and lighting, key frames were juxtaposed and superimposed strategically through fading in and out and dissolving; the sequential in-between frames of the movement were discarded, generating a unique illusion of movement akin to cinematic montage. Hu called it "the method of movement minimalization."[32] Although A Da had already used this kind of cinematic montage sparsely in *The Song of Drawings,* he used it prominently throughout *The Butterfly Spring,* making it a signature style of this film.

The omission of intermediate frames and the use of key frames only to create the illusion of movement through cinematic montage is what I have theorized elsewhere as suspended animation.[33] In terms of movement, Hu tried to break away from the full animation of Disney features by suspending the detailed in-between sequential movements. In terms of content, Hu encouraged Chinese animators to feature modern subject matter and explore the spiritual world of modern people.[34] Following this line of

32. Hu Yihong 胡依红, "Donghuapian chuangxin de keneng xing" 动画片创新的可能性 (The possibility of making innovations in animated filmmaking), in *Dianying meixue* 1984 电影美学(Film aesthetics) 1984, ed. Zhong Dianfei 钟惦棐 (Beijing: Zhongguo dianying chubanshe, 1985), 167–76.

33. Daisy Yan Du, "A Theory of Suspended Animation: The Aesthetics and Politics of (E)motion and Stillness," *Discourse: Journal for Theoretical Studies in Media and Culture* 44, no. 1 (Winter 2022): 42–77. In *The Fiery Cliff Slogans* (*Huohong de yanbiao,* 1977), suspended animation–cinematic montage was used throughout the film. In *Nezha Conquers the Dragon King* (*Nezha naohai,* 1979), Nezha's resurrection was portrayed with the aesthetics of suspended animation. See Lin Wenxiao, "Dribs and Drabs," trans. Nick Stember, in *Chinese Animation and Socialism: From Animators' Perspectives,* ed. Daisy Yan Du (Leiden: Brill, 2022), 69; and Chang Guangxi, "Tradition and Innovation," trans. Sean Macdonald, in *Chinese Animation and Socialism: From Animators' Perspectives,* ed. Daisy Yan Du (Leiden: Brill, 2022), 129.

34. Hu Yihong 胡依红, "*Xinzhuang de menling* he *Chaoji feizao*: A Da de ziwo chaoyue" 《新装的门铃》和《超级肥皂》：阿达的自我超越 (*The Newly Installed Doorbell* and *Super Soap*: A Da's self-transcendence), *Dangdai dianying* 当代电影 (Contemporary cinema) 4 (1988): 99–103.

thinking, the target audience of animation, Hu implied, should include adults as well as children. In terms of form, she advocated for experimental and philosophical animated shorts, not features. The animated shorts were mainly art films, often screened at international film festivals. Hu also espoused the collapse of boundaries between animation and live-action and proposed a primitive Chinese theory of media mix. She welcomed the integration of live-action into animated filmmaking, either by borrowing the cinematic method of montage or embedding live-action footage into animated films as A Da had done.[35]

From a feminist perspective, the debate between Hu Yihong and Qian Yunda/Ma Kexuan can be easily interpreted as a young daughter's rebellion against the National Style and socialist realism established and upheld by her "fathers" at SAFS. Although socialist animation had a maternal lineage that can be traced back to Chen Bo'er, it was gradually transformed into a patriarchal art dominated by male presidents, directors, and key animators, who were feminized by their marginalized positions in the socialist film industry. The socialist state's involvement further reinforced the patriarchal presence. The state's promotion of the National Style and socialist realism brought politics and nationalism into animation aesthetics. Hu Yihong was daring to challenge her fathers and the state rhetoric in the early 1980s, when it was still the golden age of the National Style. Her dissident status largely came from her youthfulness. As a young woman exposed to international animation aesthetics and as a newcomer to SAFS, she might not identify with the traditions long cherished at the studio. Her identity as a woman might have also granted her the capacity for oppositional thinking, as Julia Kristeva says, women are inborn "perpetual dissidents."[36]

Yet gender identity alone cannot fully explain her resistance. Strictly speaking, the new animation language Hu Yihong advocated for was not a female-feminist one, but another man's language. All the animated films

35. Hu Yihong further illustrated her views on Disney and Zagreb in her article "Liangzhong butong meixue yiyi de donghua guifan" 两种不同美学意义的动画规范 (Two different aesthetic styles of animation), *Dangdai dianying* 当代电影 (Contemporary cinema) 4 (1986): 6–20.

36. Julia Kristeva, quoted in Josette Feral, "The Powers of Difference," in *The Future of Difference*, ed. Hester Eisenstein and Alice Jardine (New Brunswick, NJ: Rutgers University Press, 1985), 92.

cited by Hu as the future direction of Chinese animation were directed by male director A Da. Even though his animated shorts did exhibit a modernist consciousness, he still worked within the framework, albeit on the edges, of the National Style at SAFS. In addition, his animated shorts only rarely dealt consciously with gender as a central issue, nor did they articulate a distinct female or feminist aesthetics-perspective, although we can argue that A Da's style was marginalized and thus feminized at the studio. Hu Yihong was challenging the male tradition by using another male language, but she had not yet formulated a female-feminist animation language of her own. In her theorization of a counter animation, gender was out of the question. Her oppositional gesture and counter thinking nonetheless made her a cine-feminist who challenged the patriarchal mainstream.

Although Hu Yihong was one of the many doubters and explorers in the 1980s, she was nonetheless the first, and perhaps the only one, who systematically and consistently theorized a counter animation and experimented with her theories in her own animated filmmaking practices throughout her career. In 1989, she independently directed her first animated short, *The Tall Wife and the Short Husband* (*Gao nüren he ai zhangfu* 高女人和矮丈夫). Targeting adults, the film reflects on the social gaze and its oppressive impact on ordinary people. The protagonists are a tall wife and a short husband. Their appearance as a couple makes onlookers feel uneasy, so they try to make the couple look like the "perfect match" by either making the husband look taller with high-heeled shoes or the wife shorter with wide, puffy clothes (fig. 6.3). In the beginning, the couple resists such intrusions, but the social gaze is so strong that it becomes persecutory. After the wife dies of stress caused by the social gaze, the husband dresses taller in line with social expectations.

In terms of formal style, the film moves away from the realist tradition of SAFS. Adopting a minimalist approach, the background is almost reduced to a blank, with only a few doors suggesting the settings and spatial relations. The characters are also caricatured as ordinary people, and they all wear the same-colored clothes. The film has indeed replicated the style of A Da. The film can be interpreted as Hu's feminist accusation of the social gaze in victimizing the female bodies that do not meet social expectations. However, such a feminist overtone was not determined by

FIGURE 6.3. A nosy neighbor giving a pair of high-heeled shoes to the short husband, in *The Tall Wife and the Short Husband* (1989).

Hu's own gender identity alone, because it was preset in the film script, written by a male author Feng Jicai 冯骥才 in 1982.

Princess Lotus Flower (*Lianhua gongzhu* 莲花公主, 1992), the second animated short directed by Hu, appears to be a return to the tradition of SAFS (fig. 6.4). Adapted from a traditional story in *Strange Stories from a Chinese Studio* (*Liaozhai zhiyi* 聊斋志异, 1740), the film features a literati scholar who saves a bee princess in a dream. Formally, the film looks like a traditional Chinese painting and seems like a departure from the counter animation Hu theorized. In an interview, Hu said that though she emulated A Da in *The Tall Wife and the Short Husband*, she tried to develop her own animation language in *Princess Lotus Flower*. Although it was adapted from traditional literature, *Princess Lotus Flower* still expressed an international "modern consciousness" in the sense that the dream was reality.[37] The new animation language of this film is strictly not a female-feminist one. Like

37. Jin Baisong 金柏松, "Meishupian liu daoyan fangtanlu" 美术片六导演访谈录 (Interview with six animation directors), *Dangdai dianying* 当代电影 (Contemporary cinema) 4 (1993): 78–82, here 80.

FIGURE 6.4. The scholar meets Princess Lotus Flower and her mother, in *Princess Lotus Flower* (1992).

many Disney princesses, the princess in this film is also a damsel in distress who needs to be saved by a man. The film per se does not articulate a distinct female or feminist perspective.

In the 1990s, Hu Yihong seemed to have abandoned her theory of counter animation by shifting her attention from animated shorts to commercial television animation series. The animated shorts were largely art films, popular at international film festivals but offering little commercial value. In 1995, SAFS, which had been state-owned and dependent on a planned economy, was fully plunged into the capitalist free market, facing fierce competition from both domestic industries and abroad. Animators at the studio left their ivory tower to make a profit. Commercialization, industrialization, and digitalization became the imperatives at the studio. Digital cinema features and television animation series were the two major forms of commercial animation at that time. After collaborating with foreign animation producers for a couple of years in the mid-1990s, Hu Yihong began to direct her own television animation series, *Music Up* (*Wo wei ge kuang* 我为歌狂, 2000) being the most famous one. *Music*

Up became a hit, with lucrative profits and audience ratings even higher than Japanese anime at that time. It was also successful in terms of media mix, as the commodities related to it, such as cards, CDs, and books, sold extremely well. The story revolves around several high school students who establish a music band on campus. Their dreams, happiness, frustrations, and confusion typical of teenagers living in big cities at that time unfold episode by episode.[38] *Music Up* tried to break away from the tradition of SAFS by adopting an anime style: it was heavily influenced by Japan's *Slam Dunk* (television animation series, 1993–1996).

Hu Yihong's tireless quest for a new animation language, which began with A Da's shorts, concluded with Japan's anime style. It is easy to say that her explorations failed if we only look at the results. Hu Yihong strove endlessly to search for a new Chinese animation language, in both theory and practice, in the 1980s and 1990s. She was one of the many pioneers and explorers on the road, probably the strongest and most persevering. As of today, no one has ever proposed a workable philosophy or new direction for domestic Chinese animation nor produced any animated films that could signal such a direction. Chinese animation has been in the process of uncertain transformation since the late 1980s.

Conclusion

Although socialist women animation directors did not articulate a distinct female or feminist aesthetics-perspective, they still tried to make a difference. In the late 1940s, Chen Bo'er inaugurated a national style by using the form of Peking opera for the making of the first animated film in socialist China, long before Te Wei and others systematically theorized and institutionalized the discourse of the National Style in the late 1950s and early 1960s. Although women directors like Tang Cheng could only codirect films with their male colleagues or their authorship was erased in the name of films being "collectively created" between the 1950s and 1970s, they

38. For more information, see Xiang Hua 向华, Hu Yihong 胡依红, and Tian Yi 天逸, "Chunzhen niandai: *Wo wei ge kuang* tanhua lu" 纯真年代：《我为歌狂》谈话录 (Innocent age: Dialogues about *Music Up*), *Dianying xinzuo* 电影新作 (New films) 6 (2002): 30–55.

still left their traces in Chinese animation history. The first ink-painting animated film, *Little Tadpoles Look for Mama,* for instance, involved the indispensable efforts of Tang Cheng, the camerawoman Duan Xiaoxuan, the female key animator Lin Wenxiao, and numerous anonymous female in-betweeners, inkers, and painters. In the 1980s, women animation directors began to direct films independently and explored a counter animation different from the mainstream style at SAFS. Lin Wenxiao's theorization and practice of lyrical animation charted a new direction for Chinese animation to focus on interiority and emotions, rather than on actions and movements. Hu Yihong was even more rebellious by directly challenging the National Style and socialist realism cherished at the studio, thus confronting its loyal advocates, such as the veteran animator Qian Yunda. Although the counter animation promoted by Hu Yihong was based on A Da's signature style, and Hu's own animated films did not articulate a distinct female or feminist perspective, Hu's challenge to the patriarchal mainstream already made her a cine-feminist. In fact, Hu has been regarded as a pioneering woman independent animator because her short films did resonate with the spirit of independent animation even though she worked at the state-owned SAFS. It was difficult for socialist women animation directors to express a distinct female or feminist aesthetics and perspective because many of the films were made for children at the studio. Also, the collective socialist mode of animated filmmaking made it difficult for women animators to mark their individual gender identities on film. Nevertheless, that these socialist women directors challenged conventions and made differences at the state-owned SAFS justifies calling them cine-feminists. After the rise of digital technologies in the 1990s, women independent animators outside the state-owned animation studios flourished, making films that expressed more explicit female and feminist aesthetics and perspectives, or what Paola Voci calls the "feminist gestures" (see chapter 7). This female and feminist tradition must be traced back to the socialist years to grasp the whole picture of gender and authorship in the history of Chinese animation.

SEVEN

When Animation is Accented and Gendered

The Feminist Gestures of Women Animateurs

Paola Voci

This chapter focuses on women animateurs and, more specifically, examines how their feminist gestures not only fracture and expand Chinese state-endorsed mainstream animation, but also meaningfully contribute accented and gendered perspectives to transnational animation practices and theories. I use the term *animateur* to refer to a conflation of artistic and artisanal qualities that are characteristic of the contemporary animation practices I examine.[1] Animateurs are characterized by liminality or, possibly more accurately, intersectionality, vis-à-vis the mainstream and the avant-garde, and also vis-à-vis China. In the current globalized context, their lives and works are marked by both self-chosen and enforced mobilities, which, I propose, situate them in an accented positionality. Within these intersectionalities, women animateurs have become increasingly visible, affirming their creative agency via minor rather than oppositional practices.[2] Applying Vilém Flusser's phenomenology of gestures to understand

1. The term *animateur* has multiple connotations in relation to animation as a film technique and a sociocultural activity. It is a close homophone with two, traditionally divergent concepts: the amateur and the auteur. See Paola Voci, "Electric Shadows Reloaded: The Post-Digital Animateur, Shadow Play and Handmade Cinema," *Journal of Chinese Cinemas* 11, no. 3 (2017).

2. I follow Alison Butler's understanding of women's cinema as minor (based on Deleuze and Guattari's conceptualisation of minor practices) as indeed applicable to animation. "To call women's cinema a minor cinema, then, is to free it from the binarisms (popular/elitist, avant-garde/mainstream, positive/negative) which result from imagining it as a parallel or

animation as a complex gesture of making, I analyze and conceptualize women animateurs' accented, gendered, minor practices as feminist gestures. I argue that these gestures point to the need for reconnecting issues of representation with those of production and distribution and embracing a critical space in which theory and practice, aesthetics and politics, art and craft are mutually determining. In a scholarly context in which a feminist approach to animation is largely undeveloped, an examination of contemporary Chinese-accented women animateurs can contribute to de-Westernizing scholarship in animation studies and also stimulate further research on the key relationship between feminism and animation.[3] I see their affirmation of corporeal presence and creative agency as part of a feminist critical approach to animation or, possibly more accurately, animation's critical approach to feminism.

Animateur Practices, Accent, Mobility, Gender

Since the beginning of this millennium and especially in the last ten years, women animateurs have contributed a wide range of innovative practices in the broader context of contemporary China's independent animation. They are neither isolated from nor oppositional to their male colleagues, with whom they share the creative multimedia apparatus and distribution channels of the digital space, arguably more equitable and gender-balanced than the film studios and television stations that dominated the production of animation in the larger part of the twentieth century.[4]

oppositional cinema." Alison Butler, *Women's Cinema: The Contested Screen*, vol. 14 (London: Wallflower Press, 2002), 21–22.

3. Chinese animateurs present specific Chinese attributes. Yet their broader theoretical relevance should not be diminished or dismissed as being "too narrow or too specialized to warrant general interest." Rey Chow, "Introduction: On Chineseness as a Theoretical Problem," *boundary 2* 25, no. 3 (1998).

4. Chinese animateur practices intersect with China's independent animation. Wu Weihua and Zhou Wenhai have analyzed and critiqued the complex, fluid alternative discourses developing outside the animation industry, convincingly framing independent animation in the sociocultural context of postsocialist and globalizing China. See Weihua Wu, *Chinese Animation, Creative Industries, and Digital Culture* (Abingdon, Oxon: Routledge, 2018); Wenhai Zhou, *Chinese Independent Animation: Renegotiating Identity in Modern China* (Cham: Palgrave Macmillan, 2020).

First, like most stakeholders in the context of the arts more broadly, women animateurs have a fluid and unsettled relationship with China. Outside ideologically driven nationalist discourses, being Chinese is mostly understood as a contested condition rather than as an unalterable, unquestionable status. Being Chinese entails a complex process of negotiations beyond dichotomies such as center and periphery, home country and host country. Although such a process challenges any rigid or essentialized notion of Chineseness, it certainly does not make being Chinese, and possibly even more crucially being seen as Chinese, inconsequential. On the contrary, localization matters, especially given that, in animation studies even more than film studies, we still need to expand and contest the predominance of Eurocentric or Americentric practices and theories.[5] However, the key is to do so without replacing it with an equally problematic and homogenizing Sinocentric experience. The concept of Sinophone has certainly significantly contributed to decentering the hegemony of Mandarin and the People's Republic of China (PRC) in Chinese studies. However, the resulting duality between Sinocentric and Sinophone perspectives may not suffice to capture the current globalized context in which cultural practices increasingly develop transversely, across this duality, often coexisting in both spaces; they are also characterized by self-chosen or imposed mobility. I propose that, instead of Chinese or Sinophone, the notion of Chinese-accented allows us to recognize a transnational positionality that can also be situated within, rather than simply departing from, the PRC, Mandarin-dominated, center.[6] In Hamid Naficy's conceptualization of accented cinema, the linguistic concept of accent is used to refer to diasporic, postcolonial, exilic cinema, as well as a marker for alternative, antihegemonic film practices outside the mainstream industry or studios.[7] By adapting and expanding the notion of

5. For more on the issue of de-Westernization, see Saër Maty Bâ and Will Higbee, *De-Westernizing Film Studies* (New York: Routledge, 2012); Myung-Jin Park and James Curran, *De-Westernizing Media Studies* (London: Routlege, 1999). Chow, "Introduction: On Chineseness."

6. Sinophone studies are "conceived as the study of Sinitic-language cultures on the margins of geopolitical nation-states and their hegemonic productions" and develop a broader critique of China-centrism and its Sinicizing discourse. Shu-mei Shih, "The Concept of the Sinophone," *PMLA* 126, no. 3 (2011): 710.

7. Hamid Naficy, *An Accented Cinema: Exilic and Diasporic Filmmaking* (Princeton, NJ: Princeton University Press, 2001).

accent beyond the diasporic or the exilic to include mobilities across and within home and host countries, I seek to capture women animateurs' deterritorialized locations as well as their nonmainstream, minor practices.

The women animateurs at the center of my study are active both in Chinese contexts (such as the PRC and Taiwan) and elsewhere, but rarely, if at all, emphasize either Sinocentric or Sinophone belongings. On their English-language websites, their Chinese-accented positionality—also evidenced by the presence of characters, and, in some cases, short Chinese-language texts—is reflected in their experiences. They inhabit declaredly transient locations, describing themselves as having been trained in different countries (e.g., in China, Taiwan, the UK, Japan, and the United States) and currently based in cosmopolitan cities, such as Beijing, London, Los Angeles, New York, Shanghai, Taipei, and Tokyo. For example, Taiwanese-born Cho Pei-Hsin 卓霈欣 and Huang Liang-Hsin 黃亮昕 both refer to their training in animation at the Royal College of Art in London; the former is "currently based in London," and the latter is "currently living in Taichung, Taiwan."[8] Mainland-born Song Siqi 宋思琪 and Wang Qieer 王切尔 describe themselves respectively as "from China, currently based in California, United States" and as "Chinese . . . currently working and living in the United States."[9] This Chinese-accented mobility is directed not only toward the West. For instance, Taiwan-born and UK-trained Liu Jiamin 刘佳旻 (aka, Miss Bowtie, *Caocao xiaojie* 曹操小姐), like many other non-PRC based animateurs, also has a Douban account.[10] Even when they are mostly active in PRC-based virtual and physical locations, they refer to their accented mobility in Vimeo channels, Instagram and Facebook accounts, and online interviews. For example, Zhu Yantong 朱彦潼 surfaces in an episode of the *Wrestling and Everything Coast to Coast* podcast, in which she introduces her unlikely audi-

8. Cho Pei-Hsin, "About," https://www.peihsincho.com/about. Huang Liang-hsin, "About," https://www.lianghsinhuang.com/about.

9. Song Siqi, "About," http://songsiqi.com/about; Wang Qieer, "About," https://www.qieerwang.com/about-qieer.

10. Liu graduated from Edinburgh College of Art and Central Saint Martins College of Art and Design. I focus here mostly on the Chinese-accented mobile localizations. Other mobilities develop within the northeast Asia region. Furthermore, practitioners not only know of each other's works, but also often collaborate across national borders.

ences to her animation work, describing herself as an itinerant practitioner who holds many jobs, has not yet been to the United States, was trained in Tokyo, and currently resides in Beijing.[11]

Unlike the big-money, critically endorsed mobility that characterizes global Chinese contemporary artists who are "setting auction records and exhibiting in art museums all around the world," women animateurs' mobile positionalities are markers of minor creative practices, developing in the space of light—neither avant-garde nor mainstream—cultures.[12] They describe themselves by referring to such light, category-resistant, hybrid, multiple belongings.[13] They often point to the wide scope of their animation practices, intersecting high-brow and low-brow visual art milieux. The words *animation* or *animator* are almost always associated with additional qualifying terms such as artist, director, producer, filmmaker, and storyteller, which in turn create connections with filmmaking, screens, multimediality, VJ live performance, digital technology, and handcrafted, artisanal materiality. As I point out elsewhere, *lightness* can be seen as a transitional, temporary condition that may or may not lead to a weightier status, that is,

11. Buddy Sotello and Evan Ginzburg, "Animator Yantong Zhu and Author Steve Verrier," *Wrestling & Everything Coast to Coast*, podcast audio, https://podcasters.spotify.com/pod/show/wrestlingandeverything/episodes/Animator-Yantong-Zhu-and-Author-Steve-Verrier-e1ij50g/a-a7udsg0.

12. The quote is from Winnie Wong, *Van Gogh on Demand: China and the Readymade* (Chicago: University of Chicago Press, 2014), 193. Wong investigates the work of copy painters, localized in Shenzhen's Dafen village as both *dagong* workers and independent artists. Like the animateurs I analyze, copy painters are characterized by hybridity, mobility, and liminality within the PRC, and can therefore also be best understood as Chinese accented. For more on light cultures, their resistance to framing (and naming) in categories or genres, and their hybrid, unstable, volatile, unendorsed, and unendorsable expressive modalities, see Paola Voci, *China on Video: Smaller-Screen Realities* (London: Routledge, 2010).

13. Lightness is not specific to the women animateurs I analyze in this essay. Most men animateurs also share the same in-between (neither mainstream nor avant-garde) location and equally resist being framed exclusively by animation or being exclusively referred to as animators. For example, Lei Lei 雷磊 describes himself as an "experimental animation artist" and notes that he has "his hands on video arts, painting, installation, music and VJ performance" (Lei Lei, "About," https://www.leilei-studio.com/about). Duan Tianran 段天然 defines himself as "a new media artist" and notes that his "work includes experimental animation, video, and installation art" (Renmin University of China School of Arts, "Lecturer Duan Tianran," http://art.ruc.edu.cn/info/1151/4005.htm).

the acquisition of financial or cultural capital associated with being established professionals or internationally renowned artists. Most often, there is fluidity between light animateur practices and avant-garde visual art, filmmaking, or commercial animation and design.

For example, Chai Mi's 柴觅 *The Sparrow and the Raven*—an improvised music and animation performed in Shanghai in 2014—can indeed be considered a turning point in Chinese independent animation and a defining work of contemporary animateur practices. Chai Mi has since established herself as an innovative, eclectic visual artist who works across multiple national and transnational physical locations as well as digital channels. While her positionality as a global experimental visual artist and her large-scale art installations place her beyond the liminal, minor, light space of animateur practices, Chai remains actively connected with the Chinese-accented space of alternative, nonmainstream, independent animation. She refers to her work as developing "in a wide variety of media, including painting, papercraft, animation, live performance and personal stylized Vjing."[14]

Also positioning herself in the space of experimental visual arts, Liu Yi 刘毅 is "a painter animator," who combines cel animation and Chinese ink painting, views "early Chinese art films and experimental animation as her primary research direction" and inhabits the space of multimedia installations.[15] By contrast, Wang Qieer, "an animation director, producer, . . . founder and director at QIE MEDIA, a creative studio specializing in custom animation, branded content, motion design, and short films" declares a much more client-oriented approach.[16] Similarly negotiating artistic motivations with commercializing necessities, Huang Liang-Hsin defines herself as a "freelance animation filmmaker" with an interest in

14. China's Stopmotion Animation, "Duli donghuaren Chai Mi zhuanfang" 独立动画人 柴觅专访 (Interview with independent animator Chai Mi), ACCR (Association des Centres Culturels de Rencontre), October 12, 2013, http://stopmotionanimationcn.blogspot.com/2013/10/blog-post.html.

15. ShanghART Gallery, "Flowing Feast: Liu Yi Solo Exhibition," ed. ShanghART Singapore (ShanghART 香格纳画廊, May 12–August 13, 2017). Liu Yi graduated from China Academy of Fine Arts (2016) in Hangzhou, where she resides. She does not have an English-language personal website and information about her work mostly circulates (under 刘毅 animation) on Chinese-language digital platforms.

16. Wang Qieer, "About."

exploring "places, poetry and rhythm."[17] In a Chinese-language interview with Art-Isle, Cai Caibei 蔡采贝 also points to her diverse experiences "working as a freelance since graduation," ranging from music video, VJ, commercials, design for animation festivals, also noting that "there is a big difference between commercial projects and personal works" and hoping to be able "to continue to create personal animations."[18] Liu Jiamin is an "animation director and multi-media artist."[19] Cho Pei-Hsin emphasizes being "a visual storyteller with a particular focus on illustration and animation."[20] Like Cho, Song Siqi views storytelling as a key drive and, like Liu and Huang, she sees herself as mainly an animation filmmaker. The word *film* indeed permeates Song's website: "Her work has been shown in numerous film festivals around the world . . . was named a Directing Fellow by Film Independent in 2018 . . . recognized by the British Academy of Film and Television Arts. . . . Song has been a juror and mentor for animation films at various film festivals."[21] In sum, Chinese-accented, on-the-move women animateurs see themselves as multimedia, hybrid practitioners.

Second, in choosing to focus on the attribute *gendered*, I want to make visible (i.e., historicize and problematize) their experience as women in a traditionally man-dominated context. I agree with Vanessa Cambier that "one of the enduring and underexamined relationships between media and feminism happens within the practice of animation."[22] In other words, being a woman working in animation needs to be understood as having historical and theoretical relevance within a feminist critique of media.

17. Huang Liang-hsin, "About."

18. "Art-Isle Talk | Cai Caibei: Banxing shifen x Pianpian mengjing 蔡采贝：半醒时分 x 翩翩梦境 (Cai Caibei: Half asleep and fluttering dream)," CareerEngine, https://posts.careerengine.us/p/611dfc0fe3095813de09b4cd. Art-Isle is claimed to be a platform focusing on sharing information about art, based in London, although the acronym "Art-Isle"—which is also associated to an Instagram account and a WeChat group—likely refers not to a platform, but to individual users. CareerEngine is a Chinese-language big data platform targeted at North American Chinese.

19. Liu Jiamin, "Info," http://missbowtie.com/info.

20. Cho Pei-Hsin, "About."

21. Song Siqi, "About."

22. Vanessa Cambier, "Women's Animation and the Creative Feminist Politics of Social Change," *LARB Los Angeles Reviews of Books*, March 25 2020, https://lareviewofbooks.org/article/womens-animation-and-the-creative-feminist-politics-of-social-change.

Even though women have been actively working in animation since its beginnings, the tradition of making women "vanish" is a long one. Men have dominated both practices and theories of animation, holding the power to erase women, often manifestly and unapologetically.[23] In the last two decades, the increased number and visibility of women in animation practices has become part of a broader—yet by no means universal—shift toward the emancipation of women in film and media, from subordinated laborers to independent creative producers. Arguably, in China as elsewhere, today men and women are working on progressively more equal grounds. Yet simply taking stock of the significantly improved status that women hold in Chinese animation risks overlooking that this shift in gender power relations is not only quite recent but also still unsettled and uneven. I argue that the increasingly visible presence of women animateurs does more than simply rectify the earlier erasure of women's subjectivities in animation and that their practices—accented and gendered—also meaningfully transform animation in its content, form, and authorship.

So, what does it mean to be a woman who creates and produces animation in the fluid, liminal Chinese-accented context that characterizes their positionality while negotiating their individual creativity in the transnational milieu of globalized animation? Can we find evidence of a feminist perspective, both in the texts—that is, their animation works and their stylistic and narrative choices—and in their contexts—that is, the channels and platforms in which these women share their works and reflect on their own practices?[24] To answer these questions, we need first to frame feminism in the context of animation studies.

23. I refer here to Karen Beckman's trope of the vanishing women, which focuses on the inescapable patriarchal repression of women' subjectivities via the erasure of their bodies—a trope that has dominated cultural discourses both on and off screens. Karen Beckman, *Vanishing Women: Magic, Film, and Feminism* (Durham, NC: Duke University Press, 2003).

24. My essay focuses on the analysis of women animateurs' feminist gestures, but all animateurs also face the broader dynamics of neoliberal capitalism and the social and economic challenges involved in completing the required technical and academic training in highly competitive international institutions, sustaining creativity by seeking employability, and finding the appropriate channels to distribute one's work. For example, in sharing their life experience as freelance both at home (in Hong Kong) and in foreign environment, Lilian Fu noted that the key challenge is developing an adaptive and real-

Women, Animation, and Feminism

In animation histories and theories, research that focuses on women is surprisingly limited, with even less research on feminist perspectives. Yet it is widely recognized that animation has been dominated by men and that women's contributions need to be recognized and examined more closely. In his book *Understanding Animation,* Paul Wells approaches the topic from the point of view of the animation text, focusing on issues of representation. He argues that women animators actively oppose the male gaze that has traditionally dominated live-action films and instead develop an alternative, more experimental, more subjective, less "hyper-real" language, using animation as a venue for auteurism.[25] Wells writes that "if men, in general, have used animation to echo and extend the premises and concerns of men in live-action filmmaking, then women have used animation to create a *specific feminine aesthetic* that resists the inherently masculine language of the live-action arena, and the most dominant codes of orthodox hyper-realist animation which also use its vocabulary" (emphasis added).[26] Conversely, he posits, "women's animation is less censored in its concerns, even when working in forms that move beyond hyper-realism, and seeks to be more subjective."[27] Wells identifies four key elements in this specific feminine aesthetic: a focus on the representation of woman as subject, a mistrust for language and a preference for "visual" expressivity, a tendency toward the creation of more "radical texts," and a focus on "reveal[ing] a woman's relationship to her own body," which he explains via a list of all-encompassing relations: "her interaction with men and other women; her perception of her private and public role; her social and political identity within the domestic and professional space, as determined by

istic career identity, "swinging between commercial and independent animation making processes." Similarly, Louise Pau pointed out the pressure of balancing one's "own art practice and commercial work." Hong Kong University of Science and Technology, "Animators' Roundtable Forum: Hong Kong Animation, Zoom Webinar," May 12–14, 2022, https://acas.world/2022/04/21/animators-roundtable-forum-hong-kong-animation-zoom-webinar-may-12-14-2022/.

25. Paul Wells, *Understanding Animation* (London: Routledge, 2013), 198–203.

26. Wells, *Understanding Animation,* 198.

27. Wells, *Understanding Animation,* 199.

law; and also, the relationship between female sexuality, desire, and creativity."[28] To illustrate these key elements, Welles focuses on Jane Aaron's *Interior Design* (1980) while referring to Suzan Pitt's *Asparagus* and listing animators such as Faith Hubley, Joy Batchelor, Sally Cruickshank, and Kathy Rose. Wells's notion of feminine aesthetic in animation is echoed in a few other studies, but it has not been significantly expanded.[29]

Beyond issues of representation, scholarship on women's animation has also taken into consideration the broader, unequal, context of production and distribution. This approach can be found in publications that have either attempted to map anthological and chronological (not quite historical) accounts of women's contributions to animation or have examined individual case studies. Anthological accounts include Jayne Pilling's *Women and Animation*, a 1992 BFI pioneering publication, which remains the first and only (although now quite dated) critical compendium of women animators.[30] Unsurprisingly, the majority of animators included in this volume are from the North American continent or Western Europe with a handful of Eastern European animators. Significantly more comprehensive, although mostly descriptive rather than analytical or critical, is Heather Kai Smith's online directory "Great Women Animators."[31] Smith includes quite a few women animators from Asia (Japan, Korea, and India) and other non-European countries (such as Iran or South Africa), but not China; a search for contemporary Chinese animators—at least at the time when this essay was written—lead to no results. The directory collects and allocates women's animation spatially (by country of origin), chronologically (by decade, starting from the 1910s and ending with the 1990s, with

28. Wells, *Understanding Animation*, 200.

29. For an earlier discussion of "feminine" quality in animation, see Bruno Edera, "L'animation au féminin," *La revue du cinéma* 389 (1983). For an alternative—from a non-Eurocentric, indigenous perspective—discussion of "feminine aesthetics" in animation, see Channette Romero, "Toward an Indigenous Feminine Animation Aesthetic," *Studies in American Indian Literatures* 29, no. 1 (2017).

30. Jayne Pilling, ed., *Women and Animation: A Compendium* (London: British Film Institute, Exhibition & Distribution Division, 1992).

31. Heather Kai Smith is a researcher and artist based in Vancouver, BC, Canada, and describes her open access, volunteer project as an "Ongoing international directory of historical and contemporary female animators." Heather Smith, "Great Women Animators," http://greatwomenanimators.com/about.

an additional category—contemporary—to cover the new millennium), as well as other more fluid and hybrid categories based on genre or style (e.g., abstract animation, clay animation, documentary animation, experimental animation, stop-motion animation).

In terms of specific case studies, examinations of individual women artists are also limited and mostly focus on European or North American animators. Among the artist-focused studies, Lotte Reiniger—as the celebrated and yet marginalized animateur who pioneered silhouette animation—has received the most significant scholarly attention.[32] As for Chinese animation, women's contributions are almost untraceable in earlier Chinese-language publications. More recently, in English-language scholarship, gender has been introduced as a critical perspective to draw attention to Chinese animation's patriarchal hegemonic discourse. For example, in her monograph, *Animated Encounters: Transnational Movements of Chinese Animation, 1940s–1970s*, Daisy Yan Du examines the representation of national(ist) masculinity and ethnic minorities' femininity in Chinese animation.[33] A renewed interest in mapping women's historical relevance by recording their voices and preserving their memories is also evidenced in the recent edited volume *Chinese Animation and Socialism: From Animators' Perspectives*, which includes several sections on Tang Cheng's 唐澄 work, beyond her contribution as one of the associate

32. Studies on Lotte Reiniger include Christiane Schönfeld, "Lotte Reiniger and the Art of Animation," in *Practicing Modernity: Female Creativity in the Weimar Republic*, ed. Christiane Schönfeld (Würzburg: Königshausen & Neumann, 2006), 169–85; Rachel Palfreyman, "Life and Death in the Shadows: Lotte Reiniger's *Die Abenteuer Des Prinzen Ahmed*," *German Life and Letters* 1, no. 64 (2011); Whitney Grace, *Lotte Reiniger: Pioneer of Film Animation* (Jefferson, NC: McFarland, 2017); Katharina Boeckenhoff and Caroline Ruddell, "Lotte Reiniger: The Crafty Animator and Cultural Value," in *The Crafty Animator: Handmade, Craft-Based Animation and Cultural Value*, ed. Caroline Ruddell and Paul Ward (Cham: Palgrave Macmillan, 2019); Chunning Guo, "The Echo of Women through Silent Paper Cut-Out Animation: "Scissorhands" Lotte Reiniger's Reflection through Body Language," in *Propaganda, Ideology, Animation: Twisted Dreams of History*, ed. Olga Bobrowska, Michał Bobrowski, and Bogusław Zmudziński (Kraków: AGH University of Science and Technology Press, 2019), 196–208.

33. See Du's analysis of patriarchal discourse in *Princess Iron Fan* or the feminization of ethnic minorities. Daisy Yan Du, *Animated Encounters: Transnational Movements of Chinese Animation, 1940s–1970s* (University of Hawai'i Press, 2019), 43–45, 166–67.

directors for *Little Tadpoles Look for Mama* (*Xiao kedou zhao mama*, 小蝌蚪找妈妈, 1960) and an interview with animation voice actress Ding Jianhua 丁建华.[34]

In this scholarly context, a feminist approach is largely undeveloped, but some significant developments in this direction have emerged. For example, in a contribution to the 2018 volume *Expanded Animation*, Suzanne Buchan engages with a declaredly feminist framework in her comparative analysis of five animators (Suzan Pitt, Tabaimo, Rose Bond, Marina Zurkow, and Miwa Matreyek).[35] Buchan revisits psychoanalytic theory from a non-essentialist theoretical perspective to examine the experience of alienation in these artists' works. She argues that the shared "trope of inside/outside specific to their animated and gendered worlds" can be interpreted as a postfeminist strategy, aimed at countering individual alienation, offering a "positive commodification of the female body."[36] Buchan points out that "by transforming the second-wave position that the personal is political into a third-wave feminist politics of the everyday, with representations of both strong and sensitive, celebratory and abject animated female figures, this animated (post-) feminism is less personal, but more embracing and inclusive of the wider audience it addresses."[37] Focusing on experimental computer animation, Birgitta Hosea has reflected on the intersection between cyberfeminism and animation by looking at the work of a multilingual multicultural diversified range of digital artists. She traces the earlier practices of female innovators in computer animation in the 1970s and examines subsequent developments in relation to the notion of

34. Daisy Yan Du, ed., *Chinese Animation and Socialism: From Animators' Perspectives* (Leiden: Brill, 2021). The Association of Chinese Animation Studies website profiles Diana Luen Wah Hui, a member of the renowned (male-dominated) animation design team of the Shanghai Animation Film Studio. Diana Luen Wah Hui, "Memories of a Socialist Inbetweener," April 17, 2020, https://acas.world/2020/04/27/memories-of-a-socialist-inbetweener. See also Daisy Yan Du's chapter 6 in this volume, "Women Animation Directors in Socialist China, 1940s–1980s."

35. Suzanne Buchan, "The Animated Female Body, Feminism(s) and 'Mushi,'" in *Experimental and Expanded Animation*, ed. Vicky Smith and Nicky Hamlyn (Cham: Springer, 2018).

36. Buchan, "Animated Female Body," 204.

37. Buchan, "Animated Female Body," 225.

écriture feminine (with reference to the Australia-based VNS Matrix), in relation to post-cyberfeminism (here, interestingly, with a reference to Lu Yang), Afrofuturism (for example, the collages and animations of Wangechi Mutu), and glitch feminism (with reference to the works of Kathleen Daniels and Lili Carré). Hosea concludes that her examination of computer animation "does not show a consistent engagement with an explicitly feminist agenda," and that it is, instead, the hand-made animation that engages more directly with feminism.[38]

More recently, in their doctoral theses (completed in 2022), Vanessa Cambier and Marie-Josée Saint-Pierre provocatively unpack issues of inequality and representation in animation practices from a declaredly feminist perspective. Both focusing on the North American context, these studies offer extensive, in-depth analyses of animation works and their symbolic, figurative choices while examining the conditions (e.g., geographical, historical, social, economic, institutional) that have produced a profoundly uneven playing field. These conditions of inequality can—at least potentially, via individual and collective actions—become channels for the promotion of alternative, antihegemonic discourses.[39] Cambier mostly focuses on the works of Sally Cruikshank and Kelly Gallagher, but also addresses the issue of race by examining the intersection between feminist politics and BIPOC animators. Saint-Pierre's PhD thesis examines a *corpus féministe* (a feminist corpus) of women animators working within the National Film Board of Canada Cinema. In an earlier article on representations of women's sexuality and desires in the work of three Quebec artists, Saint-Pierre points to the importance of understanding the conditions in which women's animation emerges and develops. She writes:

38. Birgitta Hosea, "Beyond a Digital Écriture Féminine: Cyberfeminism and Experimental Computer Animation," in *Experimental Animation: From Analogue to Digital*, ed. Miriam Harris, Lilly Husbands, and Paul Taberham (London: Routledge, 2019), 147.

39. Vanessa Cambier, "Extending the Frame: Animation, Feminism, & Politics" (PhD diss., University of Minnesota, 2022); Marie-Josée Saint-Pierre, "Femmes et cinéma d'animation: Un corpus féministe à l'Office national du film du Canada 1939–1989" (PhD diss., Les Presses de l'Université de Montréal, 2022).

> it is not trivial that image-by-image cinema allows filmmakers to occupy almost all the positions necessary for the completion of their works: scriptwriting, animation, production, photography and production. Perhaps this is one of the reasons why women have had access to this field—by working alone on their animated creations, they have been able to get out of the hegemonic and androcentric system governing the film production system in which they were mostly subjugated to men.[40]

Women in animation can and do occupy multiple positions and, crucially, can and do have agency in each of them. A feminist perspective in animation requires us to recognize the key connection between creative choices and the space of production and distribution, and to understand aesthetics and politics, art and craft as mutually determining. My examination of Chinese-accented women animateurs seeks to analyze their practices as complex gestures of making and unpack how expressive, crafting, displaying, and sharing modalities contribute to creating feminist gestures, rather than a feminine aesthetic.

Animation's Gestures of Making

As I reconnect issues of representation with those of production and distribution, I am interested in unpacking the intimate correlation between the offscreen act of handcrafting, its onscreen (trans)visualization, and the public space in which women animateurs share their work and connect among themselves and with their audiences. Vilém Flusser's phenomenology of gestures is particularly useful in bringing together all these acts and temporalities because it allows us to understand animation as a complex

40. Marie-Josée Saint-Pierre, "Quebec Animation Cinema and Women's Agentivity: An Exploration of Sexuality and Desire through the Works of Three Animators Produced at the National Film Board of Canada," *Animation Studies* (September 13, 2020). https://journal.animationstudies.org/category/volume-15/marie-josee-saint-pierre-quebec-animation-cinema-and-womens-agentivity/ (site discontinued). For the original French-language article, see Marie-Josée Saint-Pierre, "Cinéma d'animation québécois et agentivité féminine. Une exploration de la sexualité et du désir à travers trois oeuvres d'animatrices produites à l'Office National du Film du Canada," *Nouvelle vues: Revue sur les pratiques, les théories et l'histoire du cinéma au Québec* 20 (2019).

gesture of making. In the animated works of the women animateurs I examine, we are invited to contemplate and participate in the gesture of making in all its complexity, which Flusser argues "defies description" and can only be executed and ultimately presented to others.[41] Thinking of women animateurs' practices as gestures thus means understanding the making of the animation (i.e., the intersecting relationship between the off-screen subject and the on-screen object) as inseparable from its presentation, which crucially opens up and completes animation's gesture of making by including the public space in which the animated work is shared.

Flusser's phenomenology grounds itself in the materiality of the body, the hands, and their movements and relates them to meaning-making and human's ethical engagement with the world:

> We have two hands. We comprehend the world from two opposing sides, which is how the world can be taken in, grasped, intended, and manipulated. We do not comprehend it from eight sides, as an octopus does. Because of the symmetry between our opposed hands, the world is "dialectical" for us.[42]

He then elaborates on the relationship between our constantly moving hands and knowledge. Hands are not just symbolic but also material producers of a gesture of making, through which we perceive, handle, and comprehend the world. He sees this gesture as a potentially endless search for, but also a manipulation of, the objects we seek to know. It is a way of delimiting, selecting, transforming, and imposing personal agency over the world. Crucially, for Flusser, the gesture of making is not simply indexed to the maker or the object that is made. He argues that it is only via the associated gesture of presentation that the gesture of making finds its resignation, that is, the moment when "the hands stop working," when they are "no longer able to make the work better" and instead present what they have made, opening themselves to others and making their work public.[43]

Animation practices, especially the handcrafted digital animations that are the objects of my study, are arguably tangible applications of Flusser's

41. Vilém Flusser, *Gestures* (Minneapolis: University of Minnesota Press, 2014), 34.

42. Flusser, *Gestures*, 33.

43. Flusser, *Gestures*, 47.

phenomenology. Understanding animation as a gesture of making means focusing on the fundamental relationship between the hands' movement and materialities, a key relationship through which the world is perceived, grasped, understood, transformed, presented to, and shared with others. In animation "the hand at work" is central, often evoked, implied, or even explicitly revealed in the object (the animation) that is shared with the viewers.[44] As Hosea notes, "making animation by hand involves a physical activity that leaves a mark behind where the animator's body has come in contact with the surface," which affirms "not only that the hand was present, but also individual subjectivity."[45] Furthermore, while she does not find an explicit feminist agenda in contemporary digital animation, Hosea also notes that "films that engage more overtly with feminism . . . are overwhelmingly created through hand-drawn or hand-made processes" and "the majority of female students—whether feminist in outlook or not—prefer to engage with hand-drawn or hand-made aesthetics over more technical processes such as CGI or code."[46]

Feminist Gestures: Creative Agency

By recognizing the key relationship between handmade and gender, we can better understand the feminist in animation's gestures of making. Chinese-accented women animateurs emphasize the handmade as a key expressive modality in their digital animation, which they see as an embodied rather than a merely technological practice. For example, Cai

44. For more on the hand of the artist as "fundamental to the form," see Ruddell and Ward, *The Crafty Animator*, 2–4. For more on the evoked presence of the hand at work in the animation text, see Norman M. Klein, "Animation and Animorphs: A Brief Disappearing Act," in *Meta-Morphing: Visual Transformation and the Culture of Quick-Change*, ed. Vivian Sobchack, 21–39 (Minneapolis: University of Minnesota Press, 2000). For an analysis of the materialization of the hand on-screen in "para-animation," see Paola Voci, "Para-Animation in Practice and Theory: The Animateur, the Embodied Gesture, and Enchantment," *Animation* 18, no. 1 (2023): 23–41.

45. Birgitta Hosea, "Made by Hand," in *The Crafty Animator: Handmade, Craft-Based Animation and Cultural Value*, eds. Caroline Ruddell and Paul Ward (Cham: Palgrave Macmillan, 2019), 28.

46. Hosea, "Beyond a Digital Écriture Féminine," 146.

Caibei, who makes her animations by drawing on paper, projecting on fabric, printing the frames, and recoloring them, explains: "Most of my animations are hand-drawn. When I was doing *Half Asleep*, I first drew all the lines of motion with charcoal on paper and then projected them on the cloth. . . . The reason I keep going back to paper is that I feel like I can touch every frame of my film."[47] On her Vimeo channel, Zhu Yantong shares a behind-the-scene video, which shows how, after drawing a draft with a digital pen so that she can preview it on her computer, she mostly works on paper. With a pen dipped in ink, she paints lines on the images to give them "unique and random shadowing effects" and colors them, frame by frame, with pastels.[48] The completed handmade drawings are finally scanned on the computer where the final editing takes place. In each instance, the handmade is reclaimed as a key modality through which creative control and full authorship are realized.

Placing an even greater emphasis on the handmade, in a video documenting the making of her animation *The Person in Crevice [sic]*, Lu Tingting 鲁婷婷 talks about the slow labor involved in producing thousands of individually painted frames on paper, showing the massive materiality of handmade paintings, piled up on a desk, grouped by sequences, or spread in a long line across a corridor.[49] In the video, Lu explains her animation's key concerns and shares her creative agency with her collaborators, who appear to be all women, and are captured as they paint at their desks, or surround her while she discusses with them the various conceptual and technical steps of the animation. All these gendered hands and their gestures of making (i.e., pencil drawings and brushstrokes) are also visible in the texture of the completed work, which has no animation layer, allowing for "the mark left behind where the animator's body has come in contact with the surface" to be even more visible and tangible.[50] In Lu's own words, this "non-animation" aims at preserving and exposing the materiality and the labor of the

47. "Art-Isle Talk | Cai Caibei: Banxing shifen x Pianpian mengjing."

48. Zhu Yantong, "X Company Animated: Behind the Scenes with Yantong Zhu," 2016, Video, 1:30, https://vimeo.com/156761118.

49. Lu Tingting, *The Person in Crevice* (*Fengxi zhongde ren* 缝隙中的人), 2018, Video, 3:49.

50 Hosea, "Made by Hand," 28.

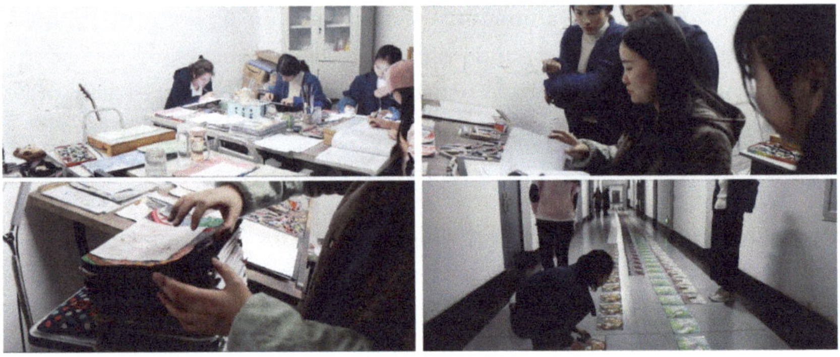

FIGURE 7.1. Gendered hands and gestures of making, in Lu Tingting's non-animation, "Documentary of *The Person in Crevice*."

individual paintings rather than merging, and thus erasing them in the process of creating motion (fig. 7.1).[51]

Expanding on Buchan's notion of a "gendered animated world" that focuses on the creative visual texts and installations, Lu's documentary video therefore points to the existence of a gendered *animating* world that refers to the act and the modalities of the creative practice. As we watch a group of women led by a woman director, working together in the making of this non-animation, it is indeed tempting to contrast them with the historical trope of women working largely as unrecognized workhands under the creative direction of male animators. Lu's video on the making of *The Person in Crevice* indeed points to a broader discourse of women's empowerment and emancipation from invisible laborers to visible subjects, in full control of their creative agency.

Beyond the moment of creation (the context of crafting and labor), as we follow these feminist gestures in the moment of presentation (the context of circulation), we can see that women animateurs are not only affirming their personal and collaborative creative agency, but are also part of a public undertaking, if not quite a call to action. To be sure, there is no organized collective of women animateurs, no manifesto that aims at creating a gendered community, no single exhibition or festival that could be seen as an extemporaneous unifying, militant event. But again, any such

51. Lu Tingting, *Fengxi zhong de ren: Lu Tingting jilu pian 15 fenzhong* 缝隙中的人：鲁婷婷纪录片15分钟 (Documentary of *The Person in Gap*), 2017, Video, 17:10, https://vimeo.com/212852551.

actions would indeed be at odds with the light, hybrid positionalities that characterize them. Yet women animateurs do indeed converge occasionally, neither accidentally nor programmatically, in the creation of public communities in which women animateurs extend their gestures to include each other as well as the audiences.

Evidence indicates that indeed Chinese-accented animateurs not only intersect with and encounter one another during their educational training or at animation festivals, but also develop active collaborations and are themselves agents of convergences. One example of these converging encounters is "Beyond Noumenon," an international experimental animation exhibition and forum that took place at the Sichuan Fine Arts Institute, in Chongqing (October 18–November 1, 2016). Although the event was not exclusively focused on women's experiences, it was clearly permeated by feminist gestures. Lu Tingting was the director and head curator; women's personal and professional connections also left a clear mark in the forum, as evidenced both by the program and the participants' narratives.[52] Another public space in which feminist gestures can be identified is the Feinaki Beijing Animation Week, also led and directed by a woman animateur, Zhu Yantong. Launched in 2019 and now in its third edition, it is "an animation festival curated by the internationally well-connected Chinese animation artists, researchers, and curators who frequently travel between animation festivals across the world."[53] In the section "Best of Feinaki (Beijing, China): Young Filmmakers from China," Chinese-accented women are making feminists gestures not only by outnumbering their men colleagues, but also by focusing on gendered animated worlds. One final example is online, on Sohu, in a 2019 screening program curated by Chai Mi, which brings together in a public space the feminist gestures of Chinese-accented women animateurs. Chai describes them as having had personal and professional impacts on her own work: "Lyric or narrative, these films have played a part in my years of experience in international animation festivals. They are about youth, aging, affection, romance, trouble (bitterness), happiness (sweetness), and transcendence. From Hers.[54]"

52. See Birgitta Hosea, "Beyond Noumenon," *Expanded Animation: Expanding Ideas about Animation*, December 14, 2016, https://expandedanimation.net/2016/12/14/beyond-noumenon-talk/.

53 "Feinaki Beijing Animation Week: About us," https://feinaki.com/about_us_en.

54. Chai Mi, "Laizi tamen: Zhongguo yishu donghua" 来自她们——中国艺术动画 (From hers: Chinese art animation), https://www.sohu.com/a/345779959_494887.

Feminist Gestures: Corporeal Presence

Last but certainly not least, feminist gestures do indeed create a "gendered animated world" that is visible in the objects of making, in the animations, on screen. Although not all animations focus on women's positionality vis-à-vis patriarchy, gendered storytelling is pervasive, as is an emphasis on the representations of women's bodies.

Zhu Yantong's *My Milk Cup Cow* (2014) centers on fragments of the everyday life of a child living with her single father, who tricks her into drinking her breakfast cup of milk—the taste of which she finds "yucky"—by telling her that a cow will magically appear at the bottom of her cup once she drinks all the milk. The child is both motivated and alarmed by the promise that a cow would indeed materialize in her cup. The animation then expands this tension between reality and imagination, showing that the father conceals other truths, which are uncomfortable or unpleasant for him (such as how children are born, or receiving money under the table). The narrative is developed from the overlapping perspectives of the child and the adult narrator, who tells the story offscreen. The narrator's voice is implicitly indexed to the animateur as being the I who remembers and crafts memories of her childhood. At the end of the animation, the narrator concludes, "I noticed that I started telling lies like my father." What the child has experienced, far from harmless tricks or inspirational fantasies, is thus described as deception, albeit with no accusatory tone, but instead with a sad awareness of these deceptions' lingering power.

On screen, the corporeal presence of the creative subject is actualized via different strategies: the convergence between the animateur and the narrator's offscreen commentary, the child's diegetic voice, the point of view in the representation of the child body (a self-reflective gaze) and that of the father (seen from the child's perspective). The bodies are gendered via visual representations that emphasize their different scales and positionalities: for example, a close-up of the child's hands squeezing her father's fingers, eyes materializing on the father's legs, the child's head inserted into her father's shoulder in recurrent acts of handling, grasping, manipulating, touching, seeing, glimpsing, spying, imagining (fig. 7.2). The animation emphasizes the expansiveness of the father vis-à-vis the smallness of the daughter, who is often shown as implanted in the father's large

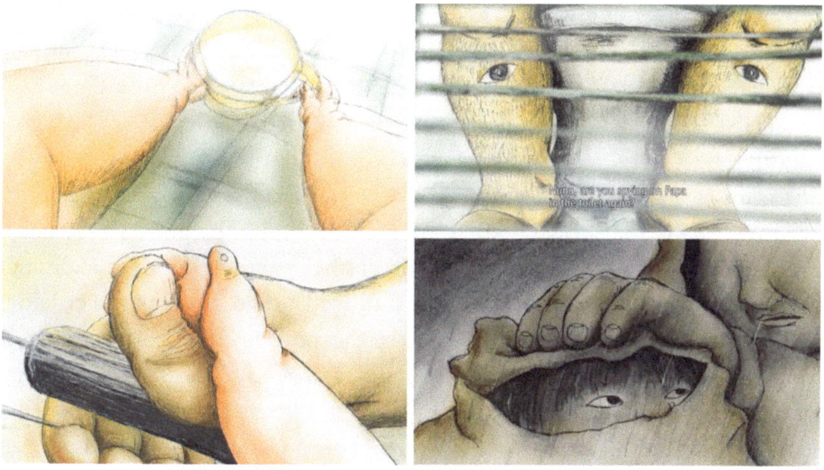

FIGURE 7.2. Recurrent acts of handling, grasping, manipulating, touching, seeing, glimpsing, spying, and imagining, in *My Milk Cup Cow* (2014). Courtesy of Zhu Yantong.

body, peeking out and then being reabsorbed into it. He is represented as a benevolent but also disconcerting patriarch who protects her, takes care of her, controls her, deceives her, worries her, and ultimately becomes a weak but undeletable memory that she carries with her that continues to shape (control?) her actions.

The gendered animated world is depicted with a soft neutral color palette, only slightly saturated with gray when evoking unsettling emotions—such as watching the legs of her father through the grate on the toilet wall and imagining her face covered by hair, riding in the bike seat under the rain anchoring herself to her father's hands. The animation seems to end with a black-and-white shot of framed photographs as the credits roll on. However, in postcredit shots, the narrator adds an epilogue, with the daughter having left home now returning to visit her father, whom she sees from the perspective of a young woman, feeble and aged, and drinking the cup of milk she never liked as a child but that he continues to give her. Power relations have changed but, without conveying nostalgia for the past, the narrator admits that she has not quite moved beyond it: "But I always drank it all down just the same."

Many of Cho Pei-Hsin's animations focus on women's stories and emotions. She describes her work as personal, seeking to create "tangible and visually tactile images," introspective and atmospheric.[55] Woman's struggle against entrapment was already a key concern in an earlier student work, *The Girl The Tree*, a stop-motion animation produced by Cho, Lin Hsin 林昕, and Chen Hsin 陈忻, which tells the story of a little girl captured by a male-gendered tree who keeps her prisoner inside his trunk. She is upset and scared but placated by the tree's roots, which feed her, give her toys, caring for her as "if she were his daughter." The girl initially feels protected and happy, but she grows increasingly tired and lonely, realizing that the world the tree created for her is indeed a cage. Missing the outside world and "her real mummy," she tries to escape, but fails. Years go by and we learn that the tree eventually allowed her to get out and see the outside world, but still keeps her tightly entangled with his trunk, so that she remains with him "forever." In *Hermit* (2016), a sad-looking woman is sitting on a bench, with a pram (albeit no baby is ever shown in the animation). She sees a small hermit crab, grabs it, and takes it home, where she places it in a bottle. Shown from the point of view of the hermit crab, the woman undresses and submerges herself in her bathtub and gazes back at the bottle with the hermit crab. Next, the woman attends to a man—likely her husband—who sits on a chair in a dark room and makes indistinguishable sounds, possibly instructing her about his needs. She walks slowly from one room to the next, sits, goes out, still pushing her pram, increasingly leaning forward under the weight of a shell-shaped hump that has grown on her back. Once at home, she opens the bottle and lets the hermit crab out. In the final mise en abyme, out of the shell emerges a miniaturized version of herself. The hermit woman is free only for a fleeting moment; she quickly retreats within the shell, going back to carry her own home and be entrapped by it.

On the one hand, these animations can be seen as addressing key oppressions in Confucian patriarchy—i.e., woman's subjugation as a daughter, a wife, and a mother. On the other, gendered animations also go beyond and outside traditional gender relations, focusing instead on women's amorphous, sensuous, and self-sufficient bodies. In Chen Jiayin's 陈佳音 *Squishy Fish Eggs*, a woman observes her own rounded body, which dilutes and separates into smaller organic, amorphous appendages simul-

55. Cho Pei Hsin, "About."

FIGURE 7.3. A woman's rounded body dilutes and separates into smaller appendages, in *Squishy Fish Eggs* (2020). Courtesy of Chen Jiayin.

taneously shown as morphing out of the squishy fish eggs she is eating. Oblong forms resembling fingers and limbs held by chopsticks then grasp and caress each other, while the woman's body duplicates, reproduces itself and merges into larger versions of her body (fig. 7.3). Similarly, in Cho Pei-Hsin's *Ego*, the female figure morphs with the grass and branches out into other organic forms (animal and microcellular shapes), then floats, duplicates, and is reabsorbed into her one (but revealed as potentially spreadable and expandable) body.

Whether by telling stories that expose the deceptions and the entrapment that patriarchal expectations impose on women, or by (re)animating and shapeshifting the woman's body to insinuate, morph into, grasp, and engulf the world, Chinese-accented women animateurs are making gendered animated gestures. These gestures differ from the gendered animated world described and analyzed by Buchan, in which "the strong and sensitive, celebratory and abject animated female figures" were seen as conveying a "less personal" animated (post-) feminism."[56] In fact, their story-based animations develop quite declaredly personal (and even autobiographical) narratives in which their female figures are neither

56. Buchan, "Animated Female Body," 225.

celebratory nor abject and are often characterized by a soft melancholy rather than by alienation. In these stories, beyond what is shown on the screen, the corporeal presence of a woman's subjectivity also materializes via gendered sounds. In almost all the animations I watched, the voice-over is a female voice (sometimes a gender-neutral child voice, but never a male voice). In more abstract, conceptual animations, the emphasis is on shapeshifting bodies rather than on the promotion of "positive commodification of the female body."[57] Animations like *Ego* or *Squishy Fish Eggs* reframe woman's subjectivity in sensuously self-reliant almost-female forms that transform and expand the female bodies both inwardly and outwardly, caressing both the world around and themselves. Making themselves (re)appear, women animateurs rematerialize both their voices and their bodies.

Conclusion

I argue that Chinese-accented women animateurs practices (the works they produce, the words that accompany them, the convergences they create) can be best understood as feminist gestures. Both on-screen and off-screen, their affirmations of corporeal presence and creative agency contribute to the reappearance of the subjectivities of women who have long been marginalized, rendered invisible, made to "vanish." On the one hand, both in narrative and conceptual animations, women are corporeally present. Women's stories are told by women's voices, drawn by women's hands; their bodies are seen, shaped, and transformed by women's perspectives and gazes. On the other hand, in the diverse temporalities and localities of physical and virtual presentations, women animateurs' affirmation of ownership and authorship completes and expands what is represented on screens. In the multiple, transnational channels through which they circulate their works, Chinese-accented women animateurs share their handmade practices ("the making of"), articulate their artistic aspirations, explain their expressive choices. They engage in a complex process of negotiations, which requires them to embrace transversal mobility—moving

57. Buchan, "Animated Female Body," 204.

in between geographical locations and artistic and commercial environments—and fluidity across multiple media and materialities. Their feminist gestures, although not connected by a unifying militant goal, challenge the many erasures, discriminations, and entrapments in the long history of male-dominated Chinese animation. With visible determination, Chinese-accented women animateurs are claiming full control over their creative agency.

SECTION THREE

Identities

EIGHT

What's in a Line?

Borders and Diffusion in Ink-Painting Animation

SHANNON BROWNLEE

Ink-painting animation is sometimes considered to be the quintessentially Chinese style of animation, primarily because it replicates the aesthetics of traditional Chinese ink painting so closely.[1] Many other animated forms draw deeply on traditional visual and performance arts, but one thing that sets ink-painting animation apart is that it required Chinese filmmakers to overcome the limitations of a Western technology. In the late 1950s, artists and technicians at the Shanghai Animation Film Studio (SAFS) worked with the multiplane animation stand to develop a technique for making ink paintings move, even though celluloid does not absorb and disperse pigmented water as paper does. They painted different opacities on multiple layers and used soft focus to replicate the diffusion effect, creating a very different aesthetic from the crisp outlines and flat colors of conventional cel animation. This thoroughly indigenized the technology.[2] The origins of ink-painting animation can thus be seen as

1. See, for example, Zhang Ruirui and Chi Cheng, "Ink Animation Art in the Digital Age," *Energy Procedia* 17 (2012): 1295–98.

2. Olga Bobrowska cites director Te Wei to this effect in "Seeking Truth in Facts: Historicizing Chinese Animation," in *Global Animation Theory: International Perspectives at Animafest Zagreb*, eds. Franziska Bruckner, Holger Lang, Nikica Gilić, Daniel Šuljić, and Hrvoje Turković (New York: Bloomsbury Academic, 2019), 67. Helen Kang notes that the precise technique is still secret because "it is one of the few animation methods that the Chinese *can call their own*" (emphasis added). See Helen Kang, "*Shui Mo Dong Hua:* The History and Development of Brush Painting Animation," *Animation Journal* 14 (2006): 64.

both a celebration of traditional aesthetics and a modern victory over Western technology and hegemony. The form stalled briefly after the late 1980s because it was unsustainable in a market economy, but digital labor-saving processes supported its revival a decade later. Although digital ink-painting animation is usually presented in less victorious terms than its analog predecessor, it continues to be seen as a quintessential Chinese aesthetic on a global stage still strongly shaped by Western interests.

This narrative of ink-painting animation is not inaccurate, but the confrontations it constructs between East and West efface aspects of the relationship and threaten to essentialize both terms. If we look at the range of aesthetics, techniques, and content of the form as well as the diversity of opinions and biographies among filmmakers and researchers, we see that ink-painting animation is deeply heterogeneous. This heterogeneity is partly intracultural, which contributes to the unraveling of essentialist definitions of Chinese culture. It is also transcultural, shaped by the East-West entanglements that are the focus of this chapter. These entanglements are sometimes oppositional and sometimes disavowed, but they blur the borders between regions and identities. Such borders are not false. They operate politically, socially, and linguistically in contexts as constructive as collaboration among peers and as adverse as international governmental conflicts. However, when lines are drawn in ways that constrict, homogenize, or essentialize, we need to look for a different story—perhaps not one that is more true, but one that is also true. As Yiman Wang writes, "the necessary divide between the Self and Other enables their mutual constitution, *which leads to border reconfiguration*" (emphasis added).[3] Ink-painting animation tells a story that reconfigures borders through its unbounded visuals. Its diffusion effects issue us a formal invitation to reflect on the transcultural entanglements that produce them: ink-painting animation is both an instance of and a metaphor for the blurriness of regional borders.

This chapter responds to that formal invitation. Broadly, the first half addresses ink painting and its cinematic translation on the animation stand, and the second half addresses the digital context. The first half starts with a brief discussion of the discursive, asymmetrical interdepen-

3. Yiman Wang, "The 'Transnational' as Methodology: Transnationalizing Chinese Film Studies through the Example of *The Love Parade* and Its Chinese Remakes," *Journal of Chinese Cinemas* 2, no. 1 (2008): 19.

dence of Chineseness and Westernness, which raises theoretical issues the chapter attempts to work through. Discussing the East-West entanglement of ink-painting animation entails a risk of simply reversing the indigenization narrative to claim, instead, that the form in fact owes a great deal to the West. To counteract this risk, I ask both how English-language animation and film theories may help us interpret ink-painting animation and its progenitor, ink painting, and also how these artistic forms can inform and edify English-language theories—specifically, theories of the still image and Tom Gunning's concept of astonishment.[4] None of this discussion is intended to be definitive. The plurality of both Chinese and Western cultures and their discursive interrelation preclude a master narrative; this chapter therefore offers multiple, even conflicting, interpretations.

The second half of this chapter turns to digital ink-painting animation. It looks first at computer scientists' work on the development of realistic digital brushes. Whereas the animation stand can plausibly be seen as a Western technology that analog ink-painting animation indigenized, even the earliest research in digital brush technology presents an entanglement of East and West. Since then, Chinese and other East Asian researchers have been the leaders in the field, but computer scientists' publications generally grant the West discursive privileges while disavowing ongoing transcultural exchange. Finally, looking at the archive of digital ink-painting animation on popular sites such as Youku Tudou and YouTube, we find diverse ways of navigating borders between cultures and between past and present. The digital tools of production and distribution amplify stylistic and cultural hybridity while remaining attentive to cultural identity and difference.

4. This discussion is a supplement to previous scholarship, especially the comprehensive mapping of the complex cultural and national position and transnational significance of ink-painting animation in the socialist era in Daisy Yan Du, *Animated Encounters: Transnational Movements of Chinese Animation 1940s–1970s* (Honolulu: University of Hawai'i Press, 2019), 114–51; and the transcultural interpretation of ink-painting animation from the earliest years into the digital age in Panpan Yang, "Animating Landscape: Chinese Ink-Painting Animation, 1960–2013," *International Journal of Comic Art* 16, no. 2 (2014): 380–97.

Chineseness-es and Westernness-es

In "On Chineseness as a Theoretical Problem," Rey Chow describes the discursivity of both Chinese and Western identities. She writes that, in response to centuries of Western imperialism, Chinese intellectuals have been compelled to emphasize Chineseness, assert cultural superiority, and draw a "boundary between China and the rest of the world"; Chow calls this "*the logic of the wound*" (emphasis in the original).[5] Conversely, Western intellectuals tend to "stigmatize and ghettoize non-Western cultures" by applying national and ethnic labels but leaving Western works unmarked and implicitly constructing them as universal or culturally neutral.[6] The West is thus hegemonic by definition, "an ambiguous and ubiquitous presence of a certain global domination whose subject can hardly be identifiable" but that "peoples in the so-called non-West have to refer to and rely on . . . so as to construct their own cultural and historical identity."[7] Chow intervenes in this discourse by arguing that Chineseness is an "open signifier" and site of difference that must be explored "not only in terms of a struggle against the West but also, increasingly, in terms of the permanently evolving mutations internal to the invocation of ethnicity itself."[8] Indeed, Chow writes that Chinese identity can be conceived as plural, as "Chineseness-es."[9] This can also prompt us to conceive of the West as plural, as Westernness-es, to challenge its hegemonic and perhaps monolithic status and to acknowledge its ongoing construction in dialogue with Chineseness-es and other identities. We cannot dispense with labels. As the editors of this volume write in the introduction, using the term *Chinese* is both a "practical necessity" and "strategic essentialism," and we could not discuss transnational entanglements without regional signifiers. However, the emphasis on discursivity in concepts such as Chineseness-es and Westernness-es may give us leeway within this necessary constraint.

5. Rey Chow, "Introduction: On Chineseness as a Theoretical Problem," *boundary 2* 25, no. 3 (1998): 6.

6. Chow, "On Chineseness," 4.

7. Naoki Sakai, *Translation and Subjectivity: On "Japan" and Cultural Nationalism* (Minneapolis: University of Minnesota Press, 1997), 61. Cited in Chow, "On Chineseness," 4.

8. Chow, "On Chineseness," 9.

9. Chow, "On Chineseness," 24.

The asymmetrical mutual dependence of Chinese and Western plays out extensively in the field of animation. As Weihua Wu writes, "the tension between Westernization and Chineseness in animation production has been in existence from the beginning, and discussions around these issues are still going on."[10] Nonetheless evidence indicates transnationalism in nationalist discourse. For example, the term *meishu dianying* 美术电影 (fine arts film) was introduced in the 1950s to replace earlier, Western-derived terms for animation, but the word *meishu* was coined in late nineteenth-century Japan.[11] The *minzu* 民族 (national) style inaugurated at this time is believed to stem from dismay that international audiences perceived the Chinese animated film, *Why the Crow Is Black* (*Wuya weishenme shi heide* 乌鸦为什么是黑的) (Wan Laiming 万籁鸣 and Wan Guchan 万古蟾, 1956), as a Soviet film.[12] However, Daisy Yan Du demonstrates that this is a foundational myth and reminds us, through this and many other stories, that what may seem essentialist is developed through encounters with others—even if that encounter demonizes the other.[13]

Ink Painting Has Always Been Animated

Just as definitions of identity are plural and dialogic, there is fluidity within definitions of ink painting (*shuimo* 水墨, also called ink-and-wash painting in English) and ink-painting animation (*shuimo donghua* 水墨动画, also ink animation). In a way, the term *donghua* is redundant. Though usually translated as "cartoon," it more literally means "moving painting"—and ink paintings are always already in motion.

Traditionally, ink painting is characterized by dynamism from creation to reception. In the sixth century, Xie He 谢赫 proposed *qiyun shengdong* 气韵生动 (vivid aliveness) as the first principle of painting. Reflecting on Song dynasty (960–1279) landscape painting, Xingming Wu writes, "Water, ink, paper and breath all work together, and they combine to produce a

10. Weihua Wu, *Chinese Animation, Creative Industries, and Digital Culture* (Abingdon, Oxon: Routledge, 2018), 26.

11. Wu, *Chinese Animation*, 27–28.

12. Wu, *Chinese Animation*, 21.

13. Du, *Animated Encounters*, 122–24.

record of the subjective quality of the whole period of time in which the painting was produced. That way, the art form is able to make use of the dynamic processes of ink application to replicate the life force that is understood to lie behind real geographic landscapes."[14] Movement also extends to the viewer, as the painting invites their eyes to roam and even "directly [affects] the rhythm of their breathing."[15] The crucial compositional principle of *liubai* 留白 (space without ink) allows the imagination to breathe.[16] Landscape, the preeminent subject matter of traditional ink painting, is often presented through scattered perspectives or multiple views within a single painting, which contrasts with the monocular perspective that dominates traditional European oil painting.[17] Insofar as ink-painting aesthetics come to represent Chineseness in contemporary animation, it is important to remember that its forms and philosophies have changed substantially over time, and have always varied in style, genre, and approach.[18] Nonetheless, this broad tradition of liveliness suggests that it is more appropriate to speak of paintings as individual rather than still images, images with their own kind of movement—as animate and even animated.

These paintings' close relation to animated film illuminates and contradicts a thread of English-language animation theory that emphasizes the deathliness of the still image. Alan Cholodenko is a particularly ardent proponent, proposing that "the first, last and enduring attraction of cinema as form of animation . . . is the uncanny reanimation of the dead as living

14. Xingming Wu, "Wrinkles in Time—Folding Song Dynasty into Contemporary Art" (PhD diss., University of Tasmania, 2018), 49.

15. Jian Cui, "The Pursuit of a National Style of Chinese Animation," *Animation Journal* 14 (2006): 46.

16. See Yang, "Animating Landscape," 382.

17. See Chen Chen, "Painterly Focused Chinese Ink Animation: Seeing Through the Cultural Lens of the Xiang System," *Animation Practice, Process & Production* 8 (2019): 146–48; Wu, "Wrinkles in Time," 49; Yang, "Animating Landscape," 3–4.

18. See, for example, an account of diversity within the Ming dynasty (1368–1644) Wu School in Kathlyn Liscomb, "Shen Zhou's Collection of Early Ming Paintings and the Origins of the Wu School's Eclectic Revivalism," *Artibus Asiae* 52, no. 3/4 (1992): 215–54. See also an account of radical departures in ink painting since the 1980s in Hung Wu's essay "Transcending the East/West Dichotomy: A Short History of Chinese Ink Painting," in *Ink Art: Past as Present in Contemporary China*, ed. Maxwell K. Hearn (New Haven, CT: Yale University Press, 2013), 19–33.

dead."[19] In this view, the individual image is dead, and the animatic machine gives it only the illusion of life and motion. This proposition holds less water in relation to a form of animation whose painterly roots are shaped by "vivid aliveness." On one hand, putting this Western animation theory into conversation with ink painting and animation elucidates its universalizing tendency. On the other, it would be a gross generalization to draw an essentialist line between Chinese vivacity and Western morbidity. For example, some Chinese stop-motion animations engage extensively with lifelessness.[20] We may also find more similarity than difference if we compare *liubai* with the early modern European painting technique of chiaroscuro, which prompts the viewer to "sort out the motions of figures from those of light, shade, and paint," and to "complete the image with his [*sic*] imagination."[21] Teasing out such variations in art and performance history and its cinematic descendants can help break down simplistic and essentialist East-West characterizations and distinctions; in this way, both similarity and difference can be productive.

Analog Ink-Painting Animation: Absence and Astonishment

If ink painting is always already animate, then in many ways the cinematic medium adds very little. The first two films that use ink animation pervasively are even adaptations of specific painters' work. *Little Tadpoles Look for Mama* (*Xiao kedou zhao mama* 小蝌蚪找妈妈) (Te Wei 特伟 and Tang Cheng 唐澄, 1960) was inspired by Qi Baishi 齐白石 (1864–1957). Li Keran

19. Alan Cholodenko, "(The) Death (of) the Animator, or: The Felicity of Felix, Part II," *Animation Studies* 2 (2007), https://oldjournal.animationstudies.org/the-death-of-the-animator-or-the-felicity-of-felix/.

20. For example, see Yiman Wang, "The Mortal Animal and the Techno-Animated Life: Chen Qiang's Experimental Zooetic Animation Trilogy *Cut Off*," *Journal of Chinese Cinemas* 11, no. 3 (2017): 210–26; Linda C. Zhang, "'Our Comrade Sun Wukong': On Fantasy and Exaggeration in *Mountain of Flames*," Association for Chinese Animation Studies, October 4, 2019, https://acas.world/2019/10/04/our-comrade-sun-wukong-on-fantasy-and-exaggeration-in-mountain-of-flames/.

21. Harry Berger Jr., "The System of Early Modern Painting," *Representations* 62 (1998): 39.

李可染 (1907–1989) was directly involved with *The Herd Boy's Flute* (*Mudi* 牧笛) (Te Wei 特伟, 1963), which adapts his paintings.[22] As Panpan Yang demonstrates, in these and the other two major analog films, *The Deer's Bell* (*Lu ling* 鹿铃) (Tang Cheng 唐澄 and Wu Qiang 邬强, 1982) and *Feelings of Mountain and River* (*Shanshui qing* 山水情) (Te Wei 特伟, 1988), slow pacing and loose story structures prioritize meditation over narrative and allow the spectator's eye and mind to rove as if over an ink painting.[23] For Chen Hailu, the slow, minimal camera movements also "effectively reenact the original way of observing ink paintings."[24] Music is an important addition, but Yang writes that it replicates the affective and meditative roles of landscape in painting.[25] In short, early ink-painting animations extend tendencies within the already animate paintings they adapt rather than investing them with entirely new dimensions of movement and time. This interpretation also suggests that the limited movement from cel to cel is not a result of a technical difficulty but instead evidence that ink-painting aesthetics are already compatible with cinematic animation. In this view, the indigenization of the animation stand is not confrontational; it is a gentler adaptation of a Western technology rather than a victory over it.

At the same time, it is valuable not to lose sight of the fact that the creation of diffusion effects on celluloid represents a technical victory over impermeability. To my mind, ink-painting animation adds one crucial, unprecedented element to ink-painting aesthetics: the element of technological wonder, or, in Tom Gunning's well-known terminology, astonishment.[26] This astonishment is of a different order from the admiration and

22. Duan Xiaoxuan, "Walking Our Own Path and Making Innovations in Chinese Animated Filmmaking," trans. Nick Stember, Association for Chinese Animation Studies, June 14, 2018, https://acas.world/2018/06/14/walking-our-own-path-and-making-innovations-in-chinese-animated-filmmaking/.

23. Yang, "Animating Landscapes," 382–85.

24. Chen Hailu, "CGI Ink-Painting Animation in Contemporary China, 1989–2019," trans. Yixing Li, Association for Chinese Animation Studies, July 24, 2020, https://acas.ust.hk/2020/07/24/cgi-ink-painting-animation-in-contemporary-china-1989-2019. See also Yang, "Animating Landscape," 383.

25. Yang, "Animating Landscape," 384.

26. Tom Gunning, "An Aesthetic of Astonishment: Early Film and the (In)Credulous Spectator," in *Viewing Positions: Ways of Seeing Film*, ed. Linda Williams (New Brunswick, NJ: Rutgers University Press, 1995), 114–33.

FIGURE. 8.1. Diffusion visible within forms, in *Little Tadpoles Look for Mama* (1960).

awe, no matter how great, that one might have for the skill with which a painter manipulates brush, ink, water, and paper. The main catalyst for astonishment is diffusion. In *Little Tadpoles Look for Mama,* this astonishing diffusion is visible within forms, as in the soft transitions between paler and darker hues of the fish's bodies, and also where forms such as tadpoles' wriggling tails meet empty space (see fig. 8.1). Diffusion should also make it impossible to achieve sufficient consistency from cel to cel. The delicate interactions of ink, water, paper, brush, and gesture present too many variables for "even the greatest artist [to] repeatedly reproduce the same paintings" as precisely as full cel animation normally requires.[27] Through these astonishing accomplishments, ink-painting animation invites "a vacillation between belief and incredulity" in that we both believe and disbelieve the magical diffusion effects before our eyes.[28] Du writes that ink painting and its animated forms follow an "aesthetics of absence" connected with minimalism and *liubai*.[29] Also absent is comprehension:

27. Kang, "*Shui Mo Dong Hua*," 64.
28. Gunning, "Aesthetic of Astonishment," 119.
29. Du, *Animated Encounters*, 131.

FIGURE. 8.2. A combination of brush and pen, in *Feelings of Mountain and River* (1988).

knowledge of the materialities of celluloid, water, and pigment provides brushstrokes of information that make the effects before eyes seem impossible even as the gaps in our understanding fill with astonishment. In this aesthetics of absence and astonishment, it is not stillness that haunts the image; it is the materialities of celluloid, water, and pigment.

Astonishment is certainly only one response among many, but it is useful insofar as its prioritization of materiality and diffusion draws attention to formal heterogeneity.[30] Granted, we can find heterogeneity even without considering astonishment. For example, Yang's excellent online archive of ink-painting animation includes many films with ink-painted backgrounds whose moving elements are created with paper cut-outs or with *danxian*

30. Another common response emphasizes nostalgia. For example, see Chen, "Painterly Focused," 142. For discussions of responses to animation that resonate with astonishment, see Panpan Yang in chapter 1 of this volume on the creation of an "enchanted space" for early filmgoers and Isabel Galwey in chapter 15 on nonnarrative attractions.

pingtu 单线平涂, the conventional cel animation technique of "single line and flat color."[31] However, the four main films created at the Shanghai Animation Film Studio receive far more scholarly attention than other analog films, and astonishment can tease out differences among them. Only *Little Tadpoles* is entirely composed in modulated rather than flat colors and with brushwork rather than the pen nib's uniformly thin lines. In *Herd Boy*, whereas the flora, fauna, and landscapes are all rendered with brushwork and extensive diffusion effects, the human figure is rendered with the single line and flat color of conventional cel animation. The last two films return to ink-painting techniques for clothing and hair, but human faces and hands are outlined with the uniform line of the pen nib (see fig. 8.2). To highlight the heterogeneity of the form, we might most accurately speak of ink-painting in animation rather than ink-painting animation films.

The concept of astonishment may also help explain why we might perceive the single line of the pen nib as an invasive, foreign body; conversely, although Gunning's theory is grounded in nineteenth-century European aesthetics, such responses to the pen's line shows how astonishment can reveal transcultural dialogues. Zhang and Chi open their article by defining this "quintessentially" Chinese form of animation as "a cartoon with[out] a contour line."[32] In fact, outlines made with the brush are fundamental to ink-painting aesthetics, but in this context, it is the absence of the penned line of conventional cel animation that signifies Chineseness.[33] Similarly, Du writes that *Herd Boy* does not "wholly follow the method of ink-painting animation"; its single line and flat color and other elements characterize the film as "modern and even Western."[34] My intuitive response is the same as Zhang's, Chi's, and Du's, but why? The

31. Panpan Yang, "Ink-and-Wash Animation," accessed June 21, 2022, https://sites.google.com/site/inkandwashanimation2013 (site discontinued). A similar range of analog films on Youku, Tencent, and Bilibili are categorized as *shuimo donghua* 水墨动画. Translation of *danxian pingtu* is from Du, *Animated Encounters*, 132.

32. Zhang and Chi, "Ink Animation Art," 1295.

33. On the importance of outlines (*goule* 勾勒) in ink painting, see Qing Huang and R. J. Balsys, "Applying Fractal and Chaos Theory to Animation in the Chinese Literati Tradition," *6th International Conference on Computer Graphics, Imaging, and Visualization* (2009): 116–17.

34. Du, *Animated Encounters*, 144–45.

minzu style more broadly accommodated single lines and flat color, so their presence alone cannot account for the sense of foreignness.[35] The uniform lines of the pen are also not dissimilar from those of linked-picture books (*lianhuanhua* 连环画), woodcuts, and even the latticework of traditional paper-cutting (*jianzhi* 剪纸). These and additional possibilities suggest that the pen nib's line is overdetermined; as Yingjin Zhang writes in the keynote essay of this book, we could plausibly trace "multiple lines of descent rather than singular origins." However, when the pen's line interrupts the astonishing diffusion effects in ink-painting animation, its aesthetic difference discursively constitutes Chineseness and Westernness in opposition to one another.

Transcultural Diffusions: A Brief History of Digital Ink-Painting Tools

In a digital context, diffusion remains a major technical challenge, but for somewhat more limited reasons. Here, the main difficulty is in achieving diffusion and other lively brush effects in "still" images rather than in reproducing these consistently from frame to frame.[36] The demo video for the Expresii painting system makes this particularly clear, its entire first half dedicated to showing how the software renders diffusion effects in real time.[37] By contrast, it is straightforward to create digital brushstrokes that are consistent from frame to frame, and animation has always been part of research on digital brush technologies. In his groundbreaking work on realistic digital brushes, Steve Strassmann incorporated several keyframe-animated tests and wrote that "one of the most important motivations for

35. See, for example, Shasha Liu, "Zooming in on the Animated Background: Mediated Dunhuang Murals with Design in *The Conceited General*," *Journal of Chinese Cinemas* 15, no. 1 (2021): 22–38.

36. This chapter focuses on digital brushes because these are most thoroughly related to ink painting, but areas such as fluid simulation are also relevant and may follow different patterns.

37. Expresii Paint, "*INCREDIBLE* Paint App Expresii Official Release Intro," July 29, 2016, YouTube video, 3:24, https://www.youtube.com/watch?v=Tu3O5qvVVHo&t=78x&ab_channel=ExpresiiPaint.

this work is the hope that creating reproducible brush strokes will allow paintings to be animated."[38] Since then, many researchers have connected ink painting with cinematic movement.[39] If ink painting has always been animate, then digital ink painting has always been cinematic: it has always moved in time rather than simply being an image of the temporal movement of brush, water, and pigment.

Nonetheless, as computer scientists and their collaborators describe the challenge of liveliness and diffusion and literally make their work move through animation, they also tend to construct static and essentialist cultural identities that belie the transnational movement that facilitates their work. This is especially ironic because an East-West encounter lies at the beginning of all realistic computer-generated brush technologies. Strassmann's work, published in 1986, was conducted in the United States and focused on reproducing the *bokkotsu* style of Japanese *sumi-e* (ink painting).[40] *Sumi-e* is itself a product of transregional East Asian dialogue, having arrived in Japan from China in the fourteenth century.[41] Strassmann accounted for the temporal interaction between paper and a pigmented medium: his software calculated each brush bristle's trajectory and pressure, the amount of ink it held, and the texture of the

38. Steve Strassmann, "Hairy Brushes in Computer-Generated Images" (master's thesis, Massachusetts Institute of Technology, 1986), 55.

39. Several researchers mention applications in films and video games, but for a more extended discussion of cinematic application, see Nelson Chu, "Expresii Watercolor," *SIGGRAPH '17 Appy Hour*, 2017. Others use animation over time more pedagogically to demonstrate brushstroke order: Lijie Yang, Tianchen Xu, and Xiaoshan Li, "An Image-Based Approach in Animating Painting Procedure of Chinese Ink Painting," *Computer Graphics International* (2011): 1–4; Fan Tang, Weiming Dong, Yiping Meng, Xing Mei, Feiyue Huang, Xiaopeng Zhang, and Oliver Deussen, "Animated Construction of Chinese Brush Painting," *IEEE Transactions of Visualization and Computer Graphics* 24, no. 12 (2018): 3019–31.

40. Steve Strassmann, "Hairy Brushes," *SIGGRAPH Proceedings* 20, no. 4 (1986): 225–32. Strassmann uses the spellings of *bokkotsu* and *sumi-e*, and these forms can also be transliterated as *mokkotsu* and *sumie*, respectively.

41. For an extensive discussion of the relation between Chinese and Japanese painting, see Aida Yuen Wong, *Parting the Mists: Discovering Japan and the Rise of National-Style Painting in Modern China* (Honolulu: Association for Asian Studies and University of Hawai'i Press, 2006).

surface it encountered. Although limited, his work is a milestone that recognizes the movement required to create ink painting.

The 1990s produced further foundational studies. In 1991, Qinglian Guo and Tosiyasu Kunii, based in Japan, extended Strassmann's method by adding calculations for the paper's structure and absorbency and accounting for the time it takes for the ink to move through the paper and to be absorbed in different ways and at different rates.[42] In 1997, Jintae Lee, a Korean- and Japanese-educated computer scientist working in Japan, presented a three-dimensional digital brush that accounted more naturally for the way degrees of pressure on bristles result in variations in the thickness of the line.[43] The same year, a U.S. team led by Cassidy Curtis published a paper on the simulation of Western watercolor painting; the scope is broad, but their work on diffusion effects and overlapping layers of translucent pigment had an impact on digital brush technologies.[44] Strassman, Guo, Kunii, Lee, and Curtis's team are widely cited by later researchers developing digital tools for use in Chinese and Japanese ink painting and calligraphy and in Western watercolor. If the animation stand was imported from the West and indigenized, digital brush technologies that produce diffusion effects were never a fully formed Western package. They have always been transcultural.

Rhetorically, however, computer graphics researchers often draw sharp borders between East and West. Strassmann's approach is typical of the Westerner Rey Chow describes: he identifies Japanese painting as such but does not mark Western media ethnically.[45] This tendency continues in later English-language articles, regardless of the cultural background or current place of residence of the writers and generally regardless of whether they focus on East Asian or Western painting traditions.[46] Many characterize

42. Qinglian Guo and Tosiyasu L. Kunii, "Modeling the Diffuse Paintings of 'Sumie,'" in *Modeling in Computer Graphics*, ed. Tosiyasu L. Kunii (Tokyo: Springer-Verlag, 1991), 329–38.

43. Jintae Lee, "Physically-Based Modeling of Brush Painting," *Computer Networks and ISDN Systems* 29 (1997): 1571–76.

44. Cassidy J. Curtis, Sean E. Anderson, Joshua E. Seims, Kurt W. Fleischer, and David H. Salesin, "Computer-Generated Watercolor," *SIGGRAPH Proceedings* (1997): 421–30.

45. Strassmann, "Hairy Brushes," 225, 230, 232.

46. Articles that culturally mark Eastern but not Western forms include Xiao-Feng Mi,

Eastern painting and calligraphy in cultural terms without mentioning the West, as in one article's opening sentence: "Chinese brush painting is a unique and fascinating form of art that has been around for more than 1500 years."[47] Articles on Eastern painting and calligraphic traditions that mark Westernness as such usually do so in a kind of ritual of cultural differentiation; for example, one states that Chinese ink painting is "unlike Western styles, such as water color and oil painting," before giving a broad overview of Chinese painting.[48] These two examples also demonstrate a slightly greater tendency to recognize diversity within Western traditions (oil painting and watercolor), whereas Eastern art is usually presented in more monolithic terms. The relationship between Japanese and Chinese ink painting is rarely addressed.[49] These discursive conventions mostly appear in the article's first page or two, framing and even justifying the computer science.

This rhetoric perpetuates ongoing global and local inequities and divisions. The tendency to mark East Asian painting and calligraphy culturally and to forgo labels for Western forms naturalizes Westernness and constructs the East in dependent opposition to that norm. When the contrast with the West is explicit, the difference is almost always presented as incommen-

Min Tang, and Jin-Xiang Dong, "Droplet: A Virtual Brush Model to Simulate Chinese Calligraphy and Painting," *Journal of Computing Science and Technology* 19, no. 3 (2004): 393; Ching Chan, Ergun Akleman, and Jianer Chen, "Two Methods for Creating Chinese Painting," *10th Pacific Conference on Computer Graphics and Applications* (2002): 403–12. Some follow this trend only inconsistently: Bill Baxter, Vincent Scheib, Ming C. Lin, and Dinesh Manocha, "DAB: Interactive Haptic Painting with 3D Virtual Brushes," *ACM SIGGRAPH* (2001): 462. Only a handful are rhetorically egalitarian: Nelson Chu and Chiew-Lan Tai, "MoXi: Real-Time Ink Dispersion in Absorbent Paper," *ACM Transactions on Graphics* 24, no. 3 (2005): 504–11; Tom Van Laerhoven and Frank Van Reeth, "Brush Up Your Painting Skills: Realistic Brush Design for Interactive Painting Applications," *Visual Computing* 23 (2007): 763–71.

47. Tang et al., "Animated Construction," 3019.

48. Lijie Yang and Tianchen Xu, "Animating Chinese Brush Painting through Generating Reproducible Brush Strokes," *Science China Information Sciences* 56, no. 1 (2013): 1.

49. I have found only one team that differentiates Chinese painting from both Japanese and Western: Chao Guo, Zeng-xuan Hou, You-zhi Shi, Jun Xu, and Dan-dan Yu, "A Virtual 3D Interactive Painting Method for Chinese Calligraphy and Painting Based on Real-Time Force Feedback Technology," *Frontiers of Information Technology & Electronic Engineering* 18, no. 11 (2017): 1843.

surable; however, this is contradicted by the cross-cultural exchanges and diasporic experience evident in the articles' bibliographies and researchers' biographies.[50] The position of the English language is also fraught. Its global dominance as a language of scientific publication enables researchers to collaborate and build on each other's work, but it also maintains privilege for native English speakers and others whose educational systems prioritize the language. Perhaps these privileges, inequities, and contradictions are noted regularly and critically in labs, classrooms, offices, and homes, but they are generally unheeded within the online archive of scientific publications.

Popular Online Diffusion

The discursive construction of China and the West is also crucial to another online archive: ink-painting animation on popular film streaming websites such as Youku, Tencent Video, Bilibili, YouTube, and Vimeo. These feature both analog and digital films; I focus on the digital and on diffusion both as a visual characteristic and in the sense of dissemination. Many digital animations on these sites are made by independent artists, academics, and students—"animateurs," as Paola Voci discusses in chapter 7 of this book.[51] The films broadly resemble analog ink-painting animation in subject matter and general aesthetic approaches but also often contain overt markers of digital production and hybridization with other forms such as photography and photorealist 3D animation. This formal diversity raises issues of cultural identity and tradition within a wide, transcultural visual landscape.

Many digital animators speak of the desire to combine tradition with innovation and cultural specificity with global reach. Master's student Lily Shen captures the outlook of numerous artists especially well:

50. As stated, most articles cite research performed in both the East and West, and transnational collaborations are common. Researchers' biographies also demonstrate migration and translocal and transregional forms of Chineseness-es and Westernness-es. Many researchers focusing on East Asian ink painting and calligraphy are based in mainland China, but some live in Special Administrative Regions, Macau, Singapore, Japan, and Korea. Evidence also indicates migration within East Asia, within the West, East to West, and West to East.

51. See also Paola Voci, "Electric Shadows Reloaded: The Post-Digital Animateur, Shadow Play and Handmade Cinema," *Journal of Chinese Cinemas* 11, no. 3 (2017): 194–95.

> 3D technology is one new approach to resurrect the old method of ink-wash animation. This new visual style does not just aim to duplicate the traditional paintings—it delivers a creative conception with strong Chinese characteristics. This creation has the potential to lead Chinese painting and ink-wash animation to the future and spread the spirit of Chinese culture. This new technique of expression could enrich the current animation market, which is largely dominated by the West. . . . Most important of all, the fact that Chinese painting itself is a significant part of Chinese long history demands that the researchers have a deep understanding of the ancient art form and the culture.[52]

In this desire for a balance between tradition and reinvention, the role of the West resonates with Chow's analysis of the logic of the wound: it appears explicitly as a hegemonic presence rather than an unmarked norm, and its role is so persistent that it effaces Japan's status as an animation superpower. Nonetheless, Shen imagines a global audience that is receptive to Chinese aesthetics and culture and that implicitly includes cultures and regions identified with the West. This constructs digital ink-painting animation—and the fusion of tradition and innovation—as a project of global outreach in response to Western cultural and economic imperialism.

Although Shen sees the project of global outreach to come from within carefully guarded cultural borders, the diverse formal and narrative strategies of digital ink-painting animation demonstrate a great deal of variety in opinions and approaches. One thing that is especially common among early landmark films, however, is a self-referential reflection on ink-painting animation's place on a global stage. For example, *Ode to Summer* (*Xia* 夏) (Ron Hui/Xu Yi 许毅, 2003), the first widely influential example of 3D ink-painting animation, dramatizes the relationships between old and new and, potentially, between the indigenous and the foreign. Its individual images are generally traditional in composition and ink techniques, with liberal use of *liubai* and diffusion, but its camera movements emphasize the 3D space. However, its most dramatic departure from the astonishment and absence of analog ink-painting animation is an ending sequence that exposes the stages of its production. Three shots from earlier in the film are replayed in a way that

52. Lily Shen, "Serenity: 3D Animation to Simulate Chinese Ink Painting" (master's thesis, Victoria University of Wellington, 2014), 5.

exposes the Maya 3D animation software used to create it. At first, we see only wireframe models; these dissolve into monochromatic shaded forms and then dissolve again into fully colored bodies. The dissolves act as cinematic correlates to diffusion effects: they trace the animator's process in the same way that diffusion on paper attests to the temporal interaction of brush, water, pigment, and paper. Insofar as Maya is perceived to be Western, *Ode to Summer* tells a story of indigenization and thus echoes the indigenization of the analog animation stand.[53] The film's status as the first mainland Chinese computer graphic animation shown at the U.S. SIGGRAPH and its continuing presence on both the Chinese-language Youku and the widely accessible, U.S.-owned platform YouTube potentially diffuse this story of indigenization to audiences around the world.[54] Its self-referentiality invites international audiences to be receptive not only to Chinese aesthetics but also to the ingenuity required to indigenize the foreign technology.

Some other early landmarks are also self-referential, but in a way that distances the audience from the art of ink painting rather than the digital technology used to achieve it. In the opening of *A Harmonious China* (*Hexie Zhongguo* 和谐中国) (Zheng Dasheng 郑大圣, 2010), ink splashes onto the title card in a temporal display of diffusion. More lively brushstrokes coalesce into a painting of the Shenzhen skyline that dissolves into live-action footage of the same. This constructs photographic indexicality as the telos of the image. Although ink painting reappears briefly toward the film's end, its brevity implies that it can coexist with the photographic only if it does not aspire to convey an immediate, globally legible truth about modernity. On the other hand, Lei Chen's master's thesis project frames an ink painter's work within a photorealistic 3D computer graphics environment. *The Brush* (2005), completed at Bournemouth University in the UK, opens in a relatively realist, 3D room where a painter

53. Although they do not discuss Maya specifically, Chen Hailu and Lily Shen both identify the 3D space in *Ode to Summer* with Western tradition. Chen, "CGI Ink-Painting Animation"; Shen, "Serenity," 11. Maya is also Western in industrial terms given that it was developed in Canada and the United States; however, identifying a company with the place where it is headquartered or traded effaces both diversity among its employees and the importance of transnational markets.

54. Apropos of the film's status at SIGGRAPH, see Shen, "Serenity," 11.

hesitates before his paper. He leaps into the paper and trudges through a white, empty space until he finds a paintbrush. Its ink flows into the air as if into water; some dissolves into invisibility, and some sticks to form a horse painting in the style of Xu Beihong 徐悲鸿 (1895–1953). The horse gallops around, displaying the Western perspectives that Xu uses extensively, and the painter collapses back into the photorealist 3D space of his studio where the horse painting on paper now hangs on the wall. Another thesis film, *Movement and Stillness* (*Dongjing* 动静) (Yi-Hsuan Kent Chiu, 2006), similarly frames ink-painting animation sequences with photorealist 3D computer graphic imagery (CGI), although without the agency of a human figure. All three films are clearly addressed to international audiences: *A Harmonious China* was shown at the 2010 World Expo and the other two were made by Chinese students studying in the West. However, whereas *Ode to Summer* constructs the intersection of ink painting and Maya, of East and West, as a technological feat worthy of display, the other three films variously construct photography or 3D CGI—with their Euclidean forms and lack of visual diffusion—as transparent visual languages that translate and explicate ink painting to a global audience. Their framing strategies also implicitly draw a border around ink painting and ink-painting animation and assert their cultural specificity.

This is not necessarily the case with another self-referential trope of ink-painting animation: the 3D animated particle effect that looks like ink dropping into water. This effect has become a kind of nondiegetic signifier of digital ink-painting animation, a status that is accentuated when it occurs during head or tail credits. Chen Hailu writes of this effect in *Believe in the Power of the Brand* (*Xiangxin pinpai de liliang* 相信品牌的力量) (Niko Tziopanos, 2009): "its methodology is completely different from Chinese ink animation, which is particular about brush strokes . . . and the five different ink textures."[55] This is absolutely true; however, it is not as clear that it is therefore a Western form of animation, as she states.[56] Its three dimensionality and photorealism adhere to the construction of space and mode of realism traditional in Western oil painting—although, as Chen points

55. Chen, "CGI Ink-Painting Animation."

56. Chen, "CGI Ink-Painting Animation." Software development in this area and that which replicates diffusion effects on paper overlap; several articles on this particle effect cite Guo and Kunii as well as Chu and Tai.

out, these aesthetic values have been partially adopted by many Chinese painters and partially rejected by many Western painters for more than a century.[57] However, the particle effect does not reproduce a specific style of Western art or animation. Instead, because the water is usually transparent and implied, it follows the principle of *liubai*; it also conjures the *shui* and *mo*, the water and ink for which Chinese ink painting is named, as well as the gestural process of painting, which is integral to vivid aliveness (*qiyun shengdong* 气韵生动). On one hand, this effect can be interpreted as an intrusion in much the same way that the single line and flat color feel foreign in analog ink painting; technical foreignness can be translated into cultural foreignness. On the other hand, its novelty and aesthetic distance from the major art forms of both China and the West pose the question of cultural neutrality. If diffusion effects in analog ink-painting animation epitomize the wonders of a technological process of indigenization, then might the seemingly endless, billowing dispersion of ink in water epitomize a new digital borderlessness—or at least the fantasy of borderlessness?

Perhaps this is a whimsical suggestion, but another early ink-painting animation offers a parallel take on the ways particle effects can mediate between the global and multiple locals. Qing Huang trained as an oil painter in Shanghai before making *The Way* (*Qiyun shengdong* 气韵生动) (2003) when studying at La Trobe University in Australia.[58] Huang's inspirations include Taoist principles, traditional Chinese aesthetic theory, modern chaos theory, and the playful paradox of 2D painterly forms in the 3D Maya environment.[59] Whereas *A Harmonious China* freezes each brush stroke once it is completed, *The Way* uses particle effects so that each brushstroke is in perpetual motion, enacting the *qiyun shengdong* that is the film's Chinese-language title. Inky brushstrokes course perpetually up the trunk of a tree and out through its branches; swimming fish grow tails that burst off their bodies, dissolve into the watery empty space, and then regrow (see fig. 8.3). Huang writes that this aims to create "an effect of contingency among forms where contrasts, variations, seemingly accidental [recombinations] and reconfigura-

57. Chen, "CGI Ink-Painting Animation."

58. Claire Smith, "*The Way*, A Dynamic Multimedia Representation of Tao," interview with Qing Huang, *Metro* 138 (2003): 96.

59. Qing Huang, "Multimedia Representation of Tao" (master's thesis, La Trobe University, 2003), 47.

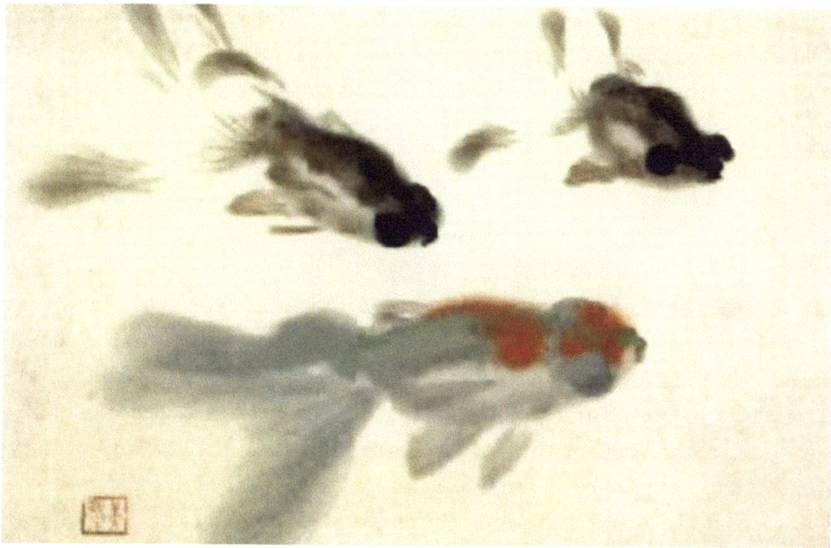

FIGURE. 8.3. Fish at different stages in their cycles of constitution and disintegration, in *The Way* (2003). Courtesy of Qing Huang.

tions ensure the effect of Chaos. This serves to create a sense of tension and ambiguity for viewers to wonder and marvel at."[60] Huang may not mean wonder and marvel in exactly the sense that Gunning uses the term astonishment, but *The Way* constructs an aesthetics of absence and astonishment that thoroughly wrangles with the limits, capabilities, and delight of ink painting moving in a digital medium. This film does not replicate ink-painting aesthetics precisely, but it extends the concept of diffusion by using particle effects as visual analogs to the movement of ink and water in paper.

Furthermore, this diffusion aims to open borders rather than police them. Huang states that his "long-time obsession" has been "to promote the Chinese tradition and aesthetics," but he is not a gatekeeper of tradition.[61] He writes, "I believe, that by using the method I have employed, a person without a classic training in Chinese ink painting can still successfully emulate past master works. Anyone who is willing to use this sophisticated new media as an expressive medium, can create a strongly stylized

60. Huang, "Multimedia Representation," 49.
61. Smith, "*The Way*," 96.

artwork following in the Traditional Chinese, Taoist aesthetic context."[62] This might meet with resistance from some, but it attests to a dedication to tradition without isolationist tendencies and an interest in broad diffusion of style, technique, and culture.

Conclusion

I have told a few stories in a relatively linear manner: the introduction of single lines and flat color into analog ink-painting animation, the development of digital brush technologies, and the strategies with which early landmarks in digital ink-painting films frame this aesthetic for a global audience. However, linearity is a construction, and the threads of each story are tied to particular emphases on East-West dialogues and on technologies such as water and paper, the animation stand, and 3D CGI. None of these stories is intended to explain everything; each is only a way of looking at the landscape, like one of many scattered perspectives in traditional ink painting. Ink-painting animation is heterogeneous, with a range of aesthetics, techniques, and content and a diversity of opinions and biographies among filmmakers and researchers. Our views of it should be similarly heterogeneous.

62. Huang, "Multimedia Representation," 45. Huang's aim to bring schools of thought together rather than draw unyielding borders is also reflected in Huang and Balsys, "Applying Fractal and Chaos Theory."

NINE

Homemaking Allegory

Animating Taiwanese Local Memory in *The Little Sun*

Jasmine Yu-Hsing Chen

How do Chinese immigrants in Taiwan—educated to actively support the return to their mainland homeland during the martial law period (1949–1987)—unexpectedly turn the island into their home and represent their local memories?[1] Animation is key to their endeavor to reframe events and memories, a medium that creates consistent meaning through disjointed images. Different from live action, animation can especially reflect the selectivity of personal memories through its imaginative and fantastical capacities. As a medium associated with childhood wonder and innocence, animated works have the effect of creating strong emotional identification in the audience. Thus animation is well suited to creating a selective narrative out of memories and enabling such a narrative to create a sense of place. This essay focuses on *The Little Sun* (*Xiao taiyang* 小太陽, 2010), a thirteen-episode animated show that represents a Chinese immigrant family in 1970s Taiwan. In this chapter, I explore how the show strategically uses the medium of animation to tell the story of homemaking in a way that transcends the China-centric imagination of homeland found in previous Taiwanese animated works.

During the martial law period, the Chinese Nationalist Party's political agenda in Taiwan was not to make a home on-site but to retake what

1. The phrase *Chinese immigrants* in this chapter is specifically used to refer to the mainlanders (*waishengren* 外省人) who arrived in Taiwan with the Chinese Nationalist Party, also known as the Kuomintang, in the mid-1940s.

its members perceived to be their homeland. That is, the Kuomintang (KMT) mainly viewed Taiwan as a springboard to restore its rule over China. In this essay, *homeland* is used as a concept rather than a distinct place, a concept that is closely linked to constructions of Chinese nationalism in that it commonly refers to the country of one's ancestors. The conceptualizations of the Chinese homeland in Cold War Taiwan were not based on shared life experiences. China, the territory that the KMT aspired to convert into a homeland, was not internal but already somewhere else, outside Taiwan itself. Taiwanese people, who had no substantial connection to or life experience in China, were made to identify with a common homeland located in China during the Cold War. In contrast to this forced homeland, *home* is the place where people are born and raised, and to which they have strong emotional ties based on life experience. Although the narrative of homeland is frequently invoked to support building a unitary national community, the notion of home, as I conceive of it, underscores an individual's affective connection based on their everyday life and memory accumulation.

With inspiration from the geographer Tuan Yi-Fu's articulation of the difference between abstract space and experience-based place, I analyze how *The Little Sun* turns Taiwan from a space into a familiar place for Chinese immigrants by evoking the audience's local memory and life experience. The augmentation of the family unit with the arrival of newborns in *The Little Sun* reflects how Taiwan has been historicized and humanized through the time-consuming process of homemaking. Animation, as a medium, brings something otherwise not fully realized into living existence, and can be used to recount factual moments in an engaging and entertaining way. Thus animation is the ideal medium to effectively vitalize the Taiwanese audience's local memories. More than simply recalling memories, the viewing process exerts meaning and influence on viewers and thereby enables a sense of place and identity in the Taiwanese context.

Through contextualizing the transition of the animation industry, this chapter argues that the homemaking narrative is a meaningful process that inspires collective memories and local identity in Taiwan. Homemaking includes double meanings in this chapter: on the one hand, *The Little Sun* represents a Chinese immigrant family's ordinary life by portraying the domestic environment and memory-evoking objects; on the other, it shows a larger sense of making Taiwan home, a place to become rooted to, rather than a temporary residence as claimed by the KMT during the martial law period.

The discussion starts with a historical overview of the animation industry in Taiwan, from its origins in the 1970s to its post-1990s industrial transformation. This concise review also explores the China-centric imagination of homeland in early Taiwanese animated films and the localization of Taiwanese animation. Then the examination moves to how the theme of homemaking in *The Little Sun* can be read as an allegory that detracted from the KMT's intention to use nostalgic sentiment toward a Chinese homeland to support their political propaganda. Finally, through an analysis of specific nostalgic objects in *The Little Sun*, I show how this animation not only uniquely portrays the main characters' growth into adulthood, but also grapples with issues of identity, family, and finding a sense of home. Such representation diversifies the political propaganda that promotes a diasporic image of Chinese immigrants staring at a distant Chinese homeland during the martial law period. Instead, their homemaking effort suggests the possibility of raising a family and rooting oneself in Taiwan. Through animation, the narrative of homemaking evokes shared local memories and transforms the meaning of homeland for Chinese immigrants in Taiwan.

The China-centric Imagination of Homeland in Early Taiwanese Animation

To understand why an original homemaking story in *The Little Sun*—an allegory of birthing Taiwanese subjectivity and cultural identity—can even exist, it is essential to understand the history of the animation industry in Taiwan. This history mainly follows the journey of transforming from the OEM model (original equipment manufacturer) to an ODM one (original design manufacturer). The OEM manufacturing model means that a company manufactures products designed by their buyer or another company, whereas an ODM company can produce and manufacture a product according to their needs and then sell the products under their own brand. Taiwan has been involved in the worldwide animation industry for decades, with a particularly tight connection to animation creation in Japan and the United States. The animation industry in Taiwan sprang up as early as the 1950s. The first known animated film created in Taiwan was *Wu Song Kills a Tiger* (*Wusong da hu* 武松打虎, 1954), which is a three-minute, black-and-white work that represents how the legendary hero of the well-known classical Chinese novel *Water Margin* bravely fights with a wild tiger.[2]

Throughout the 1960s, only a few short educational animations were released, most created by animator Chao Tse-Hsiu 趙澤修, who had studied techniques of animation at the Walt Disney Studios. The animation industry in Taiwan did not take off until the early 1970s, when the booming Japanese animation industry required considerable manpower. The low wages in Taiwan attracted Japanese animation companies to recruit animation staff from Taiwan. In 1970, The Ying Ren Cartoon Production Center (Taibei yingren guanggao yingpian zhizuo zhongxin 臺北影人廣告影片製作中心) cooperated with Tokyo Movie Shinsha (TMS) (Riben dongjing dianying gongsi 日本東京電影公司) to establish a manufacturing service site in Taiwan for the Japanese animation company. Taiwanese animators were mainly in charge of coloring and editing. Gaining experience in OEM film production was significant progress in terms of animation technique and quality in Taiwan.[3] Under the global economic system and international labor division, Taiwan thus became an inseparable part of the growth of the Japanese animation market.

The few animation films created in 1970s Taiwan reflect features of China-centric homeland-building, appealing to the KMT's aims. Animation in 1970s Taiwan was mainly produced with the OEM services of Japanese animation companies, but some were committed to creating original works and training local talent. Throughout the 1970s, most animations created in Taiwan promoted Chinese cultural heritage and young Taiwanese people's military allegiance to the government. In 1971, animators at Ying Ren made an independent short animation, *Chou Chu* (*Zhou Chu* 周處, 1972). The film portrays a legendary Chinese hero who kills a tiger

2. "Taiwan donghua fazhan nianbiao" 臺灣動畫發展年表 (The chronology of animation development in Taiwan), 2016, https://web.archive.org/web/20160401225536/http://accataiwan.com/sub4.html.

3. Hong-Chi Shiau, "The Production and Consumption of Animation in Taiwan: The Interplay of Global Political and Economic Force" (PhD diss., Temple University, 2002).

and crocodile that has caused calamities in his community.[4] The film ends with Chou's volunteering to serve in the army and Chou's master encouraging all passionate young men to do the same, asserting that it would be a bright path for their careers. Such a statement echoed the KMT's military recruitment system in Taiwan and the compulsory military service that required all men of a certain age in Taiwan to join the military for two to three years during the martial law period. In 1975, The Hsin Hong Cartoon Company (Xinhong katong gongsi 心虹卡通公司), which cooperated with the Chunghwa Cartoon Production Company (Zhonghua katong zhizuo gongsi 中華卡通製作公司), completed the television animation *Tian Dan Restores the Kingdom* (*Tiandan fuguo* 田單復國). This story centers around how historical figure Tian Dan bravely leads his people to overcome difficulties and restore their regime, a storyline meant to instill concepts of loyalty and echo the KMT's policy of striking mainland China and retaking the territory.

Another approach to shaping identities that yearn for an imaginary Chinese homeland was tracing the origin of Chinese culture. One such effort was devised in 1972 by Chunghwa Cartoon's *The Evolution of Chinese Characters* (*Zhongguo wenzi de yanbian* 中國文字的演變), a short television animation series introducing the transformation of Chinese characters. Some works that accentuated Chinese cultural origin and heritage broke through the limit of simple animated short clips, and gradually this led to full-length animated films. In 1974, in cooperation with the Nan Hai Film Company in Hong Kong (Xianggang nanhai dianying gongsi 香港南海電影公司), Chunghwa Cartoon created the first color animation film *The Story of Chinese Gods* (*Fengshen bang* 封神榜). This animation features origin stories for many deities common to the Daoist worship in Taiwan. The story suggests that the origins of Daoism can be traced back to historical China. The trailer advises that all Chinese people should feel proud of how this milestone animation demonstrates the Chinese values that evil will never prevail over the virtuous and that everyone should crusade against tyrants. Similarly, in 1979, the animated feature film *Romance of the Three Kingdoms* (*Sanguo yanyi* 三國演義) was based on a classic Chinese novel that begins with the famous line "Anything long

4. Daw-Ming Lee, *Historical Dictionary of Taiwan Cinema* (Lanham, MD: Scarecrow Press, 2012), 47.

divided will surely unite, and anything long united will surely divide." This aphorism aptly summarizes the historical and political mentality that the KMT promoted throughout martial law Taiwan, a mentality that was commonly understood as defeating the evil Chinese Communist Party and unifying mainland China and Taiwan under the KMT's rule. These films had little connection with Taiwanese people's opinions and life experiences. Due to the alienation of the audience and the limited technology and funds, most animated films of this period, unfortunately, lacked box office appeal.

Taiwan's animated films continued to underperform at the box office until the 1980s, when a major shift occurred: Taiwanese animation began to adapt bestselling comics. The first film that attracted a considerable audience was *Old Master Cute* (*Laofuzi* 老夫子, 1981), which was coproduced by Far Eastern Cartoon in Taiwan and Hong Kong Film Services.[5] In addition to the humorous plot in the original comic, the film also added fighting scenes between Bruce Lee and the blind swordsman Zatoichi. Bruce Lee, a renowned movie actor who had passed away before the production of this animation, and Zatoichi, a fictional character, were both celebrated film icons in Hong Kong and Taiwan at the time. *Old Master Cute* earned more than NT$100 million (around US$2.71 million in 1981).[6] After its success, it became very popular for animation companies to adapt comics, but films such as *Oolong Courtyard* (*Wulong yuan* 烏龍院, 1983) and *Uncle Niu and Sister Niu Busting the Diamond City* (*Niu bobo yu Niu xiaomei dapo Zuanshicheng* 牛伯伯與牛小妹大破鑽石城, 1983) either had unsatisfactory commercial achievements or were not even screened publicly.[7] Commercial performance notwithstanding, these films indicated that the representation of Chinese culture in animation had transitioned from seriously tracing a symbolic cultural origin to eliciting a relatively

5. Lee, *Historical Dictionary*, 49. For further discussions on how *Old Master Cute* reflects the modernity and medium specificity in Hong Kong, see Jessica Chan's chapter 10 in this volume, "Animation as Action: The Old Master Q Animation Trilogy in Hong Kong."

6. Tsai Cheng-Ting 蔡承汀, "Quanqiuhua xia Taiwan donghua chanye fazhan yu celüe zhi yanjiu" 全球化下臺灣動畫產業發展與策略之研究 (The development of Taiwan animation industry in the age of globalization) (master's thesis, National Taiwan Normal University, 2008), 14.

7. Lee, *Historical Dictionary*, 49.

relaxed, commercialized, and humorous tone that had less connection with Chinese nationalism.

The creative energy needed to develop original animation in 1980s Taiwan was insufficient, and the animation industry mostly relied on taking OEM orders for American animations. In 1978, the Cuckoo's Nest Studio (later renamed Hong Guang Cartoon Company) was established by Wang Chung-Yuan (James) 王中元, who had majored in audiovisual education in the United States and worked in one of the biggest television animation studios, Hanna-Barbera. Wang used his networking to establish his own company, which soon signed contracts with Walt Disney, Warner Brothers, and Universal.[8] Because Cuckoo's Nest was such an important subcontractor for many big animation companies, Taiwan thus became an important site for the global animation industry. Although numerous famous Disney animations finished the preproduction, scripts, character designs, and storyboards in Disney's headquarters in California, most of their animated production was contracted to Cuckoo's Nest in Taiwan. Since the mid-1980s, Cuckoo's Nest has participated in around 170 to 190 animation productions annually, which earned the company the name Magic Cuckoo's Nest from Hollywood at the time.[9] Although the animation industry grew tremendously in 1980s Taiwan, most Taiwanese animators only focused on drawing techniques and coloring because their experience and capacity for planning and creating original works were limited. At the same time, American and Japanese animations produced by Taiwan were aggressively dumped back into Taiwan. This further eroded the local original animation market, so few Taiwan-created animations were screened on television in 1980s Taiwan.

8. John A. Lent, "James Wang and His Crazy Climb to Taiwan's Cuckoo's Nest," in *Animation in Asia and the Pacific*, ed. John A. Lent (Bloomington: Indiana University Press, 2001), 125–29.

9. Tu Ya-Ting 涂亞庭 and He Chao-Wen 賀照文, "Zhexie Dishini dianying dou shi Taiwan zhi" 這些迪士尼電影都是臺灣製 (These Disney movies are all made in Taiwan), April 22, 2016, *The Journalist*, https://www.storm.mg/lifestyle/103893.

The Localization of Taiwanese Animation after the 1990s

Taiwanese local life experience and history have emerged as the main subject matter of animation in Taiwan since the late 1990s. Because of wage increases in Taiwan, Cuckoo's Nest's animation OEM was gradually priced out of the outsourcing market by China and Southeast Asia after the 1990s. The labor relocation trend pushed the animation industry in Taiwan to create original works to survive. Martial law in Taiwan officially ended in 1987, which enabled animators more freedom to weave their personal stories into their works. Along with the growing pursuit of a Taiwan-centric culture, animators strove to represent Taiwanese animation to the world beyond the limited market in Taiwan.

The official funding also subsidized the production of some animated films with Taiwanese features. *Zen Taipei Ah-Kuan* (*Chanshuo a'Kuan* 禪說阿寬, 1994) was the first original animated film to receive a grant from the Government Information Office. *Zen Taipei Ah-Kuan* demonstrated significant improvement in animation techniques, which helped it achieve strong numbers in video sales and gradually brought Taiwan's original animation to the attention of the international animation market.[10] The film *Grandma and Her Ghosts* (*Mofa ama* 魔法阿媽) directed by Wang Shau-Di 王小棣 in 1998 was one of the most well-known and representative works. As the first animated film that completely revolves around Taiwanese folk beliefs and the interaction between grandmother and grandchild, this work successfully resonated with the public.[11] The main character, the grandmother, was dubbed by famous Taiwanese actress Wen Ying 文英, and her natural Taiwanese accent made the audience feel a strong sense of familiarity. Director Wang recalled the unimaginable queue at the premiere, "hearing children laughing with the film, I

10. Wang Wei 王唯 and Huang Ren 黃仁, *Taiwan dianying bainian shihua* 臺灣電影百年史話 (One hundred years of Taiwan cinema) (Taipei: Taiwan Film Critics Society, 2004), 535.

11. For further discussion on how a rural Taiwanese spirit medium subverts dominant historical narratives, gender politics, geopolitical perspectives, and media theories, see Tim Shao-Hung Teng, "Psychic Grannies: Animation and Animism in Turn-of-the-Century Taiwan," chapter 5, this volume.

felt that the occasion was really heavenly."[12] The success of *Grandma and Her Ghosts* also made audiences look forward to more Taiwanese-themed animations.

Since 2000, Taiwan's animation industry has further developed toward self-branding and gradually entered the international market with films featuring local themes. In the wake of the popularization of computer-aided technologies, the production of animation has become much easier and less labor-intensive. At the same time, in response to the younger generation's interest in interactive games that integrate animation, Taiwanese animators have connected with other industries, such as advertisement, multimedia, video games, and architectural design.[13] With the transfer of animation OEM under the new order of globalization, the animation industry in Taiwan extended its ability to promote original works and aimed to brand Taiwan.

More and more, Taiwanese animators who have received international professional training have enriched the possible themes of Taiwanese animation and brought Taiwanese works to international audiences. The director of *The Little Sun*, Chiu Li-Wei 邱立偉, studied in Tainan and Beijing and worked as a researcher in Hollywood. Chiu bluntly said that the animation industry has a much more convenient drawing process due to the accessibility of digital tools. The previous labor-intensive production mode is no longer necessary, so animators can work more independently. *Grandma and Her Ghosts* inspired Chiu to rethink how animation can intimately reflect his culture and experience. He yearned to answer essential questions regarding identity and place such as "Who are you? Where do you come from? Where are you going?" through animation.[14] Chiu has been exploring the recollections of Taiwan's urban and rural landscapes in his animations. He seeks to infuse these landscapes with a distinctive style

12. Lu Hao-Ping 魯皓平, "Wang Shau-Di zhuanfang: *Mofa ama* de gandong jiang yizhi yanxu dao xiayidai" 王小棣專訪:《魔法阿媽》的感動將一直延續到下一代! (Interview with Wang Shau-Di: The emotion of *Grandma and Her Ghosts* will continue to the next generation), *Yuanjian*, November 17, 2022, https://www.gvm.com.tw/article/84293.

13. Tsai, "Quanqiuhua xia Taiwan," 14.

14. Li You 李尤, "Wushu ge 1/24 miao duiqie de qidai" 無數個1/24秒堆砌的期待 (Countless expectations piled up in 1/24 second), September 22, 2022, https://www.verse.com.tw/article/li-wei.

that is unique to Taiwan. He constantly asks, "What defines Taiwanese animation?," adding, "When I showcase my works to international audiences, I aim to narrate stories that are rooted in Taiwan, not imitations of Japanese or American stories."[15] *The Little Sun* is Chiu's first television animation series to vividly illustrate the trivial details of a middle-class, Chinese immigrant family's life in Taipei. *The Little Sun* received great acclaim after being broadcast on public television and won Chiu the Best Animation Award at the 2010 Golden Bell Awards.

Since then, Chiu has created the animated television series *Barkley the Cat* (*Xiaomao Bakeli* 小貓巴克里, 2010), in which the background was largely designed based on street scenes in Tainan City. This program has sold copyrights in more than thirty countries and laid the foundation for the later filming of a full-length feature film. The local street scenes in the animation sparked active discussions among foreign audiences. Such a reaction excited Chiu because he realized that the international audience had, albeit slowly, come to recognize Taiwanese animation as distinct from Japanese and Chinese animation.[16] Taiwanese animation has gradually demonstrated its uniqueness, distinguishing itself from other East Asian animations.

After the start of the twenty-first century, numerous Taiwanese animators have drawn their inspiration from Taiwanese history and local traditions. These works not only resonate with local audiences' remembrance and nostalgia but also attract international attention. Taiwanese animators seek to use animation to tell the story of Taiwan.[17] As an illustration-based

15. Siameses, "Zhuanfang donghua xinrui daoyan Qiu Liwei" 專訪動畫新銳導演邱立偉 (Interview with the innovative animation director Chiu Li-Wei), September 22, 2022, https://forum.gamer.com.tw/C.php?bsn=42999&snA=12.

16. Lu Chih-Fang 盧智芳, "Xiaomao Bakeli daoyan Qiu Liwei" 《小貓巴克里》導演邱立偉 (The director of *Barkley The Cat* Li-Wei Chiu), *Cheers*, March 26, 2017, https://web.cheers.com.tw/issue/2017/happiness/article/26.php.

17. For example, in 2018, the animated film *On Happiness Road* (*Xingfu lushang* 幸福路上), directed by Sung Hsin-Ying 宋欣穎, highlights Taiwanese history, including the traumatic February 28 incident and the White Terror during martial law. It portrays the identity struggle common among Taiwanese of Sung's generation. The film was well received, winning the Best Animated Feature Film at the 55th Golden Horse Awards in Taiwan, the Animated Feature Film Jury Prize at the 2018 Tokyo Animation Awards, and the Best Animation Award at the Stuttgart International Animation Film Festival in Germany.

medium, animation highlights the subjective reality that "enables it to explore the sensual responses of people to historical events rather than to show them photographically."[18] Animation can depict memory in a selective and creative approach that is impossible to replicate in live-action films because animators reconstruct painted or illustrated pieces to artistically encode elements of spatiotemporal images that retrieve the audience's memory. Animation's capacity to simultaneously mimic and defy reality allows animators to use it to strategically extend individuals' experiences and mediate people's relations to the past. Through animation, Taiwanese audiences' collective memory is activated, making a new Taiwanese cultural identity and self-confidence possible. Because of such possibilities, Taiwan has continued to promote the local film industry, especially animation, through international collaboration.

Making Taiwan Home: The Homemaking Allegory in *The Little Sun*

The Little Sun takes family life in Taiwan as its theme, which seems to be the logical outcome of Taiwanese animation, given that it has kept exploring Taiwanese characteristics and life after the new century. However, the story of how to make Taiwan home provides us with a window into the complex relationship between deviation from and submission to politics in literary and artistic works during the martial law period. *The Little Sun* was primarily adapted from a collection of essays by the same name written by the well-known Taiwanese writer Lin Liang 林良 (also known by his pen name Zi Min 子敏) and published in 1972. The essays cover the topics of Lin's ordinary family life. The animation series further visualizes Lin's words and enlivens his life details with emphasis on the domestic environment of Lin's family and street scenes of old Taipei.

The title for the essay volume was inspired by Lin's role as a father, in that his three daughters are "little suns" who bring happiness and warmth to the family. Lin served as the editor-in-chief of the *Mandarin Daily News*

18. Victoria Grace Walden, "Animation and Memory," in *The Animation Studies Reader*, ed. Nichola Dobson, Annabelle Honesse Roe, Amy Ratelle, and Caroline Ruddell (New York: Bloomsbury Publishing, 2018), 83.

publication department. The *Mandarin Daily News* was founded in 1948 to promote Mandarin education in postwar Taiwan, and young children and students were its main target readers. Most of the founding members were also members of the National Languages Committee of Taiwan Province, which was a KMT official organization. The close ties with the KMT enabled the *Mandarin Daily News* to gain government support in the early postwar period when paper was a scarce and thus highly valued resource for many presses.[19] As a semi-official newspaper press, the *Mandarin Daily News* necessarily echoed the government's cultural and political propaganda and supported Mandarin education as a vital part of the KMT's nation-building project. In 1965, Lin began to serve as one of the main columnists for Tea Talk, a new column on the Family Pages of the *Mandarin Daily News*. Except for the two essays "One-Room Home" and "Little Sun" created in the 1950s, all other works in *The Little Sun* were published in the Tea Talk column, which reflected the changing social-political atmosphere in 1960s Taiwan.

Understanding the implications of the family in *The Little Sun* animated series requires us to understand the context in which the volume that inspired it was created. In the 1960s, although the policy of literature and art still advocated anticommunism, patriotism, and nostalgia toward China, the military goal of counterattacking the mainland gradually became unrealistic. Thus the KMT urgently needed to resort to new narratives to maintain legitimacy, and the portrayal of family stability and how people live in harmony turned into a way to sustain its rule. The tendency of the Tea Talk column to pursue family order and ethics was in line with the needs of the KMT to consolidate the stability of governance and intensify the consciousness of Chinese nationalism.[20] The works in *The Little Sun* highlight the warmth, positivity, and brilliance

19. Hsueh Cheng-Hung 薛政宏, "Guofu qian Tai qianhou *Guoyu ribao* neirong zhi yanjiu (1948–1951)" 國府遷臺前後 (1948–1951) 《國語日報》內容之研究 (Research of the *Mandarin Daily News* content before and after the Nationalist government moved to Taiwan [1948–1951]) (master's thesis, National Taipei University of Education, 2012), 35.

20. Chao Hung-Yi 趙弘毅, "Anshen zai Taiwan: 1960–1970 Zimin sanwen de jiating shuxie yu rensheng yilun" 安身在臺灣：一九六〇、七〇年代子敏散文的家庭書寫與人生議論 (Settle in Taiwan: Family writing and life discussion in Zi-Min's prose in the 1960s and 1970s) (master's thesis, National Chengchi University, 2020), 46–61.

of family, thus conforming to the government's expectations for literary works to emphasize the values of filial piety, loyalty, and happiness. Lin's family-focused essays provide warm and stable images of family life, and his unpretentious writing style aligns with the feature that the government encouraged in 1960s Taiwan, yet he kept a distance from the literary trend of the anticommunism campaign.

Beyond the KMT's expectations, the family theme unexpectedly transformed the official sentiment of anticommunism and nostalgia dominant since the 1950s by increasing the visibility of Taiwan in literary and artistic works. In the 1950s and 1960s, the KMT systematically pursued literature and film in which Chinese immigrants' nostalgia for their Chinese homeland was a dominant narrative. These Chinese immigrants "set literary trends born of nostalgic longing, define a culture of pan-Chinese nationalism, and impose an imaginary geography of historical China upon the local population."[21] Although 80 percent of Taiwanese had no direct relations with China, the KMT educated people to internalize the nationalist ideology through the imagination of a "better" and more "valuable" mainland, believing that it was their mission to retake the mainland and live on it. Therefore, Taiwanese people's nostalgic imagination toward China was an essential affective resource in educating the public to support the KMT government's governance.

In contrast to the mainland theme influenced by state policies, works such as *The Little Sun* that centered on the family and everyday life experiences in Taiwan were an unintended subversive force, one that released an alternative voice. Different from the departure from reality in anticommunist and nostalgic works, one of the important features of these family writings is the recording of real life.[22] Distinct from the KMT's policy that treated Taiwan as a space to live temporarily and a springboard for retaking mainland China, the narrative of homemaking in Lin's prose turned Taiwan into a place for settling down and living. Lin's

21. Chris Wen-Chao Li, "The China That Was Not to Be: Nostalgia and the Exilic Imagination of Taiwan's Mainland Diaspora," *Diaspora Studies* 9, no. 1 (January 2, 2016): 1–14, 1.

22. Fan Ming-Ju 范銘如, *Zhong li xun ta: Taiwan nüxing xiaoshuo zonglun* 眾裡尋她：臺灣女性小說縱論 (Chronological searches of Taiwanese women's fiction) (Taipei: Rye Field, 2002), 13–48.

family-focused essays reflect the Chinese immigrants' need for respite from the war, the longing for a place to reside, and even the possibility of taking root in Taiwan.[23] The Chinese immigrant writers' portrayal of family life thus unexpectedly accumulated a rare literary legacy of local memories in Taiwan in a way that did not violate the official policy. These works steadily made Taiwan a memory assembly and built emotional attachments for the following generations.

The geographer Tuan Yi-Fu defines the difference between space and place as the extent to which people give meaning to a specific area and interact with their surrounding environments. Space is the physical site that has no social connection or immediate contact with humans. Space embodies abstract imagination and marks off the politics of inclusion or exclusion of action. Place, on the contrary, is a location created by human experiences within which people create meaning and attachment to a particular environment through interaction. Places are centers where people can satisfy their biological needs with observable boundaries and a visible expression of a specific time.[24] How people feel and perceive their surroundings is highly related to how they form attachments to home, neighborhood, and nation. For Taiwanese residents, China is an abstract space that most of them have never even visited, whereas Taiwan is a concrete place full of social connection. However, the KMT's China-centric nationalism and rule by martial law worked to alienate Taiwanese people from Taiwan by implying that it was not a place to which they were supposed to feel familiar and attached. Sharing collective life memory is a powerful, clandestine way to resist such alienation.

The Chinese immigrant's hope is to transform their family's temporary resident space into a place where they can land, raise newborns, and accumulate memories for the generations that follow. In the KMT's official vision, Taiwan was simply a space without values or personal emotional attachments during the martial law period. Thus the KMT could arbitrarily hollow out the history of Taiwan and inject the Chinese nationalist imagination. Such imagination can be used to define what is officially recognized as Chineseness and Chinese identity. However, the Chinese

23. Chao, "Anshen zai Taiwan," 76.

24. Yi-Fu Tuan, *Space and Place: The Perspective of Experience*. Reprint (Minneapolis: University of Minnesota Press, 2001).

immigrant's representation of family in literature and animation has highlighted specific life experiences and the value of personal attachment in Taiwan. The Chinese immigrant's homemaking journey in Taiwan thus turns their national identity into a dialectical search process rather than a fixed answer given by the government. The homemaking representation in *The Little Sun* and similar works progressively loosened the KMT's Chinese nationalism in Taiwan through the depiction of individuals' interaction with their family members and the surrounding environment.

As the next section details, one of the keys to this representation and place-making is animation because it is a medium that can highlight or simplify various details based on the animators' selective illustration of objects. Although animation can reproduce only a drawn version of the family, its strategic selection and omission of details evoke memories. In that regard, *The Little Sun* shows a clean and simplified living space. Such purified representation, on the one hand, embellishes the life experience in martial law Taiwan. On the other hand, it also transcends the KMT's vision of Taiwan as a vacuous space by showing it as a place where the audience can recast past local life experiences with nostalgic emotions.

Animating Local Memory in *The Little Sun* (2010)

The prose collection *The Little Sun* was adapted into an animation series in 2010; the animation further transforms Lin's family writing into a shared local memory for the Taiwanese audience and concretely shows how people's interaction with the surrounding environment converts Taiwan from space into place. The animation visually embeds Lin's family story in Taiwanese local life from 1956 to 1970, which makes Lin's writing a television animation program suitable for audiences of various ages. The animation introduces the young generation to the life of Taiwan in the 1950s through the 1970s by vividly portraying the objects and soundscape that evoke a strong sense of a specific era in domestic and public settings.

The role of animation in the series is to create a complete cinematic narrative while reshaping the truth, representation, and reconstruction of collective memories. Collective memory, based on an understanding enunciated by French sociologist Maurice Halbwachs, stresses the relation

FIGURE 9.1. A realistic portrayal of street scenes of old Taipei, including details such as verandas, red brick sidewalks, an old model scooter, and a hand-painted movie poster, in *The Little Sun* (2010), Episode 11. Courtesy of Chiu Li-Wei.

between memory and its social context and designates the shared knowledge of past experiences held by the members of a group or generation.[25] Animation, like many other mass media forms, is a site to construct collective memory by visualizing the past through its creative imaging. However, animation is an inventive style by nature in that animators recreate the material objects and conditions of reality and turn them into something new through illustration. The animated representation recreates the past through the animator's paintbrush in a way that can evoke memories in a dreamlike manner.

It is evident in the scenery that the animators meticulously drew details of objects to realistically illustrate an old version of Taipei and enliven the life memories of the past era. Considering the long-term nostalgic construction of longing for a homeland when most Taiwanese people lack a concrete memory of living in China, the signs of homemaking in *The Little Sun* are particularly meaningful for evoking memories of martial law Taiwan. In *The Little Sun*, the audience is led to be impressed by how the animation realistically portrays the street scenes of old Taipei, including

25. Maurice Halbwachs, *Collective Memory*, trans. Lewis A. Coser (Chicago: University of Chicago Press, 1992), first published posthumously in 1950.

small yet important details such as the verandas, the red brick sidewalks, the old model scooter, and the hand-painted movie poster (fig. 9.1).

The animation's realistic portrayal of objects in 1970s Taiwan stirs audience memories, shifting Chinese immigrants' focus from longing for China to settling in Taiwan. To realistically reconstruct an old Taipei in animation, director Chiu used thousands of old photos along with 3D technology to reconstruct the streets surrounding Lin's home, including Fuzhou Street, Guling Street, Heping West Road, and Chongqing South Road. This vivid depiction of the cityscape immerses the audience in the ambiance of 1950s and 1960s Taipei, re-creating the "poor but happy" era of that time.[26] Unlike documentaries or photos that record scenes in a relatively truthful approach, animation allows for a transformative form of memory, which is how Chiu strategically uses the medium.

In contrast to the realistically represented city landscape and certain objects, the figures in *The Little Sun* all have disproportionately big heads, reminding the audience that this animation is a reconstructive and symbolic portrayal of the past. As in many other animations, characters in *The Little Sun* are three heads tall, thus mimicking the exaggerated proportions of babies (fig. 9.2). As such, characters acquire the aesthetic associations of cuteness and innocence. The realistic objects make the background setting truthful, while the dramatized character designs purify people's memories of the living environment illustrated in the animation. For example, although the animation presents the cramped and crowded homes in Taipei and Taiwan's rainy climate, the audience would not see the mildew on the walls in the animation. Another example is that although political slogans appear in the street scenes, the political censorship of the brutality during the martial law period is obscured by the emphasis on warm family life. The audience would not witness the KMT government suppressing any form of political dissent, leading to the imprisonment and execution of thousands of Taiwanese intellectuals and the breaking up of countless happy families.

26. Wu Ting-I 吳亭儀 and Liang Chia-Ming 梁家銘, "Taiban *Xingfu sandingmu*: Jizai jiatingshi Lin Liang *Xiaotaiyang* gaibian donghua" 台版《幸福三丁目》：記載家庭史林良《小太陽》改編動畫 (Taiwanese version of *Always-Sunset on Third Street*: Recording family history, Lin Liang's *The Little Sun* is adapted into animation), EBC News, October 13, 2009, https://the-little-sun.blogspot.com/2009/10/.

FIGURE 9.2. Figures have disproportionately big heads, reminding the audience that this animation is a reconstructive and symbolic portrayal of the past, in *The Little Sun* (2010), Episode 6. Courtesy of Chiu Li-Wei.

The characters' oversized heads give them a sense of innocent joy, echoing the conservative style inherent in Lin's prose; the animation thus reshapes the audience's memory of the martial law period in Taiwan through a warm and bright approach.

The Little Sun also includes numerous objects to help trigger the Taiwanese audience's memory of 1960s domestic arrangements. Animating the symbolic, memory-evoking objects opens up the past and shows that other possibilities are attainable and that past and future are not rigidly fixed. Whereas live-action realism shows the world as it is, animation has a greater capacity to make audiences consider how the world could be different because the flexibility of the form allows for more fantasy thinking and more efficaciously reshapes the audience's memory. Exploring how *The Little Sun* highlights certain objects and elements sheds new light on the (trans)formation of collective memories.

One of the objects most representative of daily life in Taiwan that would first attract the audience's attention was the Tatung doll on the television in the Lin family's living room (fig. 9.3). The Tatung company was founded in 1918, and the first Tatung doll was produced in 1969 after the company

FIGURE 9.3. The Tatung doll on the television and the old-style Tatung television in the living room are memory-evoking objects, in *The Little Sun* (2010), Episode 4. Courtesy of Chiu Li-Wei.

broke away from Japan and became fully Taiwan-funded.[27] The company advertised the Tatung doll as a promotional gift for home appliance buyers. Accompanied by the patriotic slogan "Tatung's Chinese goods are the most reliable," an irresistible trend of purchasing Tatung's home appliances spread throughout Taiwan.[28] The Tatung doll became not only the symbolic logo and mascot of the company but also a shared memory among Taiwanese people, a memory of patriotically supporting locally made products and thankfully enjoying the modernized lifestyle that the KMT brought to Taiwan.

The audience would also be impressed by the old-style Tatung television with a sliding door in front of the screen (fig. 9.3). In 1960s Taiwan, television symbolized the modernized lifestyle and became the fundamental source of leisure for the entire family. Although only one channel was available (TTV, first broadcast in 1963) when the Lin family purchased

27. Chang Hsin-Chang 張信昌, *Tujie Taiwan huaijiu ganzidian* 圖解臺灣懷舊柑仔店 (The graphic illustration of nostalgic local stores in Taiwan) (Taipei: Morning Star, 2013), 105.

28. Lin Man-Chiu 林滿秋, *Chanye Taiwanren* 產業臺灣人 (Industrial Taiwanese) (Taipei: Yuan-Liou, 2001), 150.

FIGURE 9.4. A tricycle is an object in the street scenes that generates a sense of historical time and social mobility, in *The Little Sun* (2010), Episode 11. Courtesy of Chiu Li-Wei.

the television, the animation depicts how people relied on black and white television for entertainment, news, and more. This portrayal of an early television model in *The Little Sun* resonates with memories of watching limited programs with family, highlighting the transformation of television from a single-channel box to high-definition screens with diverse content. It serves as a reminder of the significant shift in Taiwanese entertainment, evoking memories of communal television watching. Even though the old model television is no longer in common use, the animation depicts it as a brand-new object that astonished Taiwanese people in the 1960s and 1970s yet made them nostalgic in the present.

Just as domestic objects can easily summon the audience's common memory, a tricycle is an object in the street scenes that generates a sense of historical time and social mobility in *The Little Sun*. In the episode "Bike to School," a tricycle school bus is frequently shown going up and down the street (fig. 9.4). In 1950s to 1970s Taipei, tricycles were a common, affordable mode of transport that relied entirely on manpower. The tricycle thus became synonymous with the lives of the common people. Because many Chinese immigrants in Taipei did not have military status after their immigration from China in 1949, the tricycle was a valuable tool in helping them earn a livelihood. Despite causing traffic issues and being banned in 1976,[29] tricycles symbolize a time when Chinese immigrants strove to make a living in Taiwan amid economic hardship. The mobility enabled by tricycles also broke the barriers between ethnic groups; this simple transportation was like a medium for communication between ordinary Chinese immigrants and local Taiwanese. The tricycle in the animation reminds the audience of this history, when numerous ordinary Chinese and Taiwanese people struggled to establish a family and a firm foothold in Taipei.

The fluidity of sound in *The Little Sun* also effectively connects interpersonal communication and aural memory. The background sounds in this animation have been carefully designed to restore the soundscape of 1950 to 1970s Taiwan, including the well-known advertisement songs on television, the sound of radio broadcasts, the vendors' Mandarin speech with a Taiwanese accent in the traditional market, and the tinny versions of the classical tune *The Maiden's Prayer* that Taiwan's trash collectors have been using to announce their arrival for decades. Among these sounds, the vendors hawking along the streets particularly linked people together. Some popular lines have been passed down through generations and become characteristic of Taiwan. The hawking line was usually straightforward, characterized by a distinctive rhythm, and the construction of the sentences usually elongated the last words of the line, followed by a momentary pause between lines. The words of the call repeated as the cassette tape looped, an effect that formed unique and intimate memories for many Taiwanese. With the change in living habits, fewer and fewer vendors hawked on the street. In a rapidly changing Taipei, the hawkers' calls have been going on for decades and have become "a rare stubborn existence, which is unforgettable" and "a common life experience of the people."[30] These sounds contribute to a transitory texture in the rich

29. Wu San-Lian 吳三連, *Wu Sanlian quanji: Taibei shizhang shiqi* 吳三連全集: 臺北市長時期 (The collected works of Wu Sanlian: The mayor of Taipei) (Taipei: Wu Sanlian Foundation of Taiwan Historical Materials, 2011), 217.

30. Hai Shen 海參, "Danchu er bubiande jietou jiaomai" 淡出而不變的街頭叫賣 (The street peddling that is fading out yet changeless), In *Erduo de qixi yu sanbu: Jiyi Taibei shengyin fengjing* 耳朵的棲息與散步: 記憶臺北聲音風景 (Taipei sound memory), ed. Li Ming-Tsung 李明璁 (Taipei: Locus, 2016), 208, 212.

soundscape, and *The Little Sun* intertwines the sensory memories with the intimate feeling of home in Taiwan.

Conclusion

Although Taiwan has participated in the animation industry by assisting top animation companies in Japan, the United States, and Europe since the 1950s, most of the original animations related to Taiwan were created after the 1990s. In recent decades, more and more Taiwanese animators have been attempting to introduce local Taiwanese culture and history to audiences through animation. The emergence of Taiwanese animation symbolizes Taiwanese animators' hope for a new self-definition and their effort to present Taiwan as an affective, experience-based homeplace.

The homemaking story in Taiwan proposes a new possibility for the audience to rethink the meaning of homeland. Homeland is significantly correlated with the place one is born and raised.[31] Nevertheless, during the martial law period, Taiwanese people were asked to identify their homeland based on an imaginary territory far away in China. This process of identity construction made Taiwanese people not only long for an unfamiliar or even uncertain homeland of which they had no memory but also made them feel alienated from the land where they were born. *The Little Sun* brings back the lost familiarity of birthplace for the readers and animation audience members. If homemaking is a journey toward hope and new possibilities, *The Little Sun* represents that journey to its audience through the process of raising a family.

The uniqueness of animation as a medium is that it is an effective way to realize imagination in a visible, shareable form. The immaterial background setting in animation differentiates the representation of memory from that in live-action movies. Although the animators put every effort into realistically reproducing Taiwan's streetscapes and domestic surroundings in *The Little Sun*, the characters' disproportionate head-to-body ratio reminds the viewer that the memory shown is selective and dramatized. *The Little Sun* shows the archetype of an ideal family: everyone is kind and the parents

31. Robert Hay, "Sense of Place in Developmental Context," *Journal of Environmental Psychology* 18 (1998): 5–29.

are patient, loving, and communicative. Even if the family is not rich, no one in the animation ever has to worry about their material needs. To a certain extent, these beautified and purified memories have the effect of loosening the abstract homeland imagination of China that the government imposed on the Taiwanese during the martial law period.

By coloring the local memory with warm tones, *The Little Sun* has endowed Taiwan with the meaning of a homeplace. No matter how real and reliable such memories are, the animation has created a feeling of "the memory of our times and place." Whether something is entirely made up or imitating the existing environment and culture, Taiwanese animators use their work to invigorate the audience's memories and creative energy for the island.

TEN

Animation as Action

The Old Master Q Animation Trilogy in Hong Kong

Jessica K. Chan

The Old Master Q Animation Trilogy (1981–1983), which includes three 2D animation feature films—*Old Master Cute* (*Qicai katong Laofuzi* 七彩卡通老夫子, 1981), *Old Master Cute Part II* (*Laofuzi shuihu-zhuan* 老夫子水虎傳, 1982), and *Old Master Cute Part III* (*Shan-T Laofuzi* 山T老夫子, 1983), is the first animation feature film series in Hong Kong cinema. The trilogy is a forgotten moment in the pioneering but marginalized work of animation in Hong Kong cinema and can be understood in terms of its modernity and medium specificity. First, it demonstrates the fluidity, elasticity, and plasmaticness of animation with an imaginative expressiveness and subversiveness that are specific to Hong Kong's colonial and capitalist modernity in the early 1980s, when the Sino-British negotiations on Hong Kong's future were unfolding. Second, by remediating various cultural icons (Bruce Lee, Wu Song, and E.T.) and traversing generic boundaries between multiple cinematic traditions (Chinese martial arts and Hollywood science fiction), the trilogy develops a global vocabulary of animation as action, seeking to create an animation paradise that is not only Disney-inspired but also identifiable and accessible across cultures. In its development from kung fu animation to *wuxia* (martial arts swordplay) animation to sci-fi animation in just three years, the trilogy experiments with the realist, supernatural, and formalist modes of animating action, thus challenging the corporeal authenticity of live action film by introducing a new animation aesthetic.

The comic strip character, Old Master Q, is often hailed as a cultural icon and a collective memory of Hong Kongers and diasporic Chinese communities. Mostly black and white, a typical *Old Master Q* comic strip is printed in a four-, six-, eight-, or twelve-panel format. Dressed in an out-of-style long gown and a tiny skullcap out of sync with the modern world, the tall and slender Old Master Q—together with the short and chubby Big Potato (Da fanshu 大蕃薯) and Mr. Dumb, aka Mr. Chun (Qin xiansheng 秦先生), *chun* being a homophone for dumb 蠢 in Cantonese—imaginatively stands in for the thousand identities of the human psyche.

The artist who created Old Master Q is Wong Chak 王澤 (aka Alfonso Wong and Wong Kar Hei, 1924–2017). Born in Tianjin, Wong Chak studied Western art at Fu Jen Catholic University in Beijing. In 1956, he moved to Hong Kong and worked as an illustrator for a Catholic publication and the children's magazine, *Joyful Vanguard* (*Le feng bao* 樂鋒報). While in this position, Wong Chak began to publish four-panel comics in local newspapers and periodicals under the pen name Bud (Mengya 萌芽). The character, Mr. Dumb, appeared as early as 1958, followed by the debut of *Old Master Q* and *Big Potato* as separate comics in four-panel format under the pen name Wong Chak (the name of the artist's eldest son, aka Joseph Wong) in 1962. In 1964, *Old Master Q and Mr. Dumb* was published for the first time as a standalone comic book.[1] A year later, *Old Master Q* moved from print publication to live-action movie. From 1965 to 1966, three black and white Cantonese film adaptations of *Old Master Q* were produced (all directed by Chan Lit Ban). From 1975 to 1978, three color Cantonese film adaptations of *Old Master Q* were released, two of which were Shaw Brothers' productions.[2] From 1981 to 1983, three 2D Old Master Q animations were produced by Wu Sau Yee 胡樹儒 (1935–2009) as the first animation feature film series in Hong Kong cinema. The digital

1. Feng Jicai argues that Peng Di, a Tianjin artist who was active in the 1930s and 1940s, is the source of direct inspiration for Wong Chak's characters in *Old Master Q manhua*. See Feng Jicai 冯骥才, *Wenhua fajue Laofuzi chutu* 文化发掘老夫子出土 (Cultural digging: The unearthing of Old Master Q) (Beijing: Xiyuan chubanshe, 2001).

2. Wendy Siuyi Wong pioneered the study of live-action films adapted from comics but her study does not discuss animations adapted from comics. See Wendy Siuyi Wong, "The History of Hong Kong Comics in Film Adaptations," in *The Oxford Handbook of Adaptation Studies*, ed. Thomas Leitch (New York: Oxford University Press, 2017), 386–403.

turn in the new millennium integrated 3D animation with live action in *Old Master Q 2001* (2001). With more than four hundred monthly comic books issued until 2000 and more than ten film adaptations, *Old Master Q* has achieved a wide readership and popularity in Hong Kong, Taiwan, and the Chinese diaspora.[3]

In examining the roots and routes of *Old Master Q* as it traveled from mainland China to colonial Hong Kong, Taiwan, and diasporic Chinese communities, one finds the emergence of a cultural icon that acquires a transnational readership, severed from mainland China and its socialist history. In his study of the appropriation of *Old Master Q* comics in Indonesia, Abidin Kusno argues that the comic was read and appropriated by ethnic Chinese communities in Indonesia in the 1970s and 1980s in the context of the Indonesian government's effort to exorcise communism by encouraging the circulation and consumption of cultural products from Hong Kong.[4] As an enduring cultural icon for Chinese-speaking communities beyond mainland China since the 1960s, Old Master Q benefited from Hong Kong's commercial print and film industry, thriving popular culture, and developing civil society with freedom of speech. Old Master Q, severed from socialist campaigns in the arts, developed in isolation from (and in parallel with) socialist cultural icons in mainland China since the 1960s. Rather than privileging Old Master Q and disparaging socialist cultural icons by suggesting that artistic creativity withered in socialist China (where it in fact thrived), I suggest that Old Master Q (as both comic and animation) and socialist animation share a marginalized position, conceived as what Daisy Yan Du calls a "minor artistic form for minors (children)."[5] The dearth of both Chinese and English language scholarship

3. Wu Jiaxiong 伍嘉雄, "Xianggang banben *Laofuzi*" 香港版本老夫子 (The Hong Kong version of *Old Master Q*), in *Laofuzi manhua yanjiu jihua* 老夫子漫畫研究計劃 (Research plan on *Old Master Q*), ed. Grace Cheng (Hong Kong: Hong Kong Arts Centre, 2003), 25.

4. See Abidin Kusno, "Master Q, *Kungfu* Heroes and the Peranakan Chinese: Asian Pop Cultures in New Order Indonesia," in *Popular Culture Co-productions and Collaborations in East and Southeast Asia*, ed. Nissim Otmazgin and Eyal Ben Ari (Singapore: National University of Singapore Press, 2012), 185–206.

5. Daisy Yan Du, *Animated Encounters: Transnational Movements of Chinese Animation, 1940s–1970s* (Honolulu: University of Hawai'i Press, 2019), 11.

on Hong Kong and mainland Chinese animation indicates that we have yet to fully comprehend the central role of animation in mediating socialist, capitalist, and colonial experiences of revolution and modernity.[6] Beyond Chinese animation, the Old Master Q Animation Trilogy sheds light on the regional and international collaboration in animation filmmaking, as well as the emerging and competing animation hubs in Asia during the Cold War.

The Pioneering but Marginalized Work of Animation

The history of Hong Kong animation has yet to be written. Daisy Yan Du explores the prehistory of Hong Kong animation by looking at the Wan brothers' (in)activity in Hong Kong in the late 1940s—a period of "suspended animation" when their animation projects were aborted because of a lack of resources, trained animators, and financial support.[7] Other than puppet animation films and postwar Cantonese films with optical animation special effects hand drawn on celluloid, hardly any local animation was produced in Hong Kong in the 1940s and 1950s. Nonetheless, commercial advertising was stimulated by the arrival of the Wan brothers, who introduced the art and equipment of animation and trained local talents (including King Hu, who worked as the Wan brothers' art assistant).[8] The 1960s witnessed the popularity of animated commercials, produced by animation departments of advertising companies. Independent animation emerged in the 1970s when filmmakers, such as Neco Lo and Roger Ho, produced animated shorts in 8mm or

6. The Hong Kong Arts Centre, together with OMQ Comics Studio in Taiwan (owned by Joseph Wong, aka Wong Chak), cosponsored the first and only edited volume about Old Master Q, titled *Research Plan on Old Master Q*, which includes essential insights and resources for researchers. See Grace Cheng, ed., *Laofuzi manhua yanjiu jihua* 老夫子漫畫研究計劃 (Research plan on *Old Master Q*) (Hong Kong: Hong Kong Arts Centre, 2003).

7. Daisy Yan Du, "Suspended Animation: The Wan Brothers and the (In)animate Mainland–Hong Kong Encounter, 1947–1956," *Journal of Chinese Cinemas* 11, no. 2 (2017): 142.

8. Du, "Suspended Animation," 152–53.

16mm.[9] These independent filmmakers became Hong Kong's first generation of professional animators when they joined television animation departments in Radio Television Hong Kong (RTHK) and Television Broadcasts Limited (TVB), which produced educational animation, such as the Chinese proverb series, *Cartooned Chinese Fables and Parables*.[10] However, a severe shortage of trained animators in Hong Kong persisted at the peak of the comics and film industry in the 1980s, when Wu Sau Yee, producer of the Old Master Q Animation Trilogy, sought collaboration with Taiwan talent. The lack of trained animators continued to haunt the local animation industry in the 1990s, prompting producer Tsui Hark to seek collaboration with a Japanese animation company that animated the 2D characters in *A Chinese Ghost Story* (Andrew Chan, 1987), whereas the Hong Kong animator and director, Andrew Chan, coordinated the film's 3D animation.[11] The 1990s and the millennium witnessed the emergence of digital special effects companies in Hong Kong, as well as the McDull animated films, including the Hong Kong production, *My Life as McDull* (Toe Yuen, 2001), and the Hong Kong–mainland coproduction, *Me and My Mum* (Brian Tse and Li Junmin, 2014), both of which are adapted from the McMug television animation series and the McMug comic strip, published in *Ming Pao Weekly* in 1991.[12]

The 1980s witnessed the peak of the comics and film industry in Hong Kong, providing an impetus for the pioneering work of cinematic animation beyond commercial advertising and television animation. This ten-year period was characterized by the emergence of the Hong Kong new wave, the modernization of the action genre (in the form of gunplay),

9. See "The Digital Turn in Hong Kong Independent Animation," chapter 14 in this volume.

10. See Keeto Lam, "A Brief Sketch of the Development of Hong Kong Animation," in *Frame After Frame: A Retrospective on Hong Kong Animation*, ed. Winnie Fu (Hong Kong: Hong Kong Film Archive, 2006), 10–27.

11. Gigi Hu, "The 'Art' Movement between Frames in Hong Kong Animation," in *Animation in Asia and the Pacific*, ed. John A. Lent (Bloomington: Indiana University Press, 2001), 110, 115–16.

12. See Hang Wu, "The Translocalized McDull Series: National Identity and the Politics of Powerlessness," *Animation: An Interdisciplinary Journal* 12, no. 1 (2017): 28–44.

and the diversification of genres such as horror, comedy, and animation, with the last discussed only rarely. The marginalization of animation in the discourse on Hong Kong cinema of the 1980s means that three important elements that define the 1980s are missing: experimentation with film form, including animation and its symbiotic relationship with the Hong Kong new wave and action cinema; international collaboration; and consciousness of the 1997 handover (frequently manifested in live-action cinema but rarely discussed in animation).

Wu Sau Yee pioneered the work of animation by producing the Old Master Q Animation Trilogy as the first animation feature film series in Hong Kong in the early 1980s. Born in Zhongshan in 1935, Wu Sau Yee moved to Hong Kong in 1949 and worked as an illustrator under the pen name Pepper (Hujiao 胡椒). As early as 1962, Wu Sau Yee established Hong Kong Film Services (Xianggang dianying gongsi 香港電影公司) to produce commercial advertisements. At the same time, he published in Hong Kong English newspapers the comics satire, *Mr. Hong Kong*, under the pen name Woo. In 1973, Wu Sau Yee entered the film industry, codirecting with James Wong *Let's Rock* (*Dajiale* 大家樂, 1975), which features the musical band, the Wynners (Wen'na yuedui 溫拿樂隊). Together with his business partners, Wu Sau Yee produced the martial arts film, *Raining in the Mountains* (*Kongshan lingyu* 空山靈雨, 1979), and the new wave film, *The Secret* (*Fengjie* 瘋劫, 1979). As a versatile film producer and director with a comics and advertising background, Wu Sau Yee traversed popular music, martial arts film, and the emerging new wave in the 1970s. In the early 1980s, Wu Sau Yee turned to his childhood passion—animation. Reminiscing about his childhood memories of Walt Disney short films and Sunday morning cartoons in the movie theaters in Hong Kong, Wu Sau Yee sought to create an animation feature film with the comics character, Old Master Q, whom he saw as a Hong Kong citizen because the character had been around for almost twenty years.[13] Wu Sau Yee believed that animation would be the best way to adapt the comic because it would be hard to "capture the spirit" of Old Master Q in live action.[14] Inspired by Walt Disney, Wu Sau Yee envisioned creating an "animation paradise"

13. Guan Baixuan 關柏煊, "'Laowantong' de Hu Shuru" "老頑童" 的胡樹儒 (Old imp Hu Shuru), *Dianying shuang zhoukan* 電影雙週刊 (Film biweekly) 64 (July 1981): 25.

14. Guan Baixuan, "'Laowantong,'" 26.

(*katong leyuan* 卡通樂園), where kung fu animation would play a central role, complemented by imported Japanese animation such as *Doraemon*, *Dr. Slump*, and *Ninja Hattori-kun*.[15]

Wu Sau Yee's pioneering animation work was premised on regional and international collaboration. Other than serving as the producer of all the films in the trilogy, Wu Sau Yee also served as a codirector of the first animation film in the trilogy, *Old Master Cute* (1981), with two Taiwan directors, Cai Zhizhong 蔡志忠 and Xie Jintu 謝金塗, who were also key animators for the film. Wong Chak served as the scriptwriter for the first animation film, but quit during production after a serious heart attack (he continued to serve as a scriptwriter and codirector of the second animation film, but made way for new talent in the third episode). Wu Sau Yee considered the first animation feature film to be a Hong Kong production rather than a Taiwan production because the conceptualization, script, character design, and animation design originated in Hong Kong.[16] Wong Chak described Hong Kong as a city well suited for animation production because its people "have a broad vision open to new things"; but due to Hong Kongers' "profit-oriented nature" and the high cost of rent and labor, the production team sought collaboration with Taiwan talent to reduce expenses for the labor-intensive animation production.[17] Under his leadership as the producer and codirector of the first two animation films in the trilogy, Wu Sau Yee unified and developed coherence in facial expressions, characterization, movement, dramatic development, special effects, music, dubbing, and editing.[18] For the first animation film in the series, a team of six was responsible for drawing key poses and a team of eighteen for drawing in-betweens. More than 80 percent of the finished layout was

15. Wei Yifeng 韋一峯, "Wang Ze haoguo Zhang Daqian: Fangwen Hu Shuru" 王澤好過張大千：訪問胡樹儒 (Wang Ze is better than Zhang Daqian: An interview with Hu Shuru), *Dianying shuang zhoukan* 電影雙週刊 (Film biweekly) 115 (July 1983): 23.

16. Guan Baixuan, "'Laowantong,'" 25.

17. Liu Chao 劉潮, "*Laofuzi* de ku yu le" 老夫子的苦與樂 (The bitterness and happiness of *Old Master Q*), *Dianying shuang zhoukan* 電影雙週刊 (Film biweekly) 89 (July 1982): 19. On the emergence of Taiwan as an animation outsourcing hub in the 1980s, see chapter 9 in this volume, "Homecoming Allegory: Animating Taiwanese Local Memory in *The Little Sun*."

18. Guan Baixuan, "'Laowantong,'" 25.

xeroxed while a team of four to eight worked on inking when it could not be done by a machine. An all-female crew was hired to focus on coloring because of their "attention to detail"—a gendered construction viewed as a professional strength.[19] There were two rounds of shooting per day: each rotation took six and a half hours with one photographer and an assistant. About twenty thousand unsatisfactory drawings from the first animation film were thrown away in the end.[20]

Wu Sau Yee's first kung fu animation film, which features Old Master Q with Bruce Lee, achieved box office success in Hong Kong. It grossed more than HK$4.5 million and won the award for best animation feature film at the 18th Taiwan Golden Horse Awards.[21] It received a warm welcome in Japan, where film distributors sought to obtain screening rights in competition with Golden Harvest, which was seeking global distribution rights of the film. In June 1981, Wu Sau Yee visited Japan to seek collaboration with the production company of *Doraemon*, and the Tokuma Shoten Publishing Company reached out to him to seek the right to publish *Old Master Q* comics in Japan.[22] In Singapore, the film broke the first three-day box office record, which had in the past been set by foreign films.[23] Encouraged by this success, Wu Sau Yee decided to make *Old Master Cute Part II* (Wu Sau Yee, Wong Chak, Xie Jintu, 1982), an animated version of Wong Chak's comics adaptation of the *Water Margin* (*Shuihuzhuan*, 水滸傳), with a budget of HK$2.5 million and more than ninety crew members in Hong Kong and Taiwan.[24]

Wu Sau Yee's experimentation in animation sparked discourse on international animation in the early 1980s, when Hong Kong cinema, mainland Chinese cinema, and Japanese cinema were experimenting

19. Guan Baixuan, "'Laowantong,'" 26.

20. Guan Baixuan, "'Laowantong,'" 26.

21. Wei Yifeng 韋一峯, "Shuqi piaofang yuce" 暑期票房預測 (Summer box office forecast), *Dianying shuang zhoukan* 電影雙週刊 (Film biweekly) 89 (July 1982): 43.

22. "*Laofuzi* zai Ri dashou zhongshi," 老夫子在日大受重視 (*Old Master Q* was greatly appreciated in Japan), *Gongshang ribao* 工商日報 (The Kung Sheung daily news), July 1, 1981, 9.

23. "*Laofuzi* zai Xing shangying," 老夫子在星上映 (*Old Master Q* is screened in Singapore), *Gongshang ribao* 工商日報 (The Kung Sheung daily news), December 8, 1981, 3.

24. "Hu Shuru Wang Ze hezuo chenggong" 胡樹儒王澤合作成功 (A successful cooperation between Hu Shuru and Wang Ze), *Gongshang ribao* 工商日報 (The Kung Sheung daily news), September 8, 1981, 5.

with animation through international coproduction and collaboration. The July issue of *Film Biweekly* (*Dianying shuang zhoukan* 電影雙週刊) in 1982 introduced international animation in the articles "News from International Animation" and "Forever Disney."[25] Single Frame, the first nonprofit organization that promoted local independent and commercial animation, was established by Neco Lo in Hong Kong in March 1982. In addition to screening foreign animation, Single Frame organized lectures, discussion panels, and production courses ranging from "Introduction to Animation" to "Comics Illustration."[26] The first China-Japan coproduced animation (also the world's first panda animation), *Doudou* (豆豆), was released in Hong Kong in 1982, adding stylistic and thematic diversity to the emerging animation film market in East Asia. Wu Sau Yee was instrumental in introducing the Japanese animation, *Doraemon*, to Hong Kong. Shortly after the release of *Old Master Cute Part II*, a critic compared the Old Master Q series with *Doraemon* and suggested that the former could learn from the latter.[27]

The international perspective on animation sparked by Wu Sau Yee's work was developed and advertised during the production of *Old Master Cute Part III* (1983), the third film in the trilogy. The film's title in Chinese, "山T," is a partially inverted E.T., formed by rotating the English letter "E" ninety degrees counterclockwise. Topping the box office in Hong Kong, Taipei, and Tokyo in April 1983, the Hollywood sci-fi film *E.T. the Extra-Terrestrial* (Steven Spielberg, 1982) became an inspiration for imitation.[28] The advertising poster of *Old Master Cute Part III* highlights its multinational talent: the film is codirected by Japanese animator Honda Toshiyuki and Taiwanese animator Cai Mingqin. An American animator,

25. See "Guoji shangye donghuajie de yixie jinkuang" 國際商業動畫界的一些近況 (Recent developments in the international commercial animation industry), *Dianying shuang zhoukan* 電影雙週刊 (Film biweekly) 90 (July 1982): 19–20; "Yongyuan de Helu Disini yishu" 永遠的和路迪斯尼藝術 (The art of Walt Disney forever), *Dianying shuang zhoukan* 電影雙週刊 (Film biweekly) 90 (July 1982): 22–23.

26. "Guoji shangye donghuajie de yixie jinkuang"; "Yongyuan de Helu Disini yishu."

27. Feng Lici 馮禮慈, "Dingdang" 叮噹 (*Doraemon*), *Dianying shuang zhoukan* 電影雙週刊 (Film biweekly) 94 (September 1982): 32.

28. "Gedi shoulun piaofang jilu" 各地首輪票房紀錄 (First round box office records by location), *Dianying shuang zhoukan* 電影雙週刊 (Film biweekly) 110 (April 1983): 38; "Gedi shoulun piaofang jilu," *Dianying shuang zhoukan* 111 (May 1983): 32.

Randy Cartwright, served as the special effects photographer.[29] Before working on *Old Master Cute Part III*, Honda Toshiyuki had served as the animation director of the television animation series *Doraemon* (1979) and the animation film *Doraemon: Nobita's Dinosaur* (1980). Impressed by the humor of *Old Master Q* comics and intrigued by Wu Sau Yee's vision of kung fu animation, Honda Toshiyuki went on board to join Wu Sau Yee.[30] Unfortunately, Wu Sau Yee's aspirations for an animation paradise in Hong Kong did not materialize due to the banking crisis from 1983 to 1986, which was exacerbated by the political uncertainties surrounding the Sino-British negotiations on the future of Hong Kong, and to the gradual emergence of Japan as a comics and animation hub in the 1980s.[31] The production of the Old Master Q Animation Trilogy is a forgotten moment in the pioneering but marginalized work of Hong Kong animation, providing a glimpse into a historical moment when the future of animation was in dialogue with emerging and competing animation hubs in Asia in the early 1980s.

Modernity and Medium Specificity

The study of animation, as Thomas Lamarre suggests, tends to oscillate between medium specificity theses (micro-aesthetic analysis) and modernity theses (macro-historical analysis). Lamarre reminds us that a productive dialogue can unfold between the two approaches, for it is often impossible to separate questions about the material and perceptual specificity of film from questions about historical formations.[32] My analysis of the

29. Before joining Wu Sau Yee's production, Randy Cartwright served as a supervising animator of the Disney animation, *The Fox and the Hound* (Ted Berman, Richard Rich, and Art Stevens, 1981). After his return to Disney, Cartwright developed with his peers the Computer Animation Production System, winning the Academy of Motion Picture Arts and Sciences Scientific and Engineering Award in 1992.

30. Wei Yifeng, "Wang Ze haoguo Zhang Daqian," 23.

31. See Cherry Sze-ling Lai and Dixon Heung Wah Wong, "Japanese Comics Coming to Hong Kong," in *Globalizing Japan: Ethnography of the Japanese Presence in Asia, Europe, and America*, ed. Harumi Befu and Sylvie Guichard-Anguis (London: Routledge, 2001), 111–20.

32. Thomas Lamarre, *The Anime Machine: A Media Theory of Animation* (Minneapolis: University of Minnesota Press, 2009), xxii–xxiii.

Old Master Q Animation Trilogy interweaves modernity and medium specificity as the two shed light on each other. In his study of *manhua*'s (comics, cartoons, and caricature) peak years in Republica-era Shanghai, John Crespi establishes the symbiotic relationship between *manhua*, pictorial magazines, and modernity. Crespi argues that *manhua* not only produced an audience that was ready to "engage the city through surface and spectacle," but also, as a "meta-picture," served as a "self-aware commentator on the relationship between power and ideology."[33] *Old Master Q* comics (and its animation) served a similar function in the context of colonial and capitalist modernity in Hong Kong. As a cheap entertainment and cultural commodity, *Old Master Q* comics were a product of the publishing boom in Hong Kong in the 1960s. The comics' highly diverse subject matter includes urban encounters, leisure, romance, horror, and the supernatural. Ann Leung suggests that the comics conveyed "the dilemma of the gap between [the rich] and [the] poor" and "the grievances of traditionalists in the Westernized metropolis."[34] The comics also often include the title "Worth pondering over" (*nairen xunwei* 耐人尋味), which interlaces the everyday with the uncanny.[35] Other than offering a kaleidoscope of urban mass culture, *Old Master Q* comics do not shy away from politics. With the freedom of speech in the comics medium, the playful and even verbally subversive Old Master Q reacted to the 1989 Tiananmen democratic movement in volumes 293 and 294.[36] Stitched into the fabric of urban life, *Old Master Q* occasionally offers political satire targeted to adults.

The discussion below seeks to understand the animated movements in the Old Master Q Animation Trilogy as an aesthetic vehicle that constructs a vision and an experience of Hong Kong's colonial and capitalist modernity. The trilogy contains a multiplicity of animated movements:

33. John A. Crespi, *Manhua Modernity: Chinese Culture and the Pictorial Turn* (Oakland: University of California Press, 2020), 16, 21.

34. Ann Y. Y. Leung, "Transformation from Comic to 2D, Then the 3D Approach: Character Representation of Old Master Q," *Asian Cinema* 18, no. 1 (2007): 160.

35. Kum-Hoon Ng and Lian-Hee Wee, "Chiaroscuro of the Uncanny: An Unknown Side of Old Master Q," in *Cultural Conflict in Hong Kong*, ed. Jason S. Polley, Vinton W. K. Poon, and Lian-Hee Wee (Singapore: Palgrave Macmillan, 2018), 213.

36. Wu Jiaxiong, "Xianggang banben *Laofuzi*," 24.

motions of the city at full speed, gravity-defying running movements, flying movements, roller-coaster movements, and aerial surveillance, all of which serve as an animated imagination of Hong Kong's territories, space, and sovereignty under colonial and capitalist modernity in the early 1980s, during the Sino-British negotiations on Hong Kong's future. The 1980s, as Akbar Abbas notes, is an era filled with "anxiety" and what he calls a "double trauma": the Sino-British Joint Declaration (1984) that announced the imminent handover of Hong Kong's sovereignty to China in 1997, and the 1989 Tiananmen democratic movement.[37] The production of the animation trilogy from 1981 to 1983 coincided with the Sino-British negotiations that began in September 1982 and ended in December 1984 with the official signing of the declaration.

In the context of the political anxiety and uncertainty about Hong Kong's future, the trilogy can be understood as a body of work that invokes the genres of martial arts and science fiction to remediate heroes of the present (Bruce Lee in episode 1), the past (Wu Song from the *Water Margin* in episode 2), and the future (E.T. in episode 3). From developing kung fu animation to *wuxia* animation to sci-fi animation, the trilogy experiments with the realist, supernatural, and formalist modes of animating action. In traversing time and space—from the modernity of kung fu and gunplay to premodern *wuxia* to futuristic sci-fi spectacle, the trilogy navigates between Hong Kong, a fictional China (through time travel), and Hollywood, developing a global vocabulary of animation as action that is identifiable and accessible across cultures. These experiments across a short span of three years can be understood in the context of Wu Sau Yee's Disney-inspired vision of an animation paradise, which, though never fully materialized, provides a glimpse into a forgotten moment in the collective efforts of pioneering animators in Hong Kong cinema.

37. Ackbar Abbas, *Culture and the Politics of Disappearance* (Minneapolis: University of Minnesota Press, 1997), 4–7.

Old Master Cute: Animating Bruce Lee in a City at Full Speed

The first film in the trilogy, *Old Master Cute* (1981), represents the high-speed, multilayered motion of the city through a combination of drawing movements and moving drawings, constructing the lifeblood of Hong Kong as an urban space and an image of Old Master Q as a powerless worker in a capitalist society. Whereas Old Master Q's morning routine in the opening sequence is animated by drawing the movements, the city traffic is animated by a combination of drawing movements and moving drawings. Lamarre uses the term *moving drawings* to refer to the way Miyazaki Hayao achieves in his animation the multi-layered "sliding of one plane over or under another—with a sense that foreground and background are in (relative) motion."[38] After his frantic but dance-like morning routine, Old Master Q finds himself amid a city filled with busy traffic. In the background is a sea of animated walking commuters; in the foreground is a rapid four-second animation of passing vehicles that almost fill the entire frame—a double-decker bus, a yellow sedan, a red taxi, and a purple pick-up truck. As he tiptoes across the street, Old Master Q becomes the midground of the shot composition. Here, almost the same cycle of the drawings of the passing vehicles is reused in the foreground (fig. 10.1). The recycling of the moving foreground is an economical and efficient way to create an illusion of speed, collision, and multilayered motion of the city in shallow space.

Lamarre describes the effect of the "sliding of figures across backgrounds, and [the] slipping of backgrounds under figures" as an "induced movement" of the spectator: "One sometimes has the sense that the background is in motion, and sometimes the character. The entire world itself seems to enter into motion."[39] Another example of induced movement as a result of moving drawings is when Old Master Q runs behind a taxi, trying desperately to catch it. The same cycle of still drawings of retail storefronts sliding behind the foreground is reused over and over again, whereas the taxi and Old Master Q drive and run in place in a repeated drive-walk

38. Thomas Lamarre, "From Animation to Anime: Drawing Movements and Moving Drawings," *Japan Forum* 14, no. 2 (2002): 360, 362.

39. Lamarre, "From Animation to Anime," 362.

FIGURE 10.1. The combination of drawing movements and moving drawings creates the vitality of the city of which Old Master Q is a part, as the clock to work is ticking. From *Old Master Cute* (1981).

cycle. Lamarre also describes the distinction between "drawing movement" and "moving drawing" as a distinction between "animating characters" and "cinematic mobility": "One way to think of this is as a distinction between an animation that focuses on animating characters (as with Donald Duck or Mickey Mouse, to use Miyazaki's examples) and an animation that aims for a cinematic mobility with manga-like drawings."[40] Drawing movements (animating characters) and moving drawings (creating cinematic mobility) are not necessarily a binary; they can be creatively combined to create multilayered motion. In a capitalist city at full speed, Old Master Q is a powerless individual from the working class, but he never succumbs,

40. Lamarre, "From Animation to Anime," 361–62.

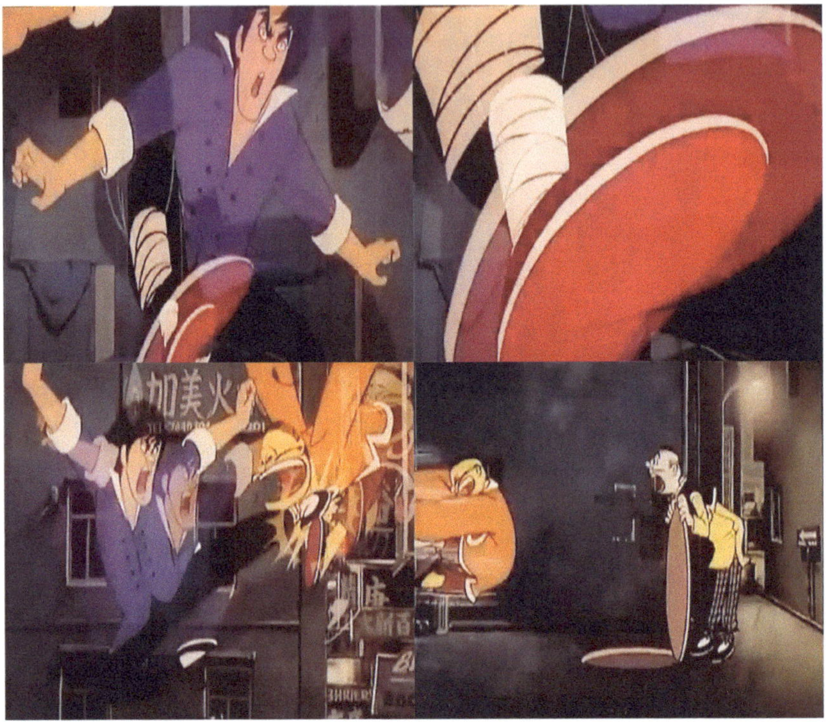

FIGURE 10.2. The experimentation with kung fu animation, highlighting animated contact and impact, might have been perceived as violent and unsuitable for children. From *Old Master Cute* (1981).

thanks to his energetic personality, work ethic, and his desire for heroic empowerment through an encounter with Bruce Lee.

Old Master Cute experiments with kung fu animation by remediating and animating Bruce Lee, an established icon in live-action cinema. Bruce Lee's kung fu in live-action cinema is centered on what Leon Hunt calls "corporeal authenticity"—the stunt work, physical risk, and fighting skills that a live actor demonstrates in a long take in a live-action film.[41] The paradox of *Old Master Cute* is that whereas the film rode the kung fu wave and cashed in on Bruce Lee with box office success, it also sought to overcome the limits of corporeal authenticity (arguably with limited success).

41. Leon Hunt, *Kung Fu Cult Masters* (London: Wallflower Press, 2003), 39.

The advertising poster of the film challenges corporeal authenticity by highlighting the "feats" and "gags" that a "live actor" (*zhenren* 真人) cannot perform.[42]

A review of *Old Master Cute* applauded Old Master Q's animated martial arts tricks (pouring wine and catching teacups flying in midair), but considered Bruce Lee's animated kicks and punches boring, violent, and unsuitable for children.[43] Whereas the former defies the natural law of gravity in the supernatural *wuxia* mode, the latter is reminiscent of a realist kung fu mode premised on physical contact. Bruce Lee's signature somersaults, nunchaku moves, and kicks are animated with dramatic sound effects, so that the visual and audio impact is exaggerated and made comedic: for example, a person flying off and hitting the sewer drain gate after receiving a powerful kick (fig. 10.2).

What might have been perceived as violent and unsuitable for children is perhaps the animated contact and impact that otherwise could have been avoided in the *wuxia* mode—a mode that the second animation in the trilogy adopts. The experimentation with kung fu animation reveals two kinds of tension: that between an animation aesthetic and corporeal authenticity from kung fu live-action cinema, and that between animated kung fu and perceived violence in a medium that caters to both young and old. These tensions were creatively resolved in the second animation in the trilogy.[44]

42. "*Qicai katong Laofuzi*" 七彩卡通老夫子 (*Old Master Cute*), *Dianying shuang zhoukan* 電影雙週刊 (Film biweekly) 64 (July 1981): 22.

43. Fu Jiang 福將, "Da heqian kan *Laofuzi*" 打呵欠看老夫子 (Yawn and watch *Old Master Q*), *Dianying shuang zhoukan* 電影雙週刊 (Film biweekly), 66 (August 1981): 38.

44. *Old Master Cute* has two endings. In one, Bruce Lee somersaults onto the kung fu world championship stage to fight a gang of thieves, ultimately winning the trophy. In the other, a detective comes in during the kung fu world championship tournament, setting off a chase sequence off stage, where Old Master Q ties up the thieves for the police to arrest. The former features Bruce Lee as the ultimate hero, whereas the latter features Old Master Q as both a hero and a good citizen collaborating with law enforcement. It is possible that the two endings were created for foreign markets because of censorship concerns.

Old Master Cute Part II: The Tiger and the Bullet Steal the Show

The second animation film in the trilogy, *Old Master Cute Part II* (1982), is an adaptation of Wong Chak's comics version of the Chinese vernacular novel, the *Water Margin*. A historical costume animation film in the *wuxia* tradition, *Water Margin* is a time-travel adventure: A scientist invents a time machine and invites Old Master Q, Big Potato, and Mr. Dumb to travel seven hundred years back in time, where they encounter (and rescue) Wu Song, a fictional hero who kills a tiger. *Old Master Cute Part II* avoids the pitfalls of its predecessor as a kung fu animation, because what might be deemed violent and unsuitable for children—animated contact and impact produced by punches and kicks—can be avoided in the supernatural *wuxia* mode, which often makes use of gravity-defying running or flying movements that are not contingent on physical contact with corporeal authenticity and therefore are best rendered with an animation aesthetic. The narrative design of time travel facilitates visual and verbal gags, made possible by the traversal in time and space and the use of a gun in a premodern context, where Old Master Q and his friends turn out to be the most modern and heroic characters in the diegetic world.

Old Master Cute II, with the playful Chinese title 老夫子水虎傳, or "Tale of the Water Tiger"—with the character for tiger (*hu* 虎) replacing the character for margin (*hu* 滸)—puts the spotlight on the animated tiger. The film can be understood in the larger context of the remediation (or lack of remediation) of the tiger in cinematic adaptations of the *Water Margin*. Referencing Julie Turnock's study of the animation tendency and photorealist tendency in predigital special effects and computer-generated image (CGI), Jason McGrath uses the term "animation aesthetic" to refer to the way in which *The Taking of the Tiger Mountain* (*Zhiqu Weihushan* 智取威虎山, 2014) uses CGI with an animation tendency to let the CG tiger steal the scene from Wu Song.[45] With an animation aesthetic (without

45. Jason McGrath, "Suppositionality, Virtuality, and Chinese Cinema," *boundary 2* 49, no. 1 (2022): 281–87. The opera film adaptation, *The Taking of the Tiger Mountain* (*Zhiqu Weihushan* 智取威虎山, 1970), does not present an actual tiger or a physical resemblance of it. See also Julie A. Turnock, *Plastic Reality: Special Effects, Technology, and the Emergence of 1970s Blockbuster Aesthetics* (New York: Columbia University Press, 2015).

the aid of CGI), *Old Master Cute II* places the kinesthetic motion of the animated tiger at the center and develops a vocabulary of animation that is identifiable across Chinese-speaking and Chinese-reading communities (both young and old), given that these communities may have a common knowledge of either the canonical literary text or adaptations of it in popular culture, including comics-based or cinematic versions.

Old Master Cute II lets the animated tiger steal the show from the unheroic Wu Song, so that Big Potato emerges as a modern hero killing the tiger with a bullet. In animating the confrontation between Wu Song and the tiger, the film not only experiments with a supernatural *wuxia* mode, but also uses montage to dramatize action—what Stephen Teo calls "the third cinematic strand" of the Chinese martial arts genre after *wuxia* and kung fu.[46] In contrast to the comics version that limits the Wu Song–tiger combat to a few panels, the film adds a chase scene in the supernatural *wuxia* mode, in which Wu Song frantically runs up to a tree, momentarily defying the law of gravity before he falls. The gravity-defying running movement is created by sliding the tree downward as Wu Song (turned 90 degrees sideways) runs in place in a repeated run cycle. Once he reaches the top, the law of gravity returns and Wu Song falls headfirst, frantically trying to grab the tree with his fingers. This gravity-defying chase scene culminates in a montage of key poses in close-up: Wu Song's leg, the tiger's big mouth and outspread front paws (filling almost the entire screen), and a flying bullet (from Big Potato's gun). The climax of the montage sequence is the flying bullet, which modernizes action in a way that allows *wuxia* and realist modes to coexist in a fictionally plausible way while avoiding contact, bloodshed, and impact that might be deemed violent. The magic and speed of the flying bullet remain invisible and incomprehensible to other premodern characters in the diegetic world. Corporeal authenticity is irrelevant here, whereas an animation aesthetic enlivens the chase scene with the animated tiger and the magic flying bullet getting all the attention.

The narrative design of time travel creates anachronism as a form of visual and verbal gag, conveying through dubbing the aspirations and value of Hong Kong's colonial and capitalist modernity in the mise-en-scène of a fictional premodern China. Other than misordering a lobster salad, an

46. Stephen Teo, *Chinese Martial Arts Cinema: The Wuxia Tradition* (Edinburgh: Edinburgh University Press, 2009), 80.

egg-and-ham sandwich, and a 7-Up in a premodern wineshop, Old Master Q and his friends express their modern, colonial, and democratic worldview when they are arrested and tried in the magistracy for hurting Simon (Ximen Qing) in an effort to help Wu Song, Pan Jinlian, and her husband to get out of trouble. When commanded by Justice Bao the Second to kneel, Big Potato refuses in defiance (in dubbed dialogue): "You're not the Queen (*si tau po* 事頭婆), why should we kneel?" The term *si tau po* (a female boss, similar to *laoban niang* 老闆娘) is a Cantonese slang expression in Hong Kong that refers to Queen Elizabeth II. The bilingual subtitles reveal a slippage in translation: "Not in a democratic society (English)/why should we kneel in a democratic era (Chinese)?" The verbal expressiveness and slippage in dubbing and subtitling suggest multivalent readings. First, at the level of subtitles, by refusing the kneeling gesture of obedience and subservience, Big Potato puts forward the idea of equality before the law in a democratic society. Second, at the level of dubbed dialogue, Big Potato does not so much contest the kneeling gesture itself, but who the real boss is—pointing to the Queen as the ultimate authority. Speaking as a colonial subject, Big Potato is effectively saying that Justice Bao the Second (and the legal system he represents) isn't the boss, but that the Queen is. The first reading at the level of bilingual subtitles would have easily passed the British censors in the colony because democracy is a key value of a modern society, even though Hong Kong had limited democracy in the 1980s. The second reading at the level of dubbed dialogue in Cantonese would have been potentially problematic to render in translation because colonialism inevitably had to end in the context of decolonization and the Sino-British negotiations in the early 1980s, when Hong Kong was one of the last colonies of the British Empire. Big Potato as a colonial subject was perhaps too outspoken in Cantonese and had to be tamed by remaining untranslated.

Old Master Cute Part III: Animating E.T. with Light

Set in an amusement park in a city filled with skyscrapers, *Old Master Cute Part III* (1983) narrates how Old Master Q, with the help of E.T., rescues an amusement park from the hands of a real estate developer. The film, filled with gravity-defying flight, roller-coaster motion, and aerial surveillance, can be read as an animated imagination of Hong Kong's territories, space, and sovereignty under colonial and capitalist modernity. By animating an aerial gaze achieved through flight, the film allegorizes capitalist and colonial surveillance of the land and Old Master Q's effort to reclaim sovereignty.

I use the term *aerial gaze* to refer to the camera's gaze from an aerial perspective. It might (or might not) involve aviation or serve as a character's point of view. The film opens with a panorama of skyscrapers in the city viewed from an aerial gaze (also the camera's gaze), followed by an extreme long shot of a rising helicopter, as the heavily accented voiceover of a real estate developer called the King of Land says, "Hong Kong is so densely populated and overcrowded! It's hard to find a nice piece of land to build properties." Similar to the animated city traffic in the first film in the trilogy, this film creates flying movements through moving drawings and sliding multiple layers. A few shots later, we see a point-of-view shot, framed by a pair of binoculars and through the surveilling eyes of the King of Land. With a big insatiable mouth smoking a cigar, the King of Land embodies the iconography of a capitalist real-estate baron, except that he is neither British nor white, but Otherized by means of a mainland Chinese accent. The King of Land can thus be read as a hybrid allegory for the capitalist, colonial, and future mainland surveillance and monopoly of Hong Kong's land. The amusement park is an allegorical metonym of Hong Kong, where citizens not only work and play but also project their fears, dreams, and aspirations. The use of an amusement park as mise-en-scène provides a context for numerous animated spectacles, such as gravity-defying flight, a roller-coaster chase, physical transformation, optical illusion, and an encounter with E.T.

Old Master Cute III remediates E.T. as a futuristic and extraterrestrial hero in the mode of sci-fi animation, thus moving beyond kung fu and *wuxia* modes to develop a global vocabulary of animation as action. Wu Sau Yee considered this film a breakthrough in photography because its animated movement is designed to be accessible to a foreign audience.[47] The film made considerable progress in animating light relative to the first film, for which all the special effects were created at the level of drawing,

47. Wei Yifeng, "Wang Ze haoguo Zhang Daqian," 23.

except for the spark of a diamond that was a "combination of photography and animation techniques."[48] Stephen Teo reminds us about direct animation in early *wuxia* films, where double exposures, composite printing, and superimpositions were often used: "Visual effects took the form of animation techniques directly drawn onto the celluloid film to denote the projection of rays and waves of energy known as *qi* or inner energy."[49] As a sci-fi animation that animates light as the locus of cinematic attraction, *Old Master Cute III* returns to animation's roots—animation as visual effects, harkening back to the early roots of cinema, when optical toys, shadow shows, and magic lanterns were exhibited in amusement parks.

A distinctive feature of ㄐT is a halo surrounding the E.T. character's entire body. Similar to an optical illusion, the luminous and animated ring of light is blue or golden yellow, moving, tracing, and trailing ㄐT's weightless movement in flight like a shooting star. I refer to the cinematic creation of this halo effect as "animating light." ㄐT's first appearance and encounter with Old Master Q is marked by an animated spark. Later on, the physical contact between their index fingers is surrounded by an animated spark of light in close-up. A similar spark of light is then given a power equivalent to magic when Old Master Q raises his fingertip to fight the enemies.

Other actions in this animation are marked by a light that moves across a character or an object. When ㄐT protects Old Master Q by intercepting a flying baseball and defying the natural law of gravity, the baseball's path of action traces a yellow path of light in an S shape (fig. 10.3). The yellow path of light is also ㄐT's path of action because ㄐT is able to shrink in size and carry the baseball as it flies. The luminous path of light and action generates an animated cinematic spectacle that creates kinesthesia and a sense of astonishment—what Tom Gunning calls the "cinema of attractions."[50]

At the end of the film, when ㄐT is ready to bid farewell and head back to outer space, the start of the rocket engine is illuminated by an animated drawing of a yellow spark that turns out to be fireworks (in

48. Guan Baixuan, "'Laowantong,'" 26.

49. Teo, *Chinese Martial Arts Cinema*, 88.

50. See Tom Gunning, "The Cinema of Attractions: Early Film, Its Spectators and the Avant-Garde," in *The Cinema of Attractions Reloaded*, ed. Wanda Strauven (Amsterdam: Amsterdam University Press, 2006), 381–88.

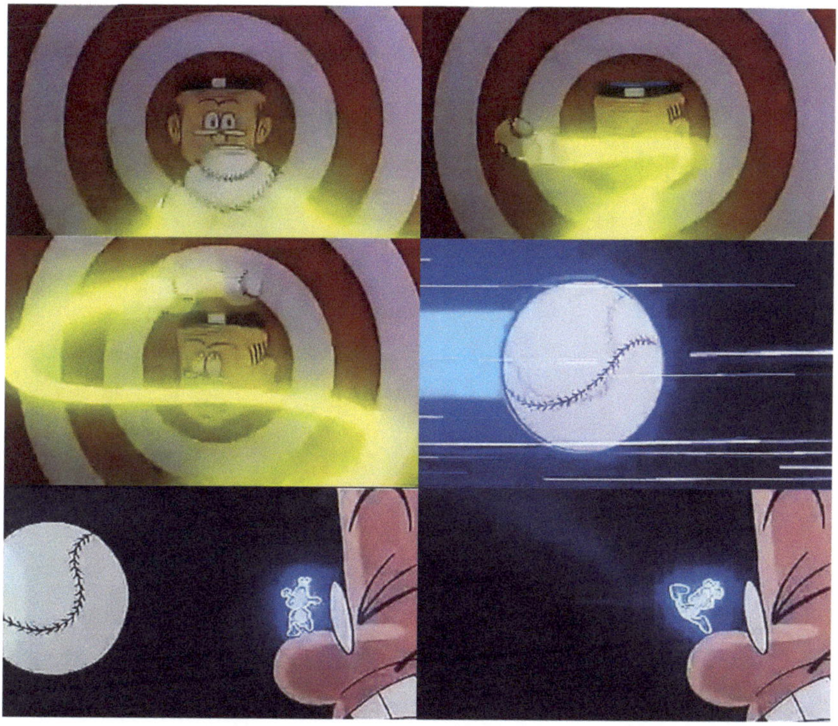

FIGURE 10.3. A luminous path of light and action creates an animated cinematic spectacle in *Old Master Cute Part III* (1983), harkening back to the early roots of cinema, where animation served as visual effects.

red), followed by two shots of raw footage of fireworks in live action (fig. 10.4). The switch from an animation aesthetic (hand-drawn fireworks) to a photorealist aesthetic (raw footage of fireworks in live action) to represent the movement of spark, light, and fireworks indicates the competing, complementary, and dialogic nature of the two aesthetics. An animation aesthetic animates by drawing movements (and moving drawings), whereas a photorealist aesthetic is premised on the mechanical process of inscribing light (emanating from actual objects and people) onto the chemical celluloid as an indexical trace. *Old Master Cute III* continues the supernatural mode of action by instilling science fiction elements but without mobilizing kung fu or *wuxia*. The film is also highly conscious of the formal aspect of animating light as a special effect. The animation

FIGURE 10.4. A switch from an animation aesthetic (hand-drawn fireworks) to a photorealist aesthetic (raw footage of fireworks in live action), integrating animation with live action in *Old Master Cute Part III* (1983).

trilogy experiments with a realist, supernatural, and formalist mode of animating action, transcending corporeal authenticity and paving the way to the digital turn that seeks to reintegrate animation with live action.

Conclusion

Sergei Eisenstein describes Disney as Paradise Regained, where the world is reconstructed according to one's fantasy and will.[51] Although his Disney-inspired vision of an animation paradise never materialized, Wu

51. Sergei Eisenstein, *On Disney*, ed. Jay Leyda, trans. Alan Upchurch (London: Seagull Books, 2017), 6–7.

Sau Yee's animation trilogy is a pioneering work that sought to develop a global vocabulary of animation as action. If anxiety, uncertainty, powerlessness, and the lack of self-determination characterized the early 1980s, when the Sino-British negotiations on Hong Kong's future were unfolding, the Old Master Q Animation Trilogy offered a fluid, elastic, and imaginative world of expressive freedom. This animated world is full of gravity-defying movements, playful transformations, strange encounters, and unlimited possibilities—what Eisenstein calls a plasmaticness that liberates all forms from the laws of logic. Eisenstein reminds us that plasmaticness, the transformation of stable forms into forms of mobility, "exceeds the boundaries of form and extends to subject and theme."[52] All the films in the trilogy convey a desire for heroic empowerment and rescue, with a powerless character such as Old Master Q (together with his friends) becoming a collective hero and embodying the aspirations and values of Hong Kong's colonial and capitalist modernity that also lie at the core of the animation universe—"what is strange is not the fact that it exists. What is strange is that it attracts."[53]

52. Eisenstein, *On Disney*, 32–34.

53. Eisenstein, *On Disney*, 32.

SECTION FOUR

Digitality

ELEVEN

Animation as Agency in the Glistening City Orb

Jia Zhangke's *The World*

Wendy Larson

With his realistic, semi-documentary focus on the lives of people living in provincial cities in his early films *Pickpocket* (*Xiaowu* 小武, 1997), *Platform* (*Zhantai* 站台, 2000), and *Still Life* (*Sanxia haoren* 三峡好人, 2006), Jia Zhangke 贾樟柯 has gained a strong following among intellectuals and film critics. In *The World* (*Shijie* 世界), Jia moves to the national capital, which becomes the backdrop for his close look at the lives of migrant workers in Beijing World Park at the edge of the metropolis. In that he continues to use a framework that concentrates on the lives of those from the provinces even in this nationally centered location, Jia has not abandoned his vision. *The World* could be seen as a devastating portrait of the meaning of globalization for migrant workers, who come to the capital seeking work only to be encapsulated within a shrunken world that produces an illusion of mobility continually fed by an imaginary fantasy of cosmopolitan, global travel.

Even in his early films, Jia associated geographic mobility with an imagined freedom that could function locally, provincially, nationally, or globally.[1] Yet the obviousness of his focus on thwarted mobility can make *The*

1. Michael Berry analyzes the train motif in *Platform* and the scuffle between two male characters as one of them tries to imitate a train whistle sound for a stage production, even though he has never seen a train: "yet another hint that this journey to modernity may not be an easy one." The imaginary train to Mao Zedong's birthplace also stands in for the

World seem pedantic and heavy-handed as viewers are treated to a profusion of shots reiterating this theme. One is taken from a car in which Cheng Taisheng 成太生 and his paramour Liao Qun 廖群 are riding, highlighting the road and a train. In another, the male construction worker Little Sister (Xiao guniang 小姑娘) and Zhao Xiaotao 赵小桃 watch a plane flying above a forest of construction where they stand. The park monorail goes round and round but never gets anywhere, and Tao angrily rebuffs Taisheng's suggestion that she can't get anywhere on her own. The worker Liu Youyou 刘友友 both literally and figuratively goes somewhere as she climbs into the car (and, it is implied, bed) of Manager Mu (Mu jingli 穆经理) as Tao watches from the sidewalk. Images of Tao and Taisheng on the virtual magic flying carpet with happy face balloons next to them fill the screen. Finally, a dancer acts out the Statue of Liberty while raising a passport rather than the torch of freedom. This ironic contrast so clearly structures *The World*—with the leitmotif of mobility appearing constantly in the form of planes, trains, cars, bicycles, passports, and bridges—that some critics have declared the film to be a failure: overly obvious and forced, these critics argue, the film has lost the connection to authentic social life that Jia skillfully illustrated in his other films.[2]

Although this belabored idea may mark the film as one of the director's least subtle, the introduction of animation sequences adds an intriguing element that, to some degree, sets the film apart from the director's earlier

---

transformation to capitalism, a change of which riders are unaware. See Michael Berry, *Jia Zhangke's "Hometown Trilogy": Xiao Wu, Platform, Unknown Pleasures* (London: BFI Publishing, 2014), 60.

2. See Chen Xiangbo 陈祥波, "Zhanzai 'shijie' wai de Zhongguo ren: Ping Jia Zhangke de dianying *Shijie*" 站在"世界"外的中国人——评贾樟柯的电影《世界》 (Chinese standing outside "The World": Critiquing Jia Zhangke's film *The World*). *Dianying pingjie* 电影评介 (Movie review) 2007 (8): 40, 39. For other interpretations, see Jason McGrath, "The Independent Cinema of Jia Zhangke: From Postsocialist Realism to a Transnational Aesthetic," in *The Urban Generation: Chinese Cinema and Society at the Turn of the Twenty-First Century*, ed. Zhen Zhang (Durham, NC: Duke University Press, 2007), 81–114; Zheng Longfu 郑隆福, "Jia Zhangke dianying zuopin *Shijie* liang banben de bijiao" 贾樟柯电影作品《世界》两版本的比较 (A comparison of two versions of Jia Zhangke's film *The World*, *Zhongguo yishu piping* 中国艺术批评 (China art criticism), April 22, 2007, https://www.jintian.net/107/d13.html; Ting Luo, "Post-realism as an Alternative Aesthetics in Contemporary Chinese Cinema" (PhD diss., University of Auckland, 2014), https://researchspace.auckland.ac.nz/bitstream/handle/2292/22738/whole.pdf.

emphasis on imaginatively capturing and illuminating something from real life. In an interview, Jia said, "Naturally, there are some directors who neglect reality in their work, but my aesthetic taste and goals don't allow me to do that—I can never escape reality."[3] However, Jia's idea of realism evolved to include both surrealism—which he came to believe was characteristic of life in a rapidly transforming Chinese society—and the world of inner experience. Some of Jia's films feature surreal images and action or odd extended moments that seemingly burst forth from the uninspiring social conditions within which his characters live. Most striking are UFO-like objects, a building that launches as if it is a rocket, and a man walking a tightrope between ruins, all in *Still Life*. These events project a sense of mystery in the environment, suppressed longing and emotional complexity in the characters, and a movement of powerful forces beyond the characters' control. Jia's tendency to deviate from the diegetic narrative trajectory can be regarded as an evolution in his depiction of space from "documenting and recording the physical, material aspects of space, as seen in Jia's earlier films, to experiencing and perceiving the psychological, emotional dimension of space."[4] His realism thus is in line with other directors of his generation who emphasize the nitty-gritty aspect of life as it occurs and also use nonprofessional actors, handheld cameras, and other strategies to move away from strict realism.[5]

Yet Jia's laser focus on reality and his indexical fidelity to the lived world has a strong presence in *The World*, despite technical innovations—high-definition digital format, 2:1 widescreen, electronic music, and, of course, the animation—that heighten the sense of artificiality in the park.[6] Counterfeit consumer items are ubiquitous and the hierarchical contrast between original and copy only hammers home the theme. It may seem

3. Berry, *Jia Zhangke's Homeland Trilogy*, 129–30.

4. Luo, "Post-realism," 150.

5. In "Post-realism," Luo credits Hao Jian 郝健 (2008) with recognizing and naming the realism of Jia's early work as stylized realism (*fenggehua jishi* 风格化纪实). For Hao's work, see Hao Jian 郝健, "Andelie Bazan zai Zhongguo: Bei yanshuo yu bei xiaojian" 安德烈．巴赞在中国：被言说与被消减 (André Bazin in China: Spoken of and forgotten), *Dangdai dianying* 当代电影 (Contemporary cinema) 8 (2008): 13–17. Hao notes that, in China, Bazin's "The Virtues and Limitations of Montage" and "The Evolution of the Language of Film" were translated and published respectively in 1962 and 1980.

6. See Luo, "Post-realism."

strange that Jia inserts animation into what otherwise is a gritty presentation that powerfully (if conventionally) zones in on the disruption of community and the individual's sense of self, belonging, and value caused by the expansion of capitalism in the postsocialist world. What does the animation cause viewers to see, feel, or sense that we cannot get from the carefully constructed realistic sequences? In a film that combines pan-documentary realism with animation and sets the story in the simulated environment of a theme park, how can we understand the animated sequences of this overwrought context of the fake+real? In the following sections, I lay out conflicting interpretations of the animation and argue that in *The World*, animation offsets the critique implicit in the realistic parts of the film, offering a burst of energy that enhances the richness of the characters' inner lives and expands their agency. In other words, the animation is not an extension of the film's realism but instead an expression of presence and creativity in a confusing and contradictory environment. Additionally, animation breaks apart the conventional interpretive habits of the intellectual art-house audience, which may see a critical realism that exposes societies' ills as the most imperative technique and thus would tend to interpret the animation as an extension of the film's realism. Finally, the theme park itself becomes a player in the nonlinear movement between the murky poles of real vs. fake, authentic vs. inauthentic, and agent vs. victim, which brings in a discourse contesting the meaning of the immersive space. Because the animation in *The World* is only a small part of the film, it is important to contextualize it within the larger environment of the film's themes and formal qualities.

Animation in the Theme Park

One interpretive strand evaluates the social life of migrant workers in *The World* as having lost any sense of organic unity, with an affective economy of despair as its central passion.[7] From this perspective, the animation can be

7. Pheng Cheah, "Entering the World from an Oblique Angle: On Jia Zhangke as an Organic Intellectual," in *What Is a World? On Postcolonial Literature as World Literature* (Durham, NC: Duke University Press, 2016), 137–64; Sijia Yao, "Pessimistic Chinese Cosmopolitanism and Jia Zhangke's *The World*," *The Comparatist* 43 (October 2019): 147–58.

thought of as simply another part of the devastating landscape of oppression. It then perfectly expresses the migrant workers' dreams of mobility, romance, and cosmopolitanism while exposing the impossibility of escape from the bondage of the park or a fake world. From this angle, because most of the animation scenes begin with the cell phone, they have a special function in enhancing and simultaneously destroying the hopes attached to the new worlds of possibility generated by digital communication. Whereas overt socialist ideals figure only briefly in the film, the animation may illustrate exactly how the material processes that would create a hopeful and equitable world for what used to be called the masses, or *qunzhong* 群众, can only be fantasies under the new capitalist regime. Thus, by transforming material and mental activity into its luminescent outline, the film shows how in real life the primacy of work, which undergirded the socialist experiment, has been gutted of its community-building significance, instead giving rise to fantasy. Everyday life finds the individual body (of women) engaged in acting out the cultural forms of others or (of men) locked in a grueling physical regime defined by the debts it leaves behind.[8]

These interpretations locate the animation within the film's realism. The realism thus shows the truth, and the animation either a stylized version of the truth or the impossible, hopeful fantasy that the capitalist transformation has produced.[9] In this analysis, the surreal works in service of the real, rendering subjective experience that "is both a continuation of and a complement to realism."[10] This understanding of the animation in *The World* may recognize its intensity and—compared with the film's realistic scenes—its ability to affect viewers differently. It also, however, encourages critics to downplay the significance of the animation because it is but a small addition to the realistic parts of the film. Furthermore, it enhances the overworked binary of an attractive mobility and the thwarted desire to attain it, presents the workers as victims, and places the viewer in a superior position. Our critical environment may encourage us to quickly

8. Although men dress up and prepare to be on stage, we do not see them perform. Their major role is to be park security or work as laborers.

9. Only the first five of the eight animation sequences could possibly be escapism. The last three concern the death of Little Sister and Taisheng's betrayal of Qun, which could be interpreted as supporting the depressing reality.

10. Luo, "Post-realism," 168.

combine the animation and the realism as an example of straightforward social critique, within which this interpretation can easily be located.

From this standpoint, any exuberance shown by the workers in the theme park can only be false consciousness that conceals the exploitation of their labor by the World Park ownership.[11] The theme park then becomes a cruel and artificial location where fake hopes are generated and sustained, a critique often leveled at immersive spaces in general:

> The critiques that have been offered of themed and immersive spaces are varied, though for the purposes of argument, we may simplify them and consider that the foundation they all share is the notion that themed and immersive spaces are inauthentic, fabricated, faux, and simulated and that (in terms of their effects on workers, guests, and society at large) such spaces result in the negative cultural, political, and economic effects of hegemony, consumerism, hedonism, and conformity.[12]

This generally accepted negative take on the theme park can be located within the Frankfurt School's dismissal of popular culture, which can become the historical imperative for viewers to reject the theme park as anything more than deception of the masses and the animation as the fantasy of escape. Walter Benjamin (1892–1940) was unsure about how to interpret popular culture in the form of the famous animated rodent Mickey Mouse. In a short fragment that he later retracted, Benjamin had no problem incorporating Mickey into his critical theory, attributing the popularity of the films not to "mechanization, their form; nor is it a misunderstanding. It is simply the fact that the public recognizes its own life in them."[13] Benjamin vacillated between regarding Mickey Mouse as undermining "the hierarchy of photographic cinema over animation," and

11. Friedrich Engels (1820–1895) used the term in a letter to Franz Mehring (1846–1919) in 1893. See Friedrich Engels, "Letter to F. Mehring," in *Karl Marx and Friedrich Engels: Selected Works in Two Volumes*, vol. 2 (Moscow: Foreign Languages Publishing House, 1949), 451. Georg Lukács (1885–1971) developed the idea in his influential *History and Class Consciousness: Studies in Marxist Dialectics*, trans. Rodney Livingstone (Cambridge, MA: MIT Press, 1972).

12. Scott A. Lukas, *A Reader in Themed and Immersive Spaces* (Pittsburgh, PA: Carnegie Mellon University ETC Press), 2016.

13. Miriam Bratu Hansen, *Cinema and Experience: Siegfried Kracauer, Walter Benjamin and Theodor W. Adorno* (Berkeley: University of California Press, 2012), 545.

as interpreting animation as generally supporting a grim reality.[14] Theodor Adorno (1903–1969) was even less accepting of the mouse, joining many others (including the Nazi Party) in branding this form of popular culture as mass deception, much as critics of *The World* tend to see the theme park only as superficial and oppressive.[15]

The possibility that viewers could recognize their own lives in the animation of *The World* opens up a more fluid and dynamic way of thinking about the relationship between the animated and realist parts of the film. Writing about cinema, Esther Leslie argues that "something has to be wrestled out of a Frankfurt School legacy that threatens to be overpowered by the aridities of philosophy, perhaps, or high cultural concerns, as Adorno and Horkheimer's 'culture industry' thesis becomes the default mode of Frankfurt thinking on popular culture."[16] Leslie is protesting the rigid dismissal of popular culture as an inferior form that downgrades vitality and energy. Jia's insertion of animation into the social reality of the theme park could be an attempt to interrupt the intellectual viewer's continuity with the "aridities of philosophy." Although the cultural derision of theme parks as shallow, imperialistic, and artificial is still the status quo, recent work has engaged with the global presence of theme parks and their invention of culture and place, their futuristic and fantastical architecture, their world-creation imagination, and the sophisticated ways that fans interact with them.[17] Thinking about theme parks as more than fake cultural constructions for dupes is a useful caution against simplification as we examine *The World*, and may also hint at new ways to interpret the surrealism in some of Jia's other films.[18]

14. Miriam Bratu Hansen, "Room-for-Play: Benjamin's Gamble with Cinema," *Canadian Journal of Film Studies* 13, no. 1 (Spring 2004): 18–19.

15. Esther Leslie, *Hollywood Flatlands: Animation, Critical Theory and the Avant-Garde* (New York: Verso, 2002). See also Esther Leslie, *Walter Benjamin Overpowering Conformism* (London: Pluto Press, 2000).

16. Esther Leslie, "Review of *Cinema and Experience: Siegfried Kracauer, Walter Benjamin and Theodor W. Adorno*," *Screen* 53, no. 3 (Autumn 2012): 318–21, https://academic.oup.com/screen/issue/53/3.

17. Rebecca Williams, *Theme Park Fandom: Spatial Transmedia, Materiality and Participatory Cultures* (Amsterdam: Amsterdam University Press, 2020); Lukas, *A Reader*.

18. Jia had a conventionally intellectual understanding of the theme park, as illustrated in his hope that *The World* was to "tell a true story in a fake environment that only reflects

Certainly, many aspects of the film reveal a depressing reality. Yet animation can provide a perspective that extends beyond the visible disheartening reality, or allow a freedom to transmogrify that is not available in realistic live action.[19] As we watch the animated sequences, the liveliness and vivacity that is missing in many—but far from all—of the real-life scenes may flood into our consciousness. The animations ironically bring to life, so to speak, an elastic quality that can transform futility and repetition into vitality. The connection between the cell phone and animation also suggests that the animated images are part of the emotional experience of the filmic character viewing the message on the phone. In other words, the texts engender a powerful subconscious vision that the film expresses through animation and that cannot be adequately addressed as part of the film's realism. This aspect of the flash scenes implies that they could function, literally, as an animating factor that recognizes energy and possibility, as if the director were searching for something to overcome the leaden, didactic liabilities of realism.

These two poles mark the interpretive possibilities of the animation sequences. One supports the film as a critique of an inequitable China under capitalist transformation, a goal of the film's realism. Under this banner, animation brings to life the vivid cosmopolitan imaginary of global mobility and its presence in the minds of the workers while showing the theme park to be part of the culture industry as it is generally understood by the Frankfurt School, a move that highlights the park's status as a copy. The cell phone (and digital communication in general) becomes

---

images." Quoted in Erik Bordeleau, "The World Without Future: Stage as Entrapment in Jia Zhangke's Film," *China Review* 10, no. 2 (2010): 163. Yet he later remarked that he does not believe theme parks such as Beijing World Park to be fakes as much as they are a way for people who cannot leave the country to see world sights: "The landscape in the World Park includes famous sights from all over the world. They're not real, but still they can satisfy people's longing for the world. They reflect the very strong curiosity of people in this country, and the interest they have in becoming a part of international culture." See Valerie Jaffee, "An Interview with Jia Zhangke," *Senses of Cinema* (July 2004), https://www.sensesofcinema.com/2004/feature-articles/jia_zhangke.

19. See Lev Manovich, *The Language of New Media* (Cambridge: MIT Press), 2001; Sean Griffin, *Tinker Belles and Evil Queens: The Walt Disney Company from the Inside Out* (New York: New York University Press, 2000); Dan Torre, "Cognitive Animation Theory: A Process-Based Reading of Animation and Human Cognition, *Animation* 9, no. 1 (March 17, 2014): 47–64.

a faux-liberatory device that promises to leap across time and space but cannot deliver. The second pole moves in two directions. First, it shifts the significance of the animation toward the interpretive conventions of a presumed intellectual audience. By disturbing the clear-cut ideological critique associated with critical realism, the animation becomes a way viewers can question interpretive conventions and evaluate their preconceptions. Second, the flash scenes become a door to experiencing the vital force of the migrants' lives, including their imagined futures, which still contain a sense of vibrancy and agency. From this position, Jia's persistent aesthetic complexity, in part formed by the mysterious elements in his films—including not only surreal happenings and scenes, but also oddness in temporality and space—"gestures toward the creative potential harbored in the unbearable banality of everyday life."[20] In the ruins of *Still Life*, this energy may be more visible given that it suggests the possibility of new life:

> Aside from the surreal visual elements and supernatural phenomena, *Still Life* reenforces its defamiliarizing effect by representing interactions and sometimes mystical connections between individuals and ruins. Usually, ruins are closely associated with destruction and decay, and they are "dead" space having nothing to do with life and living. However, *Still Life* reveals another side of ruins: ruins possess a certain vitality when they interact with people. In the process of demolition workers' [*sic*] tearing down massive ruined buildings and smashing them into piles of debris, the "dying" ruins look vibrant.[21]

Interpreting the animation in *The World* in a similar way—as possessing "a certain vitality" to people in their social world, be it ruins or a theme park—illuminates not only the film but also Jia's tendency toward the surreal in general. Many times he has stated that he wants to address real life in his work, but he persistently complicates that presentation with extraordinary scenes or sensibilities. The unreal aspects of his films show an awareness that realism cannot truly or perfectly capture reality, and that a realistic focus on those left behind in China's search for wealth and power can become simplistic and even unrealistic.

20. Wenjin Cui, "Waiting and the Duration of Time," *China Perspectives* 2, no. 121 (2020): 36.

21. Luo, "Post-realism," 164.

Two aspects of the animation challenge our experiences as intellectual viewers accustomed to the conventions of art cinema. The first is the way in which the animation comes directly from scenes of daily life, rotoscoping the real into something fantastical (and in one case—when Taisheng visits Qun at the small factory where she designs clothes—reverse-rotoscoping the animation into the real). This tight relationship between the real and the fantastical—one generating the other—encourages us to move away from our clear-cut ideological analysis toward an understanding that elevates the hopeful mentality of the workers not as false consciousness but instead as their powerful understandings of their lives. Thus, although much of the realism proposes victimhood, the animation suggests agency, bringing alive hidden aspects of quotidian life. Second, explosions of light and pulsating color characterize half of the animations, but in a way that differs from the realistic segments, where color, gleam, glitter, and light are associated with the performance of inauthenticity. If we think of the bursts as actual explosions meant to rupture, they can break through both the deadly realism and our conventions of viewing, again bringing us closer not to the experience of the migrant workers, but to a fully embodied sense of their rich subjectivity. The hierarchy of cities and the character of Tao are the keys to seeing an alternative world in which the animation is much more than escapist fantasy.

Optimism and the Glistening City Orb

Jia's narrative structure, through which he establishes the apparent dichotomies of entrepreneurship/exploitation, agent/victim, optimism/cynicism-despair, cosmopolitan city/migrant-worker city, and flight-as-travel/flight-to-work does not so much set up clear-cut categories as it shows how these areas overlap and mutually interact. It is important to recognize that the film, in addition to trauma, also exhibits happiness and exuberance in the basement costume-changing areas and the theme park. The female and male workers have formed a lively community and generally regard their jobs as a step up from the work they would have done had they stayed home. As Taisheng's cheerful boast "what do you think of my workplace?" implies as he takes hopeful new employees from his village around the park, the workers are proud to be working in the World Park. The subplots involving Little Sister, the budding affection between the Erxiao 二小 (a fellow provincial

Taisheng tries to help) and the Eiffel Tower elevator operator Afei 阿飞, the quarreling lovers Laoniu 老牛 and Xiao Wei 小魏, the career-ladder climber Liu Youyou, Liao Qun's family troubles as she waits for her passport to join her husband in France, intrigues involving Sanlai 三来, Lao Song 老宋, and others all deserve careful attention as part of the filmic narrative. The two main characters, though, Tao and Taisheng, will be my focus here because they anchor networks of experience and subjectivity that provide contrasting views of how idealism and optimism can exist under the conditions of the Beijing World Park. Whereas Taisheng has seen through everything and realizes that honest living will not improve his life, Tao refuses to relinquish her belief that by doing things right, she will build a positive, authentic, and satisfying life. Tao serves as a beacon of all that is ideally right, holding tight to her positive outlook in the face of multiple assaults. It is no coincidence that most of the animations are related to these two characters.

Within the postsocialist context—when collective idealism was quickly eroded by the individualism of capitalism—Tao's persistent optimism is especially interesting. Similar to capitalist nations, countries that adopted Marxism also embraced the idea of progress as a theory of history, which suggests that "there is a blind force in history, a force uncontaminated by historical contingency, yet dedicated to the continued improvement of man."[22] Developing out of the European Enlightenment, progress as a theory of history differs from theories of millennialism, utopianism, cyclicality, history-as-random, and so on. Optimism is the state of mind that results from believing that history will always progress. The general mobility/passport-seeking quality of most of the central characters in *The World* shows that they believe they must strive for improvement. But some are becoming cynical. Confidence in the forward movement of humanity and one's small role in that process—a state of mind characteristic of socialism—has been replaced by individual desire to get ahead at any cost. Only Tao and Liangzi 梁子, her former boyfriend from the countryside, remain as true optimists. Whereas revolutionary model worker Lei Feng 雷锋 was motivated by his desire to relinquish self-benefit and whole-heartedly "serve the people," Tao believes in the value of authentic emotions, personal morality, and always keeping alive a hope for the future, which can be

22. Theodore Olson, *Millennialism, Utopianism, and Progress* (Toronto: University of Toronto Press, 1982), 9.

summarized as flying. Tao is possessed by dreams of flying, and mobility is the mechanism of her optimistic spirit. She travels by bus and train, and earnestly participates in illusions of greater movement, from riding on a virtual flying carpet to snuggling with Taisheng in the pilot's seat of a grounded airplane. When Tao argues with Taisheng, she angrily lists her options for independent movement: bus, train, taxi. Her brightness derives not only from the possibility of spatial movement, but also from a fundamental temporal confidence that the future can be better. Tao's optimism rejects the idea that the only way to live is by striving to get rich or otherwise move up in the world at the expense of one's values.

Tao and others often travel up and down the elevator in the Eiffel Tower, but her dream of crossing and expanding space is centered on Ulaanbaatar, the Mongolian capital that is the topic of the film's theme song, "Nights of Ulaanbaatar." Ulaanbaatar is relevant to the animations because the song appears in them. Originally a Mongolian folk song, the words and tune were altered by Jia and his crew to produce a contradictory energetic yet melancholic sense of isolation, movement, speed, and stillness:

> A wind passing through the wilderness, slow down
> 穿过旷野的风啊 慢些走
> I tell you by my silence, I'm drunk with wine
> 我用沉默告诉你 我醉了酒
> Clouds drifting to faraway places, slow down
> 飘向远方的云啊 慢些走
> I tell you by my running, I won't look back
> 我用奔跑告诉你 我不回头
> Oh nights of Ulaanbaatar
> 乌兰巴托的夜啊
> So still, so still
> 那么静 那么静
> Even the wind does not know me, does not know
> 连风都不知道我 不知道
> Oh nights of Ulaanbaatar
> 乌兰巴托的夜啊
> So still, so still
> 那么静 那么静
> Even the wind does not know me, does not know
> 连风都不知道我 不知道

Why does the film, centered in Beijing, frequently reference Ulaanbaatar? A city of around 1.5 million, Ulaanbaatar was founded in 1639 as a Buddhist monastic center. Between 2000 and 2006, 220,000 people moved to the city, many of them living in traditional tents organized into informal communities. The influx of migrant workers from China led to anti-Chinese sentiment during the time *The World* was made.[23] Yet the remote city, one of the coldest capitals of the world, appears several times in *The World* in a complex and ambiguous role. Although Ulaanbaatar cannot stand with Paris, New York, London, or Rome in offering—even if only through imagination—the global pleasures of a cosmopolitan city, it is a realistic destination for a migrant worker seeking to improve his or her working conditions.

Ulaanbaatar first comes into view when Liangzi appears out of nowhere ("I bought a ticket") and goes with Tao to a restaurant, where he tells her he has a passport and is on his way to Mongolia. Because he presents himself without acrimony and with a realistic understanding of his options, Liangzi is an important character despite the brevity of his screen time. In contrast to Taisheng, he shows a commonsense approach to life improvement, going to Mongolia to seek work rather than to Beijing. The city of Ulaanbaatar also appears briefly in other scenes. As Tao looks out across the night landscape using the binoculars that the Russian woman Anna has brought, the screen flashes the words "Nights of Ulaanbaatar." In another scene, Anna tells Tao that she wants to visit her sister, who is in Ulaanbaatar. After we glimpse Anna's bruised back and she and Tao cry together in the restroom of a bar, we see Anna on an airplane on her way to Mongolia.

With its severe weather, Siberian winds and sands, and the influx of migrant workers seeking better lives, Ulaanbaatar's prominence in the film locates it as an important city of last resort. Although it does not rise to the level of the architectural monuments and ethnic performance in the national-cultural sites featured in the theme park, for migrant workers, Ulaanbaatar is emblematic of the actualized city. As such it is not merely a worksite, but also is permeated with the emotional intensity of the workers' subjective grasp of its possibilities for altering their lives, which is expressed in the melancholic song that accompanies some of the animations.

23. Victoria Whall, "Pollution Chokes Ulan Bator Skies," BBC News, February 19, 2007, http://news.bbc.co.uk/2/hi/asia-pacific/6376203.stm; "Anti-Chinese Sentiment Swelling in Mongolia," *Asian Economic News*, April 11, 2005, https://www.thefreelibrary.com/FOCUS%3a+Anti-Chinese+sentiment+swelling+in+Mongolia.-a0131327236.

FIGURE 11.1. Tao flies above Beijing, in *The World* (2004).

For women, one way out of the meaningless life in which they are entrapped is prostitution. The film implies that Anna becomes a prostitute, a "choice" enforced by violence, and Liu Youyou de facto accepts money for sex and power as she accommodates the desires of Manager Mu, who later promotes her. Despite the cynical behavior of those around her and the betrayal by Taisheng, Tao remains true to her ideals. When Taisheng complains of hardship, Tao reminds him that she slept in her plastic raincoat in a lice-ridden bed when she first arrived in Beijing, dismissing his complaint that the noise of the train makes it impossible for him to sleep by denying that a train is nearby. A piece of plastic protecting her from the rain appears in one animation, cementing viewers' understanding of her powerful desire to thrive in a difficult environment.

The most striking animation occurs when Tao and Taisheng are in the airplane that has "landed in World Park after making many international trips," the World Park announcer proclaims, and is "preserved in its original form so as to allow you to experience the beauty of air travel." Sitting in the pilot's seat with Tao on his lap, Taisheng fondles her and she pushes him away. He claims she is looking for someone better but she insists that he has misunderstood. Lao Song, Taisheng's black market collaborator, calls and Taisheng says he must go to his house. Tao decides to go along so that she will not be "stuck here all the time, like a ghost." At this point the film switches into flash animation, with Taisheng and his phone in the plane taking off and Tao in her flight attendant uniform flying across the Beijing sky with a big smile on her face (see fig. 11.1). The difference in their mode of flight, with Taisheng in control of a large machine and Tao moving through the air on her own power, suggests that Taisheng's fantasy is of control and power, whereas Tao dreams of a free, pure mobility close to creative imagination. Various aspects of Beijing appear below them, most strikingly Tiananmen Square with a statue of Mao, revolutionary placards, three national flags waving in the breeze, and the city painted dark red in the background. Connected to the visual apparatus of revolutionary optimism as she moves through the air, Tao's flying is a pure enactment of the cheerfulness she strives to sustain.

By contrast, Taisheng anchors a subjective and experiential system that is radically different than that represented by Tao. Whereas in the theme park, women are commodities to be displayed and sexually used, most men are physical laborers whose disposable status is evident in the experience of Little Sister, who works at night to earn overtime pay and is killed in an accident. The message he laboriously constructs for Taisheng on his deathbed—his final words—is nothing but a list of his debts. This list—which, as an animation, quivers as if it is alive—is deeply important to Little Sister and also expresses the profound link between the cultural role of men, who are charged with career and nation-building, at one time through revolutionary leadership and actions but more recently through economic activity.

Several scenes underline Taisheng's cultural burden and fractured, cynical subjectivity. Yet he is not an unsympathetic character. Although he pursues Qun, Taisheng is obsessed with Tao's state of mind and her physical location. He tries to retain some limited mobility, for example, to travel to Beijing and visit Qun, but Taisheng is motivated not by an imagined freedom in time and space but by a vision of control and power, as the animated airplane scene implies. He uses his walkie-talkie to ask the security guards on top of the Eiffel Tower when they last saw Tao and where she went, following her to the restaurant where she is with Liangzi. This insistent interest in fixing and controlling the mobility of women affects the other men as well. Xiaoniu argues incessantly with his girlfriend Xiaowei about where she has been and who she has seen. Both Xiaoniu and Taisheng accurately recognize the women's potential access to mobility, mostly through an ever-threatening possibility of involvement with a more accomplished man.

Tao's idealization of mobility into an open, optimistic state of mind challenges Taisheng's demand for a fixed landscape through which he aligns various players who will help him build his position as a man with a positive economic future. His biggest fear is that Tao will find someone better, an apprehension that opens a revealing window to the minute hierarchies that structure his subjectivity. The responsibilities charged to Taisheng mandate that he fulfill his role as supporter and protector of various relatives and fellow provincials. It is Taisheng, not Tao, who is tasked with finding work in the theme park for these provincial mates and who must account for their performance. When Erxiao steals money from the performers' handbags left backstage, Taisheng must confront him and ultimately send him back home. It also is Taisheng who must take responsibility for Little Sister's death and deal with Little Sister's parents, and who chastises Sanlai for his failure to protect Little Sister. Taisheng fears Tao's fantasy of mobility (as well as any male, such as Liangzi, who may have the ability to help her realize that fantasy) because it implies that the small and yet both realistic and real network of provincial relationships, black market connections, and power positioning that he has laboriously established can be pushed aside. Even as only a state of mind, female mobility refers to a bigger and more impressive reality.

Taisheng's relationship with Qun exposes his deep comprehension of what his world is made of. He quickly acquiesces when Lao Song asks him to accompany Qun on a trip to take money to her brother. After they arrive, Qun is off camera when she shrilly scolds her brother for gambling away her money, a discussion that anchors the economic basis of this world. Instead, we see Taisheng in a dark theater, walking up the stairs next to rows of seats. This disturbing episode aligns with Taisheng's distressed psychological state. Later, as Qun texts him to come by for a visit, a wildly romantic animation bursts out of his phone. Taisheng races forward on his powerful white horse, flower petals streaming from his mouth. However, although the relationship offers short-term romance, it has clear boundaries that cannot be transgressed. In that Qun is married and waiting for a passport to leave China and join her husband in Paris, she is both safe—unavailable to competitors and not a true challenge to Taisheng's bond with Tao—as well as intriguing. Taisheng's interest in seeing her passport echoes Tao's request to see Liangzi's passport, but the global status of the two cities, Paris and Ulaanbaatar, could not be more different. Despite its exuberance, the background and framing of Taisheng's animation are

FIGURE 11.2. Tao flies above red, white, and blue fabric, in *The World* (2004).

limited when compared with Tao's flying vision, suggesting that he is fixed and constrained by his cultural role.

When Tao flies, the cartoonish animation and the bright smile on her face contrast with the scenes below her body, on the ground. A reference to *Still Life* appears in the "tear-down" character *chai*, which is evident on two buildings marked for destruction underneath her flying body. More visible is the woven red, white, and blue fabric, which can be seen all over China and is associated with rural people and manual labor (fig. 11.2).

Other directors have taken advantage of the broad intelligibility of this symbol throughout China. One shot featuring the fabric—from Zhang Yimou's *Qiuju Goes to Court/Story of Qiuju* 秋菊打官司 (*Qiuju da guansi*, 1994)—brings out the vulnerability of villagers Qiuju 秋菊 and her niece as they are about to be cheated by a taxi cart driver, who approaches from behind. The fabric's connection with movement and mobility impressed Hong Kong artist Wong Wai Yin, who used it to build an art exhibition piece (fig. 11.3).[24] The fabric has taken on global iconic status, a romanticization of its working-class origins. Louis Vuitton put a bag made of the fabric on the runway, and a collaboration between CLOT and Head Porter Plus used the fabric for expensive bags.[25]

24. These images, no longer available online, were provided by Wong Wai Yin, who noted in an email to me dated August 28, 2023, that they were part of her student work at the Hong Kong Museum of Art..

25. Soo-Young, "The CLOT x Head Porter Bag Collection," Complex, February 2, 2011, accessed December 15, 2015, https://www.complex.com/style/2011/02/the-clot-head

FIGURE 11.3. The plastic red, white, and blue fabric featured in Wong Wai Yin's art exhibition of *Home Moving Furniture* (2002). Courtesy of Wong Wai Yin (Doris Wong).

A surface made up of houses that will be torn down and woven plastic fabric, as well as brief references to the socialist past, also appear in Tao's flight. But our viewing perspective is that of Tao's flying body, which moves so high above ground that the surface of the globe appears rounded, as if she were flying in space. In this context, it is important to recall that Tao rejects potential mobility—such as that of the businessman who offers to get her a passport if she will accompany him to Hong Kong—that will compromise her idealism. Her flying sequence captures the open, expansive, and energetic quality of her vision.

Conclusion: Disney, Animation, and Reality

The overarching presence of the theme park, and its saturated meaning within the lives of the workers and in the metaphoric stand-in as a world

-porter-bag-collection (site discontinued). The picture (no longer available) showed costly bags made from the plastic red, white, and blue fabric, one of which is featured in Wong Wai Yin's art installation.

of its own, draws our attention to research on theme parks and their social function, to which I have referred throughout this chapter. However, it is difficult to discuss theme parks without mentioning Walt Disney (1901–1966) and Disneyland. Long the punching bag of intellectuals, Disneyland is often mocked as the height of American cultural artificiality, and its multiplication across the globe as an embarrassing example of the worst kind of American soft power. Yet the work of Disney and the meaning of theme parks in general has been undergoing a slow process of reinterpretation in its role as a type of utopian urban space, a "perfectly realized world where fantasies and dreams are articulated and actualized."[26] In his 2002 book *Walt Disney and the Quest for Community*, Steve Mannheim argues that Disney should be compared with Le Corbusier (Charles-Édouard Jeanneret, 1887–1965). Even though Disney's EPCOT town was never built, his broader theme park vision was influential in the reanimation of small-town USA.

The recuperation of Disneyland or Disney animation is hardly universally accepted, however. The graffiti artist Banksy recently mocked Disneyland in his Bemusement Park Dismaland (open to the public August 22 through September 27, 2015, in Weston-super-Mare, UK). But we have a more enigmatic example in the well-known Austrian painter Gottfried Helnwein (1948–), who describes his encounter with Disney characters in comic books when he was five years old:

> The days . . . were gray, sticky like slime and filled with unlimited boredom - everything seemed ugly and unreal to me. I grew up in Vienna, after the war. . . . The house we lived in endured a miserable existence between an old foundry from the turn of the century and a gray monster of a factory from the Nazi era, which now bore the sign of its new masters on its roof - that very same enormous red star. In my memories everything is rusty and covered in dust. The streets looked like they were dead, nothing moved, nobody talked. The few people that I saw were bulky, misshapen and bent. I can't remember ever having heard someone sing or laugh. A world that stood still, without sounds, without colors, without movement. . . . I was dozing in this twilight-zone like in a seemingly endless trance, until one day when my father returned from his office, placed a parcel, wrapped in brown paper before me

26. Alan Bryman, *Disney and His Worlds* (New York: Routledge, 1995), 140.

> and cut the rope that was tied around it with a pocket knife. And before me the colorful splendor of the first German Mickey-Mouse comic-books gushed forth onto the parquet floor. Opening my first Donald Duck comic book felt like seeing the daylight again for someone who had been trapped underground by a mine-disaster for many days. I squinted cautiously because my eyes hadn't gotten used to the dazzlingly bright sun of Duckburg yet, and I greedily sucked the fresh breeze into my dusty lungs. . . . Walt Disney is undoubtedly the great artistic genius of the 20th century—a reincarnated Leonardo da Vinci, who came back matured and stronger, to create the most immense artwork of all times. His aesthetic empire has changed the face of this world. For him, the age-old artist's dream came true—to breathe life into his own creation, to give it a voice, and to let it dance before the whole world. . . . In retrospect, I would say from Donald Duck I have learned more about life than from all the schools I ever attended.[27]

Helnwein's admiration for Donald Duck is humorously addressed in work such as *American Prayer* (2000) (see fig. 11.4). However, his commentators, locked in their ideological perspectives, insist that his hyperrealistic paintings featuring or referring to Donald Duck and Mickey Mouse are "in part a grotesquely alienating intention" along the lines of Bertolt Brecht (1898–1956), or that Helnwein is expressing the "triviality of Disney culture."[28] But as a child, Helnwein was deeply affected by the sheer vitality and life of the Disney imaginary, and as an adult, he credits it with opening the door to his own art and thoroughly transforming his aesthetic understanding of the world. What Helnwein saw as a child is that the gray world in which he lived was not the only reality. The comic books opened the "dazzling bright sun of Duckburg."

27. Gottfried Helnwein, "Memories of Duckburg," Newshelnwein, April 12, 1989, https://www.helnwein.com/news/news_update/article_436-Memories-of-Duckburg-Memories. Originally published in *Zeitmagazin Hamburg*, 1989. Cited with permission from Studio Helnwein.

28. Walter Baier, "Capitalism's Secular Crisis and the European Social Model," Newshelnwein, February 10, 2009, https://www.helnwein.com/news/news_update/article_3922-Capitalisms-Secular-Crisis-and-the-European-Social-Model. Originally published in *Transform! European Journal for Alternative Thinking and Political Dialogue*; "The Silence of Innocence—the Artist Gottfried Helnwein," Bildersturm Film Produktion GmbH, https://www.bildersturm-film.de/en/the-silence-of-innocence.

FIGURE 11.4. *American Prayer* by Gottfried Helnwein (2000). Mixed media, oil and acrylic on canvas, 213 x 187 cm. Courtesy of Studio Helnwein. https://www.helnwein.com/works/mixed_media_on_canvas/image_13-The-American-Paintings.

Like Helnwein's interlocutors who are trained to see only the artificiality of Disney and who regard the millions who visit the theme parks as benighted, we can readily see the way the workers in the film are pushed into a gray world. By placing the animation within the realism, we end up interpreting Tao's digital "flights of fantasy" as an "illusory panacea to the loss of [a collective] world."[29] Yet much of the animation is lively, like

29. Cheah, "Entering the World," 161.

the theme park itself a colorful fake-real world that checks the intellectual viewer's tendency to deprive the workers of any possible agency to grasp and alter their lives. It is not the difficult conditions of her life that destroy Tao, but that she cannot in Taisheng find a soulmate who will be true. Ultimately the animation of *The World*, like other surreal moments in Jia's films, brings not a reiteration but a new perspective that complicates a contradictory reality.

The World's combination of fake and real is evocative, nonbinary, and hard to interpret. The theme park sets the stage for this complexity because it is much more than just an artificial setting. It provides an experience of world landmarks to those who will never have the chance to travel, as well as functioning as a small social world—with both ups and downs—for the workers, who regard their employment as a bonus. And the animation, like Duckburg for the young Helnwein, opens eyes to the possibility that there are other worlds, perceptions, and energies. My claim that in *The World* animation suggests agency only makes sense if we recognize the importance of imagination in the workers' lives. By using animation, Jia Zhangke checks our social critique tendencies to quickly regard the theme park workers as victims rather than fully embodied human beings with the ability to creatively interact with their environment and make choices about their lives.

TWELVE

When a Cat Flies

Futures of 3D Animation through *Cats and Peachtopia*

Yiman Wang

In films, there is the wind that blows and the wind that is produced by a wind machine. Computer images do not have two kinds of wind.

(Harun Farocki, *Parallel*)

From silent film to talkies, from black and white to color, from mono-channel audio to stereo, from regular aspect ratio to widescreen, from high definition to 4K, and from 2D to 3D—we are led to believe that the history of moving-image media is one of equating our phenomenological experience with the profilmic physical world or environment. One might even see this process as a testimony to André Bazin's vision of "total cinema."[1] However, diametrically opposed to Bazin's privileging of the photochemical film's indexical linkage with the profilmic world, contemporary commercial 3D films, predicated on digital rendering, tend to exploit fantastic other-than-human characters and narratives, thereby conjuring an environment far different from what we conventionally experience. 3D animated films, in particular, have harnessed digital technology to visualize fantasylands that have no indexical referents. Thus, instead of approximating the profilmic environment (a mode of realism), 3D animated films seem to have let go of realism altogether.

1. André Bazin, "The Myth of Total Cinema," in *What Is Cinema?* vol. 1, trans. Hugh Gray (Los Angeles: University of California Press, 1967), 17–22.

Yet the pursuit of realism undergirds increasingly complicated algorithmic rendering of details such as surface texture, sheen, hair, fur, and water, and in the attempt to replicate the Newtonian physics that governs how these objects move in their environment in coordination with other elements. Pixar, a leading American 3D animation studio based in the San Francisco Bay Area, uses short videos to explain to the general public the algorithmic modeling methods that have enabled its internationally acclaimed products.[2] Domee Shi, a Canadian Chinese and Pixar's first female director, known for her Academy Award-winning debut animation short *Bao* (2018) and animation feature *Turning Red* (2021), has also described how she and her team digitally generated the feel-real color and texture of Chinese culinary ingredients.[3] These prized details, elevated and separated from the narrative flow, delight the audience, offering visual and tactile cues to animate their sensuous memories and experiences, despite being no more than a sophisticated composition of pixels. The intractable incongruity between the indisputable real feel and the image's nonreferentiality both evokes and detours what traditional film scholars have theorized as cinephilia, that is, the privileged spectatorial joy of chancing upon seemingly marginal details that crack open a highly personal connection with a sliver of the profilmic environment elsewhere in another time.

How do we understand intransitive 3D digital imagery's paradoxical career of simulating real feel? This question has led media scholars to grapple, once again, with what realism is and what it does through notions such as "perceptual realism" (Stephen Prince), "second order realism" (Andrew Darley), and "anime-manga realism" (Marc Steinberg). On a different track of thinking, queer scholar Jack Halberstam embraces the creaturely world of Pixar animations, arguing that 3D technology has facilitated a "Pixavolt" that gives form to unruly childhood and collective revolutionary queer

2. See, for instance, the video of Pixar animator Rob Jenson explaining splines, the mathematical functions used in making Pixar animations: "Pixar's Animation Challenge," The Science Behind Pixar, https://sciencebehindpixar.org/pipeline/animation/challenge.

3. Lisa Wong MacAbasco, "In Domee Shi's *Bao*, Food for the Soul From Pixar's First Female Director of a Short Film," *Vogue*, April 20, 2018, https://www.vogue.com/article/pixar-bao-domee-shi-interview.

feelings. Yet a third approach excavates the material infrastructure and the government-military apparatus that undergird and spur digital visual (and other sensing) technologies, revealing the digital as not neutral, but instead imbricated with imperialist-colonialist power operations on the one hand, and with environmental extraction on the other.

These three directions of analysis represent three understandings of the real in the digital age, namely, the spectators' experience of the simulated real, the radical sociopolitical transformations that could become real as inspired by "Pixavolt," and the real underbelly of digital visual and sensing technologies. If the first two dimensions exist as the potentially real (to be activated by the situated audience), the third dimension is embedded in the historical and material genesis of the digital. They also correspond with critical engagement with three layers of digital technology. The spectatorial real feel dwells on surfaces that present composited imagery rendered legible to the human eye. The radical sociopolitical potential arises from queer studies and cultural studies informed critical reading of Pixar animations. Finally, the materialist and archeological interrogation dives into the underlying mechanisms of digital technologies, continuing the strain of apparatus study in classic film theory, but with a fresh emphasis on digital media's grounding in infrastructural, ecological, financial, and government-military operations. Unsurprisingly, the last approach has rarely been linked to commercial family-friendly animated films, given the perceived incompatibility between juvenile entertainment and concerns with media ecology and media as a war machine.

How might we cross-pollinate these three approaches? Could their dialogue lead to a more interdisciplinary framework that sheds new light on 3D digital animation? I tackle these questions by turning to the case of China's Light Chaser (Zhuiguang 追光) Animation Studios, with special emphasis on its least (box office) successful production *Cats and Peachtopia (Mao yu Taohuayuan* 猫与桃花源, 2018). Founded in 2013 by Wang Wei, former CEO of tudou.com, China's then largest streaming platform, Light Chaser was at the time China's only animation studio exclusively dedicated to developing original content rather than providing outsourced service work. Lavishly financed and equipped with cutting-edge 3D animation facilities, Light Chaser was launched with the ambition of becoming China's Pixar. If Pixar animations portend a Pixarvolt (à la Jack Halberstam) that enables us to imagine anti-heteropatriarchal and anticapitalist futures, then we must ask if Light Chaser, China's Pixar-wannabe, can go beyond technological emulation to afford such a radical interpretation. Or does the studio merely harness digital technology for the sake of maximizing feel-real simulation while partaking in this technology's problematic ecological and geopolitical implications, as diagnosed by scholars of media ecology and media archeology?

A nodal point for bringing the three approaches (as outlined) to bear on each other is Light Chaser's future imaginary and the correlated question of whose future is being imagined. In this essay, I focus on *Cats and Peachtopia*, Light Chaser's only film not modeled upon any existing legendary characters, but rather on the residential cat of the studio, with the intention to cash in on China's growing pet industry, especially cat people's devotion to their pet cats. The one visual-narrative element that is sourced from premodern Chinese culture is Taohuayuan 桃花源 (Peachtopia), originally envisioned by the Six Dynasties poet Tao Yuanming in his essay about a beautiful, harmonious utopia that he chanced upon but could not return to. Taohuayuan (Peachtopia) in the film merely serves as a Hitchcockian MacGuffin, however; it triggers the plot but is dismissed as inconsequential in the end.

The main driving force of the film stems from the genre of Bildungsroman. It revolves around the kitten Cape's decision to leave daddy cat Blanket and their confined albeit protected human owner's home in search of the mom cat, whom Cape believes has gone to Taohuayuan (Peachtopia). Cape's departure from the safe haven in search of mom (i.e., a dream) precipitates a suspenseful story in which Cape (aided by Blanket, their co-pet parrot Auntie Macaw, and the old black stray cat Wanderer) must survive the capture of a mad human artist, and eventually defeat the latter to liberate all animals in captivity. The story ends with Cape bidding a final goodbye to Blanket (who returns home with Macaw) to explore the brave new world that extends far beyond Taohuayuan (Peachtopia) and beyond what is representable within the film's diegesis.

Cats and Peachtopia engages the three approaches outlined previously. Diegetically, it imagines a future elsewhere in relation to the past-present here. Technologically, the all-animal cast showcases the studio's algorithmic modeling of the lively animal fur—a major challenge in digital animation at the time—to project a mode of phenomenological realism. Furthermore, the scene depicting the mad artist's method of modeling serves as a meta-mediatic argument for the potential advantages of digital modeling. Materially and infrastructurally, Light Chaser's resource-intensive digital rendering poses questions surrounding its environmental implications. All of this demands an analytical framework capable of addressing the significance of the surface-level phenomenological realism (or the real feel) and future imaginary in the digital age, in conjunction with the technology's underlying costs and potential.

Before diving into an analysis of *Cats and Peachtopia*, an outline of this film's position in Light Chaser's eventful history is in order. Light Chaser was launched in 2013 by Wang Wei with the ambition of becoming China's Pixar. Yet, by 2018, the board of directors pronounced the studio on the brink of failing its Pixar dream and declining into an outsourcing company due to disappointing box office performance. The studio's first three animated features, *Little Door Gods* (*Xiao menshen* 小门神, 2016), *Tea Pets* (*A'tang qiyu* 阿唐奇遇, 2017), and *Cats and Peachtopia*, all scripted and directed by Wang Wei, had raced to the bottom in box office revenues, with *Cats and Peachtopia* nearly bankrupting the studio, despite these films' distribution in the United States, both in limited theater venues and on streaming platforms such as Netflix and Amazon Prime. The failure was attributed to Wang Wei's monopolization of the concept and script development, which resulted in lackluster narratives and contrived dialogues.

Since then, Wang has let go of micromanagement and established a Braintrust (following Pixar) to develop new concepts and scripts.[4] Two recent animated features, *White Snake: The Origin* (*Baishe: Yuanqi* 白蛇：缘起, coproduced with Warner Bros., 2019) and *Green Snake* (*Baishe 2: Qingshe jieqi* 白蛇2：青蛇劫起, 2021), both directed by Huang Jiakang, have improved box office revenues. All of Light Chaser's productions (with the exception of *Cats and Peachtopia*) draw on Chinese folk stories and legends, liberally reinventing and remediating them with contemporary sentiments, discourses, and digital technology. The past is mined to appeal

4. Braintrust is Pixar's mechanism of optimizing the work environment for people to openly share and critique ideas. See Edwin Catmull and Amy Wallace, *Creativity, Inc.: Overcoming the Unseen Forces that Stand in the Way of True Inspiration* (New York: Random House, 2014).

to what the producers understand as their targeted audience's interests, which are in turn packaged as having universal value across time and space.

Unlike the productions that presume some knowledge of premodern China's folk legends, *Cats and Peachtopia* is set in contemporary China. Its cuddly animal characters and family-centered narrative are meant to be simple family-friendly entertainment. Yet an IMDB viewer's complaint, combined with the film's box office debacle in China, suggests that there is more than meets the eye. What went wrong? How could the film's failure be better understood by triangulating the three perspectives on digital technology? In what ways could my tri-perspective analysis yield an interdisciplinary framework for understanding the stakes and risks of 3D digital animation?

How to Harm a Digital Cat? The Paradox of Feel-Real Simulation

In 2019, outraged IMDB reviewer ID naphia-55531 exclaimed, "DO NOT WATCH!! Don't let the colorful cover fool you!" They went on to decry this so-called antichildren, antifamily film:

> it's a dark movie with no happy moments of singing or general happiness: instead the movie contains death, attempts to harm animals, broken family's [*sic*], loss of loved ones and will leave your child in tears. my 6yr old brother was deeply upset and troubled by this film and would not stop crying, this should NOT be a PG. a young child should not have to worry or think about death because even though it's a cartoon with a colorful cover this movie only contains heartbreaking moments with traumatic after affects on your young child. I strongly advise you do not let your child watch it unless they can handle dark and depressed scenes, which I'm sure no child can!! DO NOT WATCH.[5]

One might attribute this reviewer's overreaction to the shaping of Western audience's viewing habits by the film rating system, a system with an

5. naphia-55531, "DO NOT WATCH!!! don't let the colourful cover fool you!" IMDB review, October 25, 2019, https://www.imdb.com/user/ur109199682.

ideology of sheltering underage audiences from both real-life and fictional hardships. Yet this overreaction is also symptomatic of the film's engagement with realism and futurity, as well as its breaching of family entertainment's ideology of innocuous fantasy fabrication. The complaint about the traumatic details of animal-harming and death raises the question of what it means to inflict harm on an algorithmically composited animal figure, that is, a figure who does not exist as a physiological entity and who, logistically speaking, is not capable of suffering or death.

Writing on "anime-manga realism" as developed by Japanese animation critics Ōtsuka Eiji and Azuma Hiroki, Marc Steinberg identifies "the intersection of the semiotic body with the fleshly body," or the "paradoxical theme of expressing the fleshly body through the use of signs."[6] In other words, the semiotic body (or the signifier with no inherent profilmic referent) can impart real feel when paradoxically spliced with properties of a fleshly body (such as the ability to sustain injury). Yet this does not mean that "even unreal [i.e., animated] images can be perceptually realistic," as Stephen Prince argues in terms of "perceptual realism."[7] Instead, Steinberg suggests that anime-manga realism, understood in the Japanese animation media environment, "is not a medium capable of reproducing realism as much as it is *a medium that itself provides the basis for 'animation-like' work* within a different media form" (emphasis added).[8] That is, the real feel is already mediated by the anime-manga realism that also governs how the real feel works in other media forms. Such a real feel presumes the audience's self-aware make-believing.

If we follow this argument, then we must ask how the semiotic and animated body sustains injury and death differently from a profilmic fleshly body. Furthermore, how is this difference relevant to *Cats and Peachtopia*'s digital rendering of the furry and feathery animal characters? Here Shane Denson's analysis of "a dispersal of attention between visual surface and the

6. Marc Steinberg, "Realism in the Animation Media Environment: Animation Theory from Japan," in *Animating Film Theory*, ed. Karen Beckman (Durham, NC: Duke University Press, 2014), 294, 295.

7. Stephen Prince, "True Lies: Perceptual Realism, Digital Images, and Film Theory," *Film Quarterly* 49, no. 3 (1996).

8. Steinberg, "Realism," 289.

algorithmic operation of machine learning" is instructive.[9] It is commonly recognized that a digital image is a surface rendered legible for the human eye, and that it is made up of pixels that do not correspond to the profilmic realm (unlike a traditional photo, which directly results from the film stock registering the light reflected off a profilmic object). The intransitive digital surface is therefore emphatically removed from and therefore independent of the appearance of the physical object it purports to simulate. Instead, the surface image derives from "a deep, pre-attentional level that computation taps into with its microtemporal speed."[10] The complicated operation of computer graphics that enables the surface simulation, but that is now completely obscured for the audience, can be detected in *Kitty* (1968), the first, and quite humble, computer-animated character.[11] The kitty shape was procedurally generated (in black, white, and tiny aggregated printed frames); its motion of walking was accomplished with math calculation. In this computer-drawn 1.5-minute animation, the unrealistic robotic movement, punctuated with moments of close-up showing the kitty's face with enlarged eyes and a mouth, accentuates the uncanny feeling evoked by an eerily enlivened yet unnatural (or unreal) life. It is through this uncanny feeling that the computer-generated (CG) mechanism jumps to the surface, announcing itself as an epoch-making generative tool predicated on projective simulation rather than representational mimesis.

Swinging to the other side of the spectrum, the uncanny feeling could also arise when the simulation is too perfect, hiding the algorithm to catch the audience off guard. Japanese robotics scientist Masahiro Mori 森政弘 calls this the "uncanny valley" in his 1970 article.[12] His example is the touch of a prosthetic hand that feels different from what one expects from its visual appearance and thus triggers an uncanny feeling. He argues that an uncanny valley emerges when a person's response to a humanoid abruptly shifts from empathy to revulsion.

9. Shane Denson, "On the Embodied Phenomenology of DeepFakes," blog, October 6, 2021, https://www.blog.shanedenson.com/?p=5358.

10. Denson, "On the Embodied Phenomenology."

11. Ultimate History of CGI, "Kitty (1968)—First realistic computer animated character," YouTube video, 1:24, February 4, 2018, https://youtu.be/OYrsjc9dz3o.

12. Masahiro Mori, "The Uncanny Valley," trans. Karl F. MacDorman and Norri Kageki, *IEEE Spectrum*, June 12, 2012, https://spectrum.ieee.org/the-uncanny-valley.

Presented as surface images unavailable to touch, 3D animated characters such as those in *Cats and Peachtopia* sit in between the first computer-drawn Kitty in 1968 and Mori's near-perfect uncanny humanoid. The animated animal characters are not humanoids, but semi-anthropomorphized, though remaining animal-like with their species-specific fur, feathers, markings, and movements. Cashing in on China's booming pet industry and cat owners' shared self-identification as *maonu* 猫奴 (cat slaves), the film avails itself of 3D modeling to accentuate cats' two distinctive attractions—their plush soft fur and their perfect fit with the "baby schema."[13] To simulate the plush cat fur, Light Chaser employed what was at the time a cutting-edge algorithm specced in accordance with the Pixar-Disney standard to render six million hairs per cat. Furthermore, the way the fur moves in the wind requires a more complicated algorithm that can generate the flowing-in-response-to-wind effect compliant with Newtonian physics. According to Jordan Schonig, contemporary audience's enjoyment of the phenomenological real feel generated by digital animation technology is continuous with early cinema audience's fascination with the photochemically captured contingent movements such as the wind in the trees or the crashing ocean waves. Both rely on the medium's "temporal inscriptions that similarly transform contingent motion forms into framed temporal objects."[14]

Yet, the temporal dimension inherent in photochemical filming matters much less in 3D animation, which relies on controlled algorithms to simulate even contingent details. Furthermore, *Cats and Peachtopia* not only simulates feel-real details but also maintains a distance from realism with exaggerated rendering of the cats' baby schema features. The cats, possessing all the baby schema elements, appropriate the *moe* elements (萌え) popularized by the Japanese otaku manga culture. The manga characters, according to Hiroki Azuma, are "not unique designs created by the indi-

13. Austrian ethologist and zoologist Konrad Lorenz propose the concept of baby schema in 1943 to capture the "cute blueprint" of attention-grabbing infant features including "a large head relative to the body, chubby cheeks, a high forehead, a small nose and mouth, and rounder bodies." See Angela Saini, "The Code for Cuteness," BBC Earth, n.d., https://www.bbcearth.com/news/the-code-for-cuteness.

14. Jordan Schonig, "Contingent Motion: Rethinking the 'Wind in the Trees' in Early Cinema and CGI," *Discourse* 40, no. 1 (Winter 2018): 43.

vidual talent of the author but an output generated from preregistered elements and combined according to the marketing program of each work."[15] One of these *moe* elements is cat ears, accessorized by manga human characters. As the manga human characters take on cute animal features, the 3D animated cats also take on *moe* human baby features and the nearly perfect lip-syncing of Mandarin Chinese dialogue.

The combination of lifelike cat fur with less realistic *moe* elements and semi-anthropomorphism renders the animal characters doubly composite, not only of nonreferential pixels, but also of disparate elements attributed to different species. This interspecies simulation prevents near-perfect simulation, thus avoiding Mori's uncanny valley where empathy flips into revulsion. It also returns us to the question of the extent to which we might empathize with the suffering and potential death of digital animals, decried by the IMDB reviewer as violence against animals unsuitable for the underage audience. Here I recall Steinberg's argument that anime-manga realism paradoxically intersects "the semiotic body with the fleshly body" and at the same time keeps the fleshly experience embedded within the heavily mediated manga environment. With this in mind, I ask how we might grapple with the semiotic digital cat whose body amalgamates interspecies features (both human and feline), and which vacillates between actual suffering, as could be inflicted on a photochemically registered cat, and suffering as a simulation effect.

I tackle these questions by examining two meta-mediatic sequences in *Cats and Peachtopia*. These sequences reflect on shifting imaging technologies, thus compelling us to compare the diverse discourses and spectatorial responses to the real feel enabled by different media-making technologies. The first sequence is Cape's adventure out of his home. The second sequence is Cape's perils after being captured by the mad human artist. Both scenes evoke potential or impending harm, but affect the audience differently through different modes of real feel.

In the first sequence, Cape defies his father Blanket's lesson that cats cannot fly by literally flying out of the window of their confined home haven, riding on a propelling-gliding device he has made himself based on knowledge he has acquired online using an iPad. Cape's flying machine

15. Hiroki Azuma, *Otaku: Japan's Database Animals* (Minneapolis: University of Minnesota Press), 42.

FIGURE 12.1. Kitten Cape's winged device zooms through a simulated tunnel, in *Cats and Peachtopia* (2018).

zooms him through the labyrinthian urban topography, but eventually loses power, causing him to crash, unscathed thanks to thick bushes, right outside the gate of a Glass Sculpture Factory. This factory is to become the arena where Cape must struggle to survive life-threatening situations and defeat the mad human artist. Before crashing, however, Cape's flying, intercut with Blanket's and Auntie Macaw's frantic efforts to locate him, already places the audience on the suspenseful edge, worrying whether the flying machine can maintain its momentum without colliding with the complicated urbanscape, teeming with high-rises, freeways, a river, and a tunnel—all algorithmically modeled on the city of Chongqing in southwest China (fig. 12.1).

The dramatic suspense goes hand in hand with the wonderous shapeshifting ability of Cape's flying machine. It starts out with a set of water-filled bottles that work as a makeshift propeller, evoking what Thomas Lamarre describes as the "whimsical, implausible-looking contraptions that nonetheless fly through the skies or move over the earth."[16] When the water bottles lose power, Cape manages to drop them, then deploys a set of small wings just in time to save himself from falling into the river (fig. 12.2).

This winged machine zooms him through the urban topography at a breathtaking speed until it sputters and starts to drop again, only to be

16. Thomas Lamarre, *The Anime Machine: A Media Theory of Animation* (Minneapolis: University of Minnesota Press, 2009), 61.

FIGURE 12.2. Kitten Cape successfully drops water bottles to save himself from falling into a river, in *Cats and Peachtopia* (2018).

saved by a pair of large red wings that pop out and lift our hero kitty once again. As he glides on Superman-like, the music quickens and takes on a sublime Star Trek-esque tempo.

The spectatorial feeling of exhilaration mixed with suspense generated by the velocity is not guided by a predefined telos, as Cape's contraption is barely navigating through the complicated midair topography. The exhilarating suspense instead derives from our wonder at a DIY mishmash technology that somehow works, similar to what Tom Gunning describes as the early film audience's wonder at the cinema of attractions. This sense of wonder at technology (makeshift as it is) is further enhanced when Cape's midair gliding is intercut and contrasted with Blanket's and Auntie Macaw's chaotic gravity-hampered clumsiness as they frantically wobble down their high-rise building by holding onto a floating sun-shade canopy, then bumbling, skidding, rolling through the subway and human crowds.

A more important comparison can be made between Cape's flying and Buster Keaton's stunt sequences in his silent action comedies. Keaton performed serial death-taunting stunts of escaping one accident after another in numerous films. Some of the famous examples include the rock racing/evading scene in *Seven Chances* (1925) and the famous scene in *Steamboat Bill Jr.* (1928) where he inadvertently survives a falling wall only to be thrown into a prolonged series of escalating mishaps, dramatically engaging the audience in witnessing his breathtaking spectacles of narrow escape. His serial stunts hinge upon precise calculation of the movements of his body (running, jumping, falling, evading, grabbing, and so on) in coordination with his treacherous physical environment, whether natural or man-made. The spectatorial pleasure of watching him successfully coperforming with one crumbling object after another gives rise to the operational aesthetic.

Originally theorized by Neil Harris in his study of the nineteenth-century public hoaxes couched in pseudo-science discourses, the concept of operational aesthetic is repurposed by Tom Gunning to analyze the mechanism of the gag in early American slapstick comedy.[17] Gunning emphasizes the actor's body being implemented as a cog fitting seamlessly into the whole operation, hence the operational aesthetic. For Gunning, the operational aesthetic underscores the mechanism of the film medium itself, laying bare the working of narrative articulation. The film gag operates like the early twentieth-century American cartoonist Rube Goldberg's comic machine drawings that depict precisely interlocked steps moving unidirectionally from the starting point to the ending point. The complicated interlocked process, according to Ilka Brasch, captures the essence of the serial form related to technological marvels, including processual film.[18] In summary, the operational aesthetic encapsulates the calculated and coordinated processual mechanism of early film comedy, driving the momentum through a series of interlocked steps from the beginning to the end. In this process, the actor's body becomes enmeshed with the mechanism, its vulnerable corporeality being both accentuated in the suspenseful drama and disavowed, replaced with invulnerability if it is to survive the mishaps.

The operational aesthetic of Buster Keaton's serial stunt performances prefigures Cape's suspenseful flying through the urbanscape, especially in the latter's serial maneuvering of the shapeshifting flying machine to navigate through the tricky midair topography. The important difference, however, is that Cape's body is both mechanized in the modernist sense (enmeshed with his DIY flying machine) and digitally rendered as a postmodern simulacrum. As a digital simulacrum, it is an indestructible body,

17. Tom Gunning, "Crazy Machines in the Garden of Forking Paths: Mischief Gags and the Origins of American Film Comedy," in *Classic Hollywood Comedy*, ed. Kristine Brunovska Karnick and Henry Jenkins (New York: Routledge 1995), 87–105.

18. Ilka Brasch, *Film Serials and the American Cinema, 1910–1940: Operational Detection* (Amsterdam: Amsterdam University Press, 2018).

hence incapable of being injured or terminated. The suspense and awe that we feel for Cape's flight are therefore misplaced, carried over from our viewing habit fostered by the photochemical and referential cinematic language. Although both Keaton's serial corporeal stunts and Cape's midair navigation demonstrate the entrancing operational aesthetic, Cape is not at any real risk as Keaton was. Unlike the operational aesthetic in photochemical cinema that entails the real possibility of failure despite careful prefilming calculation, the operational aesthetic in Cape's flight is generated by algorithmic modeling, which controls even the moments of seeming loss of control only to enhance the spectatorial real feel.

Thus, Cape's flight incorporates the possibility of injury at the visual and the narrative level only then to rule it out ontologically as a result of the algorithmic technology. We might argue that digital animation's real feel rests in the schism between what Shane Denson calls the "visual surface and the algorithmic operation." Yet, for the IMDB viewer cited (who likely represents an average viewer whose central interest is the narrative), there is no distinction between the referential real and the simulated experiential real. In other words, the spectatorial experience is not specific to the media technologies, a situation that ironically converges with Harun Farocki's statement: "In films, there is the wind that blows and the wind that is produced by a wind machine. Computer images do not have two kinds of wind." Could it be that for an average viewer, the kinds of suffering inflicted on a photochemically registered cat and a digital talking cat are the same after all? Or is it rather that the difference is erased because it is mediated through the anthropocentric lens? That is, all representations of suffering (whether referential or simulacral) become comprehensible to the human viewer only when aligned with the human concept of suffering. The confluence between the cinematographic and the computational echoes Lev Manovich's observation that "the visual culture of a computer age is cinematographic in its appearance, digital on the level of its material, and computational (i.e., software driven) in its logic."[19]

Such cinematographic-digital confluence encourages anthropocentric emotional projection, which reaches a climax in a sequence following Cape's capture by the mad artist after falling into the latter's Glass Sculpture

19. Lev Manovich, *The Language of New Media* (Cambridge, MA: MIT Press, 2001), 180.

FIGURE 12.3. Kitten Cape being literally used for molding at the risk of losing his life, in *Cats and Peachtopia* (2018).

Factory that is hidden in lush foliage. The frustrated artist, who has not been able to make a marketable artwork, sees Cape as an inspiring model for a new work. Literally a model, Cape is brought into the workshop and hung up as two molding pads slam together, pressing the 3D contours of his struggling body into the pads (fig. 12.3). The mold directly imprinted by Cape's 3D body is to be used by the artist to cast a glass sculpture. This scene depicts what the IMBD reviewer decried as animal harm because Cape is left limp and lifeless after several rounds of slamming by the molds.

The experiential violence graphically conveyed in this sequence foregrounds CG imaging's effective evocation of feelings associated with life, injury, and potential death. The feeling that the digital cat could be harmed, even killed, by the molding pads forms a sharp contrast with what Sergei Eisenstein theorized as plasmaticness in Disney cel animation. Emphasizing the clay-like quality of the hand-drawn figures—a quality that lends to infinite stretching, squashing, and distorting, Eisenstein identifies a plasmatic defiance of the "definite form," a fluid transformation that happens to everything animate and inanimate alike, yielding "an unexpected rebirth of universal animism."[20] The universal animism

20. Sergei Eisenstein, *Eisenstein on Disney*, ed. Jay Leyda, trans. Alan Upchurch (Kolkata: Seagull Books, 1986), 35.

holds important revolutionary significance for Eisenstein because it departs from the oppressive grey Fordist mechanism. He writes:

> Grey, grey, grey. From birth to death. Grey squares of city blocks. Grey prison cells of city streets. Grey faces of endless street crowds. The grey, empty eyes of those who are forever at the mercy of a pitiless procession of laws, not of their own making, laws that divide up the soul, feelings, thoughts, just as the carcasses of pigs are dismembered by the conveyor belts of Chicago slaughter houses, and the separate pieces of cars are assembled into mechanical organisms by Ford's conveyor belts. That's why Disney's films blaze with color.[21]

It is against such deadening and discoloring Fordist dismemberment and rememberment (via the streamlined assembly-line method) that Eisenstein posits plasmaticity to reintroduce "universal animism" as a vital revolt against capitalist mechanization.

Logically, such plasmaticity and universal animism could be easily accomplished with digital rendering. Yet, because algorithmic modeling has been driven by the desire to simulate the real (or a specific understanding of the real), Cape the digital cat paradoxically becomes the literal fleshly model used to cast glass sculpture. Its impression left in the slamming pads points up the oxymoron—a non-indexical cat becoming the very material basis of the indexical impression that itself is digitally generated. This paradox evokes Marc Steinberg's observation of Japanese anime-manga realism, which deals with the "paradoxical theme of expressing the fleshly body through the use of signs," and results in what Azuma calls "*the real-ism of an artificial environment*" (emphasis in the original).[22] Yet, unlike otaku culture predicated on an environment of database characters composited from recombinatory elements, *Cats and Peachtopia* invites a more earnest response to its animal characters as a proxy for rather than just a simulation of the real.

Contrary to the Disney cel animation that calls attention to the technology that enables the amorphous plasmatic figures, 3D digital animation seems to disavow its technology of artifice even as it depends on it

21. Eisenstein, *Eisenstein on Disney*, 3.

22. Quoted in Steinberg, "Realism," 296.

completely. Thus, just as the vulnerably real but digitally rendered cat contrasts with the invulnerable plasmatic hand-drawn figures, the algorithmic modeling takes a direction antithetical to what Eisenstein saw in Disney animation. In fact, the resource-intense digital animation that relies on rendering farms (such as the one Light Chaser owns) and an upgraded assembly-line practice suggests that it might even resemble what Eisenstein criticized as the deadening and compartmentalizing mode of capitalist mechanization. Furthermore, spurred by the Cold War–era arms race, computational technology, which gave rise to CG animation, has been scrutinized for its problematic intertwinement with the military-industrial complex. What has taken on a cute and vulnerable face in CG animation is thus exposed to have stemmed from an ugly history.

The Cute, the Vulnerable, and the Ugly

New materialist media scholars have unearthed the problematic political and environmental ramifications of computer graphics and the hardware it depends on. The postwar rise of computational technology was directly incentivized by the government-funded arms race, especially between the United States and the former Soviet Union. Animation historian Tom Sito reveals that the Advanced Research Projects Agency (ARPA) was set up to counter the Soviet Union's launch of Sputnik, the world's first satellite, in 1957. ARPA went on to fund numerous computer graphics projects.[23] He concludes, "without the incentives and open-ended funding from the feds, the kind of computer graphics we now take for granted would not have been possible."[24] Complicating Sito's argument of the top-down transfer from government-funded military technology to popular media, science and technology historians Timothy Lenoir and Luke Caldwell deploy the concept of "military-entertainment complex" to highlight increasing mutual influence and imbrication between military and media corporations. Thus, not only does military technology enable computer graphics that support digital media, but popular digital media such as video games

23. Tom Sito, *Moving Innovation: A History of Computer Animation* (Cambridge, MA: MIT Press, 2013), 39–40.

24. Sito, *Moving Innovation*, 52.

about virtual wars have also shaped how the American public understands wars after 9/11.[25] In other words, video games have become "the training ground for what we might call post-human warfare."[26]

The congenital intimacy between computer graphics and the military imperialist regime necessitates critical disentanglement of the workings of the underlying source code. Critical code studies, as envisioned by Mark Marino, emerges precisely to apply hermeneutics to studying computer source code in order to understand code as not just what it does (its functions), but more importantly what it means (its connotations and implications).[27] Relatedly, software studies scholars such as Alex Galloway and Wendy Chun have both incisively unpacked the ways in which hegemonic ideologies undergird extrafunctional software and the digital products it generates.[28]

Furthermore, new materialist media scholars have called our attention to the environmental concerns of digital media. Busting the myth of immaterial digitality, these scholars show that the maintenance and operation of computational media depend heavily on material and energy resources, and therefore partake in the capitalist and colonialist extractive economy.[29]

It is, therefore, imperative that we approach CG animation by taking into account the environmental-political implications of both the software and the hardware of computational media-making. Light Chaser has prided itself on its own rendering farm that enables cutting-edge 3D technology. As such, its exceptionally high production values invite scrutiny of their invisible contribution to environmental extraction and tech-

25. Timothy Lenoir and Luke Caldwell, *The Military-Entertainment Complex* (Cambridge, MA: Harvard University Press, 2018).

26. Timothy Lenoir and Henry Lowood, "Theaters of War: The Military Entertainment Complex," in *Collection-Laboratory-Theater: Scenes of Knowledge in the 17th Century*, ed. Helmar Schramm, Ludger Schwarte, and Jan Lazardzig (Berlin: De Gruyter, 2005), 453.

27. Mark C. Marino, *Critical Code Studies* (Cambridge, MA: MIT Press, 2020).

28. Alexander R. Galloway, *The Interface Effect* (Cambridge: Polity Press, 2012); Wendy Hui Kyong Chun, *Discriminating Code: Correlation, Neighborhoods, and the New Politics of Recognition* (Cambridge, MA: MIT Press, 2021).

29. See, for instance, Nicole Starosielski, *Media Hot and Cold* (Durham, NC: Duke University Press, 2021); Nicole Starosielski and Janet Walker, eds. *Sustainable Media: Critical Approaches to Media and Environment* (New York: Routledge, 2016).

nological hegemony. Paying attention to these invisibilized ramifications is continuous with the agenda of apparatus studies in classic film theory. As film scholar Jean-Louis Baudry wrote in 1970, "Concealment of the [cinematographic] technical base will also bring about a specific ideological effect. Its inscription, its manifestation as such, on the other hand, would produce a knowledge effect, as actualization of the work process, as denunciation of ideology."[30] The knowledge effect Baudry calls for suggests a desire to train the mainstream film audience to see through the screen surface to become conscious of the apparatus behind the scenes that is responsible for illusion-making and ideological indoctrination.

This exposé approach of demystification is an important starting point for problematizing CG media products, including animation. Yet, given the prevalence and scale of computational technology, genuine reckoning with such technology's resource extraction and ideological impact requires that we as practitioners, consumers, and critics all become vigilant of these issues as we seek more ecological and sociopolitically responsible methods of making, imagining, and critiquing. This also entails a critique of the economy driven by teleology, technocracy, and unsustainable growth.

Whose Future? Suspending and Heterogenizing Futurity

In the remaining pages, I switch from the underlying material infrastructure of computer graphics to its visual and narrative expression to examine the future imaginary of *Cats and Peachtopia*. Here I unpack the film's politics of futurity at the intersection of the infrastructural and the representational. As stated at the beginning, *Cats and Peachtopia* presents a Bildungsroman about the growth of Cape, who ventures out of home in search of his mother in the legendary Peachtopia. After defeating the mad human artist, thus liberating himself and other captive animals, Cape embarks on another journey, this time out of Peachtopia into a future that exceeds the film's representation.

Not only were Cape and other animals meticulously modeled with state-of-art algorithms to simulate fluffy fur and feathers capable of seem-

30. Jean-Louis Baudry, "Ideological Effects of the Basic Cinematographic Apparatus," trans. Alan Williams, *Film Quarterly* 28, no. 2 (Winter 1974–1975): 41.

FIGURE 12.4. Cape's bullet-shaped rocket under construction both cues a ballistic future and suspends and questions that same future, in *Cats and Peachtopia* (2018).

ingly natural motion in the air, but the multifaceted landscape was also rendered to evoke a spectrum of topography ranging from the local to the fantastical. The urban landscape was digitally modeled upon the mountainous southwest Chinese city Chongqing famous for its futuristic high-rises. The environment around the mad artist's Glass Sculpture Factory is filled with vegetation modeled from an expansive database of flora. Peachtopia is generically fantastical and ethereal, with peach trees, pink flowers, and verdant hills suffusing the screen. Yet, after enjoying Peachtopia for a short while, all the main animal characters decide that this utopian place (a place outside of time) is "where you desire to go, but cannot stay."

Finally, the future, or the big big world elsewhere in another time, as projected by the galloping Cape, is left undefined, or unsimulatable, literally because there is no database for it to be modeled upon. In the bonus final scene inserted in between the closing credits, daddy cat Blanket and parrot Auntie Macaw are seen back at home in their high-rise apartment, connecting with Cape via the internet. At the other end, the Otaku-esque Cape is now isolated in an enclosed high-tech lab crammed with screens of different sizes showing charts and graphs, and not unlike a micro-scale 3D animation rendering farm. A cut then takes us to a wide high-angle shot of Cape overseeing a fully mechanized station where a bullet-shaped rocket-like apparatus is under construction, as Auntie Macaw marvels at the other end of the internet: "Is he really going to the Mars?!" (fig. 12.4).

With extraterrestrial travel on the horizon, Cape's future is envisioned as evolving from a barely guided low-tech DIY flying machine at the beginning of the film to a veritable military-industrial complex. The shape of the bullet rocket evokes what Lamarre calls the ballistic kinesthetic view, which draws on Paul Virilio's pessimistic critique of space-traversing high-speed technologies. Lamarre aligns the ballistic view with cinematism, even hypercinematism, associated with the simulated camera movement into the deep space enabled by closed compositing that obscures the distance between different planes (the foreground, the midground, and the background) of animation.[31] Contra cinematism, Lamarre proposes "animetism" and "animatic interval" to characterize "open" compositing that leads to a "multiplanary image," or "the separation of the image into multiple planes," which transforms the depth movement into "movement on and between surfaces."[32] Lamarre maintains that animatism often coexists with cinematism, and that it does not fantasize a departure from technology, but "promises a different way of thinking about technology and of inhabiting a technology-saturated world."[33] In other words, animetism decouples technology from teleology, thus revising Virilio's understanding of technology's overdetermined connection with militarism and power hegemony. By emphasizing animetism's thinking of and dwelling in technology, Lamarre reads Miyazaki Hayao's manga films as "antiadventure adventure films" that simultaneously narrate and critique the boy's adventure genre.

Lamarre's theory of animetism, characterized by the lateral movement produced by sliding layers of images, challenges the linear and uniperspectival drive toward a predetermined telos. The sideways and nonteleological movement at the aesthetic and technical level dovetails with Jack Halberstam's analysis of Pixar animations at the representational level. Dubbing Pixar productions Pixavolt, Halberstam argues that, despite their corporatist origin, "new forms of animation, CGI [computer-generated imagery] in particular, have opened up new narrative doors and led to unexpected encounters between the childish and the transformative and the queer."[34] Drawing on Kathryn Bond Stockton's argument that history itself "grows

31. Lamarre, *The Anime Machine*, 35, 304.

32. Lamarre, *The Anime Machine*, 6, 7.

33. Lamarre, *The Anime Machine*, 6.

34. Jack Halberstam, *The Queer Art of Failure* (Durham, NC: Duke University Press, 2011), 19–20.

sideways and outside itself,"[35] Halberstam states that Pixar animation depicts children "growing sideways," enabling "queer revolt" by "forming unusual and collective bonds beyond the family." Halberstam further links Pixavolt's queerness with socialist struggles. Zeroing in on Pixar animation's "creative anthropomorphism," Halberstam leverages "real or fantasized beasts" to "subvert the singularity of the human with the multiplicity of the unruly mob."[36] Ultimately, Halberstam aims at a "pedagogical project of creating monsters" by excavating the "silly archive," as opposed to "high cultural archives," to generate "low theory."[37]

Despite their very different approaches to animation and different technologies of animation at that, Lamarre and Halberstam both invest in the lateral and the sideways movement as a departure from teleological history and spatial single perspectivism, which portends "different ways of thinking about being, relation, reproduction, and ideology."[38] If Halberstam leverages sideways movement gleaned from the "silly archive" such as Pixar animation to challenge hegemonic heteropatriarchy, Lamarre sees lateral movement in the animatic interval as animation's ability to think and dwell in technology differently from the forward-charging technocracy.

Lamarre's and Halberstam's investment in the lateral and sideways movement is instructive for my understanding of *Cats and Peachtopia*'s future imaginary, both as a narrative drive and as an indication of the film's self-reflexive positioning vis-a-vis the technology of digital animation. As discussed previously, *Cats and Peachtopia* strives for the real feel with its high-end rendering technology. Yet it does not take the simulated real for granted, but rather self-consciously negotiates the digital technology that enables this effect of the real. The sequences presenting Cape's breathtaking flight and the mold-making of his 3D body with the slamming pads, as analyzed, suggest the film's meta-mediatic commentary on the operational aesthetics in early gag comedies and on contemporary algorithmic modeling, respectively.

35. Kathryn Bond Stockton, *The Queer Child, or Growing Sideways in the Twentieth Century* (Durham, NC: Duke University Press, 2009), 9, 10.

36. Halberstam, *Queer Art of Failure*, 51.

37. Halberstam, *Queer Art of Failure*, 19.

38. Halberstam, *Queer Art of Failure*, 42.

Similarly, the film's future imaginary lends itself to renegotiating the technology it partakes in. As a Bildungsroman, the film unsurprisingly thematizes a boy's adventure. The shot of a bullet rocket under construction suggests his impending ballistic torpedoing into deep space, the future, and elsewhere, which is coded (unsurprisingly) as Mars, referencing humanity's space travel ambitions. Although different from Miyazaki's animation technology, this 3D digital animation's overall closed compositing (à la Lamarre) minimizes the interplanary interval and leans toward cinematism. All of these evoke the militarist, imperialist, and negative environmental impact that new materialist media scholars have criticized in regard to computational imaging technology. On the other hand, however, the film's narrative is hardly assured about the goal or telos of Cape's adventure. His flight with the DIY makeshift contraption is barely guided and constantly threatens to fail. His original goal of finding Peachtopia seems duly realized toward the end; but the Peachtopia we see is the least realistic image, its modeling and coloring being flat and cartoonish. When Cape runs laterally across the screen to the big big world, the flat Peachtopia background appears dissociated, rejecting singular perspectivism and instead, suggesting Lamarre's multiplanery animetism.

The future imaginary is, therefore, left unfigurable in the film proper. It is not until the bonus scene inserted in between the closing credits, which most audiences might miss, that we catch a glimpse of the film's most high-tech and ballistic view of the telos, imagined as interstellar travel. Yet even here the grounded bullet rocket is presented mainly for appearances rather than any serious spatial expedition. Cape, who is posited as the singular hero in the film, certainly does not grow sideways to embody an unruly animal collective that might inspire a queer revolt, which Halberstam would like to see in 3D animation. Yet his high-tech ballistic future remains under construction, or more likely, in suspense.

Furthermore, Cape's future-elsewhere desire is not the only viable telos. The film ends with Blanket and Auntie Macaw returning to their urban home to continue their lives as spoiled pets, while the old black stray cat, now teamed up with a raccoon who defected from the mad artist, reopens a pub for wandering lonely animals. Thus, multiple time-spaces are validated, ranging from the pub for homeless animals who savor their brave past, the urban human home for the growing pet culture and industry, to a high-tech lab in an unknown location incubating a future that is paradoxically also in suspense. All these time-spaces are juxtaposed, signaling heterogeneous possibilities that deconstruct the hierarchy of the old and the new, the past, the present and the future, the high-tech and the low-tech.

Conclusion: When Future Fails a Viewer

Returning to the IMDB reviewer's complaint about the film's unsuitability for children, one might argue that the perceived problem—animal injury and death—symptomizes precisely the film's messiness and rejection of a clear feel-good futurity. The film harnesses cutting-edge algorithms to evoke a real feel for the animal characters, only then to make the audience stress over Cape's vulnerability, despite the character's ontological nonreferentiality. When it comes to positing a techno-future, the simulation is limited and ultimately suspended, thus failing to present a clear teleological drive.

Where *Cats and Peachtopia* fails in offering child-friendly entertainment conventionally coded as feel-good and upbeat, it succeeds in suspending and reflecting (even if inadvertently) on what it proclaims to be: a polished embodiment of 3D animation technology rivaling Pixar. In falling short of Light Chaser's Chinese Pixar dream, the film ends up being distanced from the industrial-military and entertainment complex. Although showing little environmental consciousness, the film's accommodation of heterogeneous future time-spaces does enable a critique of teleology. More specifically, the telos being questioned could be the hyperreal algorithmic simulation itself. Putting aside the Light Chaser CEO Wang Wei's Pixar dream, my tri-perspective study in this essay tells a different story of the diegetic worlding, and of the future of Chinese 3D digital animation.

SECTION FIVE

Practices

THIRTEEN

The Path to Cinematic Immersion

Creating VR Animation in China

Jake Junjie Zhang

Due to a rapid increase in virtual reality (VR) products, including games and cinematic VR, 2016 has been widely dubbed the first year of the VR industry in China. With increasing investment in the VR industry globally since 2014, especially after Facebook's purchase of Oculus, several Chinese studios have devoted themselves to this new medium, contributing to the development of a cinematic language for VR animation and its creative process. Because examples and resources regarding what VR animation should be like are limited, various approaches have been explored, including applying traditional animation principles and adding interactive components. Having been presented at top international film festivals in 2016 and 2017, VR animation creations by the first generation of Chinese creators gained international recognition. However, cinematic VR projects, including VR animation, decreased drastically after 2018 because of the immature end-user market. This chapter attempts to identify the motivations, features of development, challenges of creating VR animation, and emerging forms of VR animation in China.[1]

This research project received funding from Shanghai Jiao Tong University's USC-SJTU Institute of Cultural and Creative Industry and the Zizhu National High-Tech Industrial Development Zone via the Zizhu New Media Management Research Center and the International Association of Cultural and Creative Industry Research. The researchers acknowledge the generous financial and administrative support received from all institutions and their staff.

1. For the theorization of VR, see Akira Mizuta Lippit, "Virtual Annihilation: Optics, VR, and the Discourse of Subjectivity," *Criticism* 36, no. 4 (Fall 1994): 595–610.

In VR, audiences can enjoy a highly immersive cinematic experience. The frame or screen determined by the director does not exist, and audiences experience stories in a virtual space. This offers audiences greater freedom than traditional 2D media. However, VR narratives also face obvious challenges. Questions such as how to guide the viewer's eyes in VR, how to arrange narrative elements in space to ensure the best experience, and how to design VR framing are yet to receive definitive answers. Unlike mature narrative media, such as movies, VR still lacks solid design principles.

The first generation of VR content creators in China faced the same narrative challenges as they began to explore methods for creating VR content after VR headsets became more widely available in 2012. Their main approach was adapting to cinematic language. Initially, most VR content produced in China was based on 360° video rendering, whose pipeline is similar to that of traditional animation. Such attempts include the first 360° VR animation produced in China, *Sent* (*Zaijian biaoqing* 再见表情, 2015), and *Micro Giants* (*Weiguan jushou* 微观巨兽, 2017). Pinta Studios and Sandman Studios were the first VR content studios to create game engine–produced VR animation. *Dream Collector* (*Shimeng laoren* 拾梦老人, 2017) by Pinta Studios and *Free Whale* (*Ziyou* 自游, 2017) by Sandman Studios are representative of Chinese VR content creators' cinematic approaches to VR storytelling and exploration of methods for guiding the viewer's eyes. Although most of the early VR content creators had a filmmaking background, some independent creators, such as Hsin-Chien Huang 黄心健 and Jessien Huang 黄佳胜, had diverse backgrounds and took unique approaches to VR narratives, with an emphasis on interactivity.

Light Chaser Animation Studios: Early Approach to VR Animation

Light Chaser Animation Studios, one of the most well-known Chinese animated film production studios, launched their first VR experience based on their newly released animated movie *Little Door Gods* (*Xiao menshen* 小门神) in 2016. This is believed to have been the first narrative VR experience available to the general public in China. According to cofounder Yu Zhou 于洲, Light Chaser formed a VR team due to its attention to global VR technology trends, and *Little Door Gods* was its

FIGURE 13.1. The theater scene with emoji characters, in *Sent* (2015). Courtesy of Light Chaser Animation Studios.

first VR approach.[2] In 2015, Light Chaser completed its first 360° movie, *Sent*, which was presented at SIGGRAPH 2016.[3] *Sent* is a short animated film about the emoji Goodbye, a stamp-shaped child character with the emoji on his head who is sent on a mission during a text conversation by a boy who wants to break up with his girlfriend. Goodbye flies through a portal filled with the pictures of the two lovers but changes his mind and throws all the pictures to the other end of the portal. The "goodbye" is not sent; instead, all the sweet memories are sent to the girl. *Sent* was directed by Mi Li 米粒, who became cofounder and director of Pinta Studios in 2016. As one of the first Chinese animation studios focusing on producing Hollywood-standard, high-quality animated movies, Light Chaser adapted a mainstream character-driven animation style and pipeline to the story development and production of *Sent*. Because it is a 360° video–based VR experience, the key events follow a planned time sequence. An interesting element is the theater-like scene with a huge screen in front of the viewer, which creates the sense that they are among the emoji characters, witnessing how emoji friends are sent to the other side of the screen (fig. 13.1). Since it is important to introduce the context and the fictional world in the first act in a traditional

2. Yu Zhou, interview by Jake Junjie Zhang, June 3, 2022.

3. Ye Yuan, "Storytelling in VR," in *ACM SIGGRAPH 2016 VR Village*, 2016, 1.

narrative, using VR helps the viewer immerse themselves in the story in a short time. Because the viewer is surrounded by the emoji characters in the first scene of *Sent*, their self-identity may switch from that of an observer to that of an emoji character, thereby enhancing the feeling of presence. Using a theater-like production design in the first scene also helps the user maintain a relatively stable viewing direction due to the limited region of interest and high contrast created by the dark environment and glowing effects on the main narrative elements. Although *Sent* was not a real-time VR animation, it was the outcome of Chinese filmmakers' exploration of narratives in VR and the basis for later VR animated shorts. *Sent* was Light Chaser's last VR project. After 2015, Light Chaser tended to focus on 2D screen-based animation and storytelling.

Pinta Studios and Sandman Studios: VR Animation Produced Using Game Engines

In 2017, the 74th Venice International Film Festival organized its first VR film competition. Among the twenty-two selected films, three were made by Chinese studios: *The Dream Collector* by Pinta Studios, *Free Whale* by Sandman Studios, and *In the Pictures* (*Chuang* 窗, 2017) by VRTIMES. All three were representative of the first batch of Chinese VR animations produced in 2016. In 2014 and 2015, VR became a hot topic globally. However, with limited VR platform availability, the early exploration of VR was often in the hands of VR teams at big companies. In China, examples were Light Chaser's team, founded in 2014, and (Greater China) Digital Domain's team, founded in 2015. The necessary investment was mainly made by the companies themselves. In 2016, with increasing investment in various VR fields (technology, training, education, and entertainment), many VR companies were founded. Pinta Studios and Sandman Studios were two pioneer VR content creation studios in China and remained active till this day. According to Luo Hao 罗皓, who worked for both studios, the two studios were like sister studios and collaborated from the early days. They began similarly, focusing on VR animation production. However, after 2018, investment in VR content decreased. To survive in the market, they followed different strategies, and their content creation and collaboration patterns diverged.[4]

In 2015, Lemony Lei 雷峥蒙, then a senior operations specialist at Alibaba, watched *Sent* and saw his fellow high school alumnus Mi Li's name credited as the director. This motivated him to found Pinta Studios with Mi Li as chief creative officer and his colleague Apei 啊呸 as chief marketing officer in 2016.[5] *The Dream Collector* was their first VR project and the first Chinese game engine–produced VR animation. The main difference between 360° video–based and game engine–produced VR animation lies in the dynamics of the viewing experience. In game engine–based animation, the viewer can see perspective variations dynamically when their position changes; a 360° image sequence experience does not provide this flexibility. *The Dream Collector*, directed by Mi Li, is a VR animated short film about an old repairman who lives in an old house with his dog, collects abandoned broken objects from all over the world, fixes them, paints them, and turns them into presents ready to be sent out. Almost at the last minute, his identity as Santa Claus is revealed, and the concept of "sending dreams back" is introduced. Mi Li continued the cinematic narrative approach to VR with a sharper focus on immersive user experiences. The well-designed environment and compelling character animation capture viewers' attention and potentially enhance their engagement. In the interior scene of the old man's house, users can move and rotate their bodies to navigate the interesting setup. Viewers can clearly feel the distance between them and the objects they are looking at in the main character's room (fig. 13.2), which enhances their spatial presence. According to Mi Li's presentation at Unite Shanghai 2017, guiding viewers to experience the complete story and scene transitions were the two challenges while making their first VR animation.[6] Besides applying visual cues, sound, and

4 Luo Hao, interview by Junjie Zhang, June 3, 2022.

5 "Pingta tamen you yige xin de gushi yao dui ni jiang" 平塔他们有一个新的故事要对你讲 (Pinta has a new story to tell), in Shushi 舒适 COMFORT, January 4, 2017. https://kknews.cc/zh-mo/news/96kbz2l.html.

6. Tian Miao 田苗, "VR donghua daodi gai zenme zuo? Pingta gongzuoshi fenxiang le VR shiting yuyan de jingyan | Unite 2017 / VR 动画到底该怎么做? Pinta Studios 分享了VR 视听语言的经验 | Unite 2017" (How to create VR animation? Pinta Studios

FIGURE 13.2. The interior room, in *The Dream Collector* (2017). Courtesy of Pinta Studios.

movement to direct viewers' attention, spotlighting—an adaptation from theater—was applied to restrict users' viewing area to ensure that they were looking at the region of interest. Spotlights were also used creatively in scene transitioning. In the scene presenting the old man's and the dog's continuous performance crossing two locations (exterior and interior), an animated and progressively smaller spotlight is used as an editing tool to transition from the exterior to the interior of the house. The background finishes its transition when the cone of the spotlight becomes minimized to disable the visibility of the background.

Pinta Studios also produced *Shennong: Taste of Illusion* (*Lie shan shi* 烈山氏, 2018) in 2017 and *ELLO* in 2018. *Shennong* is an animated short based on a traditional Chinese story about the god-king of Chinese medicine. Both projects were presented at the 75th Venice International Film Festival. Many of the early employees of Pinta Studios, including Mi Li, were from the animation and game industries, and their work's main features were compelling character animation and storytelling. Facing reduced investment in VR animation projects and the difficulty of selling animated shorts due to the small number of platforms and users in 2018,

shared their experience of VR audio-visual language at Unite 2017," in *Leifeng wang* 雷锋网 (Lei Feng web), May 12, 2017. https://www.leiphone.com.

FIGURE 13.3. The long take shot, in *Free Whale* (2017). Courtesy of Sandman Studios.

Pinta Studios focused on intellectual property creation and the development of stories that could be distributed to multiple media.

Sandman Studios was founded by Eddie Lou 楼彦昕 in 2016. Its production *Free Whale* is an animated short directed by Zhang Peibin 张佩斌. In this immersive VR sci-fi narrative experience, viewers follow the main character Shem and his artificial intelligence (AI) companion Young on a mission to retrieve AI samples from a distant planet. The story starts with the two main characters walking along a dark and narrow gap between high rocks on the planet. Viewers move with Shem and Young as their companions while listening to their conversation about the meaning of "feeling" for machines and humans. They stop at the seaside, shown in a wide view, where the story reaches its climax when a giant machine whale comes out of the water. Scenes from the machine whale's memory showing its time on this planet are revealed (fig. 13.3). One of the features of *Free Whale* is the use of long shots following the characters' movements in virtual space. This experimental approach to cinematic VR editing required a careful design of narrative elements (performance, visual cues, sound sources) and viewers' path of movement. The creators also needed to perform extra tests to ensure a comfortable viewing experience that would not cause VR motion sickness. In 2018, Sandman Studios released its second VR animated short, *Fresh Out* (*Di sanxian* 地三仙), directed by Samuel Wey 魏灵强 and Tao Fangchao 陶方超, continuing its exploration of VR narratives with a greater focus on viewers' self-identification. In *Fresh Out*, the viewer is taken underground with carrot characters to confront the danger of being caught by a mysterious giant monster together. Being in a unique virtual world as one of the characters, the viewer becomes part of the story: a baby carrot in a VR world. *Fresh Out* is a representative work exploring viewers' role in cinematic VR contexts. Given the drastic reduction in investment in VR content creation after 2018, Sandman Studios focused on VR media and expanded VR content distribution to commercial VR experiences, VR concerts, and VR platforms.

Digital Domain China: Exploration of High-Quality 360° Visual-Driven Experiences

Another noteworthy piece of VR work is *Micro Giants*, directed by Zhou Yifu 周逸夫 and produced by a VR team of the well-known Hollywood-based visual effects studio Digital Domain. *Micro Giants* is a representative work of visual-driven VR animation, in which viewers are brought into a jungle with a worm's eye view to witness a series of insect activities celebrating the magnificence of nature. The insects are modeled and animated with high anatomical precision. Due to the high quality of the rendered images (4K Dual-Eye), viewers can observe these creatures from an extremely close distance. The project was completed at the end of 2016 and was officially selected for the 2017 Sundance Film Festival. Digital Domain started its VR team in Greater China after purchasing the Hong Kong–based visual effects studio Post Production Office (PO 朝霆) in 2016, which provided it with facilities and labor resources in Asia. Digital Domain had previously produced projects such as VR animation, live VR streaming events, and live-action VR in the United States. According to Zhou Yifu, the studio's early exploration of VR narratives included the project *Monkey King VR*, which was launched in 2015.[7] This experience provided it with direction and strategies for camera movement and editing,

7. Zhou Yifu, interview by Junjie Zhang, June 2, 2022.

with consideration of preventing VR motion sickness. This combination of camera movement and continuity editing was applied to *Micro Giants*. The effectiveness of the film technique of continuity editing in VR has been debated, but *Micro Giants* is a valuable example of adapting the film toolkit to VR storytelling.[8]

According to an interview that Sandman Studios chief executive officer Eddie Lou gave Lu Economics (Xiaolujiao caijing 小鹿角财经), during the "cooling down period," Chinese VR companies were affected not only by reduced investment but also by a lack of platforms for VR content.[9] As when motion pictures were first introduced to the public, accessible media and platforms are important for expanding the VR user base. With the high prices and design limitations of head-mounted display (HMD) devices and limited content availability, one of the first challenges facing Chinese VR entrepreneurs and creators was making content available to the general public. The Sandbox Immersive Festival was the first immersive content–focused international festival in China designed to draw the attention of the public and potential investors to excellent VR projects. Content platforms with vast numbers of Chinese users, such as Youku and IQIYI, launched VR channels. Technology companies PICO, HTC VIVE, and IQIYI Qiyu developed content platforms along with their own HMD devices. VeeR was founded to develop online platforms and VR arcades for exclusive immersive content.

VR channels on traditional video content platforms were one of the early ways to view VR content. Companies such as Youku, IQIYI, and Bilibili, with already large numbers of active users in China, launched such channels. However, VR content was either limited to 360° videos,

8. Aleksandra Zheleva, "Can You Make the Cut? Exploring the Effect of Frequency of Cuts in Virtual Reality Storytelling," in *Augmented Reality and Virtual Reality*, eds. M. Claudia tom Dieck, Timothy H. Jung, and Sandra M. C. Loureiro (Cham: Springer International, 2021), 45–52; Hannes Rall, "Everything Must Change? Challenges for Animated Storytelling in VR," in *2019 IEEE 2nd Workshop on Animation in Virtual and Augmented Environments: Proceedings* (Osaka: IEEE Computer Society Visualization and Graphics Technical Committee, March 24, 2019), 18–24, https://ieeexplore.ieee.org/xpl/conhome/9038148/proceeding.

9. Eddie Lou, "Shazhihe de yewang: Goujian xuni de 'daqian' shijie" 砂之盒的野望：构建虚拟的"大千"世界 (Sandbox's ambition: To build VAST, a virtual world), *Xiaolujiao caijing* 小鹿角财经 (Lu Economics), June 7, 2022.

or 360° versions were transferred from game engine–produced VR projects. HMD devices were not required to view such content. In addition to watching on screens, users could use devices such as Google Cardboard with their phones. Some platforms, such as Bilibili, developed functions similar to those of YouTube VR, allowing users to use a mouse to navigate 360° space. However, although VR channels provided wider access to 360° content in a relatively easy way, the animation content usually had low image quality, and the viewing mode did not reach the VR immersive experience standards. Therefore, the consensus among VR content creators is that platforms for exclusive VR content and devices enabling immersive experiences are preferable.

Exclusive VR content on online platforms can be divided into two categories. One is the type of platform developed by companies such as Oculus, PICO, and IQIYI Qiyu, which develop their own HMD devices. Users' activity is influenced by device functionality as well as the content and user experience on each platform. The other category consists of content-driven platforms, such as SteamVR and VeeR, which provide VR content for multiple devices. VR animation is usually found under the VR film, VR animation, or even indie game category on platforms developed by HMD developers and SteamVR. Most users of these platforms are gamers rather than cinephiles, which may negatively affect VR content purchases. Even for Pinta Studios' award-winning projects, purchases on SteamVR are low relative to many games. Founded in 2016, VeeR is a pioneer Chinese platform that focuses on providing high-quality VR content internationally. HMD devices are needed for the best experience. According to VeeR cofounder Chen Jingshu 陈婧姝, the company mostly provided 360° videos at first, including animation and live action, before developing an upgraded version to provide more interactive content on the platform.[10] VeeR has focused on developing a sustainable commercial model for original VR projects. With its own platform and distribution to device-based platforms, as well as its offline network of VR arcades, it aims to maximize the value of VR content. The profitability of original content is undoubtedly vital for investors and creators, and online platforms are playing an increasingly important role.

10. Chen Jingshu, interview by Junjie Zhang, June 1, 2022.

In 2020, the affordable standalone HMD device Oculus Quest 2 was launched, leading to renewed interest in VR. Since then, sales of increasingly user-friendly HMD devices have been growing.[11] Although by June 2022, no Chinese VR animation boom comparable to that of 2016–2017 had occurred, their positive influence was reflected in a growing user base and more VR animation content.

Investors, content creators, and platform developers set the trends and possibilities of Chinese VR animation together. Luo Hao, Zhou Yifu, and Chen Jingshu have highlighted interactivity in VR narrative animation as a strong trend in the coming years. With this trend, the content-driven platform VeeR and production company Sandman Studios are poised to significantly contribute to promoting and distributing VR content. VeeR is working on an upgraded version for more interactive VR content, and Sandman Studios presented its own VR platform, VAST, at the 4th Sandbox Immersive Film Festival in March 2022.

VR Arcades and VR Theaters

Although online platforms offer the opportunity for Chinese VR animations to be viewed by both Chinese and international audiences, offline VR arcades and theaters mainly target Chinese audiences. With few HMD device owners in China, offline VR experiences still are the mainstream for the first generation of Chinese VR users, especially before the COVID-19 pandemic. Pop-up VR experience centers, an early form of VR theater, were set up in movie theaters' open areas. The VR experience based on the animated movie *Little Door Gods* created by Light Chaser was released to movie theaters in 2015. Digital Domain launched its Digital Domain Space VR theaters in 2018, showcasing several VR works, including its own production *Micro Giants*. However, the project was later discontinued. Similarly, with limited content available and due to the high cost of rentals and devices, most VR theme park projects were discontinued, and many

11. Zhongguo dianzi xinxi fazhan yanjiuyuan 中国电子信息发展研究院 (China Center for Information Industry Development), "Xuni xianshi chanye fazhan baipishu 2021" 虚拟现实产业发展白皮书2021 (Technology white paper on virtual reality industry development 2021), in *VR+Video Art Sub-forum*, Nanchang, China, October 2021.

VR experience centers, arcades, and theaters closed down between 2018 and 2020. An accessible platform for high-quality original VR animation was still missing. Subsequently, the launch of standalone HMD devices such as Oculus Quest 2, DPVR, and PICO reduced the cost of setting up VR experience centers. VeeR started its own original content-driven online platform and established VR arcades and Zero Space theaters in big cities, such as Beijing, Shanghai, and Shenzhen, as part of its business of distributing and sublicensing global VR content.

Generally speaking, the main difference between VR arcades and VR theaters is the viewing mode. In VR theaters, viewers are usually seated in swivel chairs with no possibility of physical movement and limited or no interaction with the VR content. In VR arcades, users usually stand and experience VR content with more flexibility and interactivity; however, this requires substantial space for each user.

Both online and offline platforms are likely to continue to drive user experience, thus influencing content creation. The available VR experience environments (user interfaces and offline experience devices) and the popularity of themes on these platforms are factors to be considered by VR content creators and investors.

In the early days of VR content creation in China, Light Chaser, Pinta Studios, Sandman Studios, and Digital Domain made efforts to explore the possibilities of VR animation forms and narratives. To address challenges such as balancing between the creator's and user's flexibility, directing the user's eyes, triggering narrative events, and preventing VR motion sickness, they tested some innovative approaches. The high quality and success of works at international film festivals provided Chinese creators with recognition and, with it, motivation and confidence. Even during the period from 2018 to 2020, when big studios halted VR animation production due to a lack of investment, independent teams and creators continued to work on original VR animation, exploring diverse visual forms. VRTIMES, one of the earliest independent VR content studios, produced its first game engine–based VR animation *Black Bag* (*Heise pibao* 黑色皮包) in 2019. Director Shao Qing 邵晴 applied a unique hand-painting style to deliver an intense thriller seen from inside a black bag. With its unique space design and narrative, *Black Bag* was the only Chinese VR work presented at the 76th Venice International Film Festival.

FIGURE 13.4. The showroom, in *Hypnosis: Reveries* (2021). Courtesy of Jessien Huang.

In Taiwan, HTC VIVE ORIGINALS, a content creation brand of HTC VIVE, developed original VR content in collaboration with artists and VR production teams. With HTC VIVE's support, well-established artists from different fields (films and traditional animation) could create VR content using their own styles and unique perspectives. Directors Tang Zhi-Zhong 唐治中 and Huang Yun-Hsien 黄匀弦, two well-established stop-motion animation artists, produced a compelling 360° VR stop-motion animation titled *The Sick Rose* (*Bing meigui* 病玫瑰, 2021). Working on both VR films and installations, Taiwan-based professor and new media artist Hsin-Chien Huang approached experimental VR animation with a focus on viewers' interactive experiences. In his work *Samsara* (2021), the viewer is taken on a time travel across millions of years with different identities. A pair of unique hands that match the scene is controlled by the viewer to enhance the feeling of "being part of the story."

Further exploration of interactivity and more investment in interactive VR content creation are expected in the future. Even though more interactive game-like VR experiences have been selected in recent international film festivals, the boundary between cinematic and interactive VR could become increasingly blurry. Using interactive techniques, narrative or cinematic experiences could be combined with increased user engagement. In the 2021 Sandbox Immersive Festival, the Best Chinese Work Award went to *Hypnosis: Reveries* (*Shuishen de xiasi* 睡神的遐思), a unique interactive VR experience created by Jessien Huang, who has a strong architectural background. Users are positioned in a unique architectural space comprising two main areas: one area in which users can move around and finish interactive tasks, and another showroom area, visible through windows, in the center of the building (fig. 13.4). With handle controllers, users can teleport to a maze-like space to perform simple tasks, such as putting 3D cubes into a space on the wall outlined by a square, which triggers the cinematic performance in the showroom area by three groups of 3D geometric characters: cubes, spheres, and pyramids. More space or a door is opened once an animation scene has been played, which leads audiences to continue to the next level of storytelling. Experimenting with space, performing tasks, and viewing animation are combined in a consistent storytelling strategy. As the characters are simple geometrical shapes whose performance is based on movement, storytelling is blended with metaphors. Due to the dominant use of black and white, the appearance of red enhances the intensity. The creator embraces users' diverse ways of understanding the story and applies user input to a unique "memory mode." In this mode, a minimum interactive movement on the user's part is needed to enhance the cinematic experience. Audiences will be revealed scene by scene, and each scene is accompanied by the most quoted descriptive keywords from the *Hypnosis: Reveries* online community, who can input the keywords they think best match each scene based on their experience. *Hypnosis: Reveries* presents a novel and engaging VR narrative.

"In the future, we may not need to use VR film or interactive VR categories; they could all be in 'one VR experience' category. Storytelling certainly plays an important role in it," Luo Hao stated, highlighting the need to rethink VR narratives and VR viewers' role in them.[12] Through their thought and practice, Chinese VR content creators have helped answer the questions of how knowledge and experience from other domains can be transferred to VR content creation and what an interactive VR experience should be like. This chapter documents the early stages of the development of Chinese VR animation in anticipation of more outstanding works in the near future.

12 Luo Hao, interview by Junjie Zhang, June 3, 2022.

FOURTEEN

The Digital Turn in Hong Kong Independent Animation

Isabel Galwey

This chapter offers an overview of Hong Kong independent animation through the digital turn, which I have defined, roughly, as the decade from 1995 to 2005.[1] It focuses on the significance of independent animation as a space for new media and transmedia experimentation. This period was characterized by technological innovations that profoundly changed independent animation production, as well as by important continuities with independent animation of earlier decades—two aspects that coexisted, not always without tension. After giving some background on the history of Hong Kong independent animation and its place within the wider Hong Kong media environment, and exploring the significance of the digital turn for the field, I go on to spotlight several "animateurs," to borrow Paola Voci's portmanteau of auteur and animator, whose work has had particular impact.[2]

1. This chapter is from my MPhil thesis titled "Transmedial Attractions, Transitional Aesthetics: The Digital Turn in Hong Kong Animation," Hong Kong University of Science and Technology, January 2023. For more information about this topic, see the ACAS conference, Animators' Roundtable Forum: Hong Kong Animation, May 12–14, 2022, https://acas.world/2022/04/21/animators-roundtable-forum-hong-kong-animation-zoom-webinar-may-12-14-2022/.

2. See Paola Voci, "Electric Shadows Reloaded: The Post-Digital Animateur, Shadow Play and Handmade Cinema," *Journal of Chinese Cinemas* 11, no. 3 (2017): 192–209, as well as her chapter in this volume. Voci first used the expression "animateur" in the context of mainland Chinese animators. It is intended to simultaneously evoke amateur, animator, and auteur.

Given the slipperiness of the terms *independent* and *animation*, pinning down *independent animation* in any context, let alone Hong Kong's, is a challenge. Defining the *digital turn* is no less difficult, but I decided to focus on the mid-1990s onward, when debates about digitality and digitized practice became widespread in Hong Kong. Rather than imposing a top-down definition, I use individual *new media objects* as case studies to explore how animators used the digital technologies at their disposal to create innovative works.[3] I also include commentaries from animators active at the time—in particular, competitors' notes and jury discussions from the Hong Kong Independent Film and Video Awards (IFVA)—to give a sense of how animators themselves experienced these changes.

Of course, the turn of the millennium was also an important moment of transition for Hong Kong in other ways: these years immediately preceded and followed the city's 1997 handover. As critic Gene Ching described it, "Hong Kong cinema was on fire," as filmmakers attempted to make sense of and respond to the events unfolding around them, redefining a local Hong Kong cultural identity while forging ever-stronger connections across the global film and animation industries.[4] Victor Fan described the cultural moment as "kaleidoscopic, a media environment that was so colorful, enervative, yet volatile that nobody could make sense out of it."[5] This chapter explores and links Fan's insights to the developments taking place in Hong Kong independent animation.

A Brief History of Independent Animation in Hong Kong

Independent animation has existed in Hong Kong since at least 1947, when Zhang Guangyu 張光宇 produced the short animation *Bell Boy*.[6]

3. Lev Manovich, introduction to *The Language of New Media* (Cambridge, MA: MIT Press, 2001), 14.

4. Gene Ching, "The Weird History of a Chinese Ghost Story Franchise: Horror Comedy at Its Wildest," *Den of Geek*, October 25, 2020, https://www.denofgeek.com/movies/the-weird-history-of-a-chinese-ghost-story-franchise/.

5. Victor Fan, "The Time It Takes for Time to End," in *Extraterritoriality: Locating Hong Kong Cinema and Media* (Edinburgh: Edinburgh University Press, 2019), 156.

6. See Muyang Zhuang, "Bell Boy: Cartoonists and Animated Filmmaking in Southern

However, works were few and far between until the 1970s. Independent animation in Hong Kong has been shaped by the efforts of a dedicated group of individual animateurs, perhaps the most significant of whom is Neco Lo 盧子英. He has been heavily involved in both creating and curating Hong Kong independent animation since the 1970s. According to his account, attested to by other animators active in that period, an independent film community in Hong Kong began to emerge in the late 1960s and early 1970s. Community groups such as the Phoenix Cine Club (Huofeng dianying hui 火鳳電影會) and Single Frame animation group (Dange donghua zhongxin 單格動畫中心) came to form the backbone of independent film and animation production and appreciation.[7]

A complex network of institutional connections propelled Hong Kong independent animation forward from its earliest days. These included local universities, global organizations such as the International Animated Film Association, and local art groups such as Zuni Icosahedron (Jin'nian ershi mian ti 進念二十面體) and Videotage (Luying mengtaiqi 錄映太奇). Wenhai Zhou has theorized an "imagined community of independent animation" in mainland China.[8] In the case of Hong Kong, the community barely has to be imagined, given that it is centered around the dense locality and networks of the city itself.

In the absence of specialized animation courses at local institutions, Hong Kong independent animation education relied on animation's connections with other media forms.[9] Students of fine arts or graphic design encountered independent animation through screenings and clubs, and animation competitions provided a goal to work toward as well as a way to share their work more widely. Roger Garcia notes that one of the most important

China, 1940–1949," Association for Chinese Animation Studies, November 2, 2021, https://acas.world/2021/11/02/bell-boy-cartoonists-and-animated-filmmaking-in-southern-china-1940-1949.

7. Neco Lo, "Single Frame and the Development of Hong Kong Independent Animation," in *Frame after Frame*, ed. Winnie Fu (Hong Kong: Hong Kong Film Archive, 2006), 52–69.

8. Wenhai Zhou, *Chinese Independent Animation: Renegotiating Identity in Modern China* (Cham: Palgrave Macmillan, 2020), 46.

9. For insightful discussions of Hong Kong animation's links with short-form comics and martial arts cinema respectively, see Jessica K. Chan's chapter 10 and Jinying Li's chapter 2 in this volume.

purposes of Hong Kong independent film practice is that it "has helped to encourage and 'train' aspiring young filmmakers."[10] Independent animation also offered established professionals a platform for creative expression; one of Hong Kong's foremost commercial animators, Dick Wong 黃迪, created several personal animations which he entered into Hong Kong's IFVA.[11]

The range of works produced by Hong Kong independent animators demands an expanded definition of Hong Kong animation that takes into account its eclecticism and diversity of techniques, media, and subject matter; no single Hong Kong "school" of animation exists. Many Hong Kong animators studied abroad or worked flexibly in multiple geographical regions, combining global influences with local identity and concerns.

Despite its promising start, Hong Kong independent animation hit a dry spell from the mid-1980s to the mid-1990s.[12] Lo attributed this to the fact that Super 8 film fell out of fashion and was replaced by video, which at that time was less suited to creating animation. Funding and distribution opportunities remained limited, making independent production unsustainable. Victor Fan's documentation of the early works of Videotage confirms that some animators turned to video art, perhaps due to this technological gap.[13] Others moved back into television animation and commercial work.

The Digital Turn and Hong Kong Animateurs

The digital turn is widely credited for rejuvenating independent animation in Hong Kong, bringing in a new generation of talent and further breaking down barriers between animation and other media forms. The release of *Toy Story* in 1995 revealed the capabilities of computer animation, and

10. Roger Garcia, "Hong Kong Independent Shorts Rhythms," in *i-Generations: Independent, Experimental and Alternative Creations from the 60s to Now* (Hong Kong: Hong Kong Film Archive, 2001), 11.

11. Wong Kee-Chee, "Letters to One's Sensibility," in *Frame after Frame*, ed. Winnie Fu (Hong Kong: Hong Kong Film Archive, 2005), 75.

12. Lu Ziying 盧子英 (Neco Lo), "Duli donghua chuangzuo de yidian huiyi" 獨立動畫創作的一點回憶 (Some recollections on creating independent animation), in *i-Generations: Independent, Experimental and Alternative Creations from the 60s to Now* (Hong Kong: Hong Kong Film Archive, 2001), 18.

13. Fan, "The Time It Takes," 134–35.

ever-improving software gave animators the tools they needed to experiment. This sparked debate among established animators and inspired viewers in turn, leading to unexpected developments and connections.

From the late 1990s onward, animation in Hong Kong expanded rapidly. According to the yearly catalogs of the IFVA, an important platform for independent animation in Hong Kong, animation entries grew year on year, although, as jurors were quick to point out, this did not necessarily mean an increase in quality.

Technological innovations were changing the way that animation was made, but they were not always met favorably by those familiar with analog methods. At the 1999 IFVA, tensions emerged as judges complained of animations that were "overwhelmed by computer effects," and that they "did not know whether these images are done by the animator or the software."[14]

On the other side of this equation, a new generation of animators were excited about the possibilities offered by digital software. This is evidenced by the animators' reflections on their own work. In their credits, synopses, and film notes, animators often listed the software used, down to the exact version, and left tongue-in-cheek comments on the latest technique that they had tried out in their work.

For example, in a detailed and slightly ironic note on his 1998 animation entry *The Magician and the Rabbit*, animator Hsu Siu Chi 徐迢之 commented, "If you have to try and guess (as seems to be a favorite pastime of previous judges) what tools or software are used to create these sequences, your guesses are probably wrong. The entire animation was drawn and animated with our proprietary software and technologies."[15] Or, from the animator Toe Yuen 袁建滔, on his film on the subject of child labor in sweatshops: "I was so thrilled by [the] innovative kind of animation between 2D and 3D, that I decided to make this suicidal production. . . . I never thought that I would share the fate of those children. . . ."[16]

14. Neco Lo and Ng Chun Hong, "Panel Discussion," in *5th Independent Short Film and Video Awards Catalogue* (Hong Kong: Hong Kong Arts Centre, 1999), 96.

15. Hsu Siu Chi and Irene Lee, "The Magician and the Rabbit," in *4th Independent Short Film and Video Awards Catalogue* (Hong Kong: Hong Kong Arts Centre, 1998), 29.

16. Toe Yuen, "Foul Ball," in *2nd Independent Short Film and Video Awards Catalogue* (Hong Kong: Hong Kong Arts Centre, 1996), 30.

From Independent Animation to Animated Features

The "suicidal production" that Toe Yuen described was *Foul Ball* (1996). The animated short combined 2D characters with 3D animated backdrops, winning the silver award in that year's IFVA animation category.[17] The animation style owes much to the visual logic of advertising: it was explicitly a parody of a Nike advertisement of that year, a popular culture approach that the jurors immediately recognized. Neco Lo appraised the animation thus: "*Foul Ball* is weak in narration. But, the technique and art direction are good. I can see that the author has worked really hard on that."[18] All the jurors praised the film's strong technical skills and creative modeling, which ultimately won out over its perceived narrative shortcomings to win it the top prize. As a satire of contemporary sports consumer culture and an animated experiment for Toe Yuen, *Foul Ball* had succeeded in its creative objectives.

Foul Ball represents an important turning point in the development of Hong Kong animation. In an essay for Winnie Fu's edited volume on that topic, *Frame After Frame*, Toe Yuen recalled that *Foul Ball* also caught the attention of the creator of *McDull*, Brian Tse 謝立文.[19] Tse liked the way that Yuen had combined the 3D models of a realistically gritty city with the foregrounded cartoon characters. He persuaded Yuen to join the production of the *McDull* animation as director. *Foul Ball* was an early iteration of the visual language and animation techniques that Toe Yuen went on to use in the *McDull* animations, and proved to be an important moment of transition for Hong Kong animation. This demonstrates that some of the technical experiments undertaken by independent animators later became trendsetters for Hong Kong animation more broadly. *Foul Ball* enabled Yuen to cross media boundaries from advertising to independent shorts, and later to animated features.

Another animator who participated in the IFVA in the 1990s and went on to have a far-reaching feature animation career was Hong Kong 3D

17. Toe Yuen, "The 'Motley Crew' of *McDull* Animation Team," in *Frame after Frame*, ed. Winnie Fu (Hong Kong: Hong Kong Film Archive, 2006), 110–28.

18. Craig Au Yeung, Ku Chiu Ping, Neco Lo, Wong Ain Ling, and Wong Ying , "Panel Discussion," in *2nd Independent Short Film and Video Awards Catalogue* (Hong Kong: Hong Kong Arts Centre, 1996), 111.

19. Toe Yuen, "The 'Motley Crew'," 119.

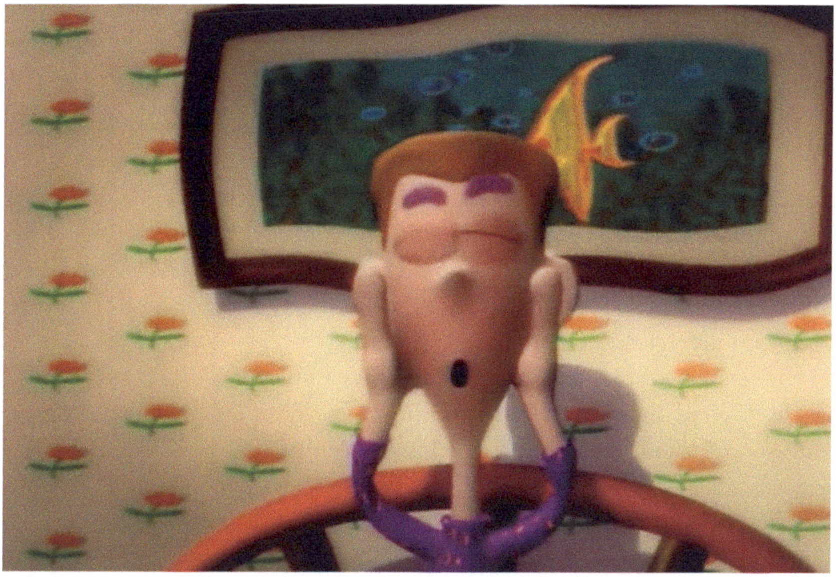

FIGURE 14.1. A young man's dreams are disturbed by increasingly irritating interruptions, in *Sleepy Guy* (1996). Courtesy of Raman Hui.

animator and director Raman Hui 許誠毅. Hui's 1996 short, *Sleepy Guy*, also won an award in the IFVA animation category. The jury commented on the high quality of the animation, which Hui had created while dividing his time between Hong Kong and North America, and working at Pacific Data Images (PDI), a forerunner to DreamWorks, where it took him "two years of after office hours to finish."[20] *Sleepy Guy* typified the style of early PDI shorts, combining a simple, humorous storyline with complex 3D character animation and a setting that shifts between a starlit dreamscape and a mundane bedroom setting (fig. 14.1). The IFVA jury commented that the animation was "complete and refined" and "very professional" with "sophisticated techniques," noting that it would be at home in "the showreel of any American computer company."[21] Indeed, *Sleepy Guy* and Hui's other shorts are now remembered largely in the context of PDI and DreamWorks' early

20. Raman Hui, "*Sleepy Guy* Notes," in *2nd Independent Short Film and Video Awards Catalogue* (Hong Kong: Hong Kong Arts Centre, 1996), 33.

21. Au Yeung et al., "Panel Discussion," in *2nd Independent Short Film and Video Awards Catalogue*, 108.

years. Hui was able to participate in and even shape the North American 3D animation industry while retaining his connection to Hong Kong independent animation.

Building on the experience gained through his production of animated shorts, Hui went on to work as a character animator for the first *Shrek* film at DreamWorks—widely regarded as an iconic animated film series that did as much to popularize 3D animation as *Toy Story* before it—after which he directed the third *Shrek* film. Later, Hui directed the Chinese box office hit *Monster Hunt,* which uses a combination of live-action footage and computer-generated creature animation.

Hui explained his trajectory in the following terms: "When I first came to the United States . . . I did commercials, TV credits, special effects, and so on. When I had time, I would make animated short films with my friends. . . . If Hong Kong animators can't find the opportunity to make 'blockbusters,' they might as well make short films first, and gradually improve the quality of their works through training."[22]

Just as in the case of *Foul Ball,* the IFVA jury was initially skeptical of *Sleepy Guy*'s light narrative. Although Hui's skills were not questioned, the jurors felt that its focus on technical experimentation led to a lack of innovative ideas, criticizing the short for its simple cartoon storyline.[23] However, the film still won a distinguished award; as in the case of *Foul Ball,* storytelling was not the only factor in either animator motivation or juror decision-making.

Independent Animation and New Media Art

Whereas *Foul Ball* and *Sleepy Guy* took a satirical approach to personal and creative exploration, other animations were more serious, such as *Love*

22. Raman Hui quoted in Wang Jiazheng 王嘉政 and Zhou Qunhuan 周群歡, "Zhuanfang Shilijia Huba zhi fu: Ni bu zhidao de *Zhuoyaoji*" 專訪史力加胡巴之父——你不知道的《捉妖記》 (Special interview with Raman Hui, the father of Shrek and Huba: What you don't know about *Monster Hunt*), January 14, 2016, https://www.hk01.com/即時娛樂/681/專訪-史力加胡巴之父-許誠毅-你不知道的-捉妖記.

23. Au Yeung et al., "Panel Discussion," in *2nd Independent Short Film and Video Awards Catalogue*, 108.

FIGURE 14.2. Two lovers part ways, in *Love* (1997). Courtesy of Hung Keung.

(1997) by Hung Keung 洪強. Born in Kunming and raised in Hong Kong, Hung Keung trained as a designer, artist, and film and video artist. *Love* was created while Hung Keung studied at Central Saint Martins in London. This was, of course, also the year of Hong Kong's historic handover. An artwork that took six months to make, *Love* explores both the personal and the political from the vantage point of this watershed moment. It was also Hung's first time making a finished animation work. Hung wrote that the animation is intended to be an exploration of interpersonal relationships, but also his love for Hong Kong: "Like Hong Kong history, *Love* was a simple thing to me when I was a child. When I grow up [*sic*], I realize that it is not the perfect thing that I expect."[24] *Love's* animation style is maximalist, with saturated neon colors and a plethora of different techniques on display.

The imagery combines a naïve directness with a fragmented structure and reliance on visual communication. As shown in figure 14.2, a nude

24. Hung Keung, "Love," in *3rd Independent Short Film and Video Awards Catalogue* (Hong Kong: Hong Kong Arts Centre, 1997), 34.

man and woman embrace, and then the man grows wings and leaves her without conflict. It suggests a transient interaction, calling to mind angelic imagery at odds with the fiery colors and sexual subject matter. *Love* is a highly colorful, kinetic work of video art that raises more questions for the viewer than it answers.

In the 1980s and 1990s, video art became a thriving art form in Hong Kong because it presented an opportunity for artists to work through their individually complex feelings about Hong Kong's traumatic historical position, poised between colonization from Britain and the ever-closer handover to China in 1997. During this period, groups like Videotage were established, and artists including Yau Ching 游靜, Ellen Pau 鮑藹倫, and May Fung 馮美華, as well as Neco Lo, first produced and exhibited their works. Video art, like independent animation, had to fight for recognition and funding in Hong Kong, but eventually became a powerful new medium through which "video artists responded to and continuously worked with the extraterritorial consciousness actively shaped and written by popular culture."[25] Hung's work can be understood in dialogue with these video artists, juxtaposing the political with the personal to underline their inseparability.

Hung has progressed from creating video artworks to ever more elaborate multimedia installations, which have moved from the "black box" of the video viewing space to the "white cube" of the gallery, and out into the public spaces of Hong Kong's cityscape. *Love* is one of the earliest examples of multimedia experimentation in his career, as well as an expression of his abiding interest in the space of Hong Kong itself.

Independent Animation and Music

Independent animation has a strong transmedial relationship with music, in Hong Kong as elsewhere. Creating an independent animation as a music video kills two birds with one stone: it provides the animator with their timings, rhythm, and emotional arc and removes the need for dialogue and Foley sound.

25. Fan, "The Time It Takes," 156.

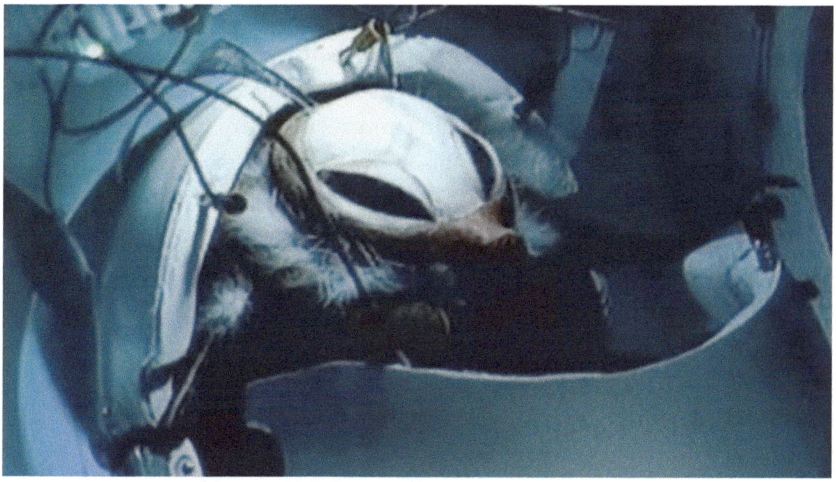

FIGURE 14.3. An insect-like creature embarks on a space voyage, in *#01* (1996). Courtesy of Siu Hak.

The audio-kinetic relationship between animation and music dates back to its earliest days, and in analog animation, the relationship between music and animation is a strict one. However, the freer production pipeline of digital animation gave animators more scope for experimentation with their music videos. Music videos are designed to attract the viewer/listener and enhance the existing soundscape rather than subjugate the music to a supporting role as a soundtrack.

One such animation that foregrounds music to great effect is *#01* (1996) by Chang Tze Hin 蔣子軒, also known as Siu Hak 小克. Siu Hak's graduation film from the Hong Kong Polytechnic University in 1996 was also selected for that year's IFVA awards. The impressively rendered 3D animation, set to Dvořák's "Songs My Mother Taught Me," portrays a science-fiction world populated by intelligent insects, some of whom are setting off on a space voyage (fig. 14.3).

Siu Hak writes that he was inspired by the inscrutability of insects, in particular one large moth that lay motionless on his wall for many hours.[26] The animation comprises a series of slow, panoramic shots, creating the

26. Chang Tze Hin, "#01," in *2nd Independent Short Film and Video Awards Catalogue* (Hong Kong: Hong Kong Arts Centre, 1996), 32.

poignant and sombre mood of the enigmatic insect world the animation portrays. Its style plays to the strengths of early 3D animation: its portrayal of expansive virtual space and use of camera movements suggests the potential of digital world-building and its nonhuman characters gloss over the shortcomings of 3D animation of that time for rendering organic forms or believable characters.

Despite its technical strengths, the fragmentary structure and at times loose relationship between music and visuals led to this animation, once again, dividing the jury at the IFVA:

> [Neco] Lo: Does anyone want to talk about *#01*? I like it very much.
> Ku [Chiu Ping]: What does the author want to tell?
> Lo: I have no idea, but it is quite interesting.
> . . . .
> Ku: The author deliberately puts fragments together, but the technique is wonderful!
> Wong [Ain Ling]: The idea of *#01* is interesting but the music does not help to enhance it.
> Lo: I find the pace quite matched. You can say the author is lazy, but the overall combination is okay.[27]

The jury conceded that the story is secondary to its technique and its skillful assembly of fragments, but was undecided on the suitability of the music. In fact, Siu Hak later repurposed the animation as part of Eason Chan's upbeat 2001 music video for his song "2001 Space Odyssey." In this music video, the animation is intercut with shots of the singer and dancers. The recut of the animated sequences and the change of the accompanying music totally alters the mood and rhythm of the animation, demonstrating the creative versatility of young digital animators in Hong Kong. Siu Hak went on to become a successful creative practitioner still active in the Hong Kong music industry.

27. Au Yeung et al., "Panel Discussion," in *2nd Independent Short Film and Video Awards Catalogue*, 110.

Conclusion

Whether operating in the realms of commercial animation, advertising, fine arts, or music, Hong Kong independent animators demonstrate an agile and multifaceted creativity. Although the later successes of independent or experimental animators should not be a litmus test for the significance of their early work, all the animators whose work is discussed here remain active in diverse creative industries. The achievements of Hong Kong animators working transnationally, such as Raman Hui, place Hong Kong at the forefront of the digital turn in animation globally. Meanwhile, animators who remained in Hong Kong used a variety of avenues, from merchandising to fine arts installation, to leave their mark on the physical cityscape as well as their own virtual spaces.

That said, despite these success stories, animation—and especially independent animation—remains a precarious creative occupation. The adaptability of Hong Kong's animators is in some part necessitated by this harsh reality, also experienced by practitioners in adjacent new media areas like video art.[28] Independent animation is a valuable space for animators to hone their creativity and skills in a variety of disciplines. It allows animators to explore complex subject matter that might be difficult or impossible to express using live-action methods or conventional narration.

For younger animators (such as myself) who have only ever worked in a digital setting, it is eye-opening to realize the extent to which digital technologies revolutionized animation. In Hong Kong, where independent animation production was often an uphill struggle, the digital turn was particularly transformative. Animateurs such as Toe Yuen and Raman Hui used animation as a testing ground for new animation styles and techniques, whereas others such as Hung Keung used new media to explore Hong Kong's political preoccupations from an intensely personal perspective. They were able to use digital methods to create works that were agile across media boundaries, sharing their animations with audiences in Hong Kong and beyond.

28. Fan, "The Time It Takes," 135–40.

FIFTEEN

Expanding Notions of Diasporic Chineseness

Toward a Singaporean Approach to VR

Hannes Rall and Emma Harper

At first glance, the decision to discuss Singapore in a book focused on Chinese animation seems relatively straightforward. Singapore is a country with a majority ethnically Chinese population—around 75 percent of residents as of 2020—and more than 30 percent of the total population speak Mandarin at home. Festivals at Lunar New Year, Qing Ming, and Mid-Autumn are widely celebrated, and Chinese-language free-to-view television channels showing local and imported content are popular.[1] However, even a cursory glance into the country's culture, and its animation industry specifically, demonstrates that any attempt to understand its artistic outputs requires an expanded concept of Chinese identity.

Scholars have interrogated the highly complex notion of Singaporean Chineseness, highlighting how the ethnically Chinese diaspora has drawn upon, or distinguished themselves from, geographical China at particular points, including in terms of artistic practices.[2] Today, Singapore's national

1. For details, see Media Development Authority Singapore, *Annual Report 2015/16*, https://www.imda.gov.sg/-/media/imda/files/about/mda-ar-2016/annex.html; Department of Statistics Singapore, "Key Indicators of Resident Population," Census of Population 2020, https://www.singstat.gov.sg/-/media/files/publications/cop2020/sr1/keyindicators.ashx.

2. For examples of such discussions, see Ng Sze Hian, "Dissecting the Singaporean Chinese Identity: After the Diaspora," *Global-is-asian*, September 1, 2020, https://lkyspp.nus.edu.sg/gia/article/dissecting-the-singaporean-chinese-identity-after-the-diaspora;

identity is distinctly multicultural—the country prides itself on its racially harmonious society and has close historical, cultural, and social ties to other Southeast Asian nations as well as a global outlook that reflects its position as a leading world financial center.[3]

The country's animation tradition is thus uniquely poised to draw on a range of influences drawn from this diverse cultural context, and the industry's relative youth has set the tone for innovation and experimentation in recent years. Recent noncommercial productions have begun to develop a distinctly Singaporean animation style, featuring local settings and dealing with issues related to contemporary identity, particularly the idea of community focused around HDB (public housing) estates.[4] Productions have also looked to artistic traditions as sources of creative inspiration—acknowledging the culture and heritage of Southeast Asia as well as a position within a broader framework that includes Chinese traditions of ink painting and papercutting, and the visual approach of Western artists including the German animator Lotte Reiniger.[5] Through a mix of traditional and digital techniques, animations produced in Singapore

---

Ashton Ng, "The Divisiveness of Chinese Identities in Singapore," *International Communication of Chinese Culture* 8 (2021): 465–81.

3. SG101, "Building a Multicultural Singapore," https://www.sg101.gov.sg/social-national-identity/multicultural/. We the authors are well aware that the concept of Singaporean identity is a much debated subject across the humanities and particularly in the social sciences. Arguably, the cultural identity of Singapore cannot really be understood as a generally fixed or ultimately defined term. We therefore treat this discussion in general terms, drawing on statistics that reflect the multicultural reality of Singapore's society, quoting from related discussions in the wider humanities whenever an animation-specific argument requires corresponding support.

4. As discussed in Qing Sheng Ang, "Infusing Local Culture in Singaporean Animation: Developing a Framework of Cultural Specifics from a Study of Contemporary Cinema in Singapore," *Animation Practice, Process & Production* 7, no. 1 (2018): 118. The term *HDB* refers to public housing built and managed by the Singapore government via the Housing Development Board. More than 80 percent of the population live in such public housing. See Singapore Housing & Development Board, "Public Housing—A Singapore Icon," https://www.hdb.gov.sg/about-us/our-role/public-housing-a-singapore-icon.

5. Hans-Martin Rall and Bernhard Schmitt, "Tradigital Shadows: Southeast Asian Silhouette Animation in the Twenty-first Century," in *Beyond Prince Achmed: New Perspectives on Animation Pioneer Lotte Reiniger*, ed. Rada Bieberstein (Marburg: Schüren Verlag, 2021), 299–325.

combine these influences to create something new, integrating the visual forms of their creators' personal cultural heritage within the framework of global animation history.

Scholarship has begun to investigate the connections between Singapore's cultural heritage and traditional screen-based animation.[6] A field that has been significantly underresearched within this wider cultural context is the emergence of expanded animation, that is, the development of fully immersive animation in virtual reality. This defines the research gap we address in this chapter.

Our approach to this broader issue has seen us combine traditional scholarly research into Singaporean cultural traditions with creative production to produce a virtual reality (VR) adaptation of Singapore's founding myth Sang Nila Utama in the style of shadow puppet play (Wayang Kulit). Although wayang puppet performance has its origins in Malaysia and Indonesia, the style can be seen as a prototypic example of the synergy of these influences on Chineseness in Singapore. As Perris notes, "in the polyglot city-state of Singapore, Chinese opera is called wayang, a Malay and Indonesian word for theatre, as in Wayang Kulit. . . . The term as used in Singapore is a solitary mark of the indigenous culture on the Chinese theatre in this Chinese-dominated nation."[7] Indeed, despite *wayang* being a Javanese term, shadow puppet play is also a long-standing part of traditional Chinese culture, reportedly from the eleventh century CE.[8] Furthermore, our research demonstrated that within Singapore, traditional Indonesian and Malaysian wayang forms have taken on unique, hybrid elements that reflect the contemporary realities of both performers and audiences. Above all, this attests to the fleeting boundaries between the diverse local cultures and their permeability as a premise for artistic creation, carrying relevance beyond the specific art form as a negotiation of how traditional regional art forms are being transformed in modern digital media.

6. See, for example, Ang, "Infusing Local Culture"; John Lui, "Time to Make an Animated Feature with Singapore DNA," *Straits Times*, April 22, 2021, https://www.straitstimes.com/life/entertainment/time-to-make-an-animated-feature-with-singapore-dna.

7. Arnold Perris, "Chinese Wayang: The Survival of Chinese Opera in the Streets of Singapore," *Ethnomusicology* 22, no. 2 (1978): 297.

8. Inge C. Orr, "Puppet Theatre in Asia," *Asian Folklore Studies* 33, no. 1 (1974): 69.

Our approach to creating a VR adaptation of a Wayang Kulit performance as a case study through which to explore the construction of a distinctly Singaporean form of expanded animation was led by several research questions: How can the underlying values, traditions, and cultural properties of Wayang Kulit in Singapore be preserved in an adaptation for immersive media? How can the tradition and techniques of animated silhouette films inform the fully immersive adaptation without compromising the tradition of the art form? What is the cultural and aesthetic impact of Singaporean Chinese animators collaborating in transcultural adaptation of local art styles in VR? Can a Singaporean style of Wayang Kulit emerge and what should it look like?

Within our discussion, we take a closer look at the specifics of our transcultural collaboration between young Singaporean Chinese and Malay artists working across performance, technical development, and creative design. The setup for our case study—within a framework of local and international research scholars—echoes the cosmopolitan environment of Singapore itself. We aim to provide transparency on how this culturally diverse teamwork is a representation of the idea of Singaporean identity that demonstrates unity through diversity, as well as situating our project within the broader context of animation—specifically expanded animation—production in Singapore.

Singaporean Animation: Historical Context and Cultural Representation

To address our research interests in cultural representation and national identity, it is necessary to begin with a short overview of Singapore's more recent animation history. During the 1990s, the government focused on attracting foreign investment, which included the development of the animation industry as part of efforts to establish the country as a high-tech hub.[9] However, as Singapore's animation scene has developed, observers have increasingly raised questions of local identity in animated

9. Gigi Hu, "Animation in Singapore," *Animation World Magazine* 1, no. 11 (1997): 32; John A. Lent, "The 'Sleeper' Status of Southeast Asian Animation," *Jurnal Komunikasi: Malaysian Journal of Communication* 20 (2004): 189.

films in terms of both design and narrative. The difficulty of defining a Singaporean animation is captured by local animator Wei Choon Goh. In an interview with animator and researcher Qing Sheng Ang, he explained it this way:

> A film can be "Singaporean" when it is about Singapore, made in Singapore, or made by a Singaporean. The term "Singaporean" is already a tricky one to maintain because Singapore could either deal strictly with the geopolitical boundaries that defines the nation, or it could deal anthropologically or culturally with the people who live in Singapore.[10]

Fewer than five animated feature films have been produced in Singapore, and "there is no apparent Singaporean trait present in them."[11] However, when a distinct local flavor is brought into visual design and narrative in independent animated short films—such as *Flats* (2011), *Foreign Plants* (2013), and *Lak Boh Ki* (2016)—several key trends can be identified. The first stresses multiculturalism and racial harmony—different groups living and working together. Another relates to the setting and environments featured in the animations—HDB estates, schools, and hawker centers function as recognizable symbols of the Singaporean landscape that facilitate the development of shared community experiences.

An alternative way in which a distinctive Singaporean identity is shown within the animation tradition is the incorporation of art styles that are culturally relevant to Singapore. The overlap between traditional arts and the multicultural environment of Singapore has recently been shown in the artistic animated short films *The Animals* (2014) and *Hair* (2019), created by young Singaporean Chinese animators Mark Wee and Caroline Ching/Ng Zhi Xin respectively. Although their foremost inspiration might have been the work of famed animation pioneer Lotte Reiniger and her classic *The Adventures of Prince Achmed* (1926), the classic artist's own well-documented reference to both Chinese traditions and Southeast Asian wayang shadow puppet play brings things full circle: these comparatively current artistic animations renegotiate the history of animation inspired by Southeast Asian shadow puppet play through a

10. Ang, "Infusing Local Culture," 135.
11. Ang, "Infusing Local Culture," 114.

Chinese Singaporean lens.[12] The film *Si Lunchai* (2014), by Hannes Rall, this chapter's first author, was his first foray into merging traditions of local shadow puppet play Wayang Kulit with the style of silhouette animation as established by Reiniger, a further example of the development of an approach to animation in Singapore drawing on elements from diverse Western and Asian artistic and performance traditions, conceptualized and developed by a project team from a range of ethnicities and nationalities in a way that can be considered uniquely Singaporean.

Although much remains at a crossroads in many aspects, the recent generation of younger filmmakers, emerging from a variety of local university programs, have energetically steered developments toward more uniquely Singaporean styles in animation. However, given its more recent origin, since roughly the 2010s, the history of fully immersive animation presents a somewhat different picture.

Fully Immersive Animation in Singapore: An Overview

Within the field of immersive media, searching for discussions of a distinctly Singaporean animation style is challenging. The government's Infocomm Media Development Authority has prioritized immersive media as one of the country's four fundamental technology frontiers, however, discussions of the role of VR and augmented reality have predominantly been motivated by industrial or commercial concerns, rather than focusing on artistic production.[13]

12. For a discussion of the relationship between Reiniger, traditional Asian puppetry, and contemporary artistic traditions, see Alfio Bastianchich, "Lotte Reiniger: An Interview with Alfio Bastianchich," in *Women and Animation: A Compendium*, ed. Jayne Pilling (London: BFI, 1992), 9; Yan Soon Lim, "Wayang Kulit and Its Influence on Modern Entertainment," in *Proceedings of MediAsia 2017* (Nagoya: IAFOR, 2017), 113, http://papers.iafor.org/wp-content/uploads/conference-proceedings/MediAsia/MediAsia2017_proceedings.pdf.

13. For an outline of the government's stance on such technologies, see Singapore Infocomm Media Development Agency, "Immersive Media," December 1, 2022, https://www.imda.gov.sg/About-IMDA/infocomm-media-landscape/SGDigital/tech-pillars/Immersive-Media. For an example of scholarly work on Singapore's industrial/commercial approach to VR, see Athirah Syamimi, Yiwei Gong, and Ryan Liew, "VR Industrial Applications: A Singapore perspective," *Virtual Reality & Intelligent Hardware* 2, no. 5 (2020): 409–20.

Despite several examples of VR being used by Singaporean museums, engaging with the broad subject matter of local culture, these experiences do not use animation as their mediation but instead rely on captured images (live action). The failure of such tours and exhibitions to bring together animation and engagement with local heritage is notable.[14] When animated VR projects do exist, it can be debated to what extent they can be considered distinctly Singaporean in style or narrative. Projects such as Mags Studios' scenario-based game *SMU Mind the Drone, which was designed to allow local students to apply the Law of Torts in a case study in an animated immersive environment, are not deeply embedded in the context of contemporary Singapore.[15] Except for a brief allusion to the skyline of the city's central business district, the visual style and narrative fail to more profoundly reflect something distinctly Singaporean.

Some very recent projects have brought together immersive animation with distinctly Singaporean themes and narratives, and perhaps set the scene for future experimentation—notably drawing on the opportunities offered by the realm of the Metaverse. This includes a virtual National Day concert produced by local designers at Pen & Paper Studios with ESPL, and the projects M Social Decentraland and the 2022 National Day Parade Metaverse, which mark collaborations between animation studios and commercial and governmental partners.[16] Developed by Singapore's

14. For details of these initiatives, see Pameyla Chan, "You Can Now Take a Virtual Tour of the Asian Civilizations Museum," *Lifestyle Asia*, June 5, 2020, https://www.lifestyleasia.com/sg/culture/asian-civilisations-museum-virtual-programmes; Art Science Museum Marina Bay Sands, "VR Gallery," https://www.marinabaysands.com/museum/exhibitions/vr-gallery.html; National Museum of Singapore, "DigiMuse Presents: Virtual Showcase," February 2018, https://www.roots.gov.sg/stories-landing/stories/digimuse-presents.

15. For an outline of this project, see Singapore Management University, "Mind the Drone," https://cte.smu.edu.sg/project/mind-drone.

16. For details, see Pen & Paper Studios, "It's been awhile folks," Facebook, August 20, 2021, https://www.facebook.com/penandpaperstudios/posts/pfbid0327AYfsSKUazMnbzd4CWyHs2SBgw421aKkmHhBmwbHy3ueaYqR5uEcHas34CbKbLRl; Finute, "Finute Creates National Day Parade Metaverse," September 17, 2022, https://finute.co/blog/finute-develops-national-day-parade-ndp-metaverse; Singapore Tourism Board, "Merlion's Virtual Vacation at M Social Decentraland Marks STB's Foray into the Metaverse," https://www.stb.gov.sg/content/stb/en/media-centre/media-releases/MERLION-VIRTUAL-VACATION-AT-M-SOCIAL-DECENTRALAND-MARKS-STB-FORAY-INTO-THE-METAVERSE.html, November 21, 2022.

self-labeled leading Metaverse-company Finute, the National Parade Metaverse allowed users to engage with the environment by exploring "a metaverse-rendition of Singapore—drive an armoured vehicle, perform free-fall as a Red Lion, fly an F16 aircraft, wear different uniforms from the SAF and Home Team, and so much more!"[17] The project is distinctly Singaporean in its references—relating to the country's National Day celebrations and a shared military identity facilitated by compulsory national service.

The production positively stands out because it takes great effort to represent Singapore as a whole, and gained major attention as an integral part of the 2022 National Day Parade campaign. Unlike the Decentraland project, which appears to anonymize the animators at the expense of the commercial partner, the project involves a local animation studio and acknowledges their role in the production. Highly stylized CG characters engage with the virtual cityscape that is, in contrast, designed rather realistically, accurately representing its real-life counterpart. However, although very competently and artistically designed, the chosen stylistic iteration does not particularly reflect local art styles or cultural heritage through corresponding design choices. Perhaps this rather neutral style was chosen to create a universality that did not appeal to one group over others, or to create relevance for an audience more familiar with international animation styles seen in games or films popular in the country.

In summary, the use of animation in fully immersive virtual environments is mostly limited to commissioned work in Singapore. Although recent examples have begun to experiment with Singaporean themes and characters to engage local audiences, commissions rarely require a deeper engagement with Singapore's rich and multicultural heritage, and instead are Singaporean having been produced in Singapore, or using internationally recognizable symbols of Singapore such as the CBD and Merlion. Topical investigations into animated VR are more confined to the state-funded research of educational institutions such as Singaporean universities. Perhaps the reason for that is obvious: VR has still not reached the point of maturity where a clear model of commercial exploitation has emerged that equals the monetization options for traditional screen-based media. A strictly heritage- or culture-oriented topicality lends itself

17. Finute, "Finute creates."

much less easily to any profitability and strictly story-based entertainment lacks the distribution channels to make costly production feasible. With this bigger picture in mind, the aim of our project was to reach beyond a merely theoretical engagement with the concept of Singaporean identity within an expanded animated environment and to practically explore a more distinctly Singaporean artistic expression in VR. Building—but also expanding—on previous experiences of adapting Wayang Kulit for single screen-based animation, we conceived a practice-led research concept, free from commercial considerations, to produce an adaptation of the story of Sang Nila Utama as fully immersive animation in VR.

Adapting Sang Nila Utama for Animated VR: A Case Study

Our project, Transforming Singaporean Wayang Kulit for Virtual Reality, funded by Singapore's National Arts Council, was completed in January 2023. The reasons for selecting this project as the case study for this discussion are multifold. One, the direct involvement of the authors in the process of creative production allows for direct and fully verifiable insights into the iterative design process and its implementation in animation and technology. Second, the framing of the project as an academic research project rather than a commercial endeavor enables a critical perspective provided by the constant dialogue between theory and practice.

Why Sang Nila Utama?

The seventeenth-century Sulalat al-Salatin, better known as Sejarah Melayu or Malay Annals, holds an important place in Singaporean collective memory. Its first six chapters provide a mythical narrative of the port-polity of Singapura and its position within the larger Malay world in the late thirteenth and fourteenth centuries.[18]

18. Derek Heng, "Sang Nila Utama: Separating Myth from Reality," *biblioasia* 16, no. 2 (2020): 59.

FIGURE 15.1. Statue of Sang Nila Utama temporarily erected at the Raffles Landing Site, Singapore, 2019. Courtesy of Daniel_Ferryanto/Shutterstock.com.

The text mentions a number of characters. Looming largest in the Singaporean imagination is Sang Nila Utama, a semi-mythical prince of Palembang.[19] Through schooling and wider public heritage initiatives—such as his inclusion within a set of statues erected as part of Singapore's 2019 bicentennial commemorations (fig. 15.1)—Singaporeans of all ages and races are familiar with the story of how Sang Nila's sighting of a lion led to the renaming of Temasek to Singapura (City of the Lion in Sanskrit), a significant moment in the heritage and identity of the modern city-state.[20]

19. Heng, "Sang Nila Utama," 59-62.
20. Heng, "Sang Nila Utama," 59.

Multicultural Representation and Uniquely Singaporean Expression

The work on this project was carried out in collaboration with a highly diverse interdisciplinary team of animators, academic researchers, and performers—including three young Singapore Chinese designers and animators, a Singapore Malay artistic technological expert, and Singapore-based researchers with origins in Europe, New Zealand, and the United States. The project also involved close collaboration with local wayang performance groups, whose performance traditions reflect the members' cultural origins in the Indonesian island of Java and the Malaysian state of Kelantan. Together, the team reflects the diverse, multicultural nature of Singaporean society.

Rather than presenting our work purely as a digital adaptation of a traditional Southeast Asian performance form, we highlight how the project can be considered a case study for the creative diversity within the broader Chinese-speaking world. It also demonstrates how design and narrative decisions drawing on Singapore's cultural diversity made within the context of VR can be considered part of an attempt to create a novel virtual experience that can be considered distinctly Singaporean in both its visual forms and storytelling methods—indebted to Chinese, Southeast Asian, and global trends yet distinctive in its approach, much like Singapore itself.

Toward a Singaporean Wayang Kulit: An Amalgamation of Styles

Wayang Kulit shadow puppet performance has erroneously been described as a vanished art in Singapore when in fact today the country is home to several performance groups working to revive the tradition for twenty-first-century audiences.[21] At the core of the project was a desire to engage with those knowledgeable about contemporary Wayang Kulit in Singapore to gain an insight into their practice within their local context,

21. Rohaniah Saini, "*Wayang Kulit* Enjoys Brief Revival at Malay Village," *Straits Times*, March 10, 1990.

as well as to gauge their responses to adapting a traditional performance art to a modern media form. To this end, our research and design process was built around a series of semi-structured interviews and feedback sessions with members of Singaporean Wayang Kulit performance groups Sri Warisan, Ethnic Shadows, and Sri Setia Pulau Singa. At every stage of the process, academic research, creative design, and practical insights from performers were closely integrated.

An important finding was the existence of two distinct performance traditions within the Singapore wayang scene. Sri Setia and Ethnic Shadows follow the Kelantanese Wayang Kulit tradition, which draws its creative influence from Kelantan in northeastern Malaysia and neighboring parts of Thailand. Sri Warisan follows the tradition of Javanese Wayang Kulit purwa. Javanese and Kelantanese wayang differ in their use of music, lighting, and above all puppet design. An important negotiation was therefore required between the two traditions and their related yet distinct cultural forms. Rather than choosing to align ourselves with a particular tradition, we chose to take an approach that brought the two together—again rooted in the broader context of Singapore and a desire to reflect its cultural diversity and position as a site for the creation of new traditions through interaction. Members of both groups were enthusiastic about this suggestion—embracing the potential of VR to create something original that reflected the reality of the living performance tradition in contemporary Singapore.

Designers Lye Hui En and Rachel Chan thus created a design style that fused influences from these two traditions mediated through their identity as Chinese Singaporeans. Initial designs for puppets taken directly from Kelantanese and Javanese traditions were brought together to create a character line-up that incorporated performers' shared concerns. Both traditions acknowledge, for example, the importance of bracelets and tall crowns as indications of status, so we worked to incorporate these elements into our design of the Prince Sang Nila Utama (fig. 15.2). Because neither tradition makes use of a lion puppet, designers were able to express their own artistic style when designing this asset, referencing the Kelantanese custom of puppets often having their tongues on display, and the importance of intricate detailing in both traditions.

Character animation was handled by another Chinese Singaporean,

FIGURE 15.2. Character line-up for puppet designs. Courtesy of designer Lye Hui En and Nanyang Technological University, Singapore.

Gelissa Loh. After consultation across the team and with performers, an approach was chosen that balances the character mobility achievable through full animation with the limited movement options of physical puppets. After completing the animation sequences, they were passed to Singaporean artistic technological expert Sulaiman Bin Abdul Rahman to model within the virtual production hub Unreal Engine (fig. 15.3).

Relative to previous adaptations of Asian shadow puppet play for silhouette animation, our VR experience more closely resembles staging for a real audience. Our goal was to expand the motion capabilities of our characters for the telling of a linear story—but also preserve the illusion of a play delivered by invisible puppeteers (*dalangs*).

This means that a movement like drawing a bow was fully animated, whereas characters dangle their feet instead of walking when they move—resembling the look of traditional wayang puppets when manipulated by a puppeteer.

To further enhance the impression of an elevated traditional performance, we also shot live-action footage of a dalang interacting with the narrative at one point in the story. Although puppeteers are typically not visible, he jumps into the virtual performance space at a moment when a puppet has fallen, picking him up again to enable the continuation of the play (fig. 15.4).

The puppeteer was first shot on high-definition video in 2D against a green screen. Subsequently, this flat image was placed into the fully immersive 3D environment in Unreal Game Engine on a billboard. We decided on this workaround to address the technological challenges of

FIGURE 15.3. A frame from the story of Sang Nila Utama shown within a virtual environment. Courtesy of Rachel Chan, Lye Hui En, Gelissa Loh, and Nanyang Technological University, Singapore.

FIGURE 15.4. Mr Mohammed Yahya Bin Haron of Sri Setia Pulau Singa as *dalang* within a virtual environment. Courtesy of Sulaiman Bin Abdul Rahman and Nanyang Technological University, Singapore.

achieving a full 3D capture and subsequent fully dimensional integration into Unreal. Moreover, we were not aiming for a photorealistic result but welcomed stylization into a 2.5D character as part of our cohesive design vision. Surprisingly, when augmented by environmental lighting and color grading, the outcome looks quite believable—the illusion of a full spatial integration broken only in extreme profile view.

To summarize, the creative production process was in many ways a reflection of Singaporean society itself: bringing together ethnically diverse artists and researchers in pursuit of a unifying outcome, drawing on cooperation spanning multiple cultural traditions and specialisms motivated by the shared desire to develop a new digital vision of a traditional art form representative of Singapore's heritage.

Conclusion and Outlook

It is hoped that our project marks an important step in the discussion of adapting Wayang Kulit for VR, as well as raising questions regarding future directions for the creation of Singaporean expanded animation. We argue that, in both cases, cultural values must inform narrative choices, aesthetics, design style, and technical implementation. In creating a fully playable VR narrative, we have shown how the cultural properties of a specific traditional art form with close links to Singapore can be respectfully adapted for new technology.

Our scholarly and artistic investigation into what could define a particularly Singaporean version of digital Wayang Kulit performance integrates Malaysian and Indonesian influences but also reflects the strong representation of Chinese culture through the lead role played by Singaporean Chinese animators and illustrators during the design process. It situates these discussions within the wider framework of Singaporean animation and a call by researchers to theorize and create a culturally Singaporean approach to animation. This fusion of cultures and traditions, together with the adoption of a narrative closely tied to the heritage of Singapore, places our project within a distinctly local context—shaped by, yet distinct from, the different influences drawn upon. Arguably, our process could also be seen as a reflection of the wider understanding of Chineseness in Singapore that transcends traditional cultural barriers versus a wider understanding as Singapore citizens first and foremost—indebted to yet distinct from China itself. Therefore, we posit that our project very much echoes the multiplicities found within the multicultural environment of Singapore itself because it combines influences from distinct strands of local cultures through artistic collaboration.

This understanding also aligns with the refusal of younger Singaporean Chinese artists to be confined to the replication of traditional Chinese art styles and their embrace of multicultural collaboration. Younger artists in particular see the cosmopolitan environment of Singapore as an integral part of their cultural DNA: this is a sentiment that Hannes Rall has heard from many of his local students in his eighteen years teaching animation in Singapore. Director Ervin Han previously described his desire to produce "something like an anthology of local short stories showcasing facets of Singapore," evoking an implicit acknowledgment of the multiplicities that need to be engaged with alongside each other to truly understand what it is to be Singaporean.[22] A particular personal conversation provides further anecdotal evidence: when questioned by an external (Western) reviewer why his designs for an animated dragon didn't resemble traditional Chinese forms, a Singaporean Chinese student answered that he understands global artistic influences as an integral part of his Singaporean identity—his Chinese ethnicity did not limit him to drawing on traditional Chinese artistic approaches. It is in the fusion of previously unconnected cultural heritage and the combination of Western and Eastern influences where often the most captivating contemporary art emerges, and it is perhaps in this tradition that Singaporean expanded animation should strive to develop.

22. Ang, "Infusing Local Culture," 132.

AFTERWORD

Lessons from Japanese Animation Studies

On the Future Directions of Chinese Animation Studies

Alexander Zahlten

First, and not unexpectedly, it is important to relativize key terms in the title of this chapter. For one, "Japanese animation studies" as a field does not really exist, or maybe instead it shouldn't. From the problem of implying a specific kind of coherence via the qualifier "Japanese" to animation associated with Japan (and its study), to the tenuous and rapidly collapsing definition of animation as a stable, recognizable media form, the designation is mainly a condensed expression of problematic assumptions. As we will see, these qualifications apply to Chinese animation studies as well, if in slightly different ways. But most of all, the aspiration of drawing lessons from Japanese animation studies for the benefit of this still-emerging field of study needs to be questioned, as that implies a quest toward charting a smooth(er) path. At the same time, the categories implemented via these field names are in use and have real force. How then, to make them useful? Maybe the most interesting and emphatically useful thing about both Japanese animation studies and Chinese animation studies is the many questions they raise and how these questions work against establishing what we might call a smooth field of inquiry.[1] At their most

1. To briefly explain the use of terms here, I use *Chinese animation studies* and *Japanese animation studies* to refer to the existing or forming institutionalized or institutionalizing fields in all their problematic dynamics; the clunky term *animation associated with Japan* refers to the (in practice) object of study of Japanese animation studies, but is meant to avoid designating it as *Japanese*, and to avoid all of the assumptions and erasures that go along with such a designation.

productive these designations and their too openly problematic assumptions become obviously, visibly, untenable and thereby unsettling.

A thickening network of scholars interested in using Chinese animation as a vehicle for asking important questions as it has begun to take shape over the last ten years can, then, better understand the possible matrix of questions and probable tensions, pressures, and epistemological traps by surveying the way these manifest or have manifested in the study of animation associated with Japan. However, Chinese animation study should not just unsettle itself, or use "lessons" learned from the study of animation associated with Japan to unsettle itself. It should actively dialogue with and unsettle the study of animation associated with Japan as well, just as it should vigorously unsettle animation studies "proper." If that is not part of the agenda from the beginning, any lessons will tend to reinforce ideas of sequence and linear development based on modernization or colonial models. In such a case, a strange doubling would take place: the anxiety about origins, influences, and trailing-behind that arguably haunts Chinese media industries and animation in the People's Republic of China (PRC) in particular will potentially be shadowed by Chinese animation studies supposedly trailing Japanese animation studies. A productive exchange and mutual unsettling of basic assumptions and frameworks will support destabilizing linear, sequential, and ultimately essentializing national framework-focused models.

In the following, I provisionally sketch several intersecting discursive contexts or backgrounds that have shaped how inquiries in the study of animation associated with Japan so far have taken shape. Centrally, these include disciplinary, national, economic, and governmental dynamics. All of these partially overlap and also traverse the methodologies, spotlights, and ultimately questions that have shaped the respective inquiries. This chapter attempts a loose mapping of the ways these lines, forces, and pressures have intersected in the case of Japanese animation studies. This will allow some speculation about the unsettling potential of Chinese animation studies, but also the potential to unsettle *it* in real time as it fully emerges and, in advance.

First, then, is the question of discipline. It is no secret that the study of animation associated with Japan has, in English-language work, been largely caught between area studies and animation studies. In Europe and in East Asia, the situation is a bit less clearly structured. The area studies–

animation studies tension has been complicated by the fact that the vast majority of work looking at animation "from Japan" has focused on what has, often in a rather loose way, been called anime.[2] The mix of centrality to the field and a looseness of the definition of the category of anime creates inconsistencies that can provide for illuminating complications. There are departures from the study of anime in the narrow sense: some work has focused on animation forms that in a more rigorous framework would not fall under anime, such as feature film-length art animation ascribed to individual auteurs; Ghibli films are commonly discussed as anime even as much has been written about Miyazaki Hayao's vigorous protest against being included under that category (which naturally is not necessarily a reason to exclude his films from the category). In Japanese-language scholarship as well, anime has variably been used as a historically highly situated form of animation tied to specific aesthetics or production and distribution practices as much as a metonym for Japanese animation, though here a different set of disciplinary dynamics is at play. Such definitional questions aside, disciplinarily speaking, at least in English, a third way has begun to open up. Hinging on its foundational connection to media mix dynamics, anime is understood to be exceptionally connective and to provide important possibilities for better understanding contemporary media dynamics and rethinking issues of nation, region, and so on. The result has been an emerging body of media studies-inflected scholarship that often self-consciously discusses the trappings of the area-animation-media dynamic, and how media studies–type approaches provide some leeway (if adjusted properly) for negotiating those trappings.[3]

The issues associated with area studies approaches have been much discussed and outlined but, being based in long institutional and disci-

2. For an in-depth discussion of that question, and of how to understand the category of anime, see Jacqueline Berndt, "Anime in Academia: Representative Object, Media Form, and Japanese Studies," *Arts* 7, no. 56 (2018): 1–13.

3. Consider especially Thomas Lamarre's discussion of such issues. Although it is not primarily about anime, see, for example, Thomas Lamarre, "Platformativity: Media Studies, Area Studies," *Asiascape: Digital Asia* 4 (2017): 285–305. For one of the most thorough arguments against applying a national framework to anime, see Stevie Suan, *Anime's Identity: Performativity and Form beyond Japan* (Minneapolis: University of Minnesota Press, 2021).

plinary histories, they persist nonetheless.[4] In the study of anime in particular, this has resulted in a strange tension because anime is profoundly networked across borders—maybe even a paradigmatic media form in this regard—but discussed predominantly within Japanese studies. Scholarship in the field has long pointed out anime's networked dynamics but remains stuck in this force field. This becomes an especially visible tension when the research centers around anime. If anime (according to Otsuka Eiji in an intervention against the understanding of anime as essentially "Japanese" in the domestic discourse on anime) is in its aesthetics the result of a fusion of Eisensteinian montage, Disney character design, and wartime fascism, it has also been understood as from its earliest stages deeply invested in media mix dynamics.[5] The animation industry in Japan from the late 1960s onward becomes fundamentally entangled with outsourcing across national borders, both in its work for U.S. animation industries and in its own outsourcing practices to East and Southeast Asia. In addition, its near-global circulation and reception as well make anime a most unlikely candidate for an almost exclusive identification as Japanese. Yet in practice, it has by and large continued to fulfill that role, be it for scholars (despite the now frequent disavowals), audiences, or policymakers. This is partly due to anime's self-marketing as a national brand, supported by the state in the wake of the government's Cool Japan policies from the early 2000s onward. Another significant factor is that Japanese area studies became the main site of the production of scholarship on anime, creating additional systemic pressure in that direction, with government institutions such as the Japan Foundation a common source of funding for research and academic conferences focusing on popular culture from Japan.

4. For a recent special journal issue that repeats and extends arguments that have been made since the 1990s, see Naoki Sakai and Gavin Walker, eds. *The End of Area*, special issue, *Positions: Asia Critique* 27, no. 1 (2019). For arguments made by Mitsuhiro Yoshimoto in the 1990s about these dynamics in film studies (arguably still not resolved) see Mitsuhiro Yoshimoto, "The Difficulty of Being Radical: The Discipline of Film Studies and the Postcolonial World Order," in *Japan in the World*, eds. Harry Harootunian and Masao Miyoshi, 242–57 (Durham, NC: Duke University Press, 1993).

5. A discussion kicked off in English by Marc Steinberg. See, for example, *Anime's Media Mix: Franchising Toys and Characters in Japan* (Minneapolis: University of Minnesota Press, 2012).

How applicable are these dynamics to a possible future Chinese animation studies? Will the same disciplinary boundaries delineate and hedge in the main approaches to Chinese animation? Will Chinese animation studies be published (in English) primarily from within area studies departments? Until animation from China achieves broad global success as a recognizable category that is likely the case; it will lead to a situation in which interactions with scholars in Chinese-language academic institutions will also have to be openly cross-disciplinary, given that animation is likely to be studied from within a broader set of disciplines there. If so, how will that inform the scholarship itself differently? Geopolitically, area studies of Japan is now more positioned to naturalize a transpacific alliance than the "know your enemy" position it inhabited as a legacy of World War II; indeed, postwar Japan studies in the United States arguably was meant to support exactly that transition. The drastically transforming global position of the PRC in the last decades puts Chinese area studies in a different and less straightforward position, as do the financial power of its media sector, the complication of the two Chinas, or the debates around categories such as the Sinophone. A location within area studies then does not by default mean a recourse to nation in the same way that Japan studies implies. In the best-case scenario, scholarship will not simply apply established methodologies and frameworks to slightly different geopolitical and economic circumstances, but instead use them to reimagine what the study of (Chinese) animation means. Petrus Liu has done as much when he outlined a vision of Marxism and Queer theory had they not developed on the basis of Euro-American power, but out of the situation of the two Chinas.[6] Will Chinese animation studies be a capable hinge for flipping naturalized assumptions and frameworks not only on their head but also in a variety of directions?

But although English-language scholarship, especially that from North America, problematically holds a position of formidable power in global academia, animation associated with Japan has nonetheless generated significant bodies of research in a variety of language contexts. At the same time, the domestic-international split in terms of the on-the-ground contexts for that research is severe. That split is likely to be reproduced in

6. See Petrus Liu, *Queer Marxism in Two Chinas* (Durham, NC: Duke University Press, 2015).

the case of Chinese animation studies, so its forms and consequences in the case of the study of animation associated with Japan may be instructive, within limits. It is nonetheless worth taking a closer look at. First, that split interacts with another binary of sorts. Roughly speaking, the study of animation associated with Japan has oscillated between theory and history, more or less corresponding to the tension between animation and media on the one side and area studies on the other. That said—and this shows the complication of mapping such a broad terrain—a certain portion of English-language scholarship is in Japan by now often perceived as more theoretically inclined, given that it has increasingly integrated larger conceptual waves of the humanities (with media studies, as mentioned, a growing presence). Recent issues of the "second arc" of *Mechademia*, a journal that was immensely formative for the early phase of the spread of the study of animation (especially anime), manga, and media mix associated with Japan reflect such broader trends: sound studies, queer studies, new materialism, media studies, and other frameworks are applied to the study of anime in particular. Anime, then, becomes a vehicle for further reproducing and refining such approaches, making anime the medium or media much like Jacqueline Berndt proposes it to be.[7] In Japan, then, the study of animation is often understood as comparably much more historically oriented, though here too recent work has integrated especially gender studies in rigorous and insightful ways.[8] This follows shifts within the field, in that the Japanese Society for Animation Studies was founded by scholars based in psychology or in film/literature studies. At the same time, especially the last decade has seen a shift in what scholarship from Japan is, as an increasing number of scholars raised in other contexts but trained in Japan make careers (also) in Japan and publish both in Japanese and in English, or Korean and Chinese, as do scholars raised in Japan but trained in institutions outside Japan, and based either in Japan or in other locations.

7. Berndt, "Anime in Academia."

8. See, for example, Ishida Minori 石田美紀, *Anime to seiyū no media-shi: Naze josei ga shōnen o enjiru no ka* アニメと声優のメディア史：なぜ女性が少年を演じるのか (A media history of anime voice actors: Why do women voice boy characters?) (Tokyo: Seikyūsha, 2020); Sugawa Akiko 須川亜紀子, *2.5 jigen bunka ron: Butai kyarakutā, fandamu* 2.5 次元文化論：舞台・キャラクター・ファンダム (Cultural theory of 2.5 dimensions: Stage, characters, fandom) (Tokyo: Seikyūsha, 2021).

In South Korea and the PRC, and to a lesser degree in Taiwan, government support for the study of media industries—in support of developing strong media industries and soft power—had considerable influence on the direction of scholarship. In tendency, industry studies and communications-inflected approaches are more prominent in these contexts than in Japanese- or English-language scholarship. This is not simply a methodological question; Korean- and Chinese-language work often has a communication studies inflection and focuses more on animation as one component in a larger media constellation. The abbreviation ACG for animation, comics, and games common in such work is a frequent marker of that thinking and takes a slightly different perspective than the more high theory-inclined media mix approaches in English. The resulting historical horizon emerging in the scholarship from these respective contexts shows the effects: in tendency, English-language scholarship can be said to be more present-focused in its aims, whereas Japanese-language scholarship is deeply committed to precise archival work (and interpreting its findings), and work in Korean and Chinese is more focused on concrete, very current and future developments, often focusing on larger industry developments.

The role of governments in shaping the conditions for both animation and for scholarship on animation is, however, not just prominent in East Asia, though that aspect has been especially well covered. Yet the effects have been quite different depending on the national context. The swell in government policies meant to support film and media industries that ensued from the late 1990s in East Asia, beginning in South Korea and emerging in full force with a simplified policy version of Joseph Nye's soft power framework as applied in the Cool Japan policies under the Koizumi government, then spreading to the PRC, Singapore, and so on, was actually fairly heterogeneous. South Korea proved most aggressive and effective in its policies, which included subsidizing setting up content-focused departments at universities as much as a range of support mechanisms for the larger film infrastructure (e.g., extensive support for film festivals). The Japanese government shied away from direct support and focused on legal adjustments to allow more flexibility in setting up media industry-focused funds or subsidizing elaborate content markets. These strategies were hampered by the fact that the majority of Japan's media industry initially remained resolutely focused on the domestic market, having only limited use for globally facing marketing events. The major exceptions were video games and anime. By the 2010s, distribution networks created by streaming supplied a strong legal distribution outlet for anime in the most lucrative markets, yet paradoxically built on a popularity that had been prepared by years of intensified pirating. Piracy, in fact, may be the single most important factor for anime's global success story. By 2020, after eight years of significant growth, foreign sales of anime accounted for more than 50 percent of the industry's total income. Central and South America together account for 16.9 percent of the anime industry's foreign sales, Europe for 21.8 percent, and Asia for 29.7 percent. Although the United States and Canada are the two largest single foreign national markets, North America actually accounts for only 5.7 percent of foreign anime sales. The relationship to the amount of scholarship produced on animation associated with Japan is interesting here. The numbers need to be treated with caution, but Manuel Hernández-Pérez found that scholars based in Japan have quantitatively speaking produced 27.6 percent of the scholarship on anime media mix between 1980 and 2018 (the largest contingent), with scholars based in the United States at second place with 23.3 percent. When the most influential journals indexed by platforms such as Scopus or Web of Science are counted, however, Hernández-Pérez finds that the vast majority is published in English and only 0.8 percent in Japanese.[9]

The PRC government also put hope in growing the media sector and making it a globally attractive product even though it arguably can rely on the domestic market even more than Japan's media industry can. Supporting scholarship on the media sector is an important part of this strategy. At this point, the building of a globally successful brand has remained largely unsuccessful in that endeavor on the level of content, though platforms such as Bilibili or Tik Tok, or select games such as Genshin Impact blazed through global markets in the 2010s. The partial exception, however, has been animation, producing a number of globally circulating successes since the late 2000s.

9. Manuel Hernández-Pérez, "Looking into the 'Anime Global Popular' and the 'Manga Media': Reflections on the Scholarship of a Transnational and Transmedia Industry," *Arts* 8, no. 2 (2019): 60.

This mode of mapping scholarship is admittedly a rather structural one. It pays little attention to the actual theoretical models, questions, and interventions that the many essays and books on animation associated with Japan have put forth. Further, the study of such animation is a thriving field, both quantitatively and qualitatively. Thus the outline might itself be seen as a media studies-inflected model that privileges channels and affordances over content. Indeed, Jacqueline Berndt has, as mentioned, repeatedly argued for understanding anime as media rather than a genre or subgenre in order to reframe many of the questions we can pose to it, if with a strategic vagueness about how we should define media.[10] Much can be said about the level of frameworks, methodologies, and concrete questions and how they have reacted to the noted force fields at different points in history. But maybe it is better to consider how future studies might react to them.

So what are points that the emerging field of Chinese animation studies can unsettle? How can it help unsettle the study of animation associated with Japan? This volume already provides a number of clues in the sheer breadth of approaches and media objects assembled here. Daisy Yan Du, John Crespi, and Yiman Wang's introduction puts a plasmatic ideal at the center of this volume's intervention. Even though a crucial long-term goal for the hopefully—in line with that goal—ever-emerging field, it is also clearly capable of more sustained interventions. At this point, what can we identify that is already happening here and to be further developed? What might still be left to do?

First, then, the volume's breadth itself is an important argument. This volume assembles animation in computer games, cel animation, computer-generated animation in live-action films, puppet animation, puppetry, virtual reality animation, and more. In contrast, the almost complete identification of scholarship on animation associated with Japan with anime continues to suggest a much more narrow view of animation. Anime is still largely identified with cel animation style and a 2D aesthetic whose recognizability has served as a useful touchstone for analysis, but also at times made it prone to being locked into fixed binaries. The anime versus Pixar opposition of Thomas Lamarre's *The Anime Machine* is a good example

10. See Berndt, "Anime in Academia."

of both the high use value and the limits of such a strategy. Interestingly, such a characterization persists at a time when anime production has been deeply affected by the use of computer graphics in production. Anime, in a sense, even in a transformed technological situation *performs* its animation stand/cel animation aesthetics and thereby makes a case for a most classical animation model. This happens precisely at the moment when the category of animation—which long existed as the Other of live-action—itself has become highly unstable. Animation has more obviously become a spectrum that runs across stylized ink brush or puppet animation to animation integrated seamlessly with live action. That anime has been able to further increase its popularity by defending the idea of a stable category called animation in this situation is in itself noteworthy—a sign perhaps of the comfort that near-defunct category can supply against the anxiety-inducing increase in the overlap of animation and live action and the breakdown of indexicality. But taking a multiplicity of media channels, historical moments, and a general diversity of materials into account helps obviate that spectrum and understand the different reactions to the current situation as much as it creates traction for rethinking the category of animation and what questions it helps us ask.

Second, the question of nation potentially plays out differently, at least in practice. Animation associated with Japan, and anime specifically, is attached to the still-persistent image of Japan as homogenous, clearly bounded, and as a repository of a supposedly more or less historically stable Japanese culture (and typical orientalist tropes). The compelling origin story of anime in the original 1963 *Tetsuwan Atomu / Astro Boy* (following Marc Steinberg also the origin story of the media mix) despite itself inevitably reinforces the idea of anime as uniquely Japanese or of Japan, in contrast to the mentioned genealogies Otsuka Eiji has traced. Even though much, though not all, contemporary scholarship disavows such associations, they also appear to still work as a background that limits or nudges scholarship in terms of where its focus lies. They additionally shape audience tastes outside Japan, both actual and imagined by the anime industry, which in turn shape production, circulation, and reception, which in turn have an effect on which works scholarship picks up on. Similarly, the large volume of animation production nominally from Japan (even if produced via elaborate outsourcing networks in East and Southeast Asia) has done much to keep animation produced outside of Japan but circulating within it out of the focus of scholars working on "Japanese animation." How does this potentially play out differently for Chinese animation studies? As Lamarre notes, the complex genealogy and the highly varied production sites counter easy identifications with nation: "The unity of 'Chinese' animation, then, is neither national nor regional, and yet somehow both, much as with 'Japanese' animation."[11] The point here is an eminently practical one. No matter the actual complexity of genealogies or the elaborate networks of production, distribution, and reception that should complicate any analysis or framework, there is a stickiness to national assignations that comply with forces exerted by states and industries and their interest in national branding, disciplinary and institutional structures, and the persistence of nation in the popular imaginary. No matter that scholars of anime have by now long critiqued a nation-centered approach, or habitually acknowledge anime as transnational (albeit often in the loosest, least rigorous usage of the term). Anime sticks, at this point, stubbornly to Japan. For Chinese animation studies, this may still play out differently, even as exactly the same force fields remain in play. The situation of the two Chinas is one factor in this complication, the considerable size and multilocatedness of a Chinese diaspora is another. The deep entanglement of the history of animation in China with Japanese colonial history is another, though one that may stand in rising future tension with state narratives. The chances for working against the split in domestic and international (primarily North American and European) research—which is only gradually giving way to increased exchange—are maybe slim. Yet hope remains, because in a sense the inevitable institutionalization of Chinese animation studies begins with that complication, whereas anime studies began with a proposed stable relationship with Japan.

Third, then, what Daisy Yan Du, John Crespi, and Yiman Wang call the plasmaticity of Chinese Animation Studies is its strength—its status as being only on the cusp of institutionalization. As scholarly networks deepen and scholarly organizations such as the recently launched Association for Chinese Animation Studies become an ever more central platform for scholarship, these structures will have to work against their

11. Thomas Lamarre, "The Animation of China: An Interim Report," *Journal of Chinese Cinemas* 11, no. 2 (2017): 123–39.

own systemic tendencies to preserve the aspiration of the plasmatic, the ever-emerging. Even though the section structure of this volume makes sense and provides a tentative order or a proposed approach, it also shows a strained coherence, one that in its tenuousness is deeply valuable and in need of perpetuation. This strength is supported—in contrast to anime—by a lack of international success of a clearly defined Chinese animation industry. Despite a number of examples of successful works of Chinese animation (be it in terms of video games, feature-length animated films, animated series, and so on), there is no real international or even domestic base of fans or dedicated base of consumers of Chinese animation in a classical sense yet (such as of animated series or feature films) in the way there is for anime. It is only beginning to be part of a global media memory shared by people growing up in many different national and regional contexts.

Chinese animation studies will feature its own specific challenges. From the role of the state for animation in the PRC and the resulting influence on archival access, or specific patterns visible in other area studies-based work on film and media in China (for example, a fixation on locating gestures of resistance in media texts as an end in itself), the list goes on and is bound to be long. But it can also challenge long-standing limitations of the study of animation associated with Japan, or of animation studies proper, or of adjacent fields such as media studies or the issues attached to the media-area dynamic. As a field in formation, it can still resist the temptation and the implications of nominal lessons in exchange for foregrounding important questions.

APPENDIX

Filmography

n.d., *The Girl The Tree*, dirs. Cho Pei-Hsin 卓霈欣, Lin Hsin 林昕, Chen Hsin 陈忻.

1905, *Dingjun shan* 定军山 (*Battle of Dingjun Mountain*), dir. Ren Jingfeng 任景丰. Beijing: Fengtai Photographic Studio.

1907, *The Haunted Hotel*, dir. James Stuart Blackton. New York: Vitagraph.

1908, *Le Rêve des Marmitons* (*Scullion's Dream*), dir. Segundo de Chomón. Paris: Pathé Frères.

1922, *Qing xu meng* 清虚梦 (*An Empty Dream*), dir. Ren Pengnian 任彭年. Shanghai: Commercial Press.

1922, *Shu Zhendong huawen daziji* 舒振东华文打字机 (*Shu Zhendong Chinese Typewriter*), dirs. Wan Laiming 万籁鸣 and Wan Guchan 万古蟾. Shanghai: Commercial Press.

1925, *Seven Chances*, dir. Buster Keaton. Beverly Hills, CA: Metro-Goldwyn.

1926, *Die Abenteuer des Prinzen Achmed* (*The Adventures of Prince Achmed*), dir. Lotte Reiniger. Germany: Comenius-Film GmbH.

1926, *Yichuan zhenzhu* 一串珍珠 (*The Pearl Necklace, aka A String of Pearls*), dir. Li Zeyuan 李泽源. Shanghai: Great Wall Film Company.

1928, *Daxia Gan Fengchi* 大侠甘凤池 (*Kan the Great Knight-Errant*), dir. Yang Xiaozhong 杨小仲. Shanghai: Great Wall Film Company.

1928, *Steamboat Bill Jr.*, dir. Charles Reisner. Hollywood, CA: United Artists.

1928–1931, *Huoshao Hongliansi* 火烧红莲寺 (*The Burning of the Red Lotus Temple*), dir. Zhang Shichuan 张石川. Shanghai: The Star Motion Picture (Mingxing Film) Company.

1935, *Dushi fengguang* 都市风光 (*Scenes of City Life*), dir. Yuan Muzhi 袁牧之. Shanghai: Diantong Film Company.

1941, *Tieshan gongzhu* 铁扇公主 (*Princess Iron Fan*), dirs. Wan Laiming 万籁鸣 and Wan Guchan 万古蟾. Shanghai: United China (Lianhua) Productions.

1947, *Huangdi meng* 皇帝梦 (*The Dream to Be an Emperor*), dir. Chen Bo'er 陈波儿. Changchun: Northeast Film Studio.

1954, *Wusong dahu* 武松打虎 (*Wu Song Kills a Tiger*), dir. Kuei Chih-Hung 桂治洪. Taipei.

1954, *Xiaomei de meng* 小梅的梦 (*The Dream of Xiaomei*), dir. Jin Xi 靳夕. Shanghai: Shanghai Animation Film Studio.

1956, *Wuya weishenme shi heide* 乌鸦为什么是黑的 (*Why the Crow Is Black*), dirs. Wan Laiming 万籁鸣 and Wan Guchan 万古蟾. Shanghai: Shanghai Animation Film Studio.

1958, *Weile haizimen* 为了孩子们 (*For the Children*), dir. Yu Zheguang 虞哲光. Shanghai: Shanghai Animation Film Studio.

1958, *Xiao faming jia* 小发明家 (*Little Inventors*), dir. Chen Zhenghong 陈正鸿. Shanghai: Shanghai Animation Film Studio.

1958, *Zhu Bajie chi xigua* 猪八戒吃西瓜 (*Pigsy Eats Watermelon*), dir. Wan Guchan 万古蟾. Shanghai: Shanghai Animation Film Studio.

1960, *Gexin mi* 革新迷 (*The Innovators*), dir. Jin Xi 靳夕. Shanghai: Shanghai Animation Film Studio.

1960, *Xiao kedou zhao mama* 小蝌蚪找妈妈 (*Little Tadpoles Look for Mama*), dirs. Te Wei 特伟 and Tang Cheng 唐澄. Shanghai: Shanghai Animation Film Studio.

1961, 1964, *Danao tiangong* 大闹天宫 (*Uproar in Heaven*), dirs. Wan Laiming 万籁鸣 and Tang Cheng 唐澄. Shanghai: Shanghai Animation Film Studio.

1963, *Mu di* 牧笛 (*The Herd Boy's Flute*), dir. Te Wei 特伟. Shanghai: Shanghai Animation Film Studio.

1964, *Caoyuan yingxiong xiao jiemei* 草原英雄小姐妹 (*Heroic Little Sisters of the Grassland*), dirs. Qian Yunda 钱运达 and Tang Cheng 唐澄. Shanghai: Shanghai Animation Film Studio.

1966, *Tieshan gongzhu* 铁扇公主 (*Princess Iron Fan*), dir. Ho Meng Hua 何梦华. Hong Kong: Shaw Brothers Studio.

1967, *Longmen kezhan* 龙门客栈 (*Dragon Inn*), dir. King Hu 胡金铨. Taiwan: Union Film Company (Lianbang Yingye).

1971, *Zhou Chu* 周處 (*Chou Chu*), dir. Wang Ming-Hui 王明慧. Taipei. Daming Animation.

1972, *Zhongguo wenzi de yanbian* 中國文字的演變 (*The Evolution of Chinese Characters*), dir. Teng Yu-Li 鄧有立. Taipei: Chunghwa Cartoon Production Company.

1974, *Fengshen bang* 封神榜 (*The Story of Chinese Gods*), dir. Chang Ying 張英. Taipei: Chunghwa Cartoon Production Company.

1975, *Dajiale* 大家樂 (*Let's Rock*), dirs. James Wong 黃霑 and Wu Sau Yee 胡樹儒. Hong Kong: Cauldron Cinematics Ltd.

1975, *Tiandan fuguo* 田單復國 (*Tian Dan Restores the Kingdom*), dir. unknown. Taipei: Hsin Hong Cartoon Company.

1978, *Hualang yiye* 画廊一夜 (*One Night in the Art Gallery*), dirs. A Da 阿达 and Lin Wenxiao 林文肖. Shanghai: Shanghai Animation Film Studio.

1979, *Fengjie* 瘋劫 (*The Secret*), dir. Ann Hui 許鞍華. Hong Kong: Unique Films Ltd.

1979, *Kongshan lingyu* 空山靈雨 (*Raining in the Mountain*), dir. King Hu 胡金銓. Hong Kong: Lo & Hu Company Productions Ltd.

1979, *Nezha naohai* 哪吒闹海 (*Nezha Conquers the Dragon King*), dirs. Wang Shuchen 王树忱, Yan Dingxian 严定宪, A Da 阿达. Shanghai: Shanghai Animation Film Studio.

1979, *Sanguo yanyi* 三國演義 (*Romance of the Three Kingdoms*), dir. Tsai Ming-Chin 蔡明欽. Taipei: Chunghwa Cartoon Production Company.

1980, *Doraemon: Nobita no kyōryū* ドラえもん: のび太の恐竜, (*Doraemon: Nobita's Dinosaur*), dir. Fukutomi Hiroshi 福冨博. Tokyo: Shin-Ei Animation.

1980, *Sange heshang* 三个和尚 (*Three Monks*), dir. A Da 阿达. Shanghai: Shanghai Animation Film Studio.

1980, *Xue haizi* 雪孩子 (*Snow Boy*), dir. Lin Wenxiao 林文肖. Shanghai: Shanghai Animation Film Studio.

1981, *Doudou/Shunmao monogatari taotao* 豆豆/シュンマオ物語タオタオ (*The Story of Panda Taotao*), dir. Shimamura Tatsuo 島村達雄. Tokyo and Tianjin: Mushi Productions and Tianjin Arts and Crafts Design Institute.

1981, *Jiuse lu* 九色鹿 (*The Deer of Nine Colors*), dirs. Qian Jiajun 钱家骏 and Dai Tielang 戴铁郎. Shanghai: Shanghai Animation Film Studio.

1981, *Qicai katong Laofuzi* 七彩卡通老夫子 (*Old Master Cute*), dirs. Wu Sau Yee (Hu Shu-ju/Hu Shuru) 胡樹儒, Tsai Chih-chung (Cai Zhizhong) 蔡志忠, and Hsieh Chin-tu (Xie Jintu) 謝金塗. Hong Kong/Taipei: Hong Kong Film Services/Far Eastern Cartoon.

1982, *E.T. the Extra Terrestrial*, dir. Steven Spielberg. Hollywood, CA: Universal Pictures.

1982, *Laofuzi shuihuzhuan* 老夫子水虎傳 (*Old Master Cute Part II*), dirs. Wu Sau Yee 胡樹儒, Wong Chak 王澤, and Xie Jintu 謝金塗. Hong Kong: Hong Kong Film Company.

1982, *Lu ling* 鹿铃 (*The Deer's Bell*), dirs. Tang Cheng 唐澄 and Wu Qiang 邬强. Shanghai: Shanghai Animation Film Studio.

1983, *Hudie quan* 蝴蝶泉 (*The Butterfly Spring*), dir. A Da 阿达. Shanghai: Shanghai Animation Film Studio.

1983, *Niu bobo yu niu xiaomei dapo zuanshicheng*, 牛伯伯與牛小妹大破鑽石城 (*Uncle Niu and Sister Niu Busting the Diamond City*), dir. Yu Wei-Cheng 余為政. Taipei: Cuckoo's Nest Studio.

1983, *Shan-T Laofuzi* 山T老夫子 (*Old Master Cute Part III*), dirs. Honda Toshiyuki 本多敏行 and Cai Mingqin 蔡名欽. Hong Kong: Hong Kong Film Company.

1983, *Wulong yuan* 烏龍院 (*Oolong Courtyard*), dirs. Tsai Chih-Chung 蔡志忠. Taipei: Dragon Animation.

1985, *Jiazi jiulu* 夹子救鹿 (*Jiazi Saves the Deer*), dirs. Lin Wenxiao 林文肖 and Chang Guangxi 常光希. Shanghai: Shanghai Animation Film Studio.
1985, *Jinhou xiangyao* 金猴降妖 (*Monkey King Conquers the Demon*), dirs. Te Wei 特伟, Yan Dingxian 严定宪, and Lin Wenxiao 林文肖. Shanghai: Shanghai Animation Film Studio.
1986, *Tenkū no shiro Rapyuta* 天空の城ラピュタ (*Castle in the Sky*), dir. Miyazaki Hayao 宮崎駿. Tokyo: Studio Ghibli.
1987, *Qiannü youhun* 倩女幽魂 (*A Chinese Ghost Story*), dir. Tsui Hark 徐克. Hong Kong: Film Workshop.
1988, *Shanshui qing* 山水情 (*Feelings of Mountain and River*), dir. Te Wei 特伟. Shanghai: Shanghai Animation Film Studio.
1989, *Gao nüren he ai zhangfu* 高女人和矮丈夫 (*The Tall Wife and the Short Husband*), dir. Hu Yihong 胡依红. Shanghai: Shanghai Animation Film Studio.
1992, *Lianhua gongzhu* 莲花公主 (*Princess Lotus Flower*), dir. Hu Yihong 胡依红. Shanghai: Shanghai Animation Film Studio.
1994, *Chanshuo a'Kuan* 禪說阿寬 (*Zen Taipei Ah-Kuan*), dir. Hsieh Hsi-Hsien 謝錫賢. Taipei: Far Eastern Cartoon.
1994, *Lan shui xiansheng* 爛睏先生 (*Sleepy Guy*), dir. Raman Hui 許誠毅.
1994, *Qiuju da guansi* 秋菊打官司 (*Qiuju Goes to Court/The Story of Qiuju*), dir. Zhang Yimou 张艺谋. Beijing: Beijing Film Academy.
1996, *#01*, dir. Chang Tze Hin 蔣子軒.
1996, *Qiumi qiyu ji* 球迷奇遇記 (*Foul Ball*), dir. Toe Yuen 袁建滔.
1997, *Heliu* 河流 (*The River*), dir. Tsai Ming-liang 蔡明亮. Taipei: Central Motion Pictures.
1997, *Love*, dir. Hung Keung 洪強.
1997, *Xiao wu* 小武 (*Pickpocket*), dir. Jia Zhangke 贾樟柯. Hong Kong: Hu Tong Communication and Radiant Advertising Company.
1998, *Chaoji gongmin* 超級公民 (*Connection by Fate*), dir. Wan Jen 萬仁. Taipei: Wan Jen Films.
1998, *Dong* 洞 (*The Hole*), dir. Tsai Ming-liang 蔡明亮. Taipei: Arc Light Films.
1998, *Mofa ama* 魔法阿媽 (*Grandma and Her Ghosts*), dir. Wang Shau-Di 王小棣. Taipei: Rice Film International Company.
1999, *Baolian deng* 宝莲灯 (*Lotus Lantern*), dir. Chang Guangxi 常光希. Shanghai: Shanghai Animation Film Studio.
2000, *Wohu canglong* 卧虎藏龙 (*Crouching Tiger Hidden Dragon*), dir. Ang Lee 李安. Hong Kong: Columbia Pictures Film Production Asia.
2000, *Yiyi* 一一 (*A One and a Two*), dir. Edward Yang 楊德昌. Taipei: Atom Film.
2000, *Zhantai* 站台 (*Platform*), dir. Jia Zhangke 贾樟柯. Hong Kong: Hu Tong Communication, T-Mark, Office Kitano.

2001, *Laofuzi 2001* 老夫子 2001 (*Old Master Q 2001*), dir. Herman Yau 邱禮濤. Hong Kong: One Hundred Years of Film Company Ltd.
2001, *Ni nabian jidian* 你那邊幾點 (*What Time Is It There?*), dir. Tsai Ming-liang 蔡明亮. Taipei: Homegreen Films.
2003, *Busan* 不散 (*Goodbye, Dragon Inn*), dir. Tsai Ming-liang 蔡明亮. Taipei: Homegreen Films.
2003, *Qiyun shengdong* 气韵生动 (*The Way*), dir. Qing Huang. Bendigo: La Trobe University.
2003, *Xia* 夏 (*Ode to Summer*), dir. Ron Hui/Xu Yi 许毅. Shenzhen: Global Digital Creations Holdings Limited.
2004, *Gong fu* 功夫 (*Kung Fu Hustle*), dir. Stephen Chow 周星驰. Hong Kong: Columbia Pictures Film Production Asia.
2004, *Shijie* 世界 (*The World*), dir. Jia Zhangke 贾樟柯. Paris: Celluloid Dreams.
2004, *Shouxia liuqing* 手下留情 (*Holding One's Hand*), dir. Ding Meiyin 丁美音.
2005, *The Brush*, dir. Lei Chen. Bournemouth: National Centre for Computer Animation, Bournemouth University.
2006, *Dongjing* 动静 (*Movement and Stillness*), dir. Yi-Hsuan Kent Chiu. Auckland: Media Design School.
2006, *Sanxia haoren* 三峡好人 (*Still Life*), dir. Jia Zhangke 贾樟柯. Shanghai: Shanghai Film Studio.
2007, *Hai zhi chuanshuo: Mazu* 海之傳說: 媽祖 (*Mazu*), dir. Lin Shi-ren 林世仁. Taipei: Chinese Cartoon Production.
2009, *Xiangxin pinpai de liliang* 相信品牌的力量 (*Believe in the Power of the Brand*), aka *Shuimo* 水墨 (*Ink*), dir. Niko Tziopanos. Beijing/Hamburg/Paris: MMIA Beijing/Weareflink/Troublemakers.
2010, *Hexie Zhongguo* 和谐中国 (*A Harmonious China*), dir. Zheng Dasheng 郑大圣. Shanghai: 2010 Shanghai World Expo.
2010, *Xiao taiyang* 小太陽 (*The Little Sun*), dir. Chiu Li-Wei 邱立偉. Tainan: Studio2.
2010, *Xiaomao Bakeli* 小貓巴克里 (*Barkley the Cat*), dir. Chiu Li-Wei 邱立偉. Tainan: Studio2.
2010, *Zhuge zaomeng* 逐格造夢 (*Pursuing Dreams Frame by Frame*), dir. C. Jay Shih 石昌傑. Taipei: Public Television Service.
2011, *Flats*, dir. Ervin Han. Singapore: Scrawl Studios.
2013, *Foreign Plants*, dir. Alex Ng. Singapore: NCHProductions.
2014, *The Animals*, dir. Mark Wee. Singapore: Nanyang Technological University.
2014, *Beizilide xiao niu* 杯子里的小牛 (*My Milk Cup Cow*), dir. Zhu Yantong 朱彦潼.
2014, *Si Lunchai*, dir. Hannes Rall. Singapore: Nanyang Technological University.

2014, *Zhiqu Weihushan* 智取威虎山 (*The Taking of the Tiger Mountain*), dir. Tsui Hark 徐克.

2015, *Xiyouji zhi dasheng guilai* 西游记之大圣归来 (*Monkey King: Hero Is Back*), dir. Tian Xiaopeng 田晓鹏. Beijing: October Animation Studio (Yancheng Shiyue).

2015, *Zaijian biaoqing* 再见表情 (*Sent*), dir. Mi Li 米粒. Beijing: Light Chaser Animation Studios.

2016, **INCREDIBLE* Paint App Expresii Official Release Intro*. Hong Kong: Expresii.

2016, *Ego*, dir. Cho Pei-Hsin 卓霈欣.

2016, *Hermit*, dir. Cho Pei-Hsin 卓霈欣.

2016, *Moana*, dirs. John Musker and Ron Clements. Burbank, CA: Walt Disney Animation Studios.

2016, *Xiao menshen* 小门神 (*Little Door Gods*), dir. Wang Wei 王微. Beijing: Light Chaser Animation Studios.

2017, *A'tang qiyu* 阿唐奇遇 (*Tea Pets*), dir. Wang Wei 王微. Beijing: Light Chaser Animation Studios.

2017, *Chuang* 窗 (*In the Pictures*), dir. Shao Qing 邵晴. Shanghai: VRTIMES.

2017, *Coco*, dir. Lee Unkrich. Emeryville, CA: Pixar Animation Studios.

2017, *Shimeng laoren* 拾梦老人 (*The Dream Collector*), dir. Mi Li 米粒. Beijing: Pinta Studios.

2017, *Weiguan jushou* 微观巨兽 (*Micro Giants*), dir. Zhou Yifu 周逸夫. Beijing: Digital Domain.

2017, *Ziyou* 自游 (*Free Whale*), dir. Zhang Peibin 張佩斌. Beijing: Sandman Studios.

2018, *Di sanxian* 地三仙 (*Fresh Out*), dirs. Samuel Wey and Tao Fangchao 陶方超. Beijing: Sandman Studios.

2018, *ELLO*, dir. Su Haodan 苏昊丹. Beijing: Pinta Studios.

2018, *Fengxi zhongde ren* 缝隙中的人 (*The Person in Crevice [sic]*), dir. Lu Tingting 鲁婷婷.

2018, *Lie shan shi* 烈山氏 (*Shennong: Taste of Illusion*), dir. Mi Li 米粒. Beijing: Pinta Studios.

2018, *Mao yu Taohuayuan* 猫与桃花源 (*Cats and Peachtopia*), dir. Wang Wei 王微. Beijing: Light Chaser Animation Studios.

2018, *Xingfu lushang* 幸福路上 (*On Happiness Road*), dir. Sung Hsin-Ying 宋欣穎. Taipei: Happiness Road Productions.

2019, *Baishe: Yuanqi* 白蛇: 源起 (*White Snake: The Origin*), dir. Huang Jiakang 黄家康. Beijing: Light Chaser Animation Studios coproduced with Warner Bros.

2019, *Hair*, dir. Caroline Ching/Ng Zhi Xin. Singapore: Nanyang Technological University.

2019, *Heise pibao* 黑色皮包 (*Black Bag*), dir. Shao Qing 邵晴. Shanghai: VR-TIMES.
2019, *Liulang diqiu* 流浪地球 (*The Wandering Earth*), dir. Guo Fan 郭帆. Beijing: China Film Group Corporation.
2019, *Nezha zhi motong jiangshi* 哪吒之魔童降世 (*Nezha*), dir. Jiaozi 饺子. Beijing: Enlight Media.
2019, *Tenki no ko* 天気の子 (*Weathering with You*), dir. Shinkai Makoto 新海誠. Tokyo: CoMix Wave Films.
2020, *Squishy Fish Eggs*, dir. Chen Jiayin 陳佳音.
2021, *Baishe 2: Qingshe jieqi* 白蛇2: 青蛇劫起 (*Green Snake*), dir. Huang Jiakang 黄家康. Beijing: Light Chaser Animation Studios.
2021, *Bing meigui* 病玫瑰 (*The Sick Rose*), dirs. Tang Zhi-Zhong 唐治中 and Huang Yun-Hsien 黄匀弦.
2021, *Lunhui* 轮回 (*Samsara*), dir. Huang Hsin-Chien 黄心健. Taiwan.
2021, *Shuishen de xiasi* 睡神的遐思 (*Hypnosis: Reveries*), dir. Jessien Huang 黄佳胜. Shenzhen: Jess Studio.
2025, *Banling feidu* 斑羚飞渡 (*Goral Flying*), dirs. Chang Guangxi 常光希 and Shi Yi 施屹. Shanghai: Shanghai Animation Film Studio.

Bibliography

"1958 nian de meishupian" 1958 年的美术片 (Animations in 1958). *Zhongguo dianying* 中国电影 (Chinese films) 6 (1958): 31.

"35 nian lai Zhongguo meishupian huo guoji dianyingjie jiang yilan biao" 35年来中国美术片获国际电影节奖一览表 (List of international film festival awards received by Chinese animations in the last 35 years). *Dangdai dianying* 当代电影 (Popular movies) 2 (1984): 159–60.

Abbas, Ackbar. *Culture and the Politics of Disappearance*. Minneapolis: University of Minnesota Press, 1997.

Andrew, Dudley. *Concepts in Film Theory*. New York: Oxford University Press, 1984.

Andrews, Julia F. "Literature in Line: Picture Stories in the People's Republic of China." *Inks: Cartoon and Comic Art Studies* 4 (1997): 17–32.

———. *Painters and Politics in the People's Republic of China, 1949–1979*. Berkeley: University of California Press, 1994.

Ang, Qing Sheng. "Infusing Local Culture in Singaporean Animation: Developing a Framework of Cultural Specifics from a Study of Contemporary Cinema in Singapore." *Animation Practice, Process & Production* 7, no. 1 (2018): 113–37.

"Anti-Chinese Sentiment Swelling in Mongolia." *Asian Economic News*, April 11, 2005. Accessed February 29, 2024. https://www.thefreelibrary.com/FOCUS%3a+Anti-Chinese+sentiment+swelling+in+Mongolia.-a0131327236.

Arnheim, Rudolf. "A Stricture on Space and Time." *Critical Inquiry* 4, no. 4 (1978): 645–55.

"Art-Isle Talk | Cai Caibei: Banxing shifen x Pianpian mengjing" 蔡采贝：半醒时分 x 翩翩梦境 (Cai Caibei: Half asleep and fluttering dream). Career Engine.us. Accessed August 15, 2024. https://posts.careerengine.us/p/611dfc0fe3095813de09b4cd.

Art Science Museum Marina Bay Sands. "VR Gallery." Accessed January 24, 2024. https://www.marinabaysands.com/museum/exhibitions/vr-gallery.html.

Au Yeung, Craig, Ku Chiu Ping, Neco Lo, Wong Ain Ling, and Wong Ying. "Panel Discussion." In *2nd Independent Short Film and Video Awards Catalogue*, 108–11. Hong Kong: Hong Kong Arts Centre, 1996.

Azuma, Hiroki. *Otaku: Japan's Database Animals*. Minneapolis: University of Minnesota Press, 2009.

Bâ, Saër Maty, and Will Higbee. *De-Westernizing Film Studies*. London: Routledge, 2012.

Baier, Walter. "Capitalism's Secular Crisis and the European Social Model." Newshelnwein, February 10, 2009. https://www.helnwein.com/news/news_update/article_3922-Capitalisms-Secular-Crisis-and-the-European-Social-Model. Originally published in *Transform! European Journal for Alternative Thinking and Political Dialogue*, "The Silence of Innocence—the Artist Gottfried Helnwein." Bildersturm Film Produktion GmbH. Accessed January 4, 2024. https://www.bildersturm-film.de/en/the-silence-of-innocence.

Bao Jigui 鲍济贵. *Zhongguo donghua dianying tongshi* 中国动画电影通史 (History of Chinese animation). Beijing: Lianhuanhua chubanshe, 2010.

Bao, Weihong. *Fiery Cinema: The Emergence of an Affective Medium in China, 1915–1945*. Minneapolis: University of Minnesota Press, 2015.

Barker, Jennifer M. *The Tactile Eye: Touch and the Cinematic Experience*. Berkeley: University of California Press, 2009.

Barthes, Roland. *Camera Lucida: Reflections on Photography*. Translated by Richard Howard. New York: Hill & McGraw, 1981.

Bastianchich, Alfio. "Lotte Reiniger: An Interview with Alfio Bastianchich." In *Women and Animation: A Compendium*, edited by Jayne Pilling, 9–15. London: BFI, 1992.

Baudry, Jean-Louis. "Ideological Effects of the Basic Cinematographic Apparatus." Translated by Alan Williams. *Film Quarterly* 28, no. 2 (Winter 1974–75): 39–47.

Baxter, Bill, Vincent Scheib, Ming C. Lin, and Dinesh Manocha. "DAB: Interactive Haptic Painting with 3D Virtual Brushes." *ACM SIGGRAPH* (2001): 461–68.

Bazin, André. "The Myth of Total Cinema." In *What Is Cinema?* Vol. 1. Translated by Hugh Gray, 17–22. Los Angeles: University of California Press, 1967.

———. "The Ontology of the Photographic Image." In *What Is Cinema?* Vol. 1. Translated by Hugh Gray, 9–16. Berkeley: University of California Press, 2004.

Beckman, Karen, ed. *Animating Film Theory*. Durham, NC: Duke University Press, 2014.

———. "Film Theory's Animated Map." *Framework* 56, no. 2 (Fall 2015): 472–91.

———. *Vanishing Women: Magic, Film, and Feminism*. Durham, NC: Duke University Press, 2003.

Bendazzi, Giannalberto. *Animation: A World History*, vol. 1. Boca Raton, FL: CRC Press, 2016.

Berger, Harry, Jr. "The System of Early Modern Painting." *Representations* 62 (1998): 31–57.

Bergson, Henri. *Creative Evolution*. Translated by Arthur Mitchell. New York: H. Holt, 1911.

Berndt, Jacqueline. "Anime in Academia: Representative Object, Media Form, and Japanese Studies." *Arts* 7, no. 4 (2018): 1–13.

Berry, Michael. *Jia Zhangke's "Hometown Trilogy": Xiao Wu, Platform, Unknown Pleasures*. London: BFI Publishing, 2014.

Bilibili. "Dianying zui TOP" 电影最TOP (Top films). Episode 132: "Cong Wukong dao Nezha, yikouqi kanwan guochan donghua fazhan shi" 从悟空到哪吒，一口气看完国产动画发展史 (From Monkey King to Nezha: The history of Chinese animation watched in one sitting). September 4, 2019. Bilibili.com. https://www.bilibili.com/video/av66591838.

Bird-David, Nurit. "'Animism' Revisited: Personhood, Environment, and Relational Epistemology." *Current Anthropology* 40, no. S1 (1999): S67–91.

———. "Persons or Relatives? Animistic Scales of Practice and Imagination." In *Rethinking Relations and Animism: Personhood and Materiality*, edited by Miguel Astor-Aguilera and Graham Harvey, 25–34. Abingdon, UK: Routledge, 2018.

Bobrowska, Olga. "Seeking Truth in Facts: Historicizing Chinese Animation." In *Global Animation Theory: International Perspectives at Animafest Zagreb*, edited by Franziska Bruckner, Holger Lang, Nikica Gilić, Daniel Šuljić, and Hrvoje Turković, 61–82. New York: Bloomsbury Academic, 2019.

Boeckenhoff, Katharina, and Caroline Ruddell. "Lotte Reiniger: The Crafty Animator and Cultural Value." In *The Crafty Animator: Handmade, Craft-based Animation and Cultural Value*, edited by Caroline Ruddell and Paul Ward, 75–98. Cham: Palgrave Macmillan, 2019.

Bordeleau, Erik. "The World Without Future: Stage as Entrapment in Jia Zhangke's Film." *China Review* 10, no. 2 (2010): 155–76.

Brasch, Ilka. *Film Serials and the American Cinema, 1910–1940: Operational Detection*. Amsterdam: Amsterdam University Press, 2018.

Breger, Claudia. "Gods, German Scholars, and the Gift of Greece: Friedrich Kittler's Philhellenic Fantasies." *Theory, Culture & Society* 23, nos. 7–8 (2006): 111–34.

Brophy, Philip. "Animation of Sound." In *Movie Music, The Film Reader*, edited by Kay Dickinson, 133–42. London: Routledge, 2002.

Bruckner, Franziska, Lang Holger, Gilić Nikica, Šuljić Daniel, and Turković Hrvoje, eds. *Global Animation Theory: International Perspectives at Animafest Zagreb*. New York: Bloomsbury Academic, 2019.

Bryman, Alan. *Disney and His Worlds*. New York: Routledge, 1995.

Buchan, Suzanne. "The Animated Female Body, Feminism(s) and 'Mushi.'" In *Experimental and Expanded Animation*, edited by Vicky Smith and Nicky Hamlyn, 203–29. Cham: Palgrave Mamillan, 2018.

———. "The Animated Spectator: Watching the Quay Brothers' 'Worlds.'" In *Animated Worlds*, 15–38. Bloomington: Indiana University Press, 2007.

———. "Animation, in Theory." In *Animating Film Theory*, edited by Karen Beckman, 111–31. Durham, NC: Duke University Press, 2014.

———. *The Quay Brothers*. Minneapolis: University of Minnesota Press, 2011.

Bukatman, Scott. "Pertaining to Cartoon Physics: Or, the Cartoon Cat in the Machine." In *Animating Film Theory*, edited by Karen Beckman, 301–16. Durham, NC: Duke University Press, 2014.

Butler, Alison. *Women's Cinema: The Contested Screen*. London: Wallflower, 2002.

Butler, Judith. *Antigone's Claim: Kinship between Life and Death*. New York: Columbia University Press, 2010.

Cambier, Vanessa. "Extending the Frame: Animation, Feminism, & Politics." PhD diss., University of Minnesota, 2022.

———. "Women's Animation and the Creative Feminist Politics of Social Change." *LARB Los Angeles Reviews of Books*, March 25, 2020. https://lareviewofbooks.org/article/womens-animation-and-the-creative-feminist-politics-of-social-change/.

Cao Di 曹迪. *Zhongguo dingge donghua* 中国定格动画 (Chinese stop-motion animation). Beijing: Communication University of China Press, 2018.

Cao Maotang 曹懋唐. "Yu Zheguang 虞哲光." In *Zhongguo dianyingjia liezhuan* No. 6 中国电影家列传第6集 (Biographies of China's filmmakers, vol. 6), edited by Chinese History Research Bureau, 496–501. Beijing: Zhongguo dianying chubanshe, 1986.

Cao Xueqin 曹雪芹. *Shitou ji* 石头记 (The story of the stone). Nanjing: Yilin chubanshe, 2017.

Catmull, Edwin, and Wallace Amy. *Creativity, Inc.: Overcoming the Unseen Forces that Stand in the Way of True Inspiration*. New York: Random House, 2014.

Cavell, Stanley. "What Photography Calls Thinking." In *Cavell on Film*, edited by William Rothman, 115–34. Albany: State University of New York Press, 2005.

———. *The World Viewed: Reflections on the Ontology of Film*, enlarged ed. Cambridge, MA: Harvard University Press, 1979.

Chai Mi 柴觅. "Laizi tamen: Zhongguo yishu donghua" 来自她们——中国艺术动画 (From hers: Chinese art animation). October 9, 2019. https://www.sohu.com/a/345779959_494887.

Chan, Ching, Ergun Akleman, and Jianer Chen. "Two Methods for Creating Chinese Painting." *10th Pacific Conference on Computer Graphics and Applications* (2002): 403–12.

Chan, Pameyla. "You Can Now Take a Virtual Tour of the Asian Civilizations Museum." *Lifestyle Asia*, June 5, 2020. https://www.lifestyleasia.com/sg/culture/asian-civilisations-museum-virtual-programmes.

Chang Hsin-Chang 張信昌. *Tujie Taiwan huaijiu ganzidian* 圖解臺灣懷舊柑仔店 (The graphic illustration of nostalgic local stores in Taiwan). Taipei: Morning Star, 2013.

Chang, Guangxi. "Tradition and Innovation." Translated by Sean Macdonald. In *Chinese Animation and Socialism: From Animators' Perspectives*, edited by Daisy Yan Du, 127–37. Leiden: Brill, 2022.

Chang Tze Hin. "#01." In *2nd Independent Short Film and Video Awards Catalogue*, 32. Hong Kong: Hong Kong Arts Centre, 1996.

Chao Hung-Yi 趙弘毅. "Anshen zai Taiwan: 1960–70 Zimin sanwen de jiating shuxie yu rensheng yilun" 安身在臺灣：一九六〇、七〇年代子敏散文的家庭書寫與人生議論 (Settle in Taiwan: Family writing and life discussion in Zi-Min's prose in the 1960s and 1970s). Master's thesis, National Chengchi University, 2020.

Cheah, Pheng. "Entering the World from an Oblique Angle: On Jia Zhangke as an Organic Intellectual." In *What is a World? On Postcolonial Literature as World Literature*, 137–64. Durham, NC: Duke University Press, 2016.

Chen, Chen. "Painterly Focused Chinese Ink Animation: Seeing through the Cultural Lens of the Xiang System." *Animation Practice, Process & Production* 8 (2019): 141–64.

Chen Hailu. "CGI Ink-Painting Animation in Contemporary China, 1989–2019." Translated by Yixing Li. Association for Chinese Animation Studies. July 24, 2020. Accessed June 21, 2022. https://acas.ust.hk/2020/07/24/cgi-ink-painting-animation-in-contemporary-china-1989-2019.

Chen Mingche 陈明彻. "Shezhi huanshu yingpian zhi changshi (weiwan)" 摄制幻术影片之常识（未完） (Common knowledge of making tricks, part one), *Sheying huabao* 摄影画报 (Photography pictorial) 7, no. 305 (1931): 7.

———. "Shezhi huanshu yingpian zhi changshi (xu)" 摄制幻术影片之常识 (续) (Common knowledge of making tricks, part two). *Sheying huabao* 摄影画报 (Photography pictorial) 7, no. 306 (1931): 7.

Chen, Shaopeng. *The New Generation in Chinese Animation*. London: Bloomsbury Academic, 2022.

———. "Industrial Transformation in Chinese Animation Cinema (1995–2015)." *New Cinemas: Journal of Contemporary Film* 15, no. 2 (2017): 157–74.

Chen Xiangbo 陈祥波. "Zhanzai 'shijie' wai de Zhongguo ren: Ping Jia Zhangke de dianying *Shijie*" 站在"世界"外的中国人——评贾樟柯的电影《世界》 (Chinese standing outside "The World": Critiquing Jia Zhangke's film *The World*). *Dianying pingjie* 电影评介 (Movie review) 2007 (8): 40, 39.

Chen Xihe 陈犀禾. "Zhongguo dianying meixue de zairenshi" 中国电影美学的再认识 (Rethinking Chinese film aesthetic). *Dangdai dianying* 当代电影 (Contemporary cinema) 1 (1986): 82–90.

Chen, Yuanyuan. "Old or New Art: Rethinking Classical Chinese Animation." *Journal of Chinese Cinemas* 11, no. 2 (2017): 175–88.

———. "The Rebel of the Chinese School: Modernist Expression in A Da's Late Animations." *Modernism / Modernity* 22, no. 1 (2015): 81–104.

Cheng, Grace, ed. *Laofuzi manhua yanjiu jihua* 老夫子漫畫研究計畫 (Research plan on *Old Master Q*). Hong Kong: Hong Kong Arts Centre, 2003.

Cheng Zhongyue 程中岳. "Mu'ou pian dongzuo biaoyan yishu sanlun" 木偶片动作表演艺术散论 (An essay on the art of puppet movements and performance). In *Meishu dianying chuangzuo yanjiu* 美术电影创作研究 (Research and production of fine arts film), edited by Ministry of Culture, Film Bureau "Film and News" Editorial Office, and the China Film Press Domestic Film Editorial Office, 66–71. Beijing: Zhongguo dianying chubanshe, 1984.

China's Stopmotion Animation. "Duli donghuaren Chai Mi zhuanfang" 独立动画人柴觅专访 (Interview with independent animator Chai Mi). ACCR (Association des Centres Culturels de Rencontre), October 12, 2013. http://stopmotionanimationcn.blogspot.com/2013/10/blog-post.html.

Ching, Gene. "The Weird History of a Chinese Ghost Story Franchise: Horror Comedy at Its Wildest," Den of Geek, October 25, 2020, https://www.denofgeek.com/movies/the-weird-history-of-a-chinese-ghost-story-franchise/.

Chion, Michel. *Audio-Vision: Sound on Screen*. Edited and translated by Claudia Gorbman. New York: Columbia University Press, 1994.

Cho, Pei-Hsin. "About." Accessed August 15, 2024. https://www.peihsincho.com/about.

Cholodenko, Alan. "The Animation of Cinema." *Semiotic Review of Books* 18, no. 2 (2008): 1–10.

———. "(The) Death (of) the Animator, or: The Felicity of Felix, Part II." *Animation Studies* 2 (2007). https://oldjournal.animationstudies.org/the-death-of-the-animator-or-the-felicity-of-felix/. (Site under construction.)

———. "'First Principles' of Animation." In *Animating Film Theory*, edited by Karen Beckman, 98–110. Durham, NC: Duke University Press, 2014.

Chow, Rey. "Introduction: On Chineseness as a Theoretical Problem." *boundary 2* 25, no. 3 (1998): 1–24.

———. *Sentimental Fabulations, Contemporary Chinese Films: Attachment in the Age of Global Visibility*. New York: Columbia University Press, 2007.

Chu, Nelson. "Expresii Watercolor." *SIGGRAPH '17 Appy Hour* (2017).

———, and Tai Chiew-Lan. "MoXi: Real-Time Ink Dispersion in Absorbent Paper." *ACM Transactions on Graphics* 24, no. 3 (2005): 504–11.

Chu Zheng 初征. "Meishu dianying geming de xin chengguo: Caise meishupian *Shihang* guanhou" 美术电影革命的新成果——彩色美术片《试航》观后 (The new achievement of fine arts films: Review of color fine arts film *Trial Voyage*). *Renmin ribao* 人民日报 (People's daily), June 9, 1976: 3.

Chun, Wendy Hui Kyong. *Discriminating Code: Correlation, Neighborhoods, and the New Politics of Recognition*. Cambridge, MA: MIT Press, 2021.

Clokey, Art. "Trimensional Animation." Unpublished typescript, 1977.

Condry, Ian. *The Soul of Anime: Collaborative Creativity and Japan's Media Success Story*. Durham, NC: Duke University Press, 2013.

Crafton, Donald. *Before Mickey: The Animated Film, 1898–1928*. Chicago: University of Chicago Press, 1993.

Crespi, John A. *Manhua Modernity: Chinese Culture and the Pictorial Turn*. Oakland: University of California Press, 2020.

Cui, Jian. "The Pursuit of a National Style of Chinese Animation." *Animation Journal* 14 (2006): 44–62.

Cui, Shuqin. *Women through the Lens: Gender and Nation in a Century of Chinese Cinema*. Honolulu: University of Hawai'i Press, 2003.

Cui, Wenjin. "Waiting and the Duration of Time." *China Perspectives* 2, no. 121 (2020): 35–42.

Curtis, Cassidy J., Sean E. Anderson, Joshua E. Seims, Kurt W. Fleischer and David H. Salesin. "Computer-Generated Watercolor." *SIGGRAPH Proceedings* (1997): 421–30.

Curtis, Scott. "The Sound of Early Warner Bros. Cartoons." In *Sound Theory, Sound Practice*, edited by Rick Altman, 191–203. New York: Routledge, 1992.

Dai, Jinhua. "Invisible Women: Contemporary Chinese Cinema and Women's Film." *Positions: Asia Critique* 3, no. 1 (1995): 255–80.

"Daxia Gan Fengchi: Changcheng chupian" 大侠甘凤池：长城出片 (*Kan the Great Knight-Errant*: A Great Wall production). *Xin yinxing* 新银星 (New silver star) 1 (1928): 43.

Deleuze, Gilles. *Cinema 1: The Movement-Image*. Translated by Hugh Tomlinson and Barbara Habberjam. Minneapolis: University of Minnesota Press, 1986.

Denson, Shane. "On the Embodied Phenomenology of DeepFakes." Blog, October 6, 2021. Accessed January 3, 2024. https://www.blog.shanedenson.com/?p=5358.

Department of Statistics Singapore. "Key Indicators of Resident Population." Census of Population 2020. Accessed January 23, 2024. https://www.singstat.gov.sg/-/media/files/publications/cop2020/sr1/keyindicators.ashx.

Descola, Philippe. "Beyond Nature and Culture." In *The Handbook of Contemporary Animism*, edited by Graham Harvey, 77–91. London: Routledge, 2014.

———. *Beyond Nature and Culture*. Translated by Janet Lloyd. Chicago: University of Chicago Press: 2013.

Ding Peng 丁鹏. "Dunhuang bihua de donghua chuangzuo yanjiu: Yi donghuapian *Jiuse lu* wei li" 敦煌壁画的动画创作研究——以动画片九色鹿为例 (A study of animation composition based on the wall painting from Dun-

huang: With reference to the *Nine Colored Deer*). *Dunhuang xue* 敦煌学 (Dunhuang research) 33 (2017): 1–16.
Doane, Mary Ann. "The Voice in the Cinema: The Articulation of Body and Space." *Yale French Studies* 60 (1980): 33–50.
Donald, Stephanie. *Little Friends: Children's Film and Media Culture in China*. Lanham, MD: Rowman & Littlefield, 2005.
Du, Daisy Yan. *Animated Encounters: Transnational Movements of Chinese Animation, 1940s-1970s*. Honolulu: University of Hawai'i Press, 2019.
———, ed. *Chinese Animation and Socialism: From Animators' Perspectives*. Leiden: Brill, 2022.
———. "The Dis/appearance of Animals in Animated Film during the Chinese Cultural Revolution, 1966–1976." *Positions: Asia Critique* 24, no. 2 (2016): 435–79.
———. "The Manchukuo Film Association and Its Afterlives: Animated Filmmaking in Wartime and Postwar Peking." *Journal of Cinema and Media Studies* 63, no.3 (Spring 2024): 119-42.
———. "On the Move: The Trans/national Animated Film in 1940s–1970s China." PhD diss., University of Wisconsin-Madison, May 2012.
———. "Suspended Animation: The Wan Brothers and the (In)Animate Mainland-Hong Kong Encounter, 1947–1956." *Journal of Chinese Cinemas* 11, no. 2 (2017): 140–58.
———. "A Theory of Suspended Animation: The Aesthetics and Politics of (E) motion and Stillness." *Discourse: Journal for Theoretical Studies in Media and Culture* 44, no. 1 (Winter 2022): 42–77.
Duan Xiaoxuan. "Walking Our Own Path and Making Innovations in Chinese Animated Filmmaking." Translated by Nick Stember. Association for Chinese Animation Studies, June 14, 2018. Accessed June 21, 2022. https://acas.world/2018/06/14/walking-our-own-path-and-making-innovations-in-chinese-animated-filmmaking/.
Dunhuang wenwu yanjiu suo 敦煌文物研究所. *Dunhuang wenwu zhanlan mulu* 敦煌文物展览目录 (Catalogue of the exhibition of Dunhuang artifacts). Beijing: Zhongyang zhengfu wenhuabu wenwuju, 1951.
"Dunhuang yizhan guanhou" 敦煌艺展观后 (After visiting the Dunhuang exhibition). *Xinjiang ribao* 新疆日报 (Xinjiang daily), November 10, 1948.

Edera, Bruno. "L'animation au féminin." *La revue du cinéma* 389 (1983).
Eisenstein, Sergei. *Eisenstein On Disney*. Edited by Jay Leyda. Translated by Alan Upchurch. Kolkata: Seagull Books, 1986.
———. *Eisenstein on Disney*. Edited by Jay Leyda. Translated by Alan Upchurch. London: Methuen, 1988.
———. *On Disney*. Edited by Jay Leyda. Translated by Alan Upchurch. London: Seagull Books, 2017.

Eisner, Ken. "Grandma and Her Ghosts." *Variety*, November 1, 1998. Accessed September 6, 2022. https://variety.com/1998/film/reviews/grandma-and-her-ghosts-1200456141/.

Elsaesser, Thomas. *Film History as Media Archaeology: Tracking Digital Cinema*. Amsterdam: Amsterdam University Press, 2016.

Engels, Friedrich. "Letter to F. Mehring." In *Karl Marx and Friedrich Engels: Selected Works in Two Volumes*, vol. 2, 451. Moscow: Foreign Languages Publishing House, 1949.

Fan Ming-Ju 范銘如. *Zhong li xun ta: Taiwan nüxing xiaoshuo zonglun* 眾裡尋她：臺灣女性小說縱論 (Chronological searches of Taiwanese women's fiction). Taipei: Rye Field, 2002.

Fan, Victor. *Cinema Approaching Reality: Locating Chinese Film Theory*. Minneapolis: University of Minnesota Press, 2015.

———. "The Time It Takes for Time to End." In *Extraterritoriality: Locating Hong Kong Cinema and Media*, 111–56. Edinburgh: Edinburgh University Press, 2019.

Farquhar, Mary Ann. "Monks and Monkey: A Study of 'National Style' in Chinese Animation." *Animation Journal* 1, no. 2 (1993): 5–27.

Felski, Rita. "Context Stinks!" *New Literary History* 42, no. 4 (Autumn 2011): 573–91.

Feng Jiannan 冯健男. "Cong changjing sheji tan donghuapian *Jiuse lu* de dansheng-mianhuai Qian Jiajun xiansheng" 从场景设计谈动画片《九色鹿》的诞生——缅怀钱家骏先生 (Discussing *The Deer of Nine Colors* by focusing on the set design: To commemorate Mr. Qian Jiajun). *Nanjing yishu xueyuan xuebao (meishu yu sheji ban)* 南京艺术学院学报 (美术与设计版) (Journal of Nanjing Arts Institute [Fine Arts & Design]) 6 (2011): 137–40.

Feng Jicai 冯骥才. *Wenhua fajue Laofuzi chutu* 文化发掘老夫子出土 (Cultural digging: The unearthing of Old Master Q). Beijing, Xiyuan chubanshe, 2001.

Feng Lici 馮禮慈. "Dingdang" 叮噹 (*Doraemon*). *Dianying shuang zhoukan* 電影雙週刊 (Film biweekly) 94 (September 1982): 32.

Feral, Josette. "The Powers of Difference." In *The Future of Difference*, edited by Hester Eisenstein and Alice Jardine, 88–94. New Brunswick, NJ: Rutgers University Press, 1985.

Finute. "Finute Creates National Day Parade Metaverse." September 17, 2022. https://finute.co/blog/finute-develops-national-day-parade-ndp-metaverse.

Fischer, Lucy. "Pre/Texts: An Introduction." In *Shot/Countershot: Film Tradition and Women's Cinema*, 3–31. Princeton, NJ: Princeton University Press, 1989.

Flusser, Vilém. *Gestures*. Minneapolis: University of Minnesota Press, 2014.

Foster, Michael Dylan. *The Book of Yōkai: Mysterious Creatures of Japanese Folklore*. Berkeley: University of California Press, 2010.

———. *Pandemonium and Parade: Japanese Monsters and the Culture of Yōkai.* Berkeley: University of California Press, 2008.

Fu Jiang 福將. "Da heqian kan *Laofuzi*" 打呵欠看老夫子 (Yawn and watch *Old Master Q*). *Dianying shuang zhoukan* 電影雙週刊 (Film biweekly) 66 (August 1981): 38.

Fu, Winnie. *Frame after Frame*. Hong Kong: Hong Kong Film Archive, 2006.

Furniss, Maureen. *Art in Motion: Animation Aesthetic*. Eastleigh, UK: John Libbey, 2007.

Furuhata, Yuriko. "Of Dragons and Geoengineering: Rethinking Elemental Media." *Media+Environment* 1, no. 1 (2019). Accessed September 21, 2022. https://doi.org/10.1525/001c.10797.

———. "*Weathering with You*: Mythical Time and the Paradox of the Anthropocene." *Representations* 157 (2022): 68–89.

Gaines, Jane M. "First Fictions." *Signs* 30, no. 1 (Autumn 2004): 1293–317.

Galloway, Alexander R. *The Interface Effect*. Cambridge: Polity Press, 2012.

———. "Love of the Middle." In *Excommunication: Three Inquiries in Media and Mediation*, by Alexander R. Galloway, Eugene Thacker, and McKenzie Wark. 25–76. Chicago: University of Chicago Press, 2013.

Galwey, Isabel. "Transmedial Attractions, Transitional Aesthetics: The Digital Turn in Hong Kong Animation." MPhil thesis, Hong Kong University of Science and Technology, January 2023.

Garcia, Roger. "Hong Kong Independent Shorts Rhythms." In *i-Generations: Independent, Experimental and Alternative Creations from the 60s to Now*, 11–17. Hong Kong: Hong Kong Film Archive, 2001.

Gaut, Berys. "Film Authorship and Collaboration." In *Film Theory and Philosophy*, edited by Richard Allen and Murray Smith, 149–72. Oxford: Oxford University Press, 1997.

"Gedi shoulun piaofang jilu" 各地首輪票房紀錄 (First round box office records by location). *Dianying shuang zhoukan* 電影雙週刊 (Film biweekly) 110 (April 1983): 38.

———. *Dianying shuang zhoukan* 電影雙週刊 (Film biweekly) 111 (May 1983): 32.

Giesen, Rolf. *Chinese Animation: A History and Filmography, 1922–2012*. Jefferson, NC: McFarland, 2015.

Giustino, Cathleen M. "Toys, Ideology, and the Avant-Garde in Socialist Czechoslovakia before 1968." In *Childhood by Design*, edited by Megan Brandow-Faller, 173–92. New York: Bloomsbury, 2018.

Godelier, Maurice. *The Metamorphoses of Kinship*. Translated by Nora Scott. New York: Verso, 2011.

Grace, Whitney. *Lotte Reiniger: Pioneer of Film Animation*. Jefferson, NC: McFarland, 2017.

Griffin, Sean. *Tinker Belles and Evil Queens: The Walt Disney Company from the Inside Out*. New York: New York University Press, 2000.

Guan Baixuan 關柏煊. "'Laowantong' de Hu Shuru" "老頑童"的胡樹儒 (Old imp Hu Shuru). *Dianying shuang zhoukan* 電影雙週刊 (Film biweekly) 64 (July 1981): 25.

Gunning, Tom. "An Aesthetic of Astonishment: Early Film and the (In) Credulous Spectator." In *Viewing Positions: Ways of Seeing Film*, edited by Linda Williams, 114–33. New Brunswick, NJ: Rutgers University Press, 1995.

———. "The Cinema of Attractions: Early Film, Its Spectators and the Avant-Garde." In *The Cinema of Attractions Reloaded*, edited by Wanda Strauven, 381–88. Amsterdam: Amsterdam University Press, 2006.

———. "Crazy Machines in the Garden of Forking Paths: Mischief Gags and the Origins of American Film Comedy." In *Classic Hollywood Comedy*, edited by Kristine Brunovska Karnick and Henry Jenkins, 87–105. New York: Routledge, 1995.

———. "Moving Away from the Index: Cinema and the Impression of Reality." *A Journal of Feminist Cultural Studies* 18, no. 1 (2007): 29–52.

———. "'Now You See It, Now You Don't': The Temporality of the Cinema of Attractions." *Velvet Light Trap* 32 (Fall 1993): 3–12.

———. "'Primitive' Cinema: A Frame-up? Or the Trick's on Us." *Cinema Journal* 28, no. 2 (Winter 1989): 3–12.

———. "Re-Newing Old Technologies: Astonishment, Second Nature, and the Uncanny in Technology from the Previous Turn-of-the-Century." In *Rethinking Media Change: The Aesthetics of Transition*, edited by David Thorburn and Henry Jenkins, 39–59. Cambridge, MA: MIT Press, 2013.

Guo, Chao, Zengxuan Hou, You-Zhi Shi, Jun Xu, and Dawei Yu. "A Virtual 3D Interactive Painting Method for Chinese Calligraphy and Painting Based on Real-Time Force Feedback Technology." *Frontiers of Information Technology & Electronic Engineering* 18, no. 11 (2017): 1843–53.

Guo, Chunning. "The Echo of Women through Silent Paper Cut-Out Animation: 'Scissorhands' Lotte Reiniger's Reflection through Body Language." In *Propaganda, Ideology, Animation: Twisted Dreams of History*, edited by Olga Bobrowska, Michał Bobrowski, and Bogusław Zmudziński, 196–208. Kraków: AGH University of Science and Technology Press, 2019.

Guo, Li, and Jinying Li. "Animating Chinese Cinemas: A Preface." *Journal of Chinese Cinemas* 11, no. 2 (2017): 115–22.

Guo, Qinglian, and Tosiyasu L. Kunii. "Modeling the Diffuse Paintings of 'Sumie.'" In *Modeling in Computer Graphics*, edited by Tosiyasu L. Kunii, 329–38. Tokyo: Springer-Verlag, 1991.

"Guoji shangye donghuajie de yixie jinkuang" 國際商業動畫界的一些近況 (Recent developments in the international commercial animation industry). *Dianying shuang zhoukan* 電影雙週刊 (Film biweekly) 90 (July 1982): 19–20.

Hai Shen 海參. "Danchu er bubiande jietou jiaomai" 淡出而不變的街頭叫賣 (The street peddling that is fading out yet changeless). In *Erduode qixi yu sanbu: Jiyi Taibei shengyin fengjing* 耳朵的棲息與散步：記憶臺北聲音風景 (Taipei sound memory), edited by Li Ming-Tsung 李明璁, 206–13. Taipei: Locus, 2016.

Halberstam, Jack. *The Queer Art of Failure*. Durham, NC: Duke University Press, 2011.

Halbwachs, Maurice. *Collective Memory*. Translated by Lewis A. Coser. Chicago: University of Chicago Press, 1992. First published posthumously in 1950.

Hansen, Miriam Bratu. *Cinema and Experience: Siegfried Kracauer, Walter Benjamin and Theodor W. Adorno*. Berkeley: University of California Press, 2012.

———. "Room-for-Play: Benjamin's Gamble with Cinema." *Canadian Journal of Film Studies* 13, no. 1 (Spring 2004): 2–27.

Hao Jian 郝健. "Andelie Bazan zai Zhongguo: Bei yanshuo yu bei xiaojian" 安德烈.巴赞在中国：被言说与被消减 (André Bazin in China: Spoken of and forgotten). *Dangdai dianying* 当代电影 (Contemporary cinema) 8 (2008): 13–17.

Haraway, Donna. "Staying with the Trouble: Anthropocene, Capitalocene, Chthulucene." In *Anthropocene or Capitalocene? Nature, History, and the Crisis of Capitalism*, edited by Jason W. Moore, 34–76. Oakland, CA: PM Press, 2016.

Hay, Robert. "Sense of Place in Developmental Context." *Journal of Environmental Psychology* 18 (1998): 5–29.

He Yi 贺宜. "Wei ertong dianying shiye de fazhan er nuli—kan mu'oupian *Xiaoxiao yingxiong* ji qita" 为儿童电影事业的发展而努力——看木偶片《小小英雄》及其他 (Working for the development of the children's movie industry—watching the puppet animation *Little Hero* and other films). *Dazhong dianying* 大众电影 (Popular movies) 22 (1954): 12–15.

Hearn, Maxwell K., ed. *Ink Art: Past as Present in Contemporary China*. New Haven, CT: Yale University Press, 2013.

Heidegger, Martin. "The Question Concerning Technology." In *The Question Concerning Technology and Other Essays*, translated by W. Lovitt, 3–35. New York: Garland, 1977.

Helnwein, Godfried. "Memories of Duckburg." Newshelnwein, April 12, 1989. https://www.helnwein.com/news/news_update/article_436-Memories.

Heng, Derek. "Sang Nila Utama: Separating Myth from Reality," *biblioasia* 16, no. 2 (2020): 59-64.

Hernández-Pérez, Manuel. "Looking into the 'Anime Global Popular' and the 'Manga Media': Reflections on the Scholarship of a Transnational and Transmedia Industry." *Arts* 8, no. 2 (2019): 57–71.

Higashiyama Kengo 东山健吾. "Dunhuang shiku bensheng gushihua de xingshi: Yi *Shanzi bensheng tu* wei zhongxin" 敦煌石窟本生故事画的形式——以睒子本生图为中心 (The forms of Jataka stories illustrated in Dunhuang grottoes: Focusing on the *Illustrations to Samaka Jataka*), translated by Li Mei 李梅, edited by Zhao Shengliang 赵声良. *Dunhuang yanjiu* 敦煌研究 (Dunhuang research) 126, no. 2 (2011): 1–11.

Hong Kong University of Science and Technology. "Animators' Roundtable Forum: Hong Kong Animation, Zoom Webinar." Association for Chinese Animation Studies, May 12–14, 2022. https://acas.world/2022/04/21/animators-roundtable-forum-hong-kong-animation-zoom-webinar-may-12-14-2022.

Hosea, Birgitta. "Beyond a Digital Écriture Féminine: Cyberfeminism and Experimental Computer Animation." In *Experimental Animation: From Analogue to Digital*, edited by Miriam Harris, Lilly Husbands, and Paul Taberham, 132–50. London: Routledge, 2019.

———. "Beyond Noumenon." *Expanded Animation: Expanding Ideas about Animation*, December 14, 2016. https://expandedanimation.net/2016/12/14/beyond-noumenon-talk/.

———. "Made by Hand." In *The Crafty Animator: Handmade, Craft-Based Animation and Cultural Value*, edited by Caroline Ruddell and Paul Ward, 17–43. Cham: Palgrave Macmillan, 2019.

Hou Dechang 侯德昌. "1974 nian Beijing pi 'heihua' shijian" 1974年北京批"黑画"事件 (Attacking "black paintings" in 1974 in Beijing). *Shiji* 世纪 (Century) (2017): 16–17.

Hou Yao 侯曜. *Yingxi juben zuofa* 影戏剧本作法 (A method of shadow play scriptwriting). Shanghai: Taidong shuju, 1926.

Hsu, Siu Chi, and Irene H. H. Lee. "The Magician and the Rabbit." In *4th Independent Short Film and Video Awards Catalogue*, 29. Hong Kong: Hong Kong Arts Centre, 1998.

Hsueh Cheng-Hung 薛政宏. "Guofu qian Tai qianhou *Guoyu ribao* neirong zhi yanjiu (1948–1951)" 國府遷臺前後 (1948–1951)《國語日報》內容之研究 (Research of the *Mandarin Daily News* content before and after the Nationalist government moved to Taiwan (1948–1951). Master's thesis, National Taipei University of Education, 2012.

Hu, Gigi. "The 'Art' Movement Between Frames in Hong Kong Animation." In *Animation in Asia and the Pacific*, edited by John A. Lent, 105–20. Bloomington: Indiana University Press, 2001.

———. "Animation in Singapore." *Animation World Magazine* 1, no. 11 (1997): 32.

"Hu Shuru Wang Ze hezuo chenggong" 胡樹儒王澤合作成功 (A successful cooperation between Hu Shuru and Wang Ze). *Gongshang ribao* 工商日报 (The Kung Sheung daily news), September 8, 1981, 5.

Hu Tai-li 胡台麗. "Shen, gui yu dutu: 'Dajiale' duxi fanying zhi minsu xinyang" 神, 鬼與賭徒: "大家樂" 賭戲反映之民俗信仰 (Gods, ghosts, and gamblers: Folk religion as reflected in the "Dajiale" gambling). In *Dierjie guoji hanxue huiyi lunwenji: Minsu yu wenhua zu* 第二屆國際漢學會議論文集: 民俗與文化組 (Collected essays from the Second International Conference on Sinology: Volume of ethnology and culture), 125–78. Taipei: Academia Sinica, 1989.

Hu Yihong 胡依红. "Cong *Hua de ge* kan donghua yuyan de tupo" 从《画的歌》看动画语言的突破 (On the innovation of animation language from *The Song of Drawings*). *Dianying yishu* 电影艺术 (Film art) 6 (1984): 44–46.

———. "Donghuapian chuangxin de kenengxing" 动画片创新的可能性 (The possibility of making innovations in animated filmmaking). In *Dianying meixue* 1984 电影美学: 1984 (Film aesthetics 1984), edited by Zhong Dianfei 钟惦棐, 167–76. Beijing: Zhongguo dianying chubanshe, 1985.

———. "Donghuapian de shenmei tezheng" 动画片的审美特征 (The aesthetic features of animated film). *Dianying yishu* 电影艺术 (Film art) 2 (1983): 48–51.

———. "Liangzhong butong meixue yiyi de donghua guifan" 两种不同美学意义的动画规范 (Two different aesthetic styles of animation). *Dangdai dianying* 当代电影 (Contemporary cinema) 4 (1986): 6–20.

———. "*Xinzhuang de menling* he *Chaoji feizao:* A Da de ziwo chaoyue" 《新装的门铃》和《超级肥皂》: 阿达的自我超越 (*The Newly Installed Doorbell* and *Super Soap*: A Da's self-transcendence). *Dangdai dianying* 当代电影 (Contemporary cinema), no. 4 (1988): 99–103.

Huang, Liang-hsin. "About." Accessed September 15, 2022. https://www.lianghsinhuang.com/about.

Huang Po-ta 黃伯達. "Xingsu *Mofa ama* de Mai Renjie" 形塑"魔法阿媽"的麥人杰 (Mai Renjie, who shapes *Grandma and Her Ghosts*). In *Mofa ama: Wo ba ama bian katong le* 魔法阿媽: 我把阿媽變卡通了 (*Grandma and Her Ghosts:* I turned grandma into a cartoon), edited by Rice Film International Co., 149–58. Taipei: Rye Field, 1999.

Huang, Qing. "Multimedia Representation of Tao." Master's thesis, La Trobe University, 2003.

———, and Ronald J. Balsys. "Applying Fractal and Chaos Theory to Animation in the Chinese Literati Tradition." *6th International Conference on Computer Graphics, Imaging, and Visualization* (2009): 112–22.

Huhtamo, Errki, and Parikka Jussi, eds. *Media Archaeology: Approaches, Applications, and Implications*. Berkeley: University of California Press, 2011.

Hui, Diana Luen Wah. "Memories of a Socialist Inbetweener." April 17, 2020. https://acas.world/2020/04/27/memories-of-a-socialist-inbetweener.

Hui, Raman. "*Sleepy Guy* Notes." In *2nd Independent Short Film and Video Awards Catalogue*, 33. Hong Kong: Hong Kong Arts Centre, 1996.

Hui, Yuk. *The Question Concerning Technology: An Essay in Cosmotechnics.* Falmouth, UK: Urbanomic, 2016.

Hung Keung. "Love." In *3rd Independent Short Film and Video Awards Catalogue,* 34. Hong Kong: Hong Kong Arts Centre, 1997.

Hunt, Leon. *Kung Fu Cult Masters.* London: Wallflower Press, 2003.

Ingold, Tim. "Hunting and Gathering as Ways of Perceiving the Environment." In *Redefining Nature: Ecology, Culture, and Domestication,* edited by Roy Ellen and Katsuyoshi Fukui, 40–60. Oxford: Berg, 1996.

———. *The Perception of the Environment: Essays on Livelihood, Dwelling and Skill.* London: Routledge, 2000.

Ishida Minori 石田美紀. *Anime to seiyū no media-shi: Naze josei ga shōnen o enjiru no ka* アニメと声優のメディア史：なぜ女性が少年を演じるのか (A media history of anime voice actors: Why do women voice boy characters?). Tokyo: Seikyūsha, 2020.

Jaffee, Valerie. "An Interview with Jia Zhangke." *Senses of Cinema,* July 2004. https://www.sensesofcinema.com/2004/feature-articles/jia_zhangke.

Jenson, Rob. "Pixar's Animation Challenge." The Science Behind Pixar. Accessed February 29, 2024. https://sciencebehindpixar.org/pipeline/animation/challenge.

Ji Hong 嵇鸿. "Kanke: Ji *Xue haizi* he tade luansheng jiejie *Ni guniang*" 坎坷：记《雪孩子》和他的孪生姐姐《泥姑娘》(Hardships: On *Snow Boy* and its twin sister *Mud Girl*), *Yishu jie* 艺术界 (Art circle) 1 (1994): 40–42.

———. "*Xue haizi* chuangzuo de qianhou" 《雪孩子》创作的前后 (The birth of *Snow Boy*). *Xiaoxue yuwen jiaoxue* 小学语文教学 (Elementary school Chinese education) 6 (2006): 29–30.

"Jin 20 nian de jingdian! Bei Jinmajiang beipan de *Mofa ama*" 近20年的經典！被金馬獎背叛的"魔法阿媽" (A classic for nearly 20 years! *Mofa ama,* the film betrayed by the Golden Horse Awards), *PTT Bulletin Board System,* August 30, 2016, https://www.ptt.cc/bbs/movie/M.1472510602.A.A47.html.

Jin Baisong 金柏松. "Meishupian liu daoyan fangtanlu" 美术片六导演访谈录 (Interview with six animation directors). *Dangdai dianying* 当代电影 (Contemporary cinema) 4 (1993): 78–82.

———. "Tan mu'ou pian meigong" 谈木偶片美工 (On the art design of puppet animation). In *Meishu dianying chuangzuo yanjiu* 美术电影创作研究 (Research and production of fine arts film), edited by Ministry of Culture, Film Bureau "Film and News" editorial office, and the China Film Press domestic film editorial office, 47–55. Beijing: Zhongguo dianying chubanshe, 1984.

Jin Xi 靳夕. "Meishu pian chuangzuo santi" 美术片创作三题 (Three topics on animation film). In *Meishu dianying chuangzuo yanjiu* 美术电影创作研究

(Research and production of fine arts film), edited by Ministry of Culture, Film Bureau "Film and News" Editorial Office, and the China Film Press Domestic Film Editorial Office, 40–46. Beijing: Zhongguo dianying chubanshe, 1984.

———. "Women gongzuo zai mu'ou zhi jia" 我们工作在木偶之家 (We work at the puppet's home). *Dazhong dianying* 大众电影 (Popular movies) 3 (1955): 12–13.

"Jinma pingshen yingdai gongbu, bufen yanlun feiyi suosi" 金馬評審影帶公布，部分言論匪夷所思 (Golden Horse jury videotapes published, some comments are mind-boggling). *Lianhe bao* 聯合報 (United daily), December 14, 1998, 26.

Johnston, Claire. "Women's Cinema as Counter-Cinema." In *Notes on Women's Cinema*, 24–31. London: Society for Education in Film and Television, 1973.

Joubert-Laurencin, Herve. "André Martin, Inventor of Animation Cinema: Prolegomena for a History of Terms," translated by Lucy Swanson. In *Animating Film Theory*, edited by Karen Beckman, 85–97. Durham, NC: Duke University Press, 2014.

Jue, Melody. *Wild Blue Media: Thinking Through Seawater*. Durham, NC: Duke University Press, 2020.

Kang, Helen. "*Shui Mo Dong Hua*: The History and Development of Brush Painting Animation." *Animation Journal* 14 (2006): 63–75.

Kaplan, Ann. "Problematizing Cross-Cultural Analysis: The Case of Women in the Recent Chinese Cinema." *Wide Angle* 11, no. 2 (January 1989): 40–50.

Keane, Michael. *Creative Industries in China: Art, Design and Media*. London: Polity, 2013.

Kessler, Frank. "The Cinema of Attractions as Dispositif." In *The Cinema of Attractions Reloaded*, edited by Wanda Strauven, 57–69. Amsterdam: Amsterdam University Press, 2007.

Klein, Norman M. "Animation and Animorphs: A Brief Disappearing Act." In *Meta-Morphing: Visual Transformation and the Culture of Quick-Change*, edited by Vivian Sobchack, 21–39. Minneapolis: University of Minnesota Press, 2000.

Kuriyama, Shigehisa. "The Imagination of the Body and the History of Embodied Experience: The Case of Chinese Views of the Viscera." In *The Imagination of the Body and the History of Bodily Experience*, edited by Shigehisa Kuriyama, 17–29. Kyoto: International Research Center for Japanese Studies, 2001.

Kusno, Abidin. "Master Q, *Kungfu* Heroes and the Peranakan Chinese: Asian Pop Cultures in New Order Indonesia." In *Popular Culture Co-productions and Collaborations in East and Southeast Asia*, edited by Nissim Otmazgin and Eyal Ben Ari, 185–206. Singapore: National University of Singapore Press, 2012.

Laack, Isabel. "The New Animism and Its Challenges to the Study of Religion." *Method and Theory in the Study of Religion* 32, no. 2 (2020): 115–47.

Lai, Cherry Sze-ling, and Dixon Heung Wah Wong. "Japanese Comics Coming to Hong Kong." In *Globalizing Japan: Ethnography of the Japanese Presence in Asia, Europe, and America*, edited by Harumi Befu and Sylvie Guichard-Anguis, 111–20. London: Routledge, 2001.

Lam, Keeto. "A Brief Sketch of the Development of Hong Kong Animation." In *Frame after Frame: A Retrospective on Hong Kong Animation*, edited by Winnie Fu, 10–27. Hong Kong: Hong Kong Film Archive, 2006.

Lamarre, Thomas. "The Animation of China: An Interim Report." *Journal of Chinese Cinemas* 11, no. 2 (2017): 123–39.

———. *The Anime Machine: A Media History of Animation*. Minneapolis: University of Minnesota Press, 2009.

———. "From Animation to Anime: Drawing Movements and Moving Drawings." *Japan Forum* 14, no. 2 (2002): 329–67.

———. "Platformativity: Media Studies, Area Studies." *Asiascape: Digital Asia* 4 (2017): 285–305.

"*Laofuzi* zai Ri dashou zhongshi" 老夫子在日大受重視 (*Old Master Q* was greatly appreciated in Japan). *Gongshang ribao* 工商日报 (The Kung Sheung daily news), July 1, 1981, 9.

"*Laofuzi* zai Xing shangying" 老夫子在星上映 (*Old Master Q* is screened in Singapore). *Gongshang ribao* 工商日报 (The Kung Sheung daily news), December 8, 1981, 3.

Latour, Bruno. *Facing Gaia: Eight Lectures on the New Climate Regime*. Translated by Catherine Porter. Cambridge: Polity, 2017.

Lee, Daw-Ming. *Historical Dictionary of Taiwan Cinema*. Lanham, MD: Scarecrow Press, 2012.

Lee, Jintae. "Physically-Based Modeling of Brush Painting." *Computer Networks and ISDN Systems* 29 (1997): 1571–76.

Lei, Lei. "About." Accessed September 15, 2022. https://www.leilei-studio.com/about.

Lenoir, Timothy, and Luke Caldwell. *The Military-Entertainment Complex*. Cambridge, MA: Harvard University Press, 2018.

Lenoir, Timothy, and Henry Lowood. "Theaters of War: The Military Entertainment Complex." In *Collection, Laboratory, Theater: Scenes of Knowledge in the 17th Century*, edited by Helmar Schramm, Ludger Schwarte, and Jan Lazardzig, 427–56. Berlin: De Gruyter, 2005.

Lent, John A., ed. *Animation in Asia and the Pacific*. Bloomington: Indiana University Press, 2001.

———. "James Wang and His Crazy Climb to Taiwan's Cuckoo's Nest." In *Animation in Asia and the Pacific*, edited by John A. Lent, 125–29. Bloomington: Indiana University Press, 2001.

———. "Ram Mohan and RM-USL: India's Change Agents of Animation." *Animation World Magazine*, August 1998. Accessed December 27, 2023. https://www.awn.com/mag/issue3.5/3.5pages/3.5lent.html.

———. "The 'Sleeper' Status of Southeast Asian Animation." *Jurnal Komunikasi: Malaysian Journal of Communication* 20 (2004): 9–17.

———, and Ying Xu. "Chinese Animation Film: From Experimentation to Digitalization." In *Art, Politics, and Commerce in Chinese Cinema*, edited by Ying Zhu and Stanley Rosen, 127–42. Hong Kong: Hong Kong University Press, 2010.

Leslie, Esther. *Hollywood Flatlands: Animation, Critical Theory and the Avant-Garde*. New York: Verso, 2002.

———. "Review of *Cinema and Experience: Siegfried Kracauer, Walter Benjamin and Theodor W. Adorno*." *Screen* 53, no. 3 (Autumn 2012): 318–21.

———. *Walter Benjamin Overpowering Conformism*. London: Pluto Press, 2000.

Leung, Ann Y. Y. "Transformation from Comic to 2D, Then the 3D Approach: Character Representation of Old Master Q." *Asian Cinema* 18, no. 1 (2007): 160–69.

Lewis, I. M. *Ecstatic Religion: A Study of Shamanism and Spirit Possession*. London: Routledge, 2003.

Leyda, Jay. *Dianying: An Account of Films and the Film Audience in China*. Cambridge, MA: MIT Press, 1972.

Li Ang 李昂. *Beigang xianglu renren cha: Dai zhencaodai de mogui xilie* 北港香爐人人插: 戴貞操帶的魔鬼系列 (Beigang incense burner of lust: The devil with a chastity belt series). Taipei: Rye Field, 1997.

Li Baozhuan 李保传 and Shu Xiaping 束霞平. *Zhongguo donghua dianying dashi* 中国动画电影大师 (The masters of Chinese animated films). Beijing: Communication University of China Press, 2012.

Li, Chris Wen-Chao. "The China That Was Not to Be: Nostalgia and the Exilic Imagination of Taiwan's Mainland Diaspora." *Diaspora Studies* 9, no. 1 (January 2, 2016): 1–14.

Li, Jie. "A National Cinema for a Puppet State: The Manchurian Motion Picture Association." In *The Oxford Handbook of Chinese Cinemas*, edited by Carlos Rojas, 79–97. New York: Oxford University Press, 2013.

Li Song 李松. "Lianhuanhua zatan" 连环画杂谈 (Discussions of *lianhuanhua*). *Meishu yanjiu* 美术研究 (Art research) 2 (1980): 10–12.

Li, Wai-Yee. *Enchantment and Disenchantment: Love and Illusion in Chinese Literature*. Princeton, NJ: Princeton University Press, 1993.

Li Yan 李燕. "Jishu shouduan de meili" 技术手段的魅力 (The charm of technology). *Dianying yishu* 电影艺术 (Film art) 5 (1988): 29.

Li You 李尤. "Wushu ge 1/24 miao duiqie de qidai" 無數個1/24秒堆砌的期待 (Countless expectations piled up in 1/24 second). September 22, 2022. https://www.verse.com.tw/article/li-wei.

Li Zhen 李镇. "Ta zi huazhong lai: Xiangei yuanxing de Qian Jiajun xiansheng" 他自画中来——献给远行的钱家骏先生 (He is from paintings: To commemorate Mr. Qian Jiajun). *Dangdai dianying* 当代电影 (Contemporary cinema) 11 (2011): 34–39.

Liang Ting-Yu 梁廷毓. "Lun 'jingguai' yu '*mô-sîn-á*' chuanwen zhong de shengtai siwei yu shenti jiexian" 論"精怪"與"魔神仔"傳聞中的生態思維與身體界限 (A study of the ecological thinking and body limits in elf and *mô-sîn-á* folklore). *Taiwan wenxue yanjiu xuebao* 台灣文學研究學報 (Journal of Taiwan literary studies) 31 (2020): 53–72.

Lim, Bliss Cua. *Translating Time: Cinema, the Fantastic, and Temporal Critique*. Durham, NC: Duke University Press, 2009.

Lim, Yan Soon. "Wayang Kulit and Its Influence on Modern Entertainment." In *Proceedings of MediAsia 2017*, 111–24. Nagoya: IAFOR, 2017. http://papers.iafor.org/wp-content/uploads/conference-proceedings/MediAsia/MediAsia2017_proceedings.pdf.

Lin Fu-shih 林富士. *Guhun yu guixiong de shijie: Bei Taiwan de ligui xinyang* 孤魂與鬼雄的世界：北台灣的厲鬼信仰 (The world of lonesome spirits and ghost heroes: Religious beliefs of malicious spirits in northern Taiwan). Taipei: Xinbeishi wenhua ju, 1995.

Lin Man-Chiu 林滿秋. *Chanye Taiwanren* 產業臺灣人 (Industrial Taiwanese). Taipei: Yuan-Liou, 2001.

Lin Mei-Rong 林美容, "Cong jitong dao tonglingren: Yu shenling goutong meijie de dianfan zhuanyi" 從乩童到通靈人：與神靈溝通媒介的典範轉移 (From *chi-tong* to *tong-ling-ren*: A paradigm shift in the medium of communication with deities), *Ciji Daxue renwen shehui kexue xuekan* 慈濟大學人文社會科學學刊 (Tzu Chi University journal of the humanities and social science) 16 (2014): 1–26.

———. *Taiwan guizaigu: Cong minsu kanjian Taiwanren de mingjie xiangxiang* 台灣鬼仔古：從民俗看見台灣人的冥界想像 (Taiwan ghost stories: Taiwanese imagination of the underworld in folk traditions). Taipei: Yuexiong, 2017.

——— and Li Chia-Kai 李家愷. *Mô-sîn-á de renleixue xiangxiang* 魔神仔的人類學想像 (The anthropological imagination of mô-sîn-á). Taipei: Wunan, 2014.

Lin Wenchi. "Taiwan dianying zhong de shijimo Taibei" 台灣電影中的世紀末台北 (Taipei at the end of the century in Taiwan cinema). In *2004 Taibeixue guoji yantaohui lunwenji* 2004台北學國際學術研討會論文集 (Collected essays from the 2004 International Conference on Taipei Studies), edited by Liao Hsien-Hao and Lin Chiu-Fan, 113–26. Taipei: Taibei wenhua ju, 2006.

Lin Wenxiao 林文肖. "Dribs and Drabs." Translated by Nick Stember. In *Chinese Animation and Socialism: From Animators' Perspectives*, edited by Daisy Yan Du, 63–74. Leiden: Brill, 2022.

———. "Zai xinling zhong boxia yike meide zhongzi" 在心灵中播下一颗美的种子 (Planting a good seed in the heart). In *Meishu dianying chuangzuo yanjiu* 美术电影创作研究 (Research and production of fine arts film), edited by Bao Lei 包蕾, 158–62. Beijing: Zhongguo dianying chubanshe, 1984.

——— and Chang Guangxi 常光希. "Donghuapian shuqing fengge de tansuo" 动画片抒情风格的探索 (On the lyrical style of animation). *Dianying* 电影 (Movie) 12 (1986): 18–20.

Lippit, Akira Mizuta. "Virtual Annihilation: Optics, VR, and the Discourse of Subjectivity." *Criticism* 36, no. 4 (Fall 1994): 595–610.

Liscomb, Kathlyn. "Shen Zhou's Collection of Early Ming Paintings and the Origins of the Wu School's Eclectic Revivalism." *Artibus Asiae* 52, no. 3/4 (1992): 215–54.

Liu Chao 劉潮. "*Laofuzi* de ku yu le" 老夫子的苦與樂 (The bitterness and happiness of *Old Master Q*). *Dianying shuang zhoukan* 電影雙週刊 (Film biweekly) 89 (July 1982): 19.

Liu, Damu, and Keeto Lam. "The One and the Many: Scriptwriters on Scriptwriting." In *The Swordsman and his Jianghu,* edited by Sam Ho, 208. Hong Kong: Hong Kong Film Archive, 2002.

Liu, Jiamin. "Info." Accessed August 15, 2024. http://missbowtie.com/info.

Liu, Petrus. *Queer Marxism in Two Chinas*. Durham, NC: Duke University Press, 2015.

Liu, Shasha. "Zooming in on the Animated Background: Mediated Dunhuang Murals with Design in *The Conceited General*." *Journal of Chinese Cinemas* 15, no.1 (2021): 22–38.

Lo, Neco, "Single Frame and the Development of Hong Kong Independent Animation." In *Frame after Frame,* edited by Winnie Fu, 52–69. Hong Kong: Hong Kong Film Archive, 2006.

———, and Ng Chun Hong. "Panel Discussion." In *5th Independent Short Film and Video Awards Catalogue*, 96–99. Hong Kong: Hong Kong Arts Centre, 1999.

Lou, Eddie. "Shazhihe de yewang: Goujian xuni de 'daqian' shijie" 砂之盒的野望：构建虚拟的"大千"世界 (Sandbox's ambition: To build VAST, a virtual world). *Xiaolujiao caijing* 小鹿角财经 (LU Economics), June 7, 2022.

Lu Chih-Fang 盧智芳. "*Xiaomao Bakeli* daoyan Qiu Liwei" 《小貓巴克里》導演邱立偉 (The director of *Barkley The Cat* Li-Wei Chiu). *Cheers,* March 26, 2017. https://web.cheers.com.tw/issue/2017/happiness/article/26.php.

Lu Hao-Ping 魯皓平. "Wang Shau-Di zhuanfang: *Mofa ama* de gandong jiang yizhi yanxu dao xiayidai" 王小棣專訪：《魔法阿媽》的感動將一直延續到下一代！(Interview with Wang Shau-Di: The emotion of *Grandma and Her Ghosts* will continue to the next generation). *Yuanjian,* November 17, 2022. https://www.gvm.com.tw/article/84293.

Lu Hongshi 陆弘石. *Zhongguo dianying: Miaoshu yu chanshi* 中国电影：描述与阐释 (Chinese cinema: Description and interpretation). Beijing: Zhongguo dianying chubanshe, 2002.

Lu Tingting 鲁婷婷. *Fengxi zhong de ren: Lu Tingting jilu pian 15 fenzhong* 缝隙中的人：鲁婷婷纪录片15分钟 (Documentary of *The Person in Gap*), 2017. Video, 17:10, https://vimeo.com/212852551.

———. *The Person in Crevice* (Fengxi zhongde ren 缝隙中的人), 2018. Video, 3:49.

Lu Ziying 盧子英 (Neco Lo). "Duli donghua chuangzuo de yidian huiyi" 獨立動畫創作的一點回憶 (Some recollections on creating independent animation). In *i-Generations: Independent, Experimental and Alternative Creations from the 60s to Now*, 18. Hong Kong: Hong Kong Film Archive, 2001.

Lü Heng 吕衡. "Mu'ou pian zuozhe de yici xuexi" 木偶片作者的一次学习 (Puppet animators go to learn). *Dazhong dianying* 大众电影 (Popular movies) 3 (1957): 28.

Lü Lü 吕律. "Duihua: Zhongguo donghua dianying de kunhuo he jietuo" 对话：中国动画电影的困惑和解脱 (Dialogue: Dilemma and resolution of Chinese animated film). *Dianying yishu* 电影艺术 (Film art) 11 (1989): 32–35.

Lui, John. "Time to Make an Animated Feature with Singapore DNA." *Straits Times*, April 22, 2021. https://www.straitstimes.com/life/entertainment/time-to-make-an-animated-feature-with-singapore-dna.

Lukács, Georg. *History and Class Consciousness: Studies in Marxist Dialectics*. Translated by Rodney Livingstone. Cambridge, MA: MIT Press, 1972.

Lukas, Scott A. *A Reader in Themed and Immersive Spaces*. Pittsburgh, PA: Carnegie Mellon University ETC Press, 2016.

Luo, Ting. "Post-realism as an Alternative Aesthetics in Contemporary Chinese Cinema." PhD diss., University of Auckland, 2014.

Ma, Jean. *Melancholy Drift: Marking Time in Chinese Cinema*. Hong Kong: Hong Kong University Press, 2010.

MacAbasco, Lisa Wong. "In Domee Shi's *Bao*, Food for the Soul from Pixar's First Female Director of a Short Film." *Vogue*, April 20, 2018. https://www.vogue.com/article/pixar-bao-domee-shi-interview.

Macdonald, Sean. *Animation in China: History, Aesthetics, Media*. London: Routledge, 2016.

———. "Artifice, Fantasy, and Exaggeration: The Boundless Limitations of Puppets." *Journal of Cinema and Media Studies* 59, no. 3 (2020): 114–18.

———. "Jin Xi: Master of Puppet Animation." *Journal of Chinese Cinemas* 11, no. 2 (2017): 159–74.

Maitra, Ani. and Rey Chow. "What's 'In'? Disaggregating Asia through New Media Actants." In *Routledge Handbook of New Media in Asia*, edited by Larissa Hjorth and Olivia Khoo, 17–27. London: Routledge, 2015.

Manovich, Lev. *The Language of New Media*. Cambridge, MA: MIT Press, 2001.

Marino, Mark C. *Critical Code Studies*. Cambridge, MA: MIT Press, 2020.

Mayne, Judith. "Female Authorship Reconsidered." In *The Woman at the Keyhole*, 89–123. Bloomington: Indiana University Press, 1990.

McGrath, Jason. "The Independent Cinema of Jia Zhangke: From Postsocialist Realism to a Transnational Aesthetic." In *The Urban Generation: Chinese Cinema and Society at the Turn of the Twenty-First Century*, edited by Zhen Zhang, 81–114. Durham, NC: Duke University Press, 2007.

———. "Suppositionality, Virtuality, and Chinese Cinema." *boundary 2* 49, no.1 (February 2022): 263–92.

Media Development Authority Singapore. *Annual Report 2015/2016*. Accessed January 23, 2024. https://www.imda.gov.sg/-/media/imda/files/about/mda-ar-2016/annex.html.

"Meishu dianying yingdang xing 'mei'" 美术电影应当姓'美' (The last name of fine arts film should be "fine arts"). *Wenhui bao* 文汇报 (Wenhui daily), March 22, 1979.

"Meishu dianying shouxian ying xing 'er': Wenxue dianying gongzuozhe taolun fuwu duixiang deng wenti" 美术电影首先应姓"儿": 文学电影工作者讨论服务对象等问题 (The last name of fine arts film should be "children": Discussing audiences and other issues by artists in the fields of film and literature). *Jiefang ribao* 解放日报 (Jiefang daily), February 10, 1982.

Metz, Christian. "On the Impression of Reality in the Cinema." In *Film Language: A Semiotics of the Cinema*, translated by Michael Taylor, 3–15. New York: Oxford University Press, 1974.

———. "'Trucage' and the Film." Translated by Françoise Meltzer. *Critical Inquiry* 3, no. 4 (Summer 1977): 657–75.

Mi, Xiao-Feng, Min Tang, and Jin-Xiang Dong. "Droplet: A Virtual Brush Model to Simulate Chinese Calligraphy and Painting." *Journal of Computing Science and Technology* 19, no. 3 (2004): 393–404.

Mori, Masahiro. "The Uncanny Valley." Translated by Karl F. MacDorman and Norri Kageki. *IEEE Spectrum*, June 12, 2012. https://spectrum.ieee.org/the-uncanny-valley.

Morris, Andrew D. *Marrow of the Nation: A History of Sport and Physical Culture in Republican China*. Berkeley: University of California Press, 2004.

———. "'To Make the Four Hundred Million Move': The Late Qing Dynasty Origins of Modern Chinese Sport and Physical Culture." *Comparative Studies in Society and History* 42, no. 4 (October 2000): 876–906.

Morris, Kathleen D. "Provincializing the Anthropocene: Eurocentrism in the Earth System." In *At Nature's Edge: The Global Present and Long-Term History*, edited by Gunnel Cederlöf and Mahesh Rangarajan, 2–14. New Delhi: Oxford University Press, 2019.

Mulvey, Laura. "Film, Feminism and the Avant-Garde." In *Women Writing and Writing about Women*, edited by Mary Jacobus, 177–95. London: Barnes & Noble Books, 1979.

Naficy, Hamid. *An Accented Cinema: Exilic and Diasporic Filmmaking*. Princeton, NJ: Princeton University Press, 2001.

naphia-55531. "DO NOT WATCH!!! don't let the colourful cover fool you!" IMDB review, October 25, 2019. https://www.imdb.com/user/ur109199682.

National Museum of Singapore. "DigiMuse Presents: Virtual Showcase." February 2018. https://www.roots.gov.sg/stories-landing/stories/digimuse-presents.

Ng, Ashton. "The Divisiveness of Chinese Identities in Singapore." *International Communication of Chinese Culture* 8 (2021): 465–81.

Ng, Kum-Hoon, and Lian-Hee Wee. "Chiaroscuro of the Uncanny: An Unknown Side of Old Master Q." In *Cultural Conflict in Hong Kong*, edited by Jason S. Polley, Vinton W. K. Poon, and Lian-Hee Wee, 211–33. Singapore: Palgrave Macmillan, 2018.

Ng, Sze Hian. "Dissecting the Singaporean Chinese Identity: After the Diaspora." *Global-is-asian*, September 1, 2020. https://lkyspp.nus.edu.sg/gia/article/dissecting-the-singaporean-chinese-identity-after-the-diaspora.

Nichols, Bill. *Introduction to Documentary*. Bloomington: Indiana University Press, 2017.

Nie Xinru 聂欣如. "Meiyou mama de haizi: Meishu dianying benti lun" 没有妈妈的孩子——美术电影本体论 (A child without a mama: The ontology of fine arts film). *Dangdai dianying* 当代电影 (Contemporary cinema) 5 (1989), republished in *Zhongguo dianying nian jian* 中国电影年鉴 (China film annals, 1990): 124–27.

Olson, Theodore. *Millennialism, Utopianism, and Progress*. Toronto: University of Toronto Press, 1982.

Orr, Inge C. "Puppet Theatre in Asia." *Asian Folklore Studies* 33, no. 1 (1974): 69–84.

Palfreyman, Rachel. "Life and Death in the Shadows: Lotte Reiniger's *Die Abenteuer Des Prinzen Ahmed*." *German Life and Letters* 1, no. 64 (2011): 6–18.

Pan Jiezi 潘絜兹. *Dunhuang Mogao ku yishu* 敦煌莫高窟艺术 (The art of Mogao grottoes at Dunhuang). Reprint. Shanghai: Shanghai renmin chubanshe, 1981.

Parikka, Jussi. *What Is Media Archaeology?* London: Polity, 2012.

Park, Myung-Jin, and James Curran. *De-Westernizing Media Studies*. New York: Routledge, 2000.

Pen & Paper Studios. "It's been awhile folks." *Facebook*. August 20, 2021. https://www.facebook.com/penandpaperstudios/posts/pfbid0327AYfsSKUazMnbzd4CWyHs2SBgw421aKkmHhBmwbHy3ueaYqR5uEcHas34CbKbLRl.

Perris, Arnold. "Chinese Wayang: The Survival of Chinese Opera in the Streets of Singapore." *Ethnomusicology* 22, no. 2 (1978): 297–306.

Pilling, Jayne, ed. *Women and Animation: A Compendium*. London: British Film Institute, Exhibition & Distribution Division, 1992.

"Pingta tamen you yige xin de gushi yao dui ni jiang" 平塔他们有一个新的故事要对你讲 (Pinta has a new story to tell), in *Shushi* 舒适 (Comfort), January 4, 2017. https://kknews.cc/zh-mo/news/96kbz2l.html.

Pong, David, ed. *Encyclopedia of Modern China*, vol. 1. Detroit, MI: Charles Scribner's Sons / Gale, Cengage Learning, 2009.

Prince, Stephen. "True Lies: Perceptual Realism, Digital Images, and Film Theory." *Film Quarterly* 49, no. 3 (1996): 27–37.

Pu Jiaxiang 浦稼祥. *Donghua chuangzuo qishilu* 动画创作启示录 (Revelation on animation creation). Beijing: Beijing lianhe chuban gongsi, 2014.

Pu Songling 蒲松龄. *Liaozhai zhiyi* 聊斋志异 (Strange tales from a Chinese studio). Facsimile reprint of the author's manuscript. Beijing, 1955.

———. *Strange Tales from a Chinese Studio*. Translated by John Minford. London: Penguin, 2006.

Qian Yunda 钱运达. "Donghua yu lianhuanhua" 动画与连环画 (Animation and lianhuanhua). *Dianying xinzuo* 电影新作 (New films) 4 (1997): 56–57.

———, and Ma Kexuan 马克宣. "*Hua de ge* yu donghua dianying guannian: Yu Hu Yihong tongzhi shangque" 《画的歌》与动画电影观念：与胡依红同志商榷 (*The Song of Drawings* and animation language: A discussion with Comrade Hu Yihong). *Dianying yishu* 电影艺术 (Film art) 6 (1985): 28–32.

Qiao Yu 乔羽. "Yibu youzhe fengfu xiangxiang de tonghuapian *Xiaomei de meng*" 一部有着丰富想象的童话片《小梅的梦》(A fairytale movie with rich imagination: *The Dream of Xiaomei*). *Dazhong dianying* 大众电影 (Popular movies) 3 (1955): 11.

"*Qicai katong Laofuzi*" 七彩卡通老夫子 (*Old Master Cute*). *Dianying shuang zhoukan* 電影雙週刊 (Film biweekly) 64 (July 1981): 22.

Qiuquemelle, Marie-Claire. "The Wan Brothers and Sixty Years of Animated Film in China." In *Perspectives on Chinese Cinema*, edited by Chris Berry, 175–86. London: British Film Institute, 1991.

Rall, Hans-Martin, and Bernhard Schmitt. "Tradigital Shadows: Southeast Asian Silhouette Animation in the Twenty-first Century." In *Beyond Prince Achmed: New Perspectives on Animation Pioneer Lotte Reiniger*, edited by Rada Bieberstein, 299–325. Marburg: Schüren Verlag, 2021.

Renmin University of China School of Arts. "Lecturer Duan Tianran," accessed October 4, 2024. http://art.ruc.edu.cn/info/1151/4005.htm.

Rippl, Gabriele. *Handbook of Intermediality: Literature-Image-Sound-Music*. Berlin: De Gruyter, 2015.

Romero, Channette. "Toward an Indigenous Feminine Animation Aesthetic." *Studies in American Indian Literatures* 29, no. 1 (2017): 56–87.

Ruddell, Caroline, and Paul Ward, eds. *The Crafty Animator: Handmade, Craft-Based Animation and Cultural Value*. Cham: Palgrave Macmillan, 2019.

Saini, Angela. "The Code for Cuteness." BBC Earth. Accessed January 3, 2024. https://www.bbcearth.com/news/the-code-for-cuteness.

Saini, Rohaniah. "*Wayang Kulit* Enjoys Brief Revival at Malay Village." *Straits Times*, March 10, 1990.

Saint-Pierre, Marie-Josée. "Cinéma d'animation québécois et agentivité féminine. Une exploration de la sexualité et du désir à travers trois oeuvres d'animatrices produites à l'Office National du Film du Canada." *Nouvelle vues: Revue sur les pratiques, les théories et l'histoire du cinéma au Québec* 20 (2019): 1–18.

———. "Femmes et cinéma d'animation: Un corpus féministe à l'Office national du film du Canada 1939–1989." PhD diss., Les Presses de l'Université de Montréal, 2022.

———. "Quebec Animation Cinema and Women's Agentivity: An Exploration of Sexuality and Desire through the Works of Three Animators Produced at the National Film Board of Canada." *Animation Studies* (September 13, 2020). https://journal.animationstudies.org/category/volume-15/marie-josee-saint-pierre-quebec-animation-cinema-and-womens-agentivity/ (site discontinued).

Sakai, Naoki. *Translation and Subjectivity: On "Japan" and Cultural Nationalism*. Minneapolis: University of Minnesota Press, 1997.

———, and Gavin Walker, eds. *The End of Area*. Special issue, *Positions: Asia Critique* 27, no. 1 (2019).

Schönfeld, Christiane. "Lotte Reiniger and the Art of Animation." In *Practicing Modernity: Female Creativity in the Weimar Republic*, edited by Christiane Schönfeld, 169–85. Würzburg: Königshausen & Neumann, 2006.

Schonig, Jordan. "Contingent Motion: Rethinking the 'Wind in the Trees' in Early Cinema and CGI." *Discourse* 40, no. 1 (Winter 2018): 30–61.

Sconce, Jeffrey. *Haunted Media: Electronic Presence from Telegraphy to Television*. Durham, NC: Duke University Press, 2000.

SG101. "Building a Multicultural Singapore." Accessed January 24, 2024. https://www.sg101.gov.sg/social-national-identity/multicultural.

ShanghART Gallery. "Flowing Feast: Liu Yi Solo Exhibition." Edited by ShanghART Singapore. ShanghART 香格纳画廊, May 12–August 13, 2017.

"Shangying chuangzuo ganbu zhanlan da bianlun" 上影创作干部展览大辩论 (Discussions by producers from the Shanghai Film Studio). *Wenhui bao* 文汇报 (Wenhui daily), January 4, 1958.

Shao Yuan 邵媛. "Donghuapian *Jiuse lu* yu Dunhuang bihua *Luwang bensheng tu* yishu fengge qianxi" 动画片《九色鹿》与敦煌壁画《鹿王本生图》艺术风格浅析 (Analyzing the artistic styles of the animation of *The Deer of Nine Colors* and the Dunhuang mural of the *Jataka Story of the Deer King*). *Dianying wenxue* 电影文学 (Film literature) 9 (2013): 54–55.

Shen, Kuiyi. "Comics, Picture Books, and Cartoonists in Republican China." *Inks: Cartoon and Comic Art Studies* 4 (1997): 2–16.

Shen, Lily. "Serenity: 3D Animation to Simulate Chinese Ink Painting." Master's thesis, Victoria University of Wellington, 2014.

Shiau, Hong-Chi. "The Production and Consumption of Animation in Taiwan: The Interplay of Global Political and Economic Force." PhD diss., Temple University, 2002.

Shih, Shu-mei. "The Concept of the Sinophone." *PMLA* 126, no. 3 (2011): 709–18.

Shu Yan 舒湮. "Sheying qiaoshu" 摄影巧术 (Cinematography tricks). *Wanying* 万影 (Ten thousand films) 6 (1937): 29–30.

Siameses. "Zhuanfang donghua xinrui daoyan Qiu Liwei" 專訪動畫新銳導演邱立偉 (Interview with the innovative animation director Chiu Li-Wei). October 2, 2010. https://forum.gamer.com.tw/C.php?bsn=42999&snA=12.

Sifianos, Georges. "The Definition of Animation: A Letter from Norman McLaren." *Animation Journal* 3, no. 2 (Spring 1995): 62–66.

Silverman, Kaja. *The Acoustic Mirror: The Female Voice in Psychoanalysis and Cinema*. Bloomington: Indiana University Press, 1988.

Silvio, Teri. *Puppets, Gods, and Brands: Theorizing the Age of Animation from Taiwan*. Honolulu: University of Hawai'i Press, 2019.

Singapore Housing & Development Board. "Public Housing—A Singapore Icon." Accessed January 23, 2024. https://www.hdb.gov.sg/about-us/our-role/public-housing-a-singapore-icon.

Singapore Infocomm Media Development Agency. "Immersive Media." Accessed December 2, 2022. https://www.imda.gov.sg/About-IMDA/infocomm-media-landscape/SGDigital/tech-pillars/Immersive-Media.

Singapore Management University. "Mind the Drone." Accessed January 29, 2024. https://cte.smu.edu.sg/project/mind-drone.

Singapore Tourism Board. "Merlion's Virtual Vacation at M Social Decentraland Marks STB's Foray into the Metaverse." November 21, 2022. https://www.stb.gov.sg/content/stb/en/media-centre/media-releases/MERLION-VIRTUAL-VACATION-AT-M-SOCIAL-DECENTRALAND-MARKS-STB-FORAY-INTO-THE-METAVERSE.html.

Sito, Tom. *Moving Innovation: A History of Computer Animation*. Cambridge, MA: MIT Press, 2013.

Smith, Claire. "*The Way*, A Dynamic Multimedia Representation of Tao." Interview with Qing Huang, *Metro* 138 (2003): 96–99.

Smith, Heather Kai. "Great Women Animators." Accessed August 15, 2024. http://greatwomenanimators.com/about/.

Sobchack, Vivian. "Animation and Automation, or, the Incredible Effortfulness of Being." *Screen* 50, no. 4 (Winter 2009): 375–91.

———. "Stop + Motion: On Animation, Inertia, and Innervation." Paper presented at *Kracauer Lectures in Film and Media Theory*, December 5, 2015.

Song Lin 松林. "Mantan meishu dianying juben de tedian" 漫谈美术电影剧本的特点 (Discussing the features of fine arts film scripts). *Dianying xinzuo* 电影新作 (New films) 2 (1979): 79–81.

———. "Meishupian yao quanmian tigao yishu zhiliang" 美术片要全面提高艺术质量 (The artistic quality of fine arts films must be improved in all respects). *Dianying tongxun* 电影通讯 (Film report) 9 (1984): 38, 41–42.

Song, Siqi. "About." Accessed August 15, 2024. http://songsiqi.com/about.

Soo-Young. "The CLOT x Head Porter Bag Collection." Complex, February 2, 2011. Accessed December 15, 2015. https://www.complex.com/style/2011/02/the-clot-head-porter-bag-collection (site discontinued).

Sotello, Buddy, and Evan Ginzburg. "Animator Yantong Zhu and Author Steve Verrier." *Wrestling & Everything Coast to Coast*. Podcast audio. Accessed August 15, 2024. https://podcasters.spotify.com/pod/show/wrestlingandeverything/episodes/Animator-Yantong-Zhu-and-Author-Steve-Verrier-e1ij50g/a-a7udsgo.

Spivak, Gayatri Chakravorty. "Subaltern Studies: Deconstructing Historiography." In *In Other Worlds: Essays in Cultural Politics*, 270–304. New York: Routledge, 2006.

Starosielski, Nicole. *Media Hot and Cold*. Durham, NC: Duke University Press, 2021.

Starosielski, Nicole, and Janet Walker, eds. *Sustainable Media: Critical Approaches to Media and Environment*. New York: Routledge, 2016.

Steinberg, Marc. *Anime's Media Mix: Franchising Toys and Characters in Japan*. Minneapolis: University of Minnesota Press, 2012.

———. "Realism in the Animation Media Environment: Animation Theory from Japan." In *Animating Film Theory*, edited by Karen Beckman, 287–300. Durham, NC: Duke University Press, 2014.

Stewart, Susan. *On Longing: Narratives of the Miniature, the Gigantic, the Souvenir, the Collection*. Durham, NC: Duke University Press, 1993.

Stiegler, Bernard. *Taking Care of Youth and the Generations*. Translated by Stephen Barker. Stanford, CA: Stanford University Press, 2010.

———. *Technics and Time, 1: The Fault of Epimetheus*. Translated by Richard Beardsworth and George Collins. Stanford, CA: Stanford University Press, 1998.

Stiegler, Bernard, and Irit Rogoff. "Transindividuation." *e-flux* 14 (2010): 1–6.

Stockton, Kathryn Bond. *The Queer Child, or Growing Sideways in the Twentieth Century*. Durham, NC: Duke University Press, 2009.

Strassmann, Steve. "Hairy Brushes." *SIGGRAPH Proceedings* 20, no. 4 (1986): 225–32.

———. "Hairy Brushes in Computer-Generated Images." Master's thesis, Massachusetts Institute of Technology, 1986.

Suan, Stevie. *Anime's Identity: Performativity and Form beyond Japan*. Minneapolis: University of Minnesota Press, 2021.

Sugawa Akiko 須川亜紀子. *2.5 jigen bunka ron: Butai kyarakutā, fandamu* 2.5次元文化論：舞台・キャラクター・ファンダム (Cultural theory of 2.5 dimensions: Stage, characters, fandom). Tokyo: Seikyūsha, 2021.

Sullivan, Michael. *Art and Artists of Twentieth-Century China*. Berkeley: University of California Press, 1996.

Sun, Shaoyi. "Chinese-language Film or Chinese Cinema? Review of an Ongoing Debate in the Chinese Mainland." *Journal of Chinese Cinemas* 10, no. 1 (2016): 61–66.

Syamimi, Athirah, Yiwei Gong, and Ryan Liew. "VR Industrial Applications: A Singapore Perspective." *Virtual Reality & Intelligent Hardware* 2, no. 5 (2020): 409–20.

"Taiwan donghua fazhan nianbiao" 臺灣動畫發展年表 (The chronology of animation development in Taiwan). 2016. https://web.archive.org/web/20160401225536/http://accataiwan.com/sub4.html.

Taiwan Film and Audiovisual Institute 國家電影及視聽文化中心. Episode 1: *Mofa ama chongfan dayinmu la!!! Ft. Wang Shau-Di daoyan* 魔法阿嬤重返大銀幕啦!!! Ft.王小棣導演 (Psychic granny returns to the big screen!!! Feat. Director Shau-Di Wang). November 21, 2021, YouTube video, 44:12, https://www.youtube.com/watch?v=7V-z_qwUr4o.

Tang, Fan, Weiming Dong, Yiping Meng, Xing Mei, Feiyue Huang, Xiaopeng Zhang, and Oliver Deussen. "Animated Construction of Chinese Brush Painting." *IEEE Transactions of Visualization and Computer Graphics* 24, no. 12 (2018): 3019–31.

Te Wei 特伟. "Meishu dianying chuangzuo fangtan" 美术电影创作放谈 (Discussions on fine arts film productions). In *Meishu dianying chuangzuo yanjiu* 美术电影创作研究 (Research and production of fine arts film), edited by Editorial Office for Film Newsletters of the Film Bureau, T. M. O. C. & Editorial Office for the Domestic Film of the Chinese Film Press, 1–11. Beijing: Zhongguo dianying chubanshe, 1984.

———. "Meishu dianying yao geng shang yicenglou" 美术电影要更上一层楼 (Fine arts film should attain a further step up). *Dianying yishu* 电影艺术 (Film art) 6 (1982): 14.

Teo, Stephen. *Chinese Martial Arts Cinema: The Wuxia Tradition*. Edinburgh: Edinburgh University Press, 2009.

Thomas, Frank, and Ollie Johnston. *Disney Animation: The Illusion of Life*. New York: Abbeville Press, 1981.

Tian Miao 田苗. "VR donghua daodi gai zenme zuo? Pingta gongzuoshi fenxiang le VR shiting yuyan de jingyan | Unite 2017 VR 动画到底该怎么做? Pinta Studios 分享了VR 视听语言的经验 | Unite 2017 (How to create VR animation? Pinta Studios shared their experience of VR audio-visual language at Unite 2017." In *Leifeng wang* 雷锋网 (Lei Feng web), May 12, 2017. https://www.leiphone.com.

Todorov, Tzvetan. *The Fantastic: A Structural Approach to a Literary Genre*. Translated by Richard Howard. Cleveland, OH: Case Western Reserve University, 1973.

Tomonari, Noboru. "Marionettes No Longer: Politics in the Early Puppet Animation of Kawamoto Kihachirō." In *Routledge Handbook of Japanese Cinema*, edited by Joanne Bernardi and Shota T. Ogawa, 231–46. London: Routledge, 2020.

Torre, Dan. "Cognitive Animation Theory: A Process-Based Reading of Animation and Human Cognition." *Animation* 9, no. 1 (March 17, 2014): 47–64.

Torri, Davide, and Sophie Roche, eds. *The Shamaness in Asia: Gender, Religion and the State*. New York: Routledge, 2021.

Tsai Cheng-Ting 蔡承汀. "Quanqiuhua xia Taiwan donghua chanye fazhan yu celüe zhi yanjiu" 全球化下臺灣動畫產業發展與策略之研究 (The development of Taiwan animation industry in the age of globalization). Master's thesis, National Taiwan Normal University, 2008.

Tu Ya-Ting 涂亞庭, and He Chao-Wen 賀照文. "Zhexie Dishini dianying dou shi Taiwan zhi" 這些迪士尼電影都是臺灣製 (These Disney movies are all made in Taiwan). *The Journalist*. April 22, 2016. https://www.storm.mg/lifestyle/103893.

Tuan, Yi-Fu. *Space and Place: The Perspective of Experience*. Reprint. Minneapolis: University of Minnesota Press, 2001.

Turnock, Julie A. *Plastic Reality: Special Effects, Technology, and the Emergence of 1970s Blockbuster Aesthetics*. New York: Columbia University Press, 2015.

Ultimate History of CGI. "Kitty (1968)—First realistic computer animated character." February 4, 2018. YouTube video, 1:24. https://youtu.be/OYrsjc9dz30.

Van Laerhoven, Tom, and Frank Van Reeth. "Brush Up Your Painting Skills: Realistic Brush Design for Interactive Painting Applications." *Visual Computing* 23 (2007): 763–71.

Viveiros de Castro, Eduardo. "Cosmological Deixis and Amerindian Perspectivism." *Journal of the Royal Anthropological Institute* 4 (1998): 469–88.

Voci, Paola. *China on Video: Smaller-Screen Realities*. New York: Routledge, 2010.

———. "DV and Animateur Cinema in China." In *DV-Made China: Digital Subjects and Social Transformations after Independent Film*, edited by Zhen Zhang and Angela Zito, 260–88. Honolulu: University of Hawai'i Press, 2015.

———. "Electric Shadows Reloaded: The Post-Digital Animateur, Shadow Play and Handmade Cinema." *Journal of Chinese Cinemas* 11, no. 3 (2017): 192–209.

———. "Para-Animation in Practice and Theory: The Animateur, the Embodied Gesture, and Enchantment." *Animation* 18, no. 1 (2023): 23–41.

———, and Hui Luo, eds. *Screening China's Soft Power*. New York: Routledge, 2018.

Walden, Victoria Grace. "Animation and Memory." In *The Animation Studies Reader*, edited by Nichola Dobson, Annabelle Honess Roe, Amy Ratell, and Caroline Ruddell, 81–90. New York: Bloomsbury Publishing, 2019.

Wan Laiming 万籁鸣, and Wan Guohun 万国魂. *Wo yu Sun Wukong* 我与孙悟空 (Monkey King and me). Taiyuan: Beiyue wenyi, 1986.

Wang, David Der-wei. *The Lyrical in Epic Time: Modern Chinese Intellectuals and Artists through the 1949 Crisis*. New York: Columbia University Press, 2015.

Wang Jiazheng 王嘉政 and Zhou Qunhuan 周群歡. "Zhuanfang Shilijia Huba zhi fu: Ni bu zhidao de *Zhuoyaoji*" 專訪史力加胡巴之父——你不知道的《捉妖記》 (Special interview with Raman Hui, the father of Shrek and Huba: What you don't know about *Monster Hunt*). January 14, 2016. https://www.hk01.com/即時娛樂/681/專訪-史力加胡巴之父-許誠毅-你不知道的-捉妖記.

Wang, Lingzhen. "Wang Ping and Women's Cinema in Socialist China: Institutional Practice, Feminist Cultures, and Embedded Authorship." *Signs: Journal of Women in Culture and Society* 40, no. 3 (2015): 589–622.

Wang Liuyi 王六一, ed. *Zhengtu: Zouxiang bainian de Zhongguo donghua* 征途：走向百年的中国动画 (March: Chinese animation enters new century): vols. 1–10. Guizhou: Guizhou renmin chubanshe, 2012.

Wang, Qieer. "About." Accessed August 15, 2024. https://www.qieerwang.com/about-qieer.

Wang Shuchen 王树忱. "*Nezha naohai* de juben gaibian he yinmu tixian" 《哪吒闹海》的剧本改编和银幕体现 (The script adaptation and screen representation of *Nezha Conquers the Dragon King*). *Dianying* 电影 (Movie) 4 (2015): 104–109.

Wang Wei 王唯, and Huang Ren 黄仁. *Taiwan dianying bainian shihua* 臺灣電影百年史話 (One hundred years of Taiwan cinema). Taipei: Taiwan Film Critics Society, 2004.

"Wang Shau-Di: Kuashidai de gongtong huiyi, ta de mingzi shi 'a ma'!" 王小棣：跨世代的共同回憶，她的名字是"阿媽" (Shau-Di Wang: Transgenerational collective memory, her name is "Grandma"). *Gongmin baoju* 公民報橘 (CitiOrange), November 9, 2021. Accessed September 20, 2022. https://buzzorange.com/citiorange/2021/11/09/magic-grandmom-4k/.

Wang, Yiman. "The Mortal Animal and the Techno-Animated Life—Chen Qiang's Experimental Zooetic Animation Trilogy *Cut Off*." *Journal of Chinese Cinemas* 11, no. 3 (2017): 210–26.

———. "The 'Transnational' as Methodology: Transnationalizing Chinese Film Studies through the Example of *The Love Parade* and Its Chinese Remakes." *Journal of Chinese Cinemas* 2, no. 1 (2008): 9–21.

Wang Yizhen 王怡蓁. "*Mô-sîn-á*, guigushi, kanjian renmen de beihuan lihe" 魔神仔，鬼故事，看見人們的悲歡離合 (Seeing people's joy and sorrow, parting and reunion in *mô-sîn-á* and ghost stories). *Yan zhi you wu* 研之有悟 (Research yowu). July 13, 2018. Accessed September 9, 2022. https://research.sinica.edu.tw/lin-mei-rong-folklore-mosina-ghost-taiwan/.

Wang Yongjun 王永钧. "Woguo meishupian xianzhuang jianping" 我国美术片现状简评 (A short review of the current status of our fine arts films). *Dianying pingjie* 电影评介 (Movie review) 6 (1989): 12–13.

Wang, Zheng. *Finding Women in the State: A Socialist Feminist Revolution in the People's Republic*. Oakland: University of California Press, 2017.

Wei, Louisa. "Women's Trajectories in Chinese and Japanese Cinemas: A Chronological Overview." In *Dekalog: On East Asian Filmmakers*, edited by Kate Taylor, 13–44. London: Wallflower, 2011.

Wei Yifeng 韋一峯. "Shuqi piaofang yuce" 暑期票房預測 (Summer box office forecast). *Dianying shuang zhoukan* 電影雙週刊 (Film biweekly) 89 (July 1982): 43.

———. "Wang Ze haoguo Zhang Daqian: Fangwen Hu Shuru" 王澤好過張大千：訪問胡樹儒 (Wang Ze is better than Zhang Daqian: An interview with Hu Shuru). *Dianying shuang zhoukan* 電影雙週刊 (Film biweekly) 115 (July 1983), 23.

Wells, Paul. *Understanding Animation*. London: Routledge, 2013.

Wen Tien Hsiang 聞天祥. "Taiwan donghua de lichengbei" 台灣動畫的里程碑 (The milestone of Taiwanese animation). In *Mofa ama: Wo ba ama bian katong le* 魔法阿媽：我把阿媽變卡通了 (*Grandma and Her Ghosts*: I turned grandma into a cartoon), edited by Rice Film International Co., 197–203. Taipei: Rye Field, 1999.

"Wenge houqi de 'pi heihua' yundong" 文革后期的"批黑画"运动 (The campaign of "attacking black paintings" in the later period of the Cultural Revolution). *Dangshi bolan* 党史博览 (Party history expo) 9 (2004): 27.

Whall, Victoria. "Pollution Chokes Ulan Bator Skies." BBC News, February 19, 2007. Accessed October 1, 2008. http://news.bbc.co.uk/2/hi/asia-pacific/6376203.stm.

Whissel, Kristen. *Spectacular Digital Effects: CGI and Contemporary Cinema*. Durham, NC: Duke University Press, 2014.

Williams, Raymond, and Michael Orrom. *Preface to Film*. London: Film Drama Limited, 1954.

Williams, Rebecca. *Theme Park Fandom: Spatial Transmedia, Materiality and Participatory Cultures*. Amsterdam: Amsterdam University Press, 2020.

Williamson, Colin. *Hidden in Plain Sight: An Archaeology of Magic and the Cinema*. New Brunswick, NJ: Rutgers University Press, 2015.

Wong, Aida Yuen. *Parting the Mists: Discovering Japan and the Rise of National-Style Painting in Modern China*. Honolulu: University of Hawai'i Press, 2006.

Wong, Kee-Chee. "Letters to One's Sensibility." In *Frame after Frame*, edited by Winnie Fu, 71–77. Hong Kong: Hong Kong Film Archive, 2005.

Wong, Wendy Siuyi. "The History of Hong Kong Comics in Film Adaptations." In *The Oxford Handbook of Adaptation Studies*, edited by Thomas Leitch, 386–403. New York: Oxford University Press, 2017.

Wong, Winnie. *Van Gogh on Demand: China and the Readymade*. Chicago: University of Chicago Press, 2014.

Wu, Hang. "The Translocalized McDull Series: National Identity and the Politics of Powerlessness." *Animation: An Interdisciplinary Journal* 12, no. 1 (2017): 28–44.

Wu, Hung. "Beyond Stereotypes: The Twelve Beauties in Qing Court Art and the *Dream of the Red Chamber*." In *Writing Women in Late Imperial China*, edited by Ellen Widmer and Kang-I Sun Chang, 306–65. Palo Alto, CA: Stanford University Press, 1996.

———. "Transcending the East/West Dichotomy: A Short History of Chinese Ink Painting." In *Ink Art: Past as Present in Contemporary China*, edited by Maxwell K. Hearn, 19–33. New Haven, CT: Yale University Press, 2013.

Wu Jiaxiong 伍嘉雄. "Xianggang banben *Laofuzi*" 香港版本老夫子 (The Hong Kong version of *Old Master Q*). In *Laofuzi manhua yanjiu jihua* 老夫子漫畫研究計劃 (Research plan on *Old Master Q*), edited by Grace Cheng. Hong Kong: Hong Kong Arts Centre, 2003.

Wu Lun 伍伦. "Meishu dianying chuangzuo suixiang 美术电影创作随想 (Discussion on fine arts film productions). *Dianying yishu* 电影艺术 (Film art) 6 (1984): 43–45.

Wu San-Lian 吳三連. *Wu Sanlian quanji: Taibei shizhang shiqi* 吳三連全集：臺北市長時期 (The collected works of Wu Sanlian: The mayor of Taipei). Taipei: The Wu Sanlian Foundation of Taiwan Historical Materials, 2011.

Wu Ting-I 吳亭儀, and Liang Chia-Ming 梁家銘. "Taiban *Xingfu sandingmu*: Jizai jiatingshi Lin Liang *Xiaotaiyang* gaibian donghua" 台版《幸福三丁目》：記載家庭史林良《小太陽》改編動畫 (Taiwanese version of *Always Sunset on Third Street*: Recording family history, Lin Liang's *The Little Sun* is adapted into animation). EBC News, October 13, 2009, https://the-little-sun.blogspot.com/2009/10/.

Wu, Weihua. "Animation in Postsocialist China: Visual Narrative, Modernity, and Digital Culture." PhD diss. Hong Kong: City University of Hong Kong Press, 2006.

———. *Chinese Animation, Creative Industries, and Digital Culture*. Abingdon, Oxon: Routledge, 2018.

Wu, Xingming. "Wrinkles in Time—Folding Song Dynasty into Contemporary Art." PhD diss., University of Tasmania, 2018.

Xiang Hua 向华, Hu Yihong 胡依红, and Tian Yi 天逸. "Chunzhen niandai: *Wo wei ge kuang* tanhua lu" 纯真年代：《我为歌狂》谈话录 (Innocent age: Dialogues about *Music Up*). *Dianying xinzuo* 电影新作 (New films) 6 (2002): 30–55.

Xu, Xiaying, and Tony Schirato. "Chinese Creative Industries, Soft Power and Censorship: The Case of Animation." *Communication, Politics & Culture* 48, no. 2 (2015): 24–43.

Yan Dingxian 严定宪, and Lin Wenxiao 林文肖. *Donghua daoyan chuangzuo* 动画导演创作 (Animation directors' productions). Beijing: Zhongguo haiyang chubanshe, 2015.

Yang, Lijie, and Tianchen Xu. "Animating Chinese Brush Painting through Generating Reproducible Brush Strokes." *Science China Information Sciences* 56, no. 1 (2013): 1–13.

———, Tianchen Xu, and Xiaoshan Li. "An Image-Based Approach in Animating Painting Procedure of Chinese Ink Painting." *Computer Graphics International* (2011): 1–4.

Yang, Mayfair. "Shamanism and Spirit Possession in Chinese Modernity: Some Preliminary Reflections on a Gendered Religiosity of the Body." *Review of Religion and Chinese Society* 2 (2015): 51–86.

Yang, Panpan. "Animating Landscape: Chinese Ink-Painting Animation, 1960–2013." *International Journal of Comic Art* 16, no. 2 (2014): 380–97.

———. "Ink-and-Wash Animation." Accessed June 21, 2022. https://sites.google.com/site/inkandwashanimation2013/ (site discontinued).

Yang Xiaozhong 杨小仲. "Yi Shangwu yinshuguan dianyingbu" 忆商务印书馆电影部 (My memory of the film department of the Commercial Press). *Zhongguo dianying* 中国电影 (Chinese film) 1 (1957): 80–84.

Yao, Sijia. "Pessimistic Chinese Cosmopolitanism and Jia Zhangke's *The World*." *The Comparatist* 43 (October 2019): 147–58.

Yin Yan 尹岩. "Donghua dianying zhong de Zhongguo xuepai" 动画电影中的中国学派 (The Chinese school of animation). *Dangdai dianying* 当代电影 (Contemporary cinema) 6 (1988): 71–79.

Yingwen zazhi 英文杂志 (English magazine) 9, no. 2 (1923): 200.

"Yongyuan de Helu Disini yishu" 永遠的和路迪斯尼藝術 (The art of Walt Disney forever), *Dianying shuang zhoukan* 電影雙週刊 (Film biweekly) 90 (July 1982): 22–23.

Yoshimoto, Mitsuhiro. "The Difficulty of Being Radical: The Discipline of Film Studies and the Postcolonial World Order." In *Japan in the World*, edited by Harry Harootunian and Masao Miyoshi, 242–57. Durham, NC: Duke University Press, 1993.

Yu Zheguang 虞哲光. *Mu'ou xi yishu* 木偶戏艺术 (The art of puppet theater). Shanghai: Shanghai Culture Press, 1957.

Yuan, Ye. "Storytelling in VR." *ACM SIGGRAPH 2016 VR Village* (2016): 1.

Yue Lu 岳路. "Mu'ou pian shi zenyang paishe de?" 木偶片是怎样拍摄的 (How are puppet animations made). *Dazhong dianying* 大众电影 (Popular movies) 5 (1957): 31.

Yuen, Toe. "Foul Ball." In *2nd Independent Short Film and Video Awards Catalogue*, 30. Hong Kong: Hong Kong Arts Centre, 1996.

———. "The 'Motley Crew' of McDull Animation Team." In *Frame after Frame*, edited by Winnie Fu, 110–28. Hong Kong: Hong Kong Film Archive, 2006.

Zeitlin, Judith. "The Ghosts of Things." In *Fantômes dans l'Extrême-Orient d'hier et d'aujourd'hui*, vol. 1, 205–21. Paris: Presses de l'Inalco, 2017.

———. "Operatic Ghosts on Screen." *The Opera Quarterly* 26, no. 2–3 (Summer 2010): 220–55.

Zhang Boqing 章柏青. "Mantan meishu dianying" 漫谈美术电影 (Discussing fine arts films). *Dianying pingjie* 电影评介 (Movie review) Z1 (1979): 2–3.

Zhang Guanhong 张关鸿. "*Danao tiangong* chushi qianhou: Fang donghuapian yishujia Wan Laiming" 《大闹天宫》出世前后：访动画片艺术家万籁鸣 (The birth of *Uproar in Heaven*: An interview with animator Wan Laiming). *Wenhui bao* 文汇报 (Wenhui daily), November 12, 1961.

Zhang Guangyu 张光宇. *Xiyou manji* 西游漫记 (The cartoon journey to the West). Beijing: Renmin meishu chubanshe, 1958.

Zhang Huilin 张慧临. *20 shiji Zhongguo donghua yishu shi* 20世纪中国动画艺术史 (The history of Chinese animated film in the twentieth century). Xi'an: Shanxi renmin meishu chubanshe, 2002.

Zhang, Linda C. "'Our Comrade Sun Wukong': On Fantasy and Exaggeration in *Mountain of Flames*." Association for Chinese Animation Studies, October 4, 2019. Accessed June 21, 2022. https://acas.world/2019/10/04/our-comrade-sun-wukong-on-fantasy-and-exaggeration-in-mountain-of-flames/.

Zhang Ruirui, and Chi Cheng. "Ink Animation Art in the Digital Age." *Energy Procedia* 17 (2012): 1295–98.

Zhang Songlin 张松林, Xu Jingda 徐景达, and Zhou Keqin 周克勤. "Cong Sagelebu guilai" 从萨格勒布归来 (Coming back from Zagreb). *Dianying tongxun* 电影通讯 (Film report) 9 (1982): 33.

Zhang, Yingjin. *Chinese National Cinema*. New York: Routledge, 2004.

Zhang, Zhen. *An Amorous History of the Silver Screen: Shanghai Cinema, 1896–1937*. Chicago: University of Chicago Press, 2005.

———. *Women Filmmakers in Sinophone World Cinema*. Amsterdam: Amsterdam University Press, 2023.

Zhang Zhenhua 张振华. "Zhongguo tuohuangzhe: Wanshi shuangxiong de dongman yishu" 中国拓荒者——万氏双雄的动漫艺术 (Chinese pioneers: Wan brothers' animation arts). Sina.com, November 25, 2011. http://blog.sina.com.cn/s/blog_89bc0f1e010106gv.html.

Zheleva, Aleksandra. "Can You Make the Cut? Exploring the Effect of Frequency of Cuts in Virtual Reality Storytelling." In *Augmented Reality and Virtual Reality*, edited by M. Claudia tom Dieck, Timothy H. Jung, and Sandra M. C. Loureiro, 45–52. Cham: Springer International, 2021.

Zheng Longfu 郑隆福. "Jia Zhangke dianying zuopin *Shijie* liang banben de bijiao" 贾樟柯电影作品《世界》两版本的比较 (A comparison of two versions of Jia Zhangke's film *The World*). *Zhongguo yishu piping* 中国艺术批评 (China art criticism), April 22, 2007. https://www.jintian.net/107/d13.html.

Zhong Dafeng 钟大丰. "Lun yingxi" 论影戏 (On shadow play). *Beijing dianying xueyuan xuebao* 北京电影学院学报 (Journal of Beijing Film Academy) 2 (1985): 54–92.

———. "'Yingxi' lilun suyuan" "影戏" 理论溯源 (Tracing the history of shadow play theory). *Dangdai dianying* 当代电影 (Contemporary cinema) 3 (1986): 75–80.

Zhongguo dianzi xinxi fazhan yanjiuyuan 中国电子信息发展研究院 (China Center for Information Industry Development). "Xuni xianshi chanye fazhan baipishu 2021" 虚拟现实产业发展白皮书2021 (Technology white paper on virtual reality industry development 2021). In *VR+Video Art Sub-forum*, Nanchang, China, October 2021.

Zhou Lixin 周立新, and Yang Wenting 杨文婷. "Qianxi donghuapian *Jiuse lu* de yishu tese" 浅析动画片《九色鹿》的艺术特色 (Analyzing the artistic features of the animation of *The Deer of Nine Colors*). *Jiangxi keji shifan daxue xuebao* 江西科技师范大学学报 (Journal of Jiangxi Normal University of Science and Technology) 5 (2010): 118–20.

Zhou, Wenhai. *Chinese Independent Animation: Renegotiating Identity in Modern China*. Cham: Palgrave Macmillan, 2020.

Zhu Yantong. "X Company Animated: Behind the Scenes with Yantong Zhu." 2016. Video, 1:30. https://vimeo.com/156761118.

Zhuang, Muyang. "Bell Boy: Cartoonists and Animated Filmmaking in Southern China, 1940–1949." Association for Chinese Animation Studies, November 2, 2021. https://acas.world/2021/11/02/bell-boy-cartoonists-and-animated-filmmaking-in-southern-china-1940-1949/.

Contributors

Shannon Brownlee is an associate professor of cinema and media studies/gender and women's studies at Dalhousie University in Mi'kma'ki, which is also known as Atlantic Canada. Her research is primarily in film adaptation and in animation; she has published articles in journals such as *Film Criticism* and *Animation: An Interdisciplinary Journal,* as well as in anthologies published by Routledge and Palgrave Macmillan. She is also part of the organizing team of the Animation Festival of Halifax.

Jessica K. Chan is an associate professor of Chinese studies at the University of Richmond. Her recent publications include *Chinese Revolutionary Cinema: Propaganda, Aesthetics, and Internationalism, 1949–1966* (I. B. Tauris, 2019) and articles in the *East Asian Journal of Popular Culture, The Journal of Chinese Cinemas, Modern Chinese Literature and Culture,* and *The Opera Quarterly.*

Jasmine Yu-Hsing Chen is an associate professor in the Department of World Languages and Cultures at Utah State University. She specializes in contemporary Chinese and Sinophone theater, film, media, visual culture, and literature. She has published peer-reviewed articles in journals including *Theatre, Dance and Performance Training; Comparative Media Arts Journal; Journal of the Oriental Society of Australia; Prism: Theory and Modern Chinese Literature;* and *Journal of Chinese Overseas.*

John A. Crespi is a professor of Chinese at Colgate University in Hamilton, New York. He is the author of *Voices in Revolution: Poetry and the Auditory Imagination in Modern China* (University of Hawai'i Press, 2010) and *Manhua Modernity: Chinese Culture and the Pictorial Turn* (University of California Press, 2020). His articles on modern Chinese poetry and

China's *manhua* (cartoons and comics) have appeared in a range of edited volumes and scholarly journals. His online publications include the path-breaking three-part illustrated essay "China's *Modern Sketch*: The Golden Era of Cartoon Art, 1934–1937," written for MIT's Visualizing Cultures project. He is the recipient of two Fulbright awards (2005–2006 and 2017).

Daisy Yan Du is an associate professor in the Division of Humanities at the Hong Kong University of Science and Technology. She is the author of *Animated Encounters: Transnational Movements of Chinese Animation, 1940s–1970s* (University of Hawai'i Press, 2019). Her refereed journal articles have appeared in the *Journal of Cinema and Media Studies, Discourse, Positions, Modern Chinese Literature and Culture, Journal of Chinese Cinemas, Women's Studies Quarterly,* and *Gender & History,* among others. She is the editor of *Chinese Animation and Socialism: From Animators' Perspectives* (Brill, 2021), and is currently working on two monographs and editing several volumes about animation and new media. She is the founder of the Association for Chinese Animation Studies (https://acas.world), established in 2015 and dedicated to introducing and promoting Chinese animation to the English-speaking world.

Isabel Galwey is an animator and researcher. She completed a foundation diploma in art and design at Leeds Arts University, followed by a BA at University of Oxford, where she studied Chinese, and an MPhil at the Hong Kong University of Science and Technology, where she researched the digital turn in Hong Kong animation, transmedia connections between different areas of the Hong Kong creative industries, and the significance of nonnarrative elements as part of animation's medium specificity. She has been involved in numerous short film and animation projects.

Emma Harper is a researcher with experience of working in universities and museums in the UK, China, and Singapore. Harper holds BA and MSt degrees from the University of Oxford. She was most recently a research associate in the School of Art, Design, and Media at Nanyang Technological University, Singapore, where she supports the delivery of cross-disciplinary projects relating to the use of immersive and interactive media within the fields of literature, culture, and education.

WENDY LARSON is a professor emeritus at the University of Oregon. She is the author of several monographs, most recently *Zhang Yimou: Globalization and the Subject of Culture* (Cambria Press, 2017) and *From Ah Q to Lei Feng: Freud and Revolutionary Spirit in 20th Century China* (Stanford University Press, 2008). Her present project is on comparative cultural optimism in 1950s China and the West.

JINYING LI is an assistant professor of modern culture and media at Brown University, where she teaches media theory, animation, and digital culture in East Asia. Her essays have been published in *Film International*, *Mechademia*, the *International Journal of Communication*, *Journal of Chinese Cinemas*, *Asiascape*, *differences*, and *Camera Obscura*. Her first book, *Anime's Knowledge Cultures: Geek, Otaku, Zhai* was published by University of Minnesota Press (2024). She is currently working on her second book, *Walled Media and Mediating Walls*.

SHASHA LIU is currently a sessional instructor at the University of Toronto (UT) and York University, after receiving her PhD degree from the Department of East Asian Studies at UT in June 2024. Her PhD dissertation investigates the reproduction and dissemination of Dunhuang in the twentieth century through the perspectives of four visual media: photography, painting, animation, and film. She published the article, "Zooming in on the Animated Background: Mediated Dunhuang Murals with Design in the Conceited General," in the *Journal of Chinese Cinemas* in 2021. One of her dissertation chapters won the Best Student Paper Award (First Place) at the Inaugural Conference of the Association for Chinese Animation Studies (Zoom Webinar, March 1–May 12, 2021).

HANNES RALL is President's Chair Professor in Animation Studies and Associate Chair (Research) in the School of Art, Design and Media at Nanyang Technological University, Singapore. He is also an award-winning director of independent animated short films, with a particular focus on animated adaptations of classic literature. Conference presentations include FMX, ACM SIGGRAPH, and the annual conferences of the Society for Animation Studies; in 2016 he was the chair of the 28th Annual Conference of the Society for Animation Studies. Hannes has published essays, chapters and books with publishers including Routledge, UVK Verlag Konstanz, and Julius Springer.

Tim Shao-Hung Teng is an assistant professor of Chinese film and media at the Chinese University of Hong Kong. He received his PhD in East Asian Languages and Civilizations at Harvard University. His book project, titled *Earthbound Mediation: Geological Entanglements in Sinophone Extractive Zones*, studies four historical sites of earth material extraction and their entanglement with media technology across China and Taiwan throughout the twentieth century. His peer-reviewed work has appeared in *positions: asia critique*, *Screen*, *New Review of Film and Television Studies*, *Journal of Chinese Cinemas*, and *Concentric: Literary and Cultural Studies*.

Paola Voci is a professor of Chinese and Asian Studies at the University of Otago, New Zealand. She specializes in Chinese cinema and visual cultures, and in particular documentary, animation, and other hybrid digital video practices. She is the author of *China on Video: Smaller-Screen Realities* (Routledge, 2010), a book that analyses and theorizes "light" movies made for and viewed on computer and mobile screens, and coeditor of *Screening China's Soft Power* (Routledge, 2018), an investigation of the role played by film and media in shaping China's global image. Her essays have been published in *Animation*, *Modern Chinese Literature and Culture*, *Journal of Chinese Cinemas*, *Screening the Past*, *Senses of Cinema*, *Global Storytelling*, *Bianco e Nero*, among others. Her current research focuses on animateur practices and examines their contribution to the theory and archaeology of the moving image.

David Der-wei Wang is Edward C. Henderson Professor of Chinese Literature at Harvard University and holds a joint appointment in comparative literature. The director of the CCK Foundation Inter-University Center for Sinological Studies and academician at Academia Sinica, Wang took his BA in foreign languages and literature from National Taiwan University, and his MA (1978) and PhD (1982) in comparative literature from the University of Wisconsin at Madison. He is the author of *The Lyrical in Epic Time: Modern Chinese Intellectuals and Artists through the 1949 Crisis* (Columbia University Press, 2014) and other works.

Yiman Wang is a professor of film and digital media and Kenneth R. Corday Family Presidential Chair in Writing for Television & Film at the University of California, Santa Cruz. She is the author of *To Be an Actress: Labor and Performance in Anna May Wong's Cross-Media World* (University of California Press, 2024) and *Remaking Chinese Cinema: Through the Prism of Shanghai, Hong Kong and Hollywood* (University of Hawai'i Press, 2013). She is coeditor of the Global East Asian Screen Cultures book series published by Bloomsbury and Associate Editor of *Journal of Chinese Cinemas*, having published numerous articles in journals and edited volumes on topics of Chinese cinema, independent documentary, ethnic border-crossing stardom, ecocinema, film remakes, and adaptation. She is an National Endowment for the Humanities award recipient (2019–2020).

Panpan Yang is a lecturer (UK equivalent of assistant professor) in the arts and visual cultures of modern China at the School of Oriental and African Studies, University of London. She received her PhD from the University of Chicago. She is currently completing her first book on the emergence of animated space in China, in which she charts the history of Chinese animation from the 1920s to the present, focusing on Chinese animation's encounters with other art forms, including photography, painting, calligraphy, and porcelain. Her writings on different aspects of Chinese animation have received a Domitor Essay Award in 2019 and an Honorable Mention from the Association for Chinese Animation Studies in 2021.

Alexander Zahlten is a professor of East Asian Languages and Civilizations at Harvard University. He received his PhD in film studies at Johannes Gutenberg University of Mainz, Germany, in 2007. He conducted dissertation research at Nihon University (2003–2005) and postdoctoral research at Meiji Gakuin University (2009–2011). Zahlten was assistant professor in the Department of Film & Digital Media of Dongguk University in Seoul, South Korea, for one and a half years before joining Harvard in 2012. He is the author of *The End of Japanese Cinema: Industrial Genres, National Times, and Media Ecologies* (Duke University Press, 2017) and a coeditor of *Media Theory in Japan* (Duke University Press, 2017).

Jake Junjie Zhang is an assistant professor of practice in digital media in computational media and arts thrust area at the Hong Kong University of Science and Technology (Guangzhou). An award-winning independent animation artist, educator, and researcher living in mainland China and Hong Kong, Zhang holds a BA in digital media from the China Central Academy of Fine Arts and an MFA in animation and digital arts from the University of Southern California. His films have been selected for and won awards at festivals all over the world, such as the Gold Award at the 8th Animation Support Program (2021) and the Jury Award at the 55th Ann Arbor Film Festival (2017), among others.

Linda C. Zhang (PhD, University of California at Berkeley, 2022) is an assistant professor of film in the Art & Media Studies program at Fulbright University Vietnam. She is currently completing a book project titled *Technological Futures: Animated Media in Socialist China*, which offers new understandings of the media history surrounding modern Chinese animation, visual culture, and popular science texts from the early Maoist era. Her work has appeared in academic and popular publications including *Journal of Chinese Cinemas*, the *Association for Chinese Animation Studies*, and *Radii China*, as well as in the edited volume *Global Film Color: The Monopack Revolution at Midcentury* (Rutgers University Press, 2024).

Yingjin Zhang (1957–2022, PhD, Stanford) was Distinguished Professor of Comparative Literature and Chinese Studies, and chair of the Department of Literature at University of California, San Diego. His works include *The City in Modern Chinese Literature and Film: Configurations of Space, Time, and Gender* (Stanford University Press, 1996), *Screening China: Critical Interventions, Cinematic Reconfigurations, and the Transnational Imaginary in Contemporary Chinese Cinema* (University of Michigan Press, 2002), *Chinese National Cinema* (Routledge, 2004), and *Cinema, Space, and Polylocality in a Globalizing China* (University of Hawai'i Press, 2010), among others.

Index

Harvard Contemporary China Series

1. Jeffrey C. Kinkley (ed.), *After Mao: Chinese Literature and Society, 1978-1981*
2. Elizabeth J. Perry and Christine Wong (eds.), *The Political Economy of Reform in Post-Mao China*
3. Merle Goldman, Timothy Cheek, and Carol Lee Hamrin (eds.), *China's Intellectuals and the State: In Search of a New Relationship*
4. Joshua A. Fogel, *Ai Ssu-chi's Contributuion to the Development of Chinese Marxism*
5. Denis Fred Simon and Merle Goldman (eds.), *Science and Technology in Post-Mao China*
6. Roderick MacFarquhar, Timothy Cheek, and Eugene Wu (eds.), *The Secret Speeches of Chairman Mao: From the One Hundred Flowers to the Great Leap Forward*
7. Deborah Davis and Ezra F. Vogel (eds.), *Chinese Society on the Eve of Tiananmen: The Impact of Reform*
8. William A. Joseph, Christine P.W. Wong, and David Zweig (eds.), *New Perspectives on the Cultural Revolution*
9. Ellen Widmer and David Der-wei Wang (eds.), *From May Fourth to June Fourth: Fiction and Film in Twentieth-Century China*
10. Christina K. Gilmartin, Gail Hershatter, Lisa Rofel, and Tyrene White (eds.), *Engendering China: Women, Culture, and the State*
11. Andrew G. Walder (ed.), *Zouping in Transition: The Process of Reform in Rural North China*
12. Merle Goldman and Roderick MacFarquhar (eds.), *The Paradox of China's Post-Mao Reforms*
13. Merle Goldman and Elizabeth J. Perry (eds.), *Changing Meanings of Citizenship in Modern China*
14. Elizabeth J. Perry and Merle Goldman (eds.), *Grassroots Political Reform in Contemporary China*
15. Kevin J. O'Brien (ed.), *Popular Protest in China*
16. Martin King Whyte (ed.), *One Country, Two Societies: Rural-Urban Inequality in Contemporary China*
17. Sebastian Heilmann and Elizabeth J. Perry (eds.), *Mao's Invisible Hand: The Political Foundations of Adaptive Governance in China*

18. Jie Li and Enhua Zhang (eds.), *Red Legacies in China: Cultural Afterlives of the Communist Revolution*
19. Prasenjit Duara and Elizabeth J. Perry (eds.), *Beyond Regimes: China and India Compared*
20. Szu-chien Hsu, Kellee S. Tsai, and Chun-chih Chang (eds.), *Evolutionary Governance in China: State-Society Relations under Authoritarianism*
21. Daisy Yan Du, John A. Crespi, and Yiman Wang (eds.), *Chinese Animation: Multiplicities in Motion*